W9-DAU-609

RIGHT TO EXIST

DOUBLEDAY

New York London Toronto Sydney Auckland

RIGHT TO EXIST

A Moral Defense of Israel's Wars

Yaacov Lozowick

PUBLISHED BY DOUBLEDAY
A division of Random House, Inc.

DOUBLEDAY and the portrayal of an anchor with a dolphin are trademarks of Random House, Inc.

Book design by Dana Leigh Treglia
Maps by Jeffrey L. Ward

Library of Congress Cataloging-in-Publication Data

Lozowick, Yaacov.
Right to exist : a moral defense of Israel's wars / Yaacov Lozowick.
p. cm.
Includes index.
1. Arab-Israeli conflict. 2. Jews—Public opinion. 3. Israel—Public opinion.
4. Public opinion—Arab countries. 5. War—Moral and ethical aspects. 6. Zionism.
7. Antisemitism. 8. Jews—Palestine—History—20th century. 9. Israel—History, Military.
I. Title.

DS119.7.L69 2003
956.9405—dc21 2003048477

ISBN 0-385-50905-7

PRINTED IN THE UNITED STATES OF AMERICA

October 2003
First Edition

1 3 5 7 9 10 8 6 4 2

To Malka Lozowick,

who taught me the imperative to be moral.

CONTENTS

MAPS

INTRODUCTION

Why I Voted for Sharon

The war against the Jews goes on. Jewish children are shot in their beds, and the shooters are celebrated as heroes. Jewish teenagers are blown up, and the mothers of their murderers exult. Elderly Jews are burned to death, and the killers gloat on their Web sites. And across the Arab world from Pakistan to Morocco, hundreds of millions have nothing better to do than to chant for the death of the Jews. If there was one thing to be learned from the twentieth century, it is that when people consistently say that they want the Jews dead, they may actually mean it. And when the rest of the world looks away or pretends not to hear, the killers take silence for acquiescence, acquiescence for concurrence, and concurrence for support.

Yet in our generation the Jews are quite capable of defending themselves, and that confuses the issue. The irrationality of wishing the Jews gone can hide—just barely—behind political considerations: the Jews must change before one can live with them. The immorality of passive support for the killers can hide—almost plausibly—behind censure of the way the Jews wield power: the Jews have brought their enemies' ire upon themselves. Worst of all, the resolve of the Jews never to succumb can be whittled away by their own doubts about the wisdom of surviving by the sword and by their hopes of buying acceptance with political gambles: if only we were more benign and accommodating, our enemies would accept us.

The Jews cannot decide for the Arabs to accept Israel's right to exist. They cannot decide for Israel's Western detractors to accept the morality of the choices she makes. But Israel can and must do her utmost to ensure that her choices are moral and wise; when they're not, they must be corrected. Jews care deeply about morality and always have; this has been a source of their strength in the face of enduring adversity. Since the adversity continues unabated, the strength that comes from being moral is as essential as ever.

My initial understanding of Zionism, while childish, was shared by most adults I knew. It had a good side, the Israelis, and a bad side, the Arabs, and they were so bad that their motives seemed almost inexplicable. The Arabs kept trying to destroy Israel, but Israel, partly by virtue of her moral methods of waging war, repeatedly rebuffed the heinous Arab attacks. The events of spring 1967—bombastic Arab speeches about destroying Israel, total international ineptitude in stopping them, if not even acquiescence, and then the seemingly miraculous Israeli deliverance and victory—these were the formative events of my childhood.

My arrogant complacency took its first blow on the gray afternoon of February 21, 1973, when our fighter pilots shot down a civilian Libyan airliner that had strayed into Israeli airspace over the Sinai. I was appalled by the deaths of everyone aboard and horrified by the total lack of remorse exhibited by the head of the army and the two civilians above him, Defense Minister Moshe Dayan and Prime Minister Golda Meir. The plane had no reason to be there, they said. It had flown over a military installation. It could have been spying. There was no way to know—so they had ordered it shot down.

I was a teenager at the time, and in the first political act of my life I faced my peers with the demand that they agree that while Zionism was still fine, these particular Zionists must go. Almost no one agreed.

From 1975 I spent three years in the armored corps. The army I was in was still reeling from the ferocity of the 1973 Yom Kippur War, in which people I knew had been killed; we spent most of our time in the Sinai desert, training to stop and rout another Egyptian attack, should it come. To listen to Israel's critics today, we were already a decade into the brutal occupation of the Palestinians, but neither I nor anyone I knew had any military encounters with occupied Palestinians. We served on the borders and faced Arab armies or Palestinian forces in Lebanon; the Palestinians under our occupation went to work in Israel, and while undoubtedly disliking us intensely, they did very little that called for brutal oppression. On vacations we would roam freely wherever we wished, at times taking Palestinian buses between Palestinian towns. One image stands out: eight or nine of us standing in a Palestinian town and Avi Greenwald cracking jokes in Yiddish, to the tremendous amusement of the young Palestinians grouped around us. Avi was killed a few years later, fighting the Syrians; I have no doubt that some of those young Palestinians were later killed fighting us. That simple scene is hard to conceive of today.

A few years later, out of the army and at university, I took to reading history, particularly the history of the Jewish state. The good guys vs. bad guys version of the story on which I had been raised lost its appeal; the story of Zionism acquired darker hues, and Arab rejectionism became less inexplicable. They hadn't asked us to come to their part of the world; the simplistic version of Zionism as a national movement that never did anything wrong, so I learned, was not the full story. As time went on, it seemed to me that saving the soul of the Zionist project required—indeed demanded—that Israel address the Arab predicament. That we reach a mutual accommodation that would address the basic needs not only of the Jews, but of their neighbors, especially the Palestinians. The Egyptian case was a shining example that this could happen.

In 1978, a trio of American, Egyptian, and Israeli leaders cloistered themselves at Camp David; the result was a treaty that has withstood some pretty severe tests. Those were heady days. Upon his return, Prime Minister Menachem Begin was greeted at the airport by thousands of cheering demonstrators; a representative of the Peace Now movement announced: "We didn't vote for Begin, but as he has risen to the historic moment, we'll marshal all our forces to support him." The image was in black and white: color TV came to Israel only a few years later. The physical sensation was unforgettable. I was overcome by tears of emotion at the prospect of life in a country not at war—"a normal country." Though not actively interested in politics in those days, I was inclined to support whoever was willing to seek negotiating partners for peace, even if this meant handing over additional chunks of the territory we'd been holding since 1967. This put me to the left of the political center, since most people didn't see any additional partners to discuss peace with, beyond the Egyptians.

Any final wavering about my political position was beaten out of me in 1982, when we went to war in Lebanon. The Lebanese war was Israel's fifth since 1947, but it was the first war that many of us wondered about even before it had started. For one thing, it didn't seem an unavoidable war of self-defense as the others had been. For another, it was brewing just as we were completing our evacuation of the Sinai as part of the agreement with Egypt, a peace that as yet showed no sign of spreading to the rest of the Arab world. The final stages of that agreement included the dismantling of settlements in Sinai set up after the Six-Day War and was presided over by an unlikely duo of hawks, Menachem Begin and Ariel Sharon, his minister of defense. Sharon, already nicknamed "the Bulldozer" for his ability to get things done, quite literally bulldozed the settlements lest the settlers return, he said—or lest the Egyptians try to use them, some of us speculated. Then, within two months, these peacemakers took us to war.

The plan seemed straightforward enough. We were going to push the brigades and artillery of the Palestinian Liberation Organization (PLO) away from our northern border, whence they had been shelling and infiltrating northern Israel for several years; the war would be a limited affair, not very costly in blood and quickly over. We wouldn't tangle with the Syrians unless they chose to tangle with us, and the whole thing had the fine title Operation Peace for Galilee.

Yet within a few days, doubts began to gnaw at us. Rumors coming from units facing the Syrians suggested that some of the provocations had been ours, not theirs. The government had assured us that the goal was to reach a line forty kilometers north of our border, but we were obviously not stopping at that line—nor was the operation over within a few days, or a week, or a month. About then, we had our first taste of a totally new phenomenon: A group of reserve officers, freshly demobilized from active duty at the front, announced to an incredulous nation that they thought this was a stupid war.

As weeks turned into months, the pictures got worse. Every evening we would watch on television as our aircraft pounded Beirut: there were high-rise buildings there. How can you bomb them without hitting the wrong people? The wife of a lieutenant colonel whom I had known in high school published his letters of dissent in *Haaretz,* our left-leaning highbrow newspaper; he was abruptly thrown out of the army. Then the rebellious reservists were joined by a career officer, a full colonel who resigned rather than lead his troops into house-to-house combat in Beirut. Even cabinet ministers began to mutter that this was not the operation they had authorized and refused to countenance any further advances.

Begin, meanwhile, seemed increasingly out of touch. Visiting some crack troops who had just taken a very tough PLO position in an old crusader fortress called Beaufort, where they had lost their commanding officer, he inquired if the enemy had used "firing machines"—an archaic word for machine guns. Then he compared Yasser Arafat in his bunker to Hitler, prompting author Amos Oz to publish his famous article, "Hitler Is Dead, Mr. Prime Minister!" Soon he would visibly start to wither, eventually fading from the public eye and then out of office entirely. For better or worse, we were left with one major villain, Ariel Sharon, minister of defense and the architect of the entire campaign.

People like myself decidedly didn't like Sharon even before 1982. Though he had fought heroically in the War of Independence and was an acknowledged tactical genius, there was something brutal about him. He set goals and reached them, no matter what the cost in human lives, whether in the Arab town of Kibiya in 1953, the Mitla Pass battle of 1956, or the subduing of the Gaza refugee camps in 1970. Even his brilliant turning of the tide in the Sinai in 1973 was rumored to have been the result of crass insubordination at a human cost that was not necessary. Perhaps most disturbing of all, he was completely free of any doubts, always certain that he was right and everyone else wrong, and since leaving the army and entering politics after the war of 1973, he had been a hard-line cabinet minister, the chief architect of the new settlements springing up throughout the West Bank. The political Right loved him, and the Left hated him, for the same reason: He represented Zionism's transformation of weak but moral Jews into immoral power users.

At the end of September 1982, Lebanese president-elect Bashir Gemayel, perceived as pro-Israeli, was assassinated by Syrian proxies. For reasons still unclear, the Israelis allowed units of Gemayel's paramilitaries into the Sabra and Shatila refugee camps near Beirut, where they massacred hundreds of defenseless Palestinian civilians. For a moment of panic we feared that our own men were implicated, but even when we understood that the murderers were Arabs, we were still horrified that we had somehow become allied to such thugs. The growing sense of unease and rejection that had been building all summer exploded in a nauseating attack of guilt and an acute sense of moral defilement. How could anyone have dared to drag us so incredibly low? With a sense of doom, we turned our fury on the man who epitomized the whole morass: Ariel Sharon.

There was a tidal wave of demonstrations, culminating in what is still referred to as the "Rally of the 400,000," although the square where it took place couldn't contain more than half that number. But even two hundred thousand people made up a full 5 percent of the population, equivalent to having fourteen million Americans at one rally. The government bowed to the pressure and appointed a commission of inquiry headed by Chief Justice Yitzhak Kahan. Then began a very tense period of waiting.

The winter of 1983 was unusually bleak. The misadventure in Lebanon was proving a quagmire akin to the American experience in Vietnam. The populace was sharply divided: the enthusiastic supporters of Menachem Begin, until recently a charismatic leader and hypnotic orator, had no patience for what they saw as spinelessness in the face of a hostile Arab world; we in the opposition were deeply mortified by what seemed our encroaching moral integration into the surrounding Middle East. Then in February the Kahan Commission recommended that Sharon leave the Ministry of Defense for his failure to foresee the danger in allowing the Phalange forces into those camps. What remained was for the government to accept the recommendations.

The tension in the air was palpable. Walking down Ben Yehuda Street in the center of Jerusalem, I saw an ugly crowd of gesticulating and cursing men. Edging my way in, I recognized the man at their epicenter: we were reservists together. Short, dark, and of Iraqi descent, Nathan did not at all resemble your stereotypical light-skinned academic peace activist. But he was proudly and furiously holding his own, damning Sharon and his failures and drawing the holy wrath of the surrounding ring of men. Hoping to reduce the pressure, I told some of the hecklers that Nathan, in one of the toughest battles of the war he was now lambasting, had proven himself a bona fide hero; but this was like water off the back of a duck. "Maybe he's shell-shocked out of his senses," they said, then shrugged and turned back to scream at him. That evening, Peace Now demonstrators, grimly bound together in a compact phalanx, marched through the streets of Jerusalem, surrounded by jeering crowds, all the way to the prime minister's office, where the government was still deliberating. Yonah Avrushmi, who saw himself as a protector of Sharon, hurled a grenade at them, wounding many and killing Emil Grynzweig.

It was the first political murder I had experienced in Israel, and I can think of only one since then. Faced with the looming mayhem, the government removed Sharon from his post. We swore that he'd never be back.

Eighteen years later, in July 2000, Prime Minister Ehud Barak set off for a second set of trilateral Camp David peace talks with the American president, Bill Clinton, and PLO chairman Yasser Arafat. Thousands of us converged in front of his residence to demonstrate our support. The first speaker, Tzali Reshef, had been prominent in Peace Now since its inception; now he was in his late forties. He reminded his audience of more than two decades of activism for peace—often in an atmosphere of severe public animosity, since the movement had demanded that the dream of retaining control of the West Bank be dropped. And now an elected prime minister with a mandate to withdraw from the territories was off to reach an agreement with Arafat. *"This is the moment!"* he thundered.

A few weeks later Barak was home, but there were no crowds to greet him at the airport. Israel had been dismantling her control over the Palestinians since the Oslo Accords in 1993. At Camp David, Barak had effectively offered an end to the occupation, with Israel to evacuate whatever territory she still held in Gaza and at least 90 percent of the West Bank, while dismantling many settlements; Israel would recognize an independent Palestinian state in all of the evacuated areas. In Jerusalem, Barak offered to divide the city, insisting only on Israel's retaining some sort of connection, even symbolic, with the Old City and the Temple Mount. In return, he expected the Palestinians officially to declare that the conflict was over. Bill Clinton praised Barak for his far-reaching offers, while dejectedly noting that Arafat had simply turned them down without making any counteroffers.

Shlomo Ben-Ami, acting foreign minister, took off on a whirlwind tour of foreign capitals, to explain what had happened at Camp David. Wherever he went, he was congratulated on the positions Israel had taken while being encouraged not to give up. And indeed, the diplomatic activity between the sides was still going on. On September 24, Barak hosted Arafat at his home; after the meeting, negotiators from both sides flew to talks in Washington.

On September 27, an Israeli soldier, nineteen-year-old David Biri of Jerusalem, was killed by a bomb at Netzarim, an island of Israeli-controlled territory in the Gaza Strip. It was the first such attack since Barak had offered to dismantle and evacuate it, along with the other remaining settlements in Gaza. In other words, every single casualty there from August 2000 onward will be senseless, as the Palestinians are fighting for something they could have had without bloodshed. The second *intifada* had begun.

The next day, opposition leader Ariel Sharon and his entourage visited the Temple Mount. The visit had been cleared in advance with Palestinian authorities. Shlomo Ben-Ami, no friend of Sharon, had spoken personally about it to Jibril Rajoub, one of the top Palestinian security officials; Rajoub had told him that as long as Sharon stayed away from the mosques, there would be no problem. The visit itself was short and uneventful; Sharon told reporters how important the Temple Mount is to Jews, and left.

Friday, September 29: Muslim rioters on the Temple Mount dump rocks on Jews praying at the Western Wall below. A picture on my desk shows a four-year-old girl, crying with terror, being pulled away from the wall by her mother; other women are racing off; a policeman is screaming at them all to get away. Up on the mountain, five demonstrators were killed in the ensuing clash with police. Yossi Tabaja, an Israeli policeman on a joint patrol near the town of Kalkilya, was killed when one of his Palestinian colleagues simply walked over and shot him.

For the next two days I heard no news. It was Rosh Hashanah, one of the most solemn dates of the year, and we spent long hours in the synagogue. The climax of the day, I have always felt, is the segment written in the eleventh century by Amnon of Magenza, as he lay dying from torture inflicted for his refusal to convert to Christianity. Magenza was the Jewish name of the German town of Mainz, although I have yet to meet a single German who recognizes it. A few years later, the whole community was destroyed by Crusaders on their way to Jerusalem. The survivors fervently adopted Rabbi Amnon's powerful passage about the awesomeness of the day each year on which God decides who will live and who will die. Fittingly enough, the possibility of living for another year is noted briefly, while the possibilities of death are multiple: "who by water, who by fire, who by the sword, by the beast, by hunger, by thirst. . . . Man is as a broken shard, as hay on the wind, as a wilted flower, as a passing shadow, as a fleeting dream." A tradition that calls forth such poetry from the bloody rubble is surely worth living—and fighting—for. Some cultures would call forth only hatred.

Sunday night, with the two days of prayer and reflection behind me, I got on the Internet and visited *The New York Times.* The horrifying picture of a twelve-year-old Palestinian boy named Muhammad al-Durrah huddling in terror next to his father, moments before he was shot, struck me like a fist in my face. As a liberal humanist, a lover of peace, and a seeker of justice, and as the father of a twelve-year-old son, I recoiled from the image. My first response was an internal cry of pain; externally, a compressing of the lips and a grim condemnation of our inability to keep the children out of our wars. That picture is on my desk as I write, and I have spent many hours studying it, etching it on my mind and soul. It is an incredibly powerful image—so powerful, indeed, that it took me weeks to understand the truth of it: that it happened at Netzarim, a place that had already been surrendered. That Muhammad's father had been screaming *to his own compatriots* for a brief pause in the firing; that a French cameraman—mysteriously alerted to the attack ahead of time—had been standing a few yards away but rather than join in the pleas of the anguished father had merely kept his camera trained on the picture of his career; that the Palestinian fighters themselves were so intent on redeeming by bloodshed what they had refused to accept by negotiation that it never crossed their minds to stop shooting; and that given the terrain and the range, it was highly unlikely that the Israeli soldiers had any idea a child was there. Hunkered in their trenches, being shot at from three sides just a few days after David Biri's death at the same place, they could not be accused of having calmly and maliciously shot down a child; only a fool would say otherwise.

But that is precisely what my good friend Arthur turned out to be. Arthur is an English academic who takes his non-Jewish students each year to visit the Nazi death camps in Poland. In a heated exchange, he placed the entire blame for the violence on Sharon and, implicitly, on Israel's insistence on occupying Palestinian territory; he further declared that Sharon was a war criminal and that in a normal country he would have been tried for his crimes. Going over the top, he likened Sharon to Slobodan Milošević, the Serbian leader who has the blood of hundreds of thousands on his conscience, the dynamo of an entire decade of calculated murder of civilians, concentration camps, and systematic ethnic cleansing. This was too much, and for the first time in decades I found myself defending Sharon by replying that these events were a bit too grave to be glibly assigned to him and that if one were looking for a leader with the blood of innocents on his hands, Arafat would easily qualify. In response, Arthur severed his relations with me—a decade of friendship, gone in the puff of an e-mail.

Also gone forever was my second, laboriously constructed, revised understanding of the Zionist project. In this version, so typical of my own post-1967 generation, powerful Israel had to reach out her hand to the aggrieved Palestinians and offer them generous terms of peace and reconciliation, and if she did so, the Palestinians would inevitably return the gesture in kind, because after all, everybody prefers peace with dignity to war with suffering. Nothing to come in the months and years ahead would allow me to get back to where I had been.

On October 12, Yosef Avrahami and Vadim Novesche, two reservists who mistakenly entered Ramallah, where Arafat has his headquarters, were lynched by a mob in the center of town. The purportedly wild and uncontrollable mob had the presence of mind to confiscate the film from all of the cameramen present, except for an Italian who smuggled out video images of the killers exultantly bathing their hands in Jewish blood. It was a deeply shocking illustration of the savage hatred of the enemy we had thought we were making peace with: say what you like about Israeli policies, we could not think of a single case where Jews washed their hands in the blood of their enemies. The army warned the Palestinians to clear the police building where it happened and rocketed it from the air. No one was hurt, but the pictures told their own story: here the impotent mob, there the arrogant helicopters; there the almighty occupiers firing from the safety of the air, below the despairing occupied people, venting their frustration with their bare hands.

The Palestinians seemed to feel that they were winning. Superficially, they were. That one image of twelve-year-old Muhammad al-Durrah was more powerful than seven years of Israel transferring real power to the Palestinians; Barak's proposals at Camp David were as nothing when compared with the deaths of children confronting Israeli soldiers. In the first *intifada,* the working assumption had been that since it was an unarmed population facing the Israelis, the tremendous power of their army had been neutralized; should the Palestinians use firearms, however, the Israelis would be free to react with force and crush the uprising. This time, in the second *intifada,* the Palestinians were using automatic weapons from the first, the Israelis were responding with the tiniest fraction of the firepower at *their* disposal, and still the world reacted with abhorrence. In other words, the Palestinians had nothing to lose except lives and much to gain. They realistically assumed that no Israeli government would offer them dramatically more than Barak had, so they were trying the double track of violent pressure at home and massive pressure abroad, on the reasonable assumption that this would lead to even better terms: when you hold a winning hand, why stop playing?

But they had badly miscalculated. After all the speeches and declarations and resolutions, the Palestinians must make peace with Israel, not with the UN or the European Union. The opinion of the American president is reasonably important, but at the end of the day, the Israeli electorate is the only body that can agree or disagree with the terms the Palestinians seek. Now, however, the Israeli electorate was furious at the Palestinians—and nowhere near breaking.

The first group to tire in this cruel war of attrition was that of the large numbers of Palestinian men who daily went out of their way to seek Israeli military outposts beyond the perimeters of the enclaves ruled by the Palestinian Authority (PA), there to taunt the soldiers and to act as live shields for the armed men firing from their midst. After a month or two, however, they dropped out of the confrontation. From then on, it was armed men against Israelis—though preferably not Israelis of the lethal kind. The settlers in their civilian vehicles were a much easier target, and much of the international community regarded them as legitimate prey, since the Palestinians were purportedly resisting occupation and displacement.

No one gets worse press than the settlers. They are portrayed as the evil and violent edge of Israeli society, their greed for Palestinian land the engine of the entire conflict. My own relationship with them has long been ambivalent: I objected to their goals but liked many of them personally. Almost all the people I went to school with grew up to be settlers. Two weeks into the violence I had lunch with three or four of them, and they were complimenting themselves on their prescience: they had known the Palestinians were not going to make peace and had managed to provoke them into showing their hand. "Stop kidding yourselves," I responded. "This has nothing to do with you. If the Palestinians had been willing to make peace with me and my kind, you wouldn't have impeded us. The truth is that the peace efforts blew up over Jerusalem, over the right of return, perhaps over our very existence here—anything but the settlements, which Barak was willing to dismantle."

By November, settlers were being shot down on the roads to their homes. Colleagues who live in Efrat or Ofra took to leaving work early in order to be home before nightfall; one of my staff didn't come to work one day at all, going instead to the funeral of her neighbor, murdered in his car the evening before. Yet contrary to their image as Zionist fanatics no less militant than their Palestinian counterparts, they restrained themselves. Practically every household in the settlements owns a firearm or three, and many are armed with automatic weapons loaned on a permanent basis by their reserve units. There are forty-five thousand armed Palestinians, we were told. The number of armed settlers was at least as high, many with military training and experience far exceeding anything the Palestinians can offer. Yet surrounded by violence that threatens the lives of their wives and children, these supposed warmongering extremists refrained from using their firepower, even when faced with the most outrageous provocations.

Dr. Shmuel Gillis, forty-two years old and father of five, was a hematologist at Haddassah Hospital. His colleagues told of his outstanding professionalism and his contribution to the international research team he belonged to; his patients told of his warm bedside manner. After he was shot down as a settler, even his Palestinian patients mourned with the others, sharing their grief openly with the media. His funeral set out from Haddassah with thousands of participants; additional thousands lined the road south of Jerusalem on which he had been shot, standing in silence.

A few days later, Zachi Sasson was killed, again just south of Jerusalem. Also a settler, he had formerly been a congregant at my synagogue, so someone put up an announcement of the funeral details, including the promise of bulletproof buses. Yet ironically, the attacks on the settlers may have achieved the opposite of what their perpetrators intended. The murderous campaign had spread to Jerusalem and the Israeli towns of Hadera,

Holon, and Netanya, blurring the line between the settlers and the general population. The settlers, by virtue of their restraint, had driven home the feeling that their predicament was shared by all of us and was part of a strategic Palestinian move against all Israelis—indeed, against the very existence of the Jewish state.

For decades I had been voting for candidates and parties who promised to leave no stone unturned in their efforts to achieve peace. The violence of the second *intifada* had totally undermined the agreements on which the peace process agreed to at Oslo had been predicated, but one might still hope that by offering them everything we could possibly afford to give, they might conclude that they had reached their utmost realistic goals and make peace. It is hard to think of a worse way to negotiate, but in order to save lives on both sides and to rectify the injustices we had done over the years, perhaps this was the last stone we must turn. But as the Palestinians began to murder Israeli civilians deep inside Israel while proclaiming that they were struggling against an unjust occupation that we had just tried to end, this position seemed increasingly irrational.

As Barak fell from power in December and new elections were set for February 2001, I was forced to admit that the rational choice would be to vote in a way that reflected what was happening around me; sticking to my liberal guns might be what my heart wanted, but it was not what my mind dictated.

There were to be no blank ballots for me. It is duty of the citizen to vote, I have always felt, and if you can't make up your mind, then agonize over it until you can. But could my heart survive a vote for Sharon?

Zeituni is an uncommon name, and the family that bears it has a long history: they can prove that their forebears never left this land during the entire two thousand years when most Jews were elsewhere. In recent centuries, they resided in the Galilean village of Peki'in; today, the synagogue of Peki'in is their only relic. The populace is Arab, and the Zeitunis live elsewhere.

In January 2001 a young man named Etgar Zeituni, owner of a restaurant in Tel Aviv, went to the Palestinian town of Tulkarm on business with his cousin Motti Dayan and an Arab Israeli. Sitting in a restaurant, they

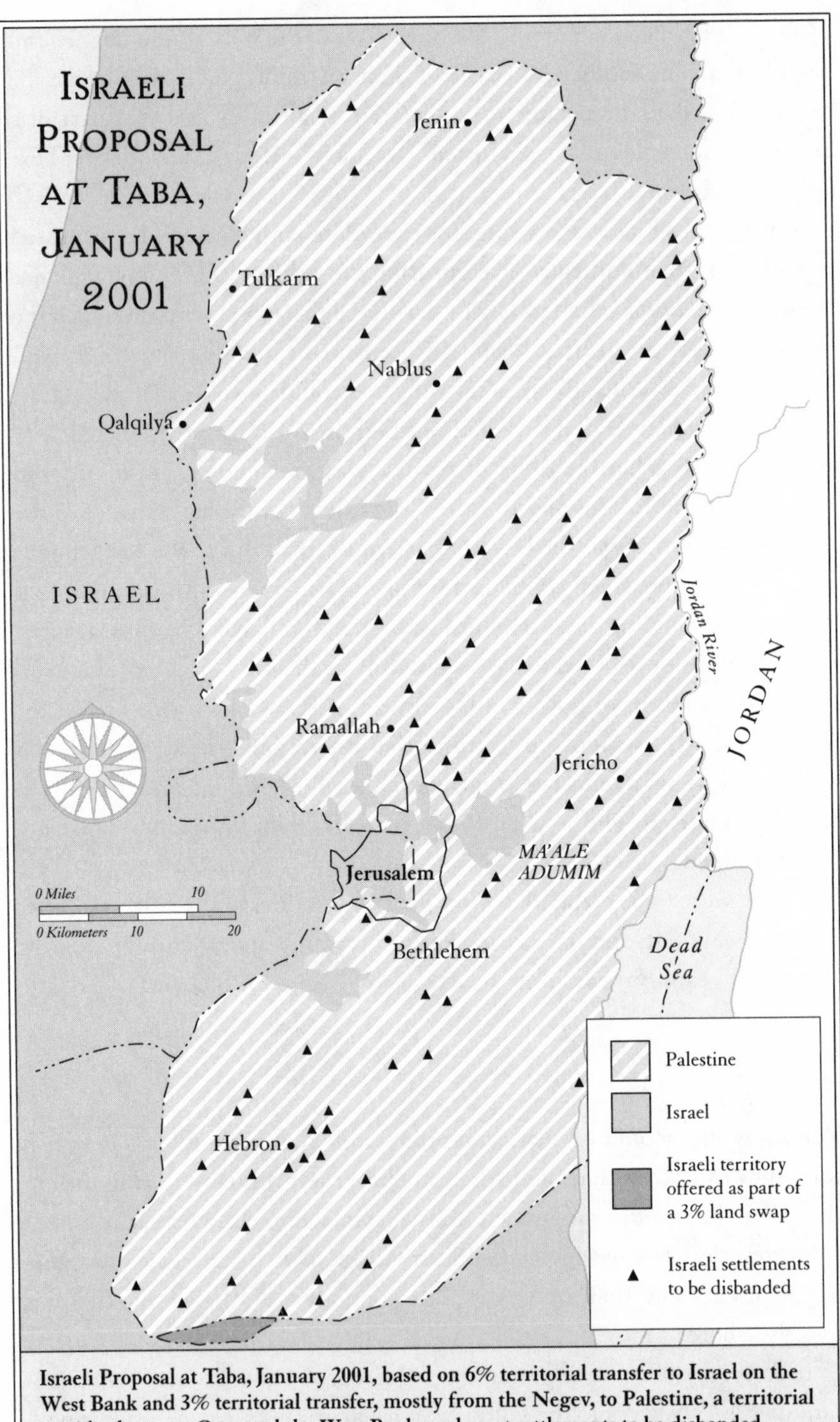

Israeli Proposal at Taba, January 2001, based on 6% territorial transfer to Israel on the West Bank and 3% territorial transfer, mostly from the Negev, to Palestine, a territorial corridor between Gaza and the West Bank, and most settlements to be disbanded.

were abducted by local thugs, given two minutes to pray, and shot. The Arab Israeli was sent home.

A young Jew whose family has been here for millennia, uprooted from the ancestral village that has become Arab, trying peacefully to do business with individual Palestinians in spite of the national tensions, and being murdered for his efforts. A true story to fly in the face of every platitude you have ever heard about the conflict in the Middle East.

The murder took place while high-ranking teams from both sides were convened at Taba, just over the Egyptian border. Barak froze the negotiations for thirty-six hours, and these—so the optimists claimed—were all that were lacking to clinch a deal.

Barak had not been backed by a majority of the Knesset when he went to Camp David; but neither had he been toppled, and in any case he could plausibly say that he was doing precisely what he had said he would do before being elected by a large majority a year earlier. Yet his efforts to make peace had resulted in war, and by January 2001, the polls were unanimous that he was going to be severely thrashed. Only a treaty could save him.

Bill Clinton's proposals for bridging the gap addressed the two crucial issues: Israel would have to acquiesce in a clear division of Jerusalem, with no Israeli connection, not even symbolic, to the Old City irrespective of what was holy for the Jews; the Palestinians, for their part, would have to renounce their right of return. Whether Barak had a mandate to agree to such a proposal was unclear, but it was also irrelevant, as the Palestinians rejected it without making a counterproposal. The discussions at Taba were Barak's last desperate attempt to reach an agreement by moving even closer toward the Palestinians than Clinton's proposals: territories would be swapped so that the Palestinians would have the equivalent of 100 percent of the occupied territories; most significant, however, the Israelis were willing to discuss formulas that would recognize a legal Palestinian right of return, though perhaps not an unlimited practical right. All the Palestinians had to do was halt the violence, presenting the Israeli electorate with a harsh choice between Barak, poised on the cusp of a treaty, and Sharon. Instead, the murders went on.

The positions of the two sides were clearly set out at a press conference at Taba, on the final evening of the talks. Shlomo Ben-Ami, our foreign minister, spoke Hebrew; Abu Ala, the senior Palestinian negotiator, spoke Arabic and was translated simultaneously. Each spoke to his own constituency. Ben-Ami was full of sweetness: our mutual trust has been reestablished, he proclaimed. Vote for Barak next week, and peace will come shortly thereafter, he almost added. Abu Ala was less sanguine. Yes, progress had been made toward putting an end to Israeli aggression, he announced, but the main sticking point remains the right of return. The Israelis, he told his people, were not yet ready to accept this inalienable right; if they did not, he asserted, the Palestinians had assorted methods to force them. Vote for Sharon next week, Abu Ala had more or less told us, since peace is not going to happen, and he's the candidate who knows it. Despite Sharon's unsavory past and my aversion to him personally, the new reality required that I vote for him.

There were four reasons for this choice: two for voting against Barak and two for supporting Sharon.

First, the putative Israeli peacemakers had to be ousted—nay, overwhelmingly routed—in order to demonstrate to the Palestinians that the proper response to violence and perfidy cannot be further concessions. Concessions are a possible component only of a process of mutual compromise. Barak had offered concessions at Camp David, but the Palestinians demolished the underpinning of the entire Oslo process by returning to the violence they had irrevocably forsworn in 1993. The only acceptable response should have been to halt negotiations as long as the violence continued.

The concessions suggested by Israeli negotiators at Camp David were probably greater than the mandate given democratically to Barak in 1999; but had he brought peace, he would easily have swayed the electorate. The concessions made after the violence began went much further, and by throwing him out by the widest landslide imaginable, the electorate stated clearly that whatever he had offered in those last few months had been the desperate manipulations of a small group out of touch with the popular will.

These were two reasons to vote against Barak. One reason to vote for Sharon was precisely his image in the Arab world as a dangerous warmonger: since the Palestinians were obviously reading Barak as an appeaser who could be pushed to the limit and beyond, they must be shown that the Israeli public was in no mood for appeasement. Finally, in the event of any future negotiations, our representatives must be of the hard-boiled skeptical sort, since the trusting, optimistic, peace-seeking ones had proved disastrously naive.

All this, however, was merely political tactics. I had not yet resolved my existential turmoil. Whatever the Palestinians were doing could not erase my memory of our own wrongs, as I had learned of or experienced them since that afternoon in 1973 when we shot down that Libyan airplane; but nothing I had learned could really explain the situation we were in, and I concluded that once again my own Zionism had to be thoroughly reevaluated.

Meanwhile, things went from bad to much worse.

The Palestinians greeted the election of Sharon with more violence. In the month between his victory at the polls and the presentation of his new government, there were five lethal attacks on Israelis, with fourteen noncombatants dead, one of them eighty-five years old. This is not to count the botched attempts, such as the bomb in Mea Shearim that merely wounded four pedestrians. Arafat had freed all the Hamas and Islamic Jihad terrorists who had been in Palestinian prisons since the previous wave of violence in 1996, and it took them only a few weeks to start sending new suicide murderers against Israeli targets.

Much of the international press, meanwhile, was declaring that Sharon's electoral victory meant war. On March 7, 2001, CNN announced with a straight face: "Sharon Can Choose Between Peace and Violence, Arabs Say." Given that Barak had chosen peace and received violence, this assertion was rather startling. *The Economist* (London) had warned us before the election that if we chose Sharon, we would be saying no to peace; the following week, they greeted our democratic decision by adorning their front page with a picture of Sharon against a black background and the headline SHARON'S ISRAEL, THE WORLD'S WORRY. Once in office, Sharon laid down new rules for the renewal of negotiations: First, there had to be an end to violence. *The Economist* characterized this reasonable demand, consistent with the Oslo Accords, as "unadorned extortion." *The Guardian* greeted the election with a caricature of Sharon leaving bloody handprints on the Western Wall and ran an article by Seamus Milne calling for sanctions against Israel for daring to elect a war criminal worse than Chile's Augusto Pinochet.

Less than three weeks into Sharon's term, the Danish foreign minister explained that the Israeli occupation was the reason for the conflict. The context of his statement were discussions at the UN about sending an international force to protect the Palestinians. At the Arab summit at

Amman in March 2001, the UN secretary-general, Kofi Annan, harshly criticized Israel for her occupation of Arab land and said that Israel's "collective punishment" had fed Palestinian anger and despair. Pierre Sane, Amnesty International's secretary-general, made a series of demands, including armed international observers in the West Bank and Gaza and the right of return for Palestinian refugees. Yasser Arafat must have felt like a mainstream leader when stating in his speech at the Arab summit that "Israel's occupation is the greatest terrorism possible, while the Palestinians reject terrorism and seek peace."

Those were the speeches. The actions on the ground over the same two days seemed to be taking place on a different planet. In Hebron, a Palestinian sniper shot and killed ten-month-old Shalhevet Pass in her stroller on a playground. A bomb was defused successfully in the center of Petach Tikva. Another bomb went off but killed no one in southern Jerusalem. In the early afternoon—precisely as Arafat was giving that speech, which was broadcast live—a suicide bomber detonated himself on a number six bus headed into our neighborhood. Both of my sons and I take that bus every day.

The first few weeks of Sharon's government were characterized by a serious attempt to lighten restrictions on the Palestinian populace, including the careful lifting of blockades around Palestinian cities. In the old, pre-Oslo days, such blockades had been unnecessary, since Israeli security forces ruled the towns directly and were free to do their utmost to get at potential terror cells. This had caused countless ugly scenes and made people like myself eager to find a way to get out of there, but in retrospect it had been far cheaper in human lives on both sides and had also been easier for the Palestinians to live with: as long as there wasn't a curfew—and most of the time there wasn't—they were free to lead their normal lives, and large numbers of them daily entered Israel to work. The second *intifada* saw the Palestinians armed and organized as they hadn't been in the first, and the Israelis were forced to work with blunter tools.

The lightened restrictions were accompanied by a sharp rise in Palestinian attacks on civilian targets inside Israel. There were six suicide attacks and six car bombs in two months. In the past, one might have said that terror was the price for Israeli control over the Palestinians. But what did the murder of civilians in Netanya, Kfar Saba, and Hadera have to do with negotiations in which Israel had already ceded just about everything there was to cede and had clearly stated that she did not want control over the Palestinians? Was there anything we were withholding that could by any stretch of imagination justify this?

Sharon's government was caught between the impossibility of appeasing the Palestinians, which in any case it had been elected not to do, surrendering to the strident demands of the international community, and fulfilling the fundamental task of government: protecting the lives of its citizens. After the murder of five civilians doing their shopping on a Friday morning in Netanya, F-16s were sent to bomb a police station in nearby Nablus. The shrieks of international protest were deafening. Then, on June 1, 2001, a suicide bomber finally managed to kill lots of Israelis, almost all of them children, at the Dolphinarium discotheque in the middle of Tel Aviv.

In an unimaginable act of self-restraint, Sharon did nothing. Joschka Fischer, the German foreign minister who was coincidentally down the block when the bombing occurred, beseeched the Israelis not to retaliate and shouted at Arafat that the violence had to cease. The Israelis waited, proving to those who already knew that there was no "cycle of violence" in the Arab-Palestinian conflict, merely one-sided aggression. The lull lasted four days, and on June 5, five-month-old Yehuda Shoham had his head smashed by a rock thrown at his parents' car. That week, *Le Monde* put a caricature on its front page by Plantu, its prize-winning cartoonist. Captioned "Kamikazes," it showed two equally repulsive individuals, one with explosives strapped around his hips and the second with the houses of a settlement strapped around his. By the end of June, eight more Israelis had been killed, four of them civilians, as well as a Greek Orthodox priest who was driving a car with Israeli plates.

By training I am a historian, but by occupation I'm the director of an archive. In mid-August, a friend showed me the results of some family research that had recently been carried out in a Polish archive. Someone had dug up the registration forms that the Jews in one town were forced to fill out when the Germans arrived; most of the forms contain snapshots. It was the first time my friend had ever seen a picture of his father as a young man, before the Shoah. It was also the first time he had seen pictures of his aunts, who did not survive. For him, the astonishing thing was the incredible similarity of his own daughter to one of the aunts. It was almost as if she had been given a second chance at life. For his daughter, the discovery served as a trigger to develop a serious sense of her own participation in the flow of Jewish history. Fifteen-year-old Malki Roth was murdered at the Sbarro pizzeria in the center of Jerusalem.

The awesome Israeli response to the second mass murder of civilians in ten weeks? To shut down the unofficial Palestinian "foreign office" in Jerusalem, at the Orient House. The number of dead Palestinian civilians: none. The number of wounded Palestinians: none. The number of dead or wounded Palestinian gunmen: none. The irrevocability of the action: until decided otherwise. Yet inexplicably, the BBC led the pack in screaming about Israeli revenge. Yossi Klein Halevy found a fine metaphor for being an Israeli in 2001: like being trapped in a soundproof room with a psychopathic killer, while outsiders peered in and clucked about the lunatics.

On September 11, 2001, terrorism on an unimaginable scale reached America. Clyde Haberman of *The New York Times,* recently back from Jerusalem, asked his readers, "Do You Get It Now?" Our enemies, and those who pretend to be our critical friends, gloated that this was retribution for the one-sided American support for Israel. The French ambassador to Israel caused an uproar when he stated the European line that Osama bin Laden was evil incarnate, but the Palestinians had a case. Yet in America, a growing number of people now felt that terrorism cannot "have a case." No one who chooses to pursue political ends by such immoral means deserves a civilized hearing, no matter what the grievance.

The next month, at a conference on Nazism in Hamburg, a participant told me that where people live in fear, they will also hate. I responded sharply: "My teenage children are growing up with fear, and rightly so, but they're not allowed to hate."

On December 1, 2001, two suicide murderers and a car bomb struck in the center of Jerusalem. Eleven teenagers were killed. Meir, my seventeen-year-old son, was standing around the corner of a building, so that he and his friends emerged physically unscathed. But they saw things that one should live an entire life without seeing.

Before it hit the radio, he called to tell us he was all right. Even as he was on the phone, we heard them taking stock: "Efi's over there. He's all right! Did you see Itai? Where's Itai?" So what he had to tell us was that he was all right, but also, "I can't find lots of my friends, and there are dead bodies lying around." There was a tone of panic in his voice. When we finally reached him, he kept telling us, over and over, how someone with a torn leg was leaning on him until a medic appeared, thanked him, and then shouted, "Now get the hell out of here!"

The next day he tried to work it over. "We should send them all to Afghanistan. All these Palestinians. They can have as many square miles as they want, they won't be crowded there."

"You'll uproot millions of them?" I asked.

A few minutes later, he had dropped that solution and was searching for another. "Let's go in there and arrest all the able-bodied men from eighteen to forty and put them in a big ravine. Then we'll bring in all of the judges we have, and we'll stand each of them before a judge. There will be three verdicts: to be shot, to spend the rest of your life in jail, or to go home. Some we'll shoot, most will go to jail, and a very few we'll send home."

"Hundreds of thousands of people? Doesn't sound like justice to me."

"Well, what can we do? What kind of a people is this that proudly sends its men to blow up children?" I had no answer to that one. "I want them gone! All of them!"

"Meir, you know I'm not willing to hear such talk, even tonight."

He wandered off to his room—until he came back with another harebrained scheme, knowing it was unacceptable but having to say it, having to hear it rejected.

He had encountered evil, in its pure and unadulterated form. Most of his contemporaries in the West, along with their parents, their politicians, their journalists and academics, never have and never will; going by the things they say and write, they will never understand what Meir did at seventeen.

Sometime in March 2002, as the suicide murderers were hitting us daily and their compatriots were deliriously celebrating their heroes, I sent an e-mail to some twenty or thirty non-Israelis, Jews and non-Jews, Americans and Europeans: "Can any of you give me one compelling argument why Israel should not militarily dismantle the Palestinian Authority, throw out Yasser Arafat, collect all the arms she can, and kill all the Palestinian arms bearers who won't hand over their weapons?" I was surprised how many replied with a weary "No," but some reiterated the accepted wisdom about the impossibility of achieving anything by force of arms, though it flies in the face of the entire history of mankind. It also overlooked, willfully or foolishly, the truth about the Palestinian violence: that they had every intention of achieving quite a bit by force of arms and that by early 2002 their hopes were rising daily. Israel surely couldn't go on much longer under the strain of daily, and soon hourly, mass murders of civilians by seemingly unstoppable suicide bombers. Soon she must either start to collapse or, at the very least, plead for a cessation of hostilities in return for vastly worse terms than she had offered at Taba, terms that would lead to her future demise. Either that or she would retaliate with such brutality that the international community would be forced to step in and save the Palestinians, who would be free to continue their campaign from behind the apron of external forces unfriendly to Israel. The conventional view was that the suicide bombers were motivated by "despair," but as columnist Charles Krauthammer noted, the real motivating force of these attacks was not despair but hope. Hope that Israel could be broken and, ultimately, hope that she could be destroyed. It was crucial that they be knocked out of their hallucinations.

What remained was the response of one of my more naive friends, a Jew living in Europe, who objected to my suggestion because "I wouldn't want to live in a world where people do things like that." Meaning, I think, that it would be immoral, though for the life of me I couldn't see how.

A week later, a suicide murderer struck at the Park Hotel in Netanya, killing twenty-nine Israelis as they sat down to the Passover seder table—the most family-oriented moment in the year. So Israel finally did what she had to do. By going after the master terrorists and their thugs in their own lairs, she changed the rules of engagement. The symbol of this was the battle of Jenin—actually a battle for a small section in a small town, about the size of a football field, where the worst of the murderers were holed up in a residential area, surrounded by tons of carefully laid explosives and booby traps. Rather than vaporize them safely from the air, as they were well equipped to do, the Israelis fought inch by inch. Battle in such conditions is more than anything else a test of mettle, tenacity, and, ultimately, the resolve to win, as the Palestinians knew what was coming and had time to prepare. This explained the near parity in casualties—fifty-two Palestinians to thirty-three Israelis. The Israeli victory in this brutal contest of wills hammered home the understanding that things would not continue as they had. The tide had turned.

Which may have been precisely the reason for the orgy of hatred directed at Israel by most of the world that week. Shrieks of loathing told of an Israeli massacre of hundreds of civilians (the Palestinians told of thousands). Television panelists and newspaper pundits expounded with smirks of satisfaction that "the Butcher of Beirut" was finally showing his true colors. So-called peace activists flocked to the assistance of the Palestinians; one sent me an e-mail about how she was saving Palestinian lives from Israeli aggression, as once a handful of righteous Europeans had saved Jews from the Nazis. Leaders of nations got on the phone to Sharon to protest the siege of Arafat, never once inquiring after the dozens of wounded from the real massacre of civilians that had just taken place in Netanya. Tens of thousands of demonstrators poured onto the streets of European capitals to protest Israel's supposed war crimes, and a prominent German politician castigated our *Vernichtungskrieg,* a Nazi word that means war of annihilation. The United Nations set up a commission of inquiry into the "crimes" committed at Jenin, headed by a Swiss official by the name of Saramuga who had in the past compared the Magen David to the swastika.

My friend Esther Golan is a Holocaust survivor in her late seventies. On the afternoon of Yom HaShoah, the day of remembrance of the Holocaust, we were to appear together at a public event where she would donate to Yad Vashem a sheaf of letters written by her mother sixty years ago. The mother, despairing of ever again seeing her children, had clung to the hope that somehow, someday, they could be "reunited in our own land," right up until she was sent to Auschwitz. Esther did not appear that afternoon. Her grandson, Eyal Joel, was killed that morning in Jenin. When I visited her a few days later, she asked me if she was losing her grip on reality or was it the world? I assured her it was the world. By this time, I had been grappling with the issues for more than a year, and I felt that I knew how to prove this.

The Jews were humanity's first monotheists, and monotheism, in its complex way, is universal. It does not necessarily expect everyone to believe in it, but it does allow anyone to do so. It states that there is one God who created us all, and it welcomes anyone, irrespective of race, gender, status, or wealth. It also asserts that there is a universal morality. There are countless caveats, but this is the fundamental position. Living in a Jewish context means accepting that cognition and morality both are fundamentally universal.

The premise of this book is that there is, at least sometimes, an objective truth that can be known; there are modes of investigation and deliberation that are open to all, which can be used to determine it. Morality too is universal; while not everyone will agree about what is moral in every circumstance, anyone can, potentially, identify it. Truth and morality are not owned by any group, although it is conceivable that some individuals or groups will be moral more often than others. But this will be something that anyone can test empirically, if one is honest about it.

Some readers will disagree that morality is universal, but if that were so, there would be no way to make any judgments at all. Given the intensity and pervasiveness of opinions on Israel's behavior, however, most people obviously do feel that there are moral criteria by which it can be measured and judged.

The case against Israel is varied, detailed, and harsh. Most Westerners subscribe only to some of the main accusations; some of the allegations are mutually incompatible, but inconsistency has never stopped people from voicing opinions.

Zionism is rejected by definition, regardless of its policies or actions. It is cast as a European colonial project, which is about as devastating a critique as possible in this age of postcolonial guilt. Israel is actually the worst of all colonial projects, because it is the only one still around, after the others saw their errors and disbanded. Arabs compound this culpability by claiming that there is no evidence for a Jewish past in Palestine; Westerners cannot agree to this because it undermines Christianity and their own history, but they agree with the Arabs that even if there was a Jewish past, it is too ancient to be meaningful today. Finally, people who regard themselves as proponents of a universal humanism dislike Zionism for concentrating on the well-being of Jews alone: such concentration on a single ethnic group can only be an instance of racism.

Having denied the Jews the right to national expression in their land, the detractors bolster their position with claims about the practice of Zionism. The Palestinians, they say, were peacefully living their national life until they were invaded by Jews, who drove them off and stole their land. The Zionists always intended to destroy the Palestinians and won't desist until this has been accomplished. Zionism is thus a genocidal movement with a long-standing penchant for terror against defenseless Palestinian civilians. As soon as British forces left Palestine in 1948, this view asserts, the Zionists did their best to evict the Palestinians from their homeland, and afterward they continued the persecution so as to stave off any possibility of peace before the task had been completed. In 1967, it is said, Israel provoked another war in which she conquered the parts of Palestine she did not yet control and evicted additional masses of Palestinians. When this still didn't break the backs of the Palestinian people, the Israelis launched a program of settlement on expropriated land, cleverly planned to strangle the Palestinians. Even when Israel ostensibly negotiates with the Palestinians, she never does so in good faith; her real goals are to subjugate the Palestinians, directly or indirectly.

This version of history is so breathtakingly hostile to the Jews that most Westerners wouldn't profess it in such a condensed form, but every one of its tenets can be found in the pages of many European newspapers. Its power lies in the kernels of truth it contains and is abetted by the ignorance of the readers—and perhaps of the writers themselves—who accept these distortions of fact since they fit traditional preconceptions about the Jews.

Given the inhumane policies of the Israelis, you begin to see why the conflict is so protracted. The Palestinians are infuriated by the injustice of the Zionist invasion, the brutality of Israeli occupation, and the violence of the settlers perched strategically on every hilltop. Their resistance is only natural, but since the Israelis insist on answering them with redoubled force, a vicious cycle has been created that can only get worse. The conflict has become an intractable blood feud that feeds on itself, and the protagonists on both sides have lost their senses. Morality no longer matters, since one man's terrorist is another man's freedom fighter, but it makes all the difference, since the only way to end the conflict is for Israel to redress the injustices she has done. Since Israel is the powerful aggressor, she can afford to be magnanimous toward the Palestinians, who are weak and do not threaten her. Yet Israel rejects all this good sense, because her goal remains the destruction of the Palestinians and the annexation of their land in fulfillment of Zionist prophecies.

I have repeatedly asked critics of Israel to explain how they reconcile this view with the electoral victories of Rabin or Barak or the offers Barak made in 2000. Those who are willing to respond tell me that the whole thing was a hoax, Israeli propaganda; all Barak really wanted was to control the Palestinians indirectly instead of directly. It is astonishing how deep-seated the fear of covert Jewish power really is.

It is this primordial fear of the Jews, inculcated during centuries of animosity, that inflates the global importance of this conflict to irrational proportions. From the volume of vituperation hurled at her, one would think that tiny Israel threatens world peace and stability (as the French ambassador to the United Kingdom put it: "Why should we all be in danger because of shitty little Israel?"). People who hate the United States often hate Israel for being an American outpost. In recent years, however, a more potent strain of this theory has been raising its all-too-familiar head, as stated clearly in the letter of Saddam Hussein to the United Nations of September 19, 2002: "In targeting Iraq, the United States Administration is acting on behalf of Zionism, which has been killing the heroic people of Palestine, destroying their property, murdering their children, and seeking to impose their domination on the whole world. . . . You may notice how the policy of the Zionist Entity, which has usurped Palestine and other Arab territories since 1948, and afterward, has become now as one with the policies and capabilities of the United States."

There can no more be a debate with such a viewpoint than there could have been in the early 1940s, when Nazi propaganda referred to the president of the United States as Franklin Rosenfeld. You might expect Western public opinion to be more sensitive to the dangers of such viewpoints, but you would be sadly mistaken. Saddam's allegations, which are standard fare in Arab propaganda, failed to cause any consternation in the ranks of Israel's detractors, no second thoughts about their partners in bile. As if the history of Jew-hatred never happened, they continue to assure us that the moment we redress all the Palestinian grievances, peace and serenity will reign. Or perhaps it's the other way around: they frequently reprimand the Israelis for not learning the proper lessons from their own history. The Jews, of all people, should know better, goes the refrain. Having themselves suffered so grievously, they should be the last ones to inflict suffering on anyone else.

The maliciousness of this statement is complex. It insinuates that the Israelis are somehow treating the Palestinians as the Nazis treated them; it further intimates that the Palestinians are as innocent of evil designs as were the Jews of Europe; and while quite overlooking the fact that the Jews never murdered their tormentors, it excuses Palestinian crimes as the result of persecution. All of which leads to the conclusion that since the Jews so obstinately refuse to behave, Zionism has failed demonstrably and must be undone.

Take Oxford professor Tom Paulin, who in February 2001 published a poem about the "Zionist SS" who shoot down defenseless Palestinian children. When Paulin makes such comparisons, he is calling for the violent destruction of the Jewish state. What's more, his vitriol is dangerously approaching mainstream discourse, as illustrated by the spat between some local politicians in Wales in January 2003.

A minor Labour politician, Ray Davies, called upon two midlevel Welsh politicians not to travel to Israel, which he characterized as an "apartheid state." "Hitler's Nazi regime occupied Europe for four years only. Palestine and the West Bank have been occupied for 40 years. . . . I do draw that comparison because [this is] one group of people who should understand what oppression is and what it is like living under occupation." Davies himself had participated in a fact-finding trip to the occupied territories but proudly explained why he had "utterly resisted" the idea of going to Israel proper: "When they go out there they will be treated like lords and taken to the Holocaust museum to try to engineer as much sympathy as they can and shown the bright side and the pleasant side and the sort of life the Israelis are enjoying. . . . Anybody who goes to Israel will be taken to the Holocaust museum and shown what has happened to the Israelis. . . . But that does not give the Israeli government any right to do what they are doing to the poor beleaguered Palestinians for over 40 years. Life in Palestine and the occupied territories at the moment is nothing short of disgraceful." He was joined in his plea by Welsh children's poet laureate Menna Elfyn.

The refusal even to listen to the Israeli side indicates the irrational depth of the animosity and the impossibility of responding to it through dialogue—which has of course been a hallmark of antisemitism for centuries. As long as Israel can protect herself, the fact that she is despised by irrational people need not be a source of despair; if enlightened rationality is important, it should be a source of pride. The danger is that eventually rational people will begin to doubt the truth of what they know.

This book addresses itself to anyone open to a moral evaluation of the facts. Since the story of Zionism is intertwined with the story of its wars, an attempt to evaluate Zionism must be anchored in assumptions about the morality of war.

There are four main schools of thought on justifying war.

First, there are religious justifications, whereby wars are viewed as the enactment of God's will. The Islamic conquests of the seventh to ninth centuries, or the Crusades that responded to them from 1095 onward, are prime examples. The modern atheists of this school replace God with the inevitability of History, as in Nazism and some stages of communism. These justifications are usually not universal, as the unbelievers or the losers of History are shut out—the Jews and other subhumans in Nazism; the bourgeois and kulaks in communism; and eventually the alleged intellectuals in Communist Cambodia. By definition, these wars will not be justifiable by universal standards of morality.

Others view warfare as an inevitable part of realpolitik—an extension of politics by other means—and therefore not a subject of moral considerations. Since they feel unbound by such considerations, the practitioners of this form of warfare often wage immoral wars. Most of Europe's wars from the eighteenth century on were of this sort, climaxing in World War I, which started as just another war for the balance of power but got horribly out of hand because of the unnoticed advance of military technology in the decades preceding it. Africa's unnoticed wars these days are also of this type: they are about power or greed.

Pacifists condemn all war, for any reason. This is an appealing school of thought, and if it could somehow be simultaneously inculcated in all of humanity, the world would be a much better place. In the meantime, pacifists allow themselves to stand aloof from unjust wars, effectively supporting the aggressors. Where they themselves are targets of aggression, they must either surrender whatever is being demanded of them, including possibly their lives and the lives of fellow citizens whom they are not willing to defend, or rely on someone else to do their fighting. The defeatism of the French in 1940, for example, was influenced by pacifism, with the result that the Nazi war machine routed them with an ease that belied their actual military potential and then deported seventy thousand Jews to the camps before the Allies fought the French war for them and stopped the murder. The Western European refrain of appeasers of the Soviet Union, "Better Red Than Dead," was fortunately never tried, since others were willing to face the Reds and force them to back down. Refusing to use one's power to stop murderers caused the deaths of tens of thousands in Bosnia in the 1990s and of hundreds of thousands in Rwanda. In such a world, pacifism is not morally defensible.[1]

Finally, there is the moral war school of thought, which recognizes that wars are a part of the human condition but seeks to regulate their conduct

1 The German pacifists of the Jehovah's Witnesses group in Nazi Germany are an interesting exception, not only because they refused to fight in an exceptionally immoral war, but particularly because they were willing to pay the ultimate price for their convictions and to languish for years in Nazi concentration camps when they could have walked free at will merely by changing their convictions. They are the exception that demonstrates the rule.

according to moral considerations. (I have drawn heavily, though not exclusively, on Michael Walzer's account of this tradition in *Just and Unjust Wars: A Moral Argument with Historical Illustrations,* though I cannot say whether Walzer would be pleased at my adaptation of his thoughts.) This is the camp with which I and most other Israelis identify. As a school of thought, the moral war tradition is rooted in Christian theology, but its ultimate roots are in Jewish monotheism. The concept of war as a human activity that must be regulated by moral constrictions first appears in Deuteronomy, in chapter 20, for example, which regulates how the army should prepare for battle, how to lay siege and negotiate lifting it, and the relation to prisoners of war.

A crucial distinction in the discussion of morality and war is that between *jus ad bellum,* or justice in going to war, and *jus in bello*, or justice in waging war. The first asks whether one is ever justified in going to war in the first place and answers that nations may protect themselves against aggression and thereby ensure their right to define for themselves the kind of communal life they wish to live—the American Revolution being an obvious example. Intervention in the wars of others can also be justified, when the intervention is meant to put an end to aggression—the Kosovo campaign in 1999 being perhaps the clearest example, or expelling Iraq from Kuwait in 1991. Another point, not made by Walzer, is the price of ending the war, be it by surrender, negotiated settlement, or victory. The price each side will pay for peace can indicate what the original goals of being at war were and the degree of their morality. The American behavior after winning World War II speaks volumes about the morality of their fighting it in the first place; the fate of Czechoslovakia after Munich, in 1938–1939, proves how moral (though futile) a war against Germany would have been.

Jus in bello is the attempt to wage war according to a code, lest one's actions nullify whatever justification there may have been for the original decision to fight. This is a separate issue from *jus ad bellum* and reaches down to the individual behavior of soldiers in the field, irrespective of whether the war they are engaged in is just. A just war can be waged unjustly, and an unjust war could conceivably be justly waged. The decisive issue is that war is to be waged by soldiers against other soldiers. Civilians and captured soldiers are not legitimate targets.

What I found in my review of Israel's wars was that Zionism has mostly tried to be moral. Sometimes it made mistakes, from which it generally (but not always) learned. While being continuously at war, it was surprisingly, though not fully, successful at all sorts of other projects, such as the building of a reasonably healthy society out of widely diverse communities. Precisely because its overall record is basically positive, its citizens are deeply committed to its success, even in the face of violent rejection from its neighbors and widespread international condemnation. Much of this stems from ancient Jewish traditions that remain powerfully influential in modern Israel. As a country, it is not religious, but it is very Jewish, especially in the choices it makes.

For at the heart of all morality is choice. The biblical story of Creation underlines that choosing between good and evil is the essence of being human. (Marxist historical imperatives diminish our humanity by reducing our responsibility to choose morally.) The original Zionist choice was that the goal of Jewish national existence was worthy of considerable effort; subsequent choices have been concerned mainly with the permissible means for preserving it.

In April 2002, the government of Saudi Arabia tried to convince the rest of the Arab world to adopt an initiative to recognize Israel and make peace with her, under certain circumstances. The proposal was accompanied by considerable fanfare and an Arab Conference in Beirut. Whether the Saudis were sincere is hard to say, but even if they were, the fanfare obscured the underlying fact that after waging one war a decade since the 1940s, most of the Arab world has still not made the choice to accept Israel's right to exist. The means chosen to affirm this lack of recognition were demonstrated some four hours after the discussion in Beirut, when twenty-nine Jews were murdered in Netanya at the seder table. The howls of protest in the West as Israel then decided to use force to protect her citizens were also a moral decision, as recognized by Arabs and Jews alike.

So if our enemies dispute our right to exist, let's at least make certain that we can defend our actions to ourselves. This will add fiber to our resilience, fortitude to our determination, and encouragement to those allies still left with us. Ensuring that our wars are just will also ensure that those of our enemies are not, and this knowledge will strengthen our hand until the day they tire of spilling blood for what should not be achieved anyway.

CHAPTER

I

Early Zionism: The Decision to Have and Use Power

From the Palestinian National Charter (1968): **Article 20:** . . . Claims of historical or religious ties of Jews with Palestine are incompatible with the facts of history and the true conception of what constitutes statehood. Judaism, being a religion, is not an independent nationality. Nor do Jews constitute a single nation with an identity of its own; they are citizens of the states to which they belong.

Article 22: Zionism is a political movement organically associated with international imperialism and antagonistic to all action for liberation and to progressive movements in the world. It is racist and fanatic in its nature, aggressive, expansionist, and colonial in its aims, and fascist in its methods. Israel is the instrument of the Zionist movement, and geographical base for world imperialism placed strategically in the midst of the Arab homeland to combat the hopes of the Arab nation for liberation, unity, and progress. Israel is a constant source of threat vis-à-vis peace in the Middle East and the whole world. . . .

The charter of the PLO is the single most important document in the history of the Palestinians, since for decades it was the governing document of their national institution; parts of it may have been modified during the 1990s, but it has yet to be superseded by any other. Yet as written, the charter does not make clear what the Palestinians think their enemy is. The Jews: Are they merely a religious group, as stated clearly in article 20, or are they an insidious, unseen network of malevolent conspirators à la *The Protocols of the Elders of Zion*—racist, fanatic, aggressive, expansionist, colonial, and Fascist—whose goals, among others, include the destruction of all that is beautiful in the Arab world, as article 22 implies?

They are, of course, none of these. Yet in the time-honored tradition of all propaganda, the closer the propagandist sails to the truth, the more potent his or her message will be. The truth is, the Jews have been unusual for a very long time, and Zionism has been assiduously creating new levels of complexity from its inception. They started as a nation with a religion, went on to become a religion with a nation, then spent centuries as a religious community that looked more like a nation than any of the societies surrounding it. With the Enlightenment, many of them pretended to be merely a religion until that seemed not to be working, and then some of them invented Zionism in order to be merely a nation. Unsurprisingly, Zionism as a national movement has been deeply influenced by its religious heritage, to the degree that some of its strands now see it as more religious than national, while others see it as a tool to rid the nation of religion.

This confusion about what sort of social group the Jews really are began about three thousand years ago. At that time, a young nation calling itself the tribes of Israel created what would become some of humanity's most famous and enduring religious texts, and at the precise geographic spot that lies at the heart of today's Middle East conflict. Since thousands of years later the fate of Jerusalem was to prove divisive enough to destroy the best-laid plans for peace, its importance and centrality in the conflict must be clarified.

For the first two thousand years of its five-thousand-year history, Jerusalem was a small and insignificant hamlet. It was situated on a low hill with steep sides to the east, south, and west, so that it needed to be defended only from the north. The valley to the south broadened for a mile or two, so it had enough good agricultural land to support the small number of people who could have lived on the narrow crown of the hill. To the east, just above where the valley broadened, there was a spring, the only one of reasonable size for a number of miles in any direction. It was slightly unusual in the propitious combination of easy defense, good land, and enough water—but not unique. I can think of two or three similar sites within twenty miles or so, and you've never heard of them.

All the hills in the area were higher, and in an era when travel was always on foot, this ensured that no main road led through it, as such a road would have required too much climbing. A mile or two to the west, along the top of a ridge, there was indeed a regional road, but the region was small and the road was of no great significance. All in all, it was an unimportant place, with nothing to indicate that it would ever be otherwise. So insignificant was it that when Joshua and his armies rolled over the land, they didn't bother to conquer it, leaving it as a Canaanite enclave. And so it remained for another few generations.

The hour of destiny struck almost exactly three thousand years ago. David son of Ishai had been anointed king in Judea. But he had been accepted only by his own tribe, the Judeans, and by the small tribe of Benjamin. The other ten tribes still proclaimed their allegiance to the house of Saul, recently dead in battle, or to no one. Needing a neutral base, David proclaimed Jerusalem his capital—sort of a District of Columbia, outside the jurisdiction of any tribe and more centrally located than his Judean capital of Hebron.

Sometime thereafter it became apparent that the City of David, as some were now calling it, had another unusual characteristic. The hill to its west also had a deep ravine to *its* west; to the north, it connected to the ridge Jerusalem was on. This meant that should there ever be a reason for the city to grow, it could preserve its tactical advantages: ravines on three sides, water, and agricultural land in a number of directions. Not long thereafter, some unsung hero invented plaster, allowing water to be stored in cisterns, and the size of the spring was no longer a limit to the growth of population.

Once he had a capital, David wished to build a Temple for the Lord. The tradition says that God turned him down, since David was a man of war and the Temple needed to be built by a man of peace. In the biblical story, David's life is divided between that of the heroic young rogue and the unmitigated disaster that was his life as king, from the arranged death of Uriah onward. It was in these years, sitting in his palace in Jerusalem, that he wrote many of the psalms and became one of humanity's foremost poets.

Solomon built the Temple on the hilltop known as Mount Moriah, north of the City of David. It was completed about 950 B.C.E., or some fifty years after his father had taken the city. Afterward, Jewish tradition imposed earlier events on the spot, the most important being the story of Abraham's near sacrifice of his son Isaac. The original version, in Genesis, merely states that it took place on one of the mountains three days' walk north of Beer Sheva, which could have been any one of dozens of other hilltops in Judea. The point of the story, however, was to engage not in geographic research but in religious meaning, by tying the story of David into the central tradition of the Jewish people, drawing a direct line between the founding fathers, the builders of the Temple, and the future Messiah. Essentially, Jerusalem is at the epicenter of what Judaism is all about.

How much of this is fact and how much merely myth? There is little archaeological evidence for the stories of the Patriarchs. But it is hard to see how there could be. Seventy nomads living in tents 3,300 years ago hardly lend themselves to archaeological verification—or repudiation, one might add. Hundreds of thousands of nomads wandering through the Sinai for forty years should have left more evidence than they apparently did, although they also built no long-standing structures that archaeologists could be expected to dig up.

Israeli surveys in the West Bank, however, do seem to have uncovered evidence of a new wave of settlements in about the eleventh century B.C.E. Most archaeologists do not read the evidence as telling of a single military invasion by outsiders. Rather, it speaks of a process. They are also skeptical about the violence described in the Bible, but clearly something was afoot that changed the pattern of habitation in the hills of today's West Bank. There does not seem to be much evidence that Jerusalem under David was the capital of a regional power. However, the existence of a house of David has been verified by evidence uncovered at Dan, near today's Lebanese border.

From the ninth century B.C.E. onward, there *is* limited external evidence that confirms the outlines of the biblical story—ever more so as one advances in time. From the seventh century, most archaeologists agree on the basic correctness of the story, even as they continue to disagree on specifics and remind themselves that the Bible is a subjective version of events. The Bible itself, they roughly concur, was repeatedly edited from the fifth century B.C.E.; yet the language of the stories of the Patriarchs differs significantly from that of the Scribes, so they must have inherited them from an earlier age.

Only a small group of researchers, referred to as the Copenhagen school or the minimalists, denies the Jewish connection to the land until much later. Academically they play a useful role as a foil for much of the mainstream research and discussion, but their political line is that mainstream archaeological research is unacceptable because it serves the political interests of Israel and supports its oppression of the Palestinians.

Archaeologists have not come up with an explanation for monotheism or its origin, leaving believers untroubled at the most crucial points. The Jewish idea of freedom from bondage predates its appearance elsewhere by millennia. The point about David was not that he forged a small empire, but that he forged a national tradition, founded a capital, and wrote the psalms. Most surprising of all, however, is that the onus of the earliest, violent era seems to have been removed. The tradition told of a bloody war of conquest, which would have been a standard practice in the context of its day but may actually never have happened, even if Jews 2,500 years ago felt they needed such a chapter in their past. Anti-Zionists sometimes point to the conquest of Canaan as a precursor to the Zionist invasion of Palestine. Yet the growing Hebrew presence in the land now appears to have been the result of a gradual process, not a genocidal war. If those first centuries of violence never happened, the Jews seem to have a history of three thousand years, in which mass murder was never employed as a political tool, not for domination and not for resisting oppression. Astonishing, and unparalleled anywhere else on the face of the globe.

Hezekiah, a direct descendant of David and Solomon who reigned in Jerusalem about 250 years after them, was a great builder. When the marauding Assyrian army was known to be approaching, Hezekiah undertook various fortification projects, two of which are worth noting. The first was to divert the water of the spring away from the eastern side of the town, which lay beyond the walls, to the western side of the same hill. The second was to build a new wall on the western ridge; the gully to the west was now inside the city. In order to divert the water, Hezekiah's builders dug a tunnel under the city, which shouldn't have been complicated: dig into the hill with the spring always behind you, and soon enough you'll come out on the other side.

It wasn't done that way, however. Instead, the engineers started simultaneously from both sides, digging consistently at a grade that would allow the water to flow freely. They dug in a rough S shape, with a few extra curves thrown in. Zigzagging under the mountain, neither party ever erred or backtracked, and they met about 250 meters from each side, deep under the mountain; at the spot where they met a stone plaque was placed, telling of the excitement in Hebrew anyone can understand, 2,700 years later. Still inexplicable is how they did it, in the middle of the Iron Age; engineers in the twenty-first century tell me they would not be able to repeat the achievement. I once took a group of Israel Air Force pilots through the tunnel, which is still there, the water still flowing, and they suggested that perhaps our forefathers were navigating with the stars, a hundred meters under the rock.

The prophet Isaiah, who also lived at this time, saw his mission as correcting the world, not forecasting the future. He can plausibly be called the single most important advocate of justice in human history. "Wash yourselves clean: put your evil doings away from my sight. Cease to do evil. Learn to do good. Devote yourselves to justice; aid the wronged. Uphold the rights of the orphan; defend the cause of the widow." (chapter 1, verses 16–17) Yet Isaiah was rooted in the very particular events of his long life in Jerusalem. Listen to his admonitions to remain just and serious in the face of approaching war: "And you counted the houses of Jerusalem and pulled down houses to fortify the wall . . . my Lord God of Hosts summoned on that day to weeping and lamenting, to tonsuring and girding with sackcloth. Instead, there was rejoicing and merriment, killing of cattle and slaughtering of sheep, eating of meat and drinking of wine: 'Eat and drink, for tomorrow we die!' " (chapter 22, verses 10–13)[1] War cannot come at the expense of the poor or without good reason. It requires reflection and moral seriousness.

The water project was rediscovered in the nineteenth century; the wall was discovered in the 1970s, in the middle of what is today the Jewish Quarter of the Old City. It was hurriedly thrown up along the crest of the hill on a line marked by the military engineers. You can see it to this day and see where it cuts through a residential neighborhood, even through individual homes: you are looking at the very stones that provoked Isaiah's

[1] Translations from *JPS Hebrew-English Tanakh* (Philadelphia: Jewish Publication Society, 1999).

ire. The power of eternal moral precepts is that they address the lives of real people; if they don't, they become sterile platitudes.

Eternal precepts are also realistic: for all his fury at how things were being done, Isaiah was in favor of the war and strengthened the resolve of the wavering king and his lieutenants when the outlook seemed bleakest. Is there a moral to that tale? Perhaps that war is not the worst thing that can happen, but that it must be waged justly. There is something essentially Jewish about the fact that the prophet who castigated our forefathers for their weaknesses remains a living figure, his words still ringing with urgency and truth, while the king who built the walls and dug the tunnel is merely a king who built and dug.

The Assyrian king whose looming invasion set the backdrop for all this came in 701 B.C.E., failed (alone of all his targets) to take Jerusalem, and left. But in 586 B.C.E., Nebuchadnezzar of Babylon did manage to destroy the city and its Temple. He put out the eyes of the last king of the house of David, breaking a dynasty of four hundred years, and exiled many of the people, who mourned their misfortune:

By the rivers of Babylon
There we sat
Sat and wept
As we thought of Zion
[. . .]
If I forget thee, O Jerusalem
Let my right hand wither
Let my tongue stick to my palate
If I cease to think of you
If I do not keep Jerusalem in my memory
Even at my happiest hour

The first verse has turned into an archetypal lament, an allegory of the human yearning for better times. Verdi in *Nabucco* wrote the "Chorus of the Hebrew Slaves" from it. The sentences about Jerusalem get less publicity. But for Jews, of course, they are not allegorical.

Fifty years later, in 538 B.C.E., Cyrus the Great, king of Persia, conquered Babylon and decreed that the exiled Jews could return to their land. Some chose not to do so, and their descendants were still living in

Iraq until they were expelled from that country in 1949. The Second Temple was inaugurated in 516 B.C.E., seventy years after the First Temple was destroyed, on the same spot. The Jews of Judea multiplied and prospered, and their capital also grew. From time to time, such growth required the building of new outer walls to enclose the new neighborhoods. The Hasmoneans presided over the greatest growth of the city until the twentieth century, and they built three walls, each farther flung (to the north) than its predecessor. (Golgotha, where Jesus is thought to have been crucified, lay between the second and third walls.) The ensuing centuries have smothered the hill and the first wall with deep layers of urban debris.

The greatest builder the Jews ever had was Herod, known to the Romans as "the King of the Jews," although most of his subjects would not have regarded him as Jewish. His subjects generally detested him, yet in addition to being a brutal man, he was also a devious politician. So alongside such megalomaniacal projects as palaces built on remote desert cliffs (Masada), a deep-sea port on a straight coastline (Caesarea), and an artificial mountain for his burial spot (Herodian), he also rebuilt the Second Temple.

The triannual Jewish pilgrimages to Jerusalem and the Temple were growing too large, and the area around the Temple was no longer able to accommodate the visitors. Herod's solution was radical: He simply made the mountain bigger. He built a tremendous retaining wall around it and filled it up so as to create a gigantic artificial plateau whose center rose slightly to the peak of the natural mountain, on which the First and Second Temples had been sitting for some nine hundred years. Since the top of the wall needed to be a uniform height, while the bottom followed the contours of the mountain, at some points the wall was probably higher than any other building in the world. In order to hold the weight of the fill, it was built with large stones, each weighing several tons; at one place in the wall, opposite the Temple, is a thirteen-meter rock that probably weighs about five hundred tons, more than the obelisk taken from Egypt to Paris by Napoleon. It was brought there and raised to its permanent spot, manually.

The construction proved so sturdy that nothing has ever affected it. Neither wars, earthquakes, nor the elements have left any mark on it. Although Jerusalem has repeatedly been razed, rebuilt, and razed again, the Temple Mount still stands. It is an immovable object that by some accounts now has the power to destroy the best-laid plans of peace-seeking men, whose noble intentions are dashed on its inscrutable walls.

Jewish sovereignty on the mountain ended abruptly, and violently, in the summer of 70 C.E., after more than one thousand years. It was the culmination of a three-year campaign in which the Roman armies had been inching inexorably southward from the Galilee, smothering every pocket of resistance in their way. The brunt of the attack on Jerusalem came from the north, where there had never been any natural obstacles, merely a succession of walls. Weeks after the outer walls had been breached, the butchery raged in the narrow streets and across the rooftops. Finally, on the evening of the ninth of the Jewish month of Av, according to Jewish tradition, the legionnaires broke onto the Temple Mount and torched it. There was no way they could destroy the Mount itself, but a group of them did gather around the capstone at the top of the southwestern corner. Straining and huffing, they levered the heavy boulder from its place and toppled it over the edge. It plunged some 130 feet onto the pavement below, which was laid with gigantic flagstones. So great was the force that it cracked the flagstone, and to this day it remains where it fell, only now you have to climb down into an archaeologist's pit to see it.

The Roman generals went home, had their triumphal parades, and built the Colosseum to mark their victory over the Jews. It was a fitting epitaph: an arena of mass murder to commemorate their victory over the people who had suggested to the world, "You shall not judge unfairly; you shall show no partiality; you shall not take bribes, for bribes blind the eyes of the discerning and upset the plea of the just. Justice, justice shall you pursue." (Deuteronomy, chapter 16, verses 19–20)

Jerusalem was destroyed, and the Jews were left with no Temple. The world must have seemed at an end. Even the most optimistic Jews hoped for no more than somehow to find the strength to continue another day, week, or month. Even Rabbi Akiva, the greatest scholar of his age, who set the Jews on a new path, never realized what he was doing. He and his disciples were convinced that redemption was imminent: it *had to be.* God was angry but had not abandoned them; soon the punishment would be over, and He would rectify everything. Soon: Tomorrow! Today! Now! When Simon Bar Kochba rose in revolt in 132 C.E., Rabbi Akiva declared that he was the Messiah. They all perished in the conflagration, never knowing how wrong they were.

The Romans had had enough of the tiresome Jews with their insistence on being different and their penchant for revolts. The full brunt of their awesome power was brought to bear, and the legions were ordered systematically to wipe out the whole Jewish populace. Faced with guerrilla fighters based in hundreds of villages and towns, the Romans razed everything. One by one, each town and village was surrounded and demolished. No quarter was given, and no mercy. Week after week, month after month, for three bloody years the hillsides were denuded of their inhabitants. Pillage, rape, and murder were the order of the day. The destruction of Carthage, centuries earlier, still echoes through the ages, yet this destruction of Judea, gone now from the memory of the West, was of far greater dimensions. Anywhere from five hundred thousand to one million Jews died; so many survivors were sold into slavery that the going rate for slaves fell all over the Roman Empire.

By the time the campaign was over, in 135 C.E., Judea was empty of Jews for the first time in over a thousand years. Hillsides cultivated lovingly from generation to generation stood orphaned, their terraces soon to be eroded by the elements back into wilderness. Even the name Judea was erased, and by order of Emperor Hadrian it was now called Palestine. Eventually new inhabitants moved in, and far in the future their descendants would assume Hadrian's name, claiming that they had been here from time immemorial—but that would merely underscore the limits of their memory.

Hadrian retired to his villa to study the arts, secure in the knowledge that he had broken the back of the tiresome Jews. Eighteen centuries later, a unit of Jewish soldiers from Judea passed through Rome in 1945 as soldiers of the British Empire. They took the time to visit Titus's arch, which they smeared with paint in Hebrew: *Am Yisrael chai*. "The people of Israel live." It was a weird way of celebrating the liberation of Auschwitz.

Bar Kochba's revolt and the Shoah are the two greatest catastrophes in more than three thousand years of Jewish history. They also bookend the period of Jewish powerlessness. Until the Hadrianic genocide, the Jews had been a people on their land like any other. Afterward, the survivors turned themselves into something quite unusual: a national community without the geographic or political trappings of a nation. In the dialectic of history, this was to give them an unsurpassed longevity. No other nation or community would make it from antiquity into modernity, not even the Romans themselves.

The essence of this unlikely survival strategy was to create a vital culture common to all Jews and set apart from everyone else. Lacking all the usual trappings of a nation, this culture was primarily religious. It dealt with individual and communal issues such as birth, life, and death, or communal welfare and education. It did not deal with military, diplomatic, or economic matters. Yet the Jewish way of life was common to Jews wherever they were, so that ultimately a Jew felt at home among other Jews no matter how far from home and uneasy among non-Jews a stone's throw down the road. What had once been a nation on its land with a common religion had evolved into a religion that was preserving a nation—in very unusual conditions.

Although they were a well-defined nationality more than a millennium before the surrounding populace began once more to think in such terms, they never acted accordingly. There was no national leadership (although for the first few centuries the Jewish community in Babylon may have thought of itself as such), no national representatives, no promoting of national self-interest. And of course, no use of power in the defense of the nation. Jewish leaders grew adept at local political machinations for the benefit of their people, but these rarely succeeded in times of major crisis, when the host nations wanted the Jews gone or severely restricted. But the Jews had learned how to adapt, and they achieved a surprising stability.

Nowhere were Jews ever treated as equals by the surrounding society. Medieval Jews in Muslim societies were easily distinguishable by their appearance and relegated by Muslim law to second-class status, called *dhimmi.* In Christian lands their position at the best of times was similar; often it was far worse. Although anti-Jewish violence was an oft recurring phenomenon, most Jews must have lived their whole lives without being direct victims of it. But the memory of earlier events, or the hearsay of violence elsewhere, would have been part of their daily reality. Yet this continuing violence, persecution, discrimination, and segregation called forth more resolution than self-pity. They responded by looking inward to their community, backward to their glorious past, and forward to an even greater future. In the meantime, they were not prone to violence and did not see it as an acceptable option.

A popular cliché among Israel's critics is that Jews suffer from a deeply ingrained culture of alleged Jewish victimhood. According to Uri Avneri, one of Israel's most prominent homegrown critics:

> The Israeli-Palestinian conflict has become a kind of championship fight between two grand masters of victimization. But the phenomenon is more profound. For generations the Jews were persecuted in many countries and developed the consciousness of victims. It could almost have been said that most of the Jewish culture created during the last two or three centuries revolves around this axis.[2]

Avneri mistakes disdain for victimhood. Indeed, Jews often held a low opinion of their persecutors. But to portray the persecutors themselves as the axis around which Jewish culture revolves is radically to inflate their importance. In the halachic literature there is but limited discussion of non-Jews one way or the other, and that was the overwhelming bulk of Jewish literature until recent centuries; afterward, many Jews were exhilarated by the new vistas that seemed to be opening to them, and victimhood was anything but the axis of their creativity.

The Italian Renaissance seems largely to have bypassed the Jews; nor was the scientific revolution of the seventeenth century of any relevance to them (Spinoza, who was rejected by the Jews of his day, is the only exception). With the Enlightenment of the eighteenth century, however, Christian society undertook a reassessment of its own traditions that was to revolutionize everything, from the structures of power to the daily routines of individual life. The essence of the Enlightenment was the belief that nature was governed by natural law and that human reason could unravel it. Rational and scientific inquiry would be the tools of choice in dealing not only with nature, but with politics, history, economics, and society in general. Religion would cease to be the primary principle by which society organized itself and would eventually become part of the private decisions made by each individual. Since reason was a universal potential, everyone might benefit from using it. Even Jews.

The Jews were thus faced with a novel challenge. They could integrate

[2] Published on-line, July 17, 2001, at Palestine Media Watch (www.pmwatch.org).

into the broader society, but only on condition that they, too, free themselves of outdated religious ideas. Essentially, they were being offered emancipation as individuals, not as a community, or at least not as a Jewish community. They could be a religion, if Judaism were to change significantly, but they must cease being a nation.

Some accepted both the option and its price; many of their descendants do not know they were ever Jewish. Others sought ways of accommodating Judaism to eighteenth-century rationalism, emphasizing proto-Enlightened strands of Jewish thought while downplaying the isolationist elements. One such attempt, the Reform movement in Germany, turned Judaism from a religion based on halachic behavior into a pseudo-Protestant sect based on faith and with scant need for ritual. Others repudiated modernity entirely, freezing their style of life exactly as it was. More than two hundred years later, they still wear the same clothes: long black coats, outmoded headgear.

The Zionists accepted the Enlightenment, only to be rejected by it in the end. Theodor Herzl, the founder of political Zionism, perfectly epitomized this process. Born into a German-speaking Jewish family in Budapest in 1860, he was highly educated as a citizen of the West while being an ignoramus in the traditions of the Jews. One of his earliest schemes was to lead the Jews of Vienna in a ceremony of mass conversion to Christianity at St. Stephen's Cathedral. In 1894, as a journalist on the prestigious *Freie Presse,* he covered the trial in Paris of Alfred Dreyfus and the accompanying uproar. Dreyfus was an assimilated Jew who managed to become a staff officer in the French army. To Herzl, he must have seemed the epitome of what an enlightened Jew could strive for. Yet here he was, accused of treason and tried in an atmosphere that reeked of anti-semitism—and this in France, the most Enlightened of all lands. The moral of the story, it seemed to him, was that there was nothing the Jews could do short of total rejection of their identity that would allow them to be accepted, and even that might not suffice. If the societies of Europe were not capable of making room for the Jews, then the Jews must return to the political stage and fend for themselves.

Herzl soon found that there were quite a few Jews in Eastern Europe who had reached similar conclusions. Many had been influenced by the Enlightenment, with the concomitant weakening of traditional Jewish modes of thought and behavior; yet under the malignant and Jew-hating regime of the czars, they had never been able to convince themselves that by improving their behavior, they would be accepted as equals. (Since the 1880s, there had been a series of large-scale pogroms such as had not been seen in Western Europe for generations.) Coming as they did from the margins of Europe, however, these Russian Jews lacked the audacity of Herzl, who proposed to create a Zionist movement that would promote its goals through negotiations with the "great powers." They had, however, already begun to take initial steps toward this goal.

The land of Israel at this time was part of the Ottoman Empire. The Galilee in the north was part of the region of Beirut. The area roughly comparable to ancient Judea was called the Senjak (county) of Jerusalem and was subordinated directly to Constantinople. Muslims, not being cultural descendants of the Romans, did not generally refer to it as Palestine, as the Europeans did, and the fact that they now do so is a small irony of history: from the very beginning of their struggle with the Jews, they understood the importance of Western public opinion. The Jews for their part called it *Eretz Yisrael,* "the Land of Israel," as they always had.

The total population of Palestine in 1800 has been estimated at about three hundred thousand, a mere five thousand of them Jews, their largest community being in Galilean Safed. By the eve of World War I, the total population had more than doubled to about seven hundred thousand; but the Jews had multiplied by a factor of seventeen and now numbered eighty-five thousand, with the largest concentration in Jerusalem. The most significant settlements, however, were the small, rural ones. Petach Tikva had been founded on the coastal plain in 1878 by a group of Orthodox Jews from Jerusalem. In the same year, a similar group from Safed tried to settle in Rosh Pina, in the northern Jordan valley. Rishon LeZion, south of Petach Tikva, was founded in 1882 by a group of young Jews from Russia; Zichron Yaacov, on the southern Carmel, was founded in 1882 by a group from Romania; Yesod Hamaala was founded in the Hula marshes, east of Rosh Pina, by Safadians and immigrants from Miedzyrzecz in Poland. Altogether, about two dozen settlements were set up. In some of them, groups of Jews from Yemen had joined the settlers; they were better adapted both to the climate and to the hard labor of agriculture.

In retrospect, this movement was to be called the first aliyah, the first wave of Zionist immigrants. Most of them did not see themselves as heralds of a national movement, certainly not one that would lead to political independence and generations of warfare. Yet they *were* aware of the novelty of their actions—witness the names they gave to their settlements: Petach Tikva means "Opening of Hope," Rishon LeZion is "First in Zion," Rosh Pina and Yesod Hamaala are both variations on "Foundation."

Zionism thus began as an intertwining of revolutionary hope and deep cultural pessimism. The Enlightenment had disconnected many Jews from their forefathers' belief in a miraculous messianic redemption. Yet irrational hatred of them was clearly not dissolving in the warm bath of Enlightenment rationalism. Their solution was to revive the traditional Jewish hope of redemption, this time with the tools of modern rationalists. No longer necessarily believing in God, or with any messianic expectations, they could fulfill His promise on their own.

Herzl played three roles in jump-starting Zionism. Being a journalist, he started by writing a short book, *The Jewish State* (1896), in which he proposed creating a Jewish entity in Palestine, under the suzerainty of the Ottoman Empire, in which the Jews could go about their own business far from the antisemitism of Europe. In 1897, a few hundred self-selected delegates from Jewish communities all over the world responded to his call and convened for the first Zionist congress at Basle, which then became an annual affair. Thus was Zionism launched as a political movement. His third role was to negotiate with non-Jewish power brokers so as to convince them to support the new movement. He met various European officials—Ottomans, Italians, British, and even the German kaiser Wilhelm—but most did not take him particularly seriously. In 1903, however, the British tentatively offered him a territory in Uganda in which the Jews could create an autonomous region.

Herzl, Jewish ignoramus that he was, brought the offer before that year's Zionist congress, which narrowly adopted it in deference to his status and with the understanding that it would be a temporary solution, a shelter for the persecuted Jews who had to get out of Europe. But the Russian delegates revolted. Their communities were the most threatened by antisemitic violence, but they were adamant that a Jewish national undertaking must be based in *Eretz Yisrael* or nowhere. It was an early indication of the inherent tension in Zionism, between pure pragmatists whose intention was to improve the conditions of the Jews and more

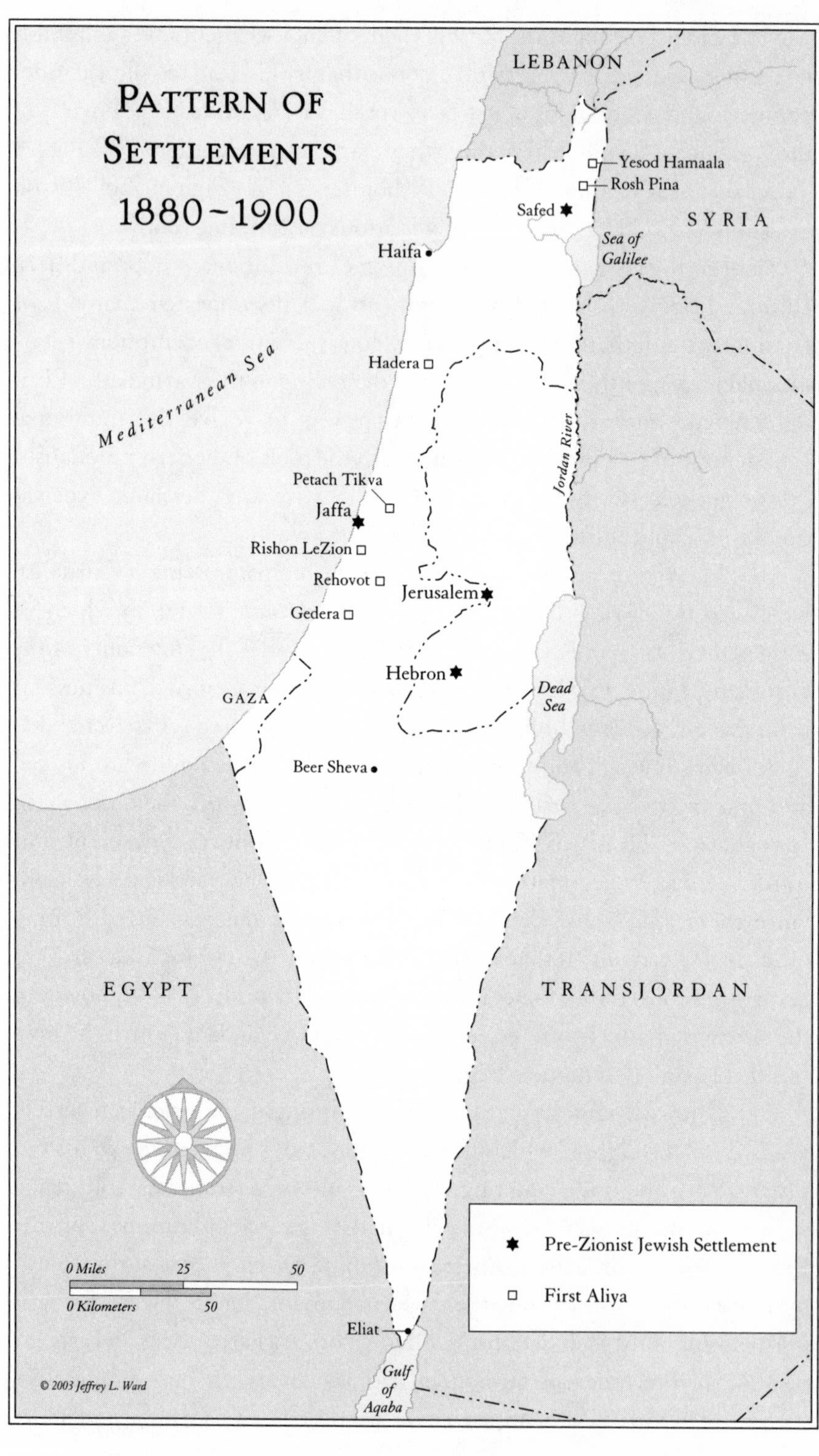

PATTERN OF SETTLEMENTS 1880~1900
LEBANON
SYRIA
Yesod Hamaala
Rosh Pina
Safed
Sea of Galilee
Haifa
Hadera
Mediterranean Sea
Jordan River
Petach Tikva
Jaffa
Rishon LeZion
Rehovot
Jerusalem
Gedera
Hebron
Dead Sea
GAZA
Beer Sheva
EGYPT
TRANSJORDAN
Pre-Zionist Jewish Settlement
First Aliya
0 Miles
25
50
0 Kilometers
50
Eliat
Gulf of Aqaba
© 2003 Jeffrey L. Ward

tradition-minded Zionists whose intention was to improve the condition of the Jews in the ancestral homeland. Herzl died in 1904, overworked and frustrated at his lack of real progress.

By the turn of the twentieth century, the conceptual components of the Zionist revolution were already in place. Jews would try to resolve their inability to live in peace as Jews by a combination of political action in Europe and settlement in *Eretz Yisrael.* Political parties were being created, with local chapters, dues, and publications; Jewish national institutions were also created, such as a head office in Jaffa to coordinate the activities, and a bank.

In 1906, twenty-year-old David Ben-Gurion got off a boat in the ancient port city of Jaffa (Tel Aviv did not yet exist). He refused to spend even one night in town, preferring to walk the ten to fifteen miles to Petach Tikva to be with the farmers (or rather the laborers, the farmers of the previous generation having become the capitalist landowning class: a good socialist is always aware of such distinctions). Not only were they capitalists, they were callous ones and given the choice were liable to prefer Arab day laborers to Jews, since the Arabs were peasants by birth, while the Jews had been raised as shopkeepers' sons in small Russian towns, and their heads were full of revolutionary slogans.

The backbone of the new wave of immigrants that began to arrive at the beginning of the twentieth century consisted of young men and women from Eastern Europe who chose *Eretz Yisrael* over America for idealistic reasons. Unlike their predecessors of the first aliyah, they had every intention of creating a socialist Utopia. In order to achieve this, the Jews themselves would have to be redeemed along with the land. Their spiritual leader was Aharon David Gordon, or A. D. Gordon, as he was more generally known. Born in 1856, he was considerably older than the pioneers who were to be so deeply influenced by him. Moreover, unlike them, he had been the manager of an agricultural estate back in the old country. He came to Petach Tikva in 1904 and spent the rest of his life (until 1922) as an agricultural laborer, thereby setting a personal example for an entire generation for whom he became a father figure. The image of this elderly man with a long white beard, laboring in the intense heat and exhorting his far younger peers not to lose spirit and never give up, inspired generations and took on patriarchal proportions. He had a mystical philosophy, whereby a nation rejuvenates itself by digging its roots as deep as possible into the very earth from which it has sprung. Yet his mysticism had the most practical application: no matter how great the hardships, one must somehow wrench a living from the soil.

Settlers in the American West had wrestled a living from tracts of virgin land that in most cases had never been cultivated; within a few generations they were to create the breadbasket of the world. The Fertile Crescent had been the source of more of humanity's basic foodstuffs than anywhere else on the globe, but that lay millennia in the past. In the eyes of the new Jewish settlers, the land was a priceless wreck that had to be restored to its mythological greatness. One advantage they had over their predecessors of the first aliyah was that they were backed, to an extent, by the institutions of political Zionism. That backing was still rudimentary, but it was there and had the potential for growth.

In the spirit of building a new society, and not just a group of settlements, the pioneers insisted on using a new language: ancient Hebrew, reawakened as the tongue of daily discourse. This was to prove an immensely powerful tool of nation building. All future Jewish immigrants were required to use the same language, no matter what their mother tongue, and who could argue against Hebrew? Another innovation was the invention of political parties within the Jewish community—actually, ideological debating clubs and support groups. The pioneers had two of them, with the usual amount of acrimony.

During the fifteen years or so of the second aliyah, about twenty new settlements were founded, although a number would not survive the tribulations of World War I. Two that would survive stand out in particular. Tel Aviv was founded in 1909 as a Jewish neighborhood north of Jaffa, by middle-class immigrants who came at the same time as the more ideologically motivated pioneers. At the opposite end of the country, and of the ideological spectrum, Degania was created also in 1909: the world's first kibbutz.

The disintegrating Ottoman Empire viewed the Jewish immigration and settlement efforts with disfavor, nominally forbidding much of it. Yet it was preoccupied with the turmoil at its heart and with its loosening control over territories nearer to home, such as the Balkans. The reality was that until the hostilities of World War I, Jews with European passports enjoyed partial immunity from the Turks and could find ways to do mostly what they wanted. Great-power politics being what they were, even Russian Jews enjoyed their country's protection, far more than they had at home.

Meanwhile, in this process of redeeming the Jews by redeeming the land, the local Arabs played a minor role. The absentee landlords in Beirut or Cairo would sell the land, and the local peasants were welcome to partake in the fruit of the reconstruction if they wished. This was admittedly a patronizing attitude, but it was neither anti-Arab nor colonial, and certainly not racist, even if Palestinian spokesmen like Edward Said allege that the early Zionists were not capable of seeing the Arabs as fully human.[3] (The same thing could be said of Arab attitudes toward Jews, by the way, and with much greater justification.)

Indeed, the main victims of the second aliyah were the pioneers themselves. An estimated 80–90 percent of the starry-eyed idealists did not survive. Many were carried off by local illnesses, like malaria, to which their European systems had no immunity. Some—an unusually high proportion—could not sustain the effort and chose suicide. Many others were willing to admit defeat and simply left. Born on the plains of Eastern Europe, they had looked out from the towns of their childhood across broad rivers at endless expanses of fields and forests; arriving in rocky fields of thistles and brambles, many found the intensity of the glaring sunlight and relentless heat unbearable.

Those who held on were the toughest of the tough. With decades of productive years ahead of them, they were to lead—and overshadow—the Zionist project all the way to political sovereignty, a goal quite unformulated when they first embarked at Jaffa. The ethos they created contained a determination that seems almost larger than life, though one could also call it simple stubbornness. It demanded a single-minded commitment to revolutionary goals that would override many more mundane requirements, such as family life, intimacy, sensitivity. They were mythological figures even in their lifetimes, and many of their descendants were to be burdened by the legacy that had been thrust upon them. To be honest, there was also a touch of cruelty about them. But then, the course of history is rarely diverted by nice people. And they usually made the harshest demands on themselves. This severe and demanding ethos, superimposed on the ancient dream that needed no explaining to the masses of Jews, was to prove one of the most potent tools that the Zionists could have invented.

It would also be the starting point for a potent strain of criticism later

[3] Edward W. Said, *The Question of Palestine* (New York: Vintage Books, 1980).

directed at Zionism by Jews themselves. In 1988, a young Israeli historian named Benny Morris announced the advent of a new school of thought, which he dubbed the New Historians, foremost among whom were Ilan Pappe, Avi Shlaim, and Morris himself. Their project, Morris explained, was to critically reexamine the Zionist myths in order to uncover their falsity. Soon they were joined by scholars from other disciplines, such as sociology, anthropology, journalism, and law. All set out to prove that Zionism had never been the moral movement its adherents claimed. Rather, it had been conniving in its colonialism, imperious in its wars, arrogant in its relations with the Arabs, callous in its treatment of immigrants, hardhearted in relation to those European Jews who looked to it for succor in the late 1930s, and so on. Since many of them were not historians, they called themselves post-Zionists.

The post-Zionists seem to have practically no traditional Jewish education; at any rate, there is no echo in their writing of the thousands of years of intellectual deliberations in which their forefathers engaged so intensely. Instead, much of their writing is infused with the faddish terminology of postmodernism: gender, narrative, ethnicity, and, of course, hegemony, couched within the boundaries of political correctness, though this is neither here nor there in terms of the validity of their findings. The quality of their research has been uneven, as you would expect from such a varied group. The discussion of the Palestinian refugee problem below leans heavily on Morris's indispensable research; elsewhere, their claims may serve as foils for focusing attention on essential aspects of unfolding events.

The post-Zionists take pride in their irreverent iconoclasm. No unthinkable or unspeakable ideas for them; they'll dare to suggest anything. Upon closer inspection, however, this claim rings distinctly hollow. No traditional Israeli claim is protected from their scrutiny, but anti-Israeli claims mostly are. The Zionists are castigated for not seriously seeking peace in the early 1950s, while the frequently stated Arab intention to destroy Israel is brushed aside. The assertion that Israel is a Jewish state is constantly criticized by post-Zionists, who would prefer her to be "a state of all its citizens," shorn of anything particularly Jewish. Suggest to them, however, that by the same token a Palestinian state should also be a state of all its citizens, including hundreds of thousands of Jewish settlers, and you have entered the realm of the truly unthinkable.

Likewise, their understanding of human motives and actions is highly deterministic. In this view, people hold the opinions they do because they are manipulated by hegemonic powers in society. Free will is apparently a luxury only they and their colleagues possess, as attested to by the unthinkable thoughts they hatch. Thus, one of the post-Zionists admits in a recent publication the role his father played in transferring Arab land to Jewish control in the 1950s. The father was an eminently decent man, but as a judge he was caught up in the hegemonic interpretation of the legal establishment and so could not see that his verdicts were not decent. Perhaps. More likely, the father, intelligent enough to become a judge, and Zionist enough to choose to emigrate from South Africa as early as the 1930s, felt his verdicts to be both legal and just, and also to promote the interests of his country.[4]

Inasmuch as they've uncovered unnoticed aspects of Israel's history, their perspectives have contributed something valuable to the understanding of our society and its past. Yet their real project is not to analyze so much as to moralize—and they find much that is immoral in Zionism.

Even this would have some value, if only their moral criteria were universal and clear. Being postmodernists, however, who are uneasy with concepts such as objective truth or varying shades of good and evil, they take a murkier path. Often they merely assert their claims, condescendingly assuming that their readers must agree on what is good or right and what is not. This dogmatic tendency is reinforced by the common use of weighted terms—colonialism, hegemony, and so on—that have been allotted a negative moral value and thus require no further examination. Perhaps most significant of all, they are attracted to the victimhood of the weak. Suffering bestows moral superiority, especially the suffering of the weak. The sufferings of the strong have a different moral quality, since the strong have the power to liberate themselves from oppression while the weak do not. This moral outlook has echoes of the determinism noted above: one's acts are the result of one's condition, not one's decisions. Finally, there is the assumption that power is inevitably corrupting, so that weak victims hold the moral high ground by virtue of their longevity as victims. Should there ever be a reversal of positions, with the strong and the weak changing places, this would not be noticed for some time.

An excellent example appears near the end of the above quoted book by

[4] Dan Rabinowitz and Kwala Abu Baker, *The Stand-Tall Generation: The Palestinian Citizens of Israel Today* [Hebrew] (Jerusalem: Keter, 2002).

Rabinowitz and Baker. In one of the rare moments where the Palestinians are criticized, Rabinowitz gives his assessment of the Oslo process: "Yasser Arafat and his cronies took over every positive aspect of Palestinian society, and under the aegis of the Israelis and the Americans steadily subordinated the populace of the territories to a paralyzing, corrupt, and corrupting control system. The Palestinian Authority became a subcontractor for Israeli security. She worked alongside Israel in the service of the 'Pax Americana'—a steamroller of pressure that often suffocates authentic social forces. What is called 'regional geo-political stability in the Middle East' is a pseudonym for the American ambition, perfectly personified by the Texan family Bush, that the oil continue to flow." (p. 171, my translation)

Given this frame of mind, you begin to see why the Zionists in general, the second aliyah leadership especially, and David Ben-Gurion above all must be cast as historical villains. Their entire enterprise stemmed from their determination to change the Jews from powerless victims to powerful promoters of their own interests. They fully understood that this could not be achieved merely by suggesting to the world that the existing situation was not pleasant and could the rules please be changed. It was a revolutionary project, and its success would cost blood, sweat, and tears. To make matters worse, these revolutionaries were not gentle, sensitive, or pleasant people.

For the post-Zionists, the end of Jewish victimhood means the end of Jewish morality. When you lack an objective moral system whereby to judge the actions of a powerless and persecuted nation determined to take its destiny in its own hands, you are left to make judgments about the symbolic aspects of their actions. More than anything else, the post-Zionists seem to be acutely embarrassed by the power that Zionism allows itself to use, irrespective of its justification or results. The use of power itself is the problem.

For those of us who wish to be Zionists while also being moral in our actions, there is something comforting in all this. No group of critics knows Zionism as well as the post-Zionists, who live here, speak the language, and follow events as closely as anyone else. If this is the worst they can muster, perhaps the use of universal moral criteria might show that we're not doing so badly.

When did the Arab-Zionist war begin? This question is not as easy to answer as it sounds. Are we talking about Arabs or Palestinians? Jews or Zionists? I have referred to the Arabs, since much of the conflict to come involved Arab forces outside of Palestine; and I have referred to the Zionists so as to distinguish the violence involving them from the occasional killing of individual Jews at the hands of Arabs, which had been going on for centuries.

There was, of course, some animosity against the proto-Zionist immigrants from the very beginning, in the 1880s. A few farsighted Arabs may have seen in them the harbingers of something much greater, but much of the animosity against them at this time was the result of what was regarded as their arrogance, disrespect, and general unseemliness. Unlike the local Jews, who were urban, poor, and aware of their place in a Muslim society, the newcomers were cut from a different cloth: striving for agricultural success, revolutionary, confident in the protection of their European passports, and quite unawed by the local Arabs.

There were often scuffles between Jewish settlers and local Arab peasants, mainly over boundaries of land. Occasionally people were killed. Yet if there was a pattern to these conflicts, after the initial disagreements both sides usually settled down to living alongside each other. In many cases, the Jewish settlements became a source of employment and income for local Arabs, leading to the growth of both populations; some Arab villages, which had been semideserted before the arrival of the Jews, now blossomed. Still, during the final years before World War I, there was a real rise in violence, even if the number of casualties was still small—probably no more than ten dead in the last two years.

All this changed after World War I, when the land itself went from an insignificant backwater in a crumbling empire to a well-defined geopolitical unit with an undetermined future. Previously, the Jews had been trying only to create some sort of autonomy within the Ottoman Empire, while the local Arabs, if they gave any thought to a post-Ottoman era, spoke in terms of a new pan-Arab entity. The British suddenly created a geographic unit called Palestine and, in a convoluted way, put it up for grabs.

CHAPTER

2

The British Mandate: The Decisions to Build and Destroy

The British general Edmund Allenby conquered Palestine from the Turks in 1917, entering Jerusalem just before Christmas. In November 1947, the United Nations adopted a resolution ending British control over Palestine. During the thirty-year interval, Zionists and Palestinians both made many of the key decisions regarding each other. The Jews made settlements a central element of their efforts; the Palestinians chose violent rejection of Zionism as *their* hallmark. These decisions remain mostly unchanged eight decades later, long after the British departure.

In retrospect, the British role was nowhere near as important as they like to imagine, and their present insistence on broadcasting their opinions on the conflict is both conceited and misplaced. In 1917, they stumbled into a charged situation, meddled unproductively for thirty years, and stumbled out. History didn't begin with them, and it continued quite intensely after they left. The same goes for the broader conceit of framing the conflict in terms of European colonialism. Forcing such an ancient story into the framework of a brief European presence that was over almost as quickly as it started takes an impressive amount of Eurocentric arrogance.

This is not to say that the British intervention had no importance. For thirty years they were the ruling power, and both sides had to devise ways to take advantage of them or minimize their damage. At the outset, the

Palestinians would have seemed to be in the better position, since they were the larger group, they were part of the surrounding region, and they had no external enemies. The Jews were a small minority, they owned almost none of the land, and beyond the borders of Palestine any political or financial backing they briefly had in the early 1920s was totally to disappear, to be replaced by the greatest helplessness conceivable. They did initially have one asset, of which they made optimal use: the Balfour Declaration. Even that, however, was the result of their efforts, not an inexplicable stroke of luck.

The Balfour Declaration was a cornerstone of the British Mandate in Palestine, but the foundation on which it stood were the Zionist efforts of the previous decades. When at the turn of the century Theodor Herzl worked himself to death trying to convince someone to let him set up a Jewish entity under Ottoman suzerainty, no one had taken any notice. When, during World War I, Herzl's successor, Chaim Weizmann, negotiated with the British as they began their conquest of Palestine, he was backed by a political movement with branches in many countries and could point to dozens of new Jewish settlements on the ground, populated by those obstinate settlers. In other words, the Zionists had already completed the first step of their revolution and by dint of their achievements had proved worthy of a place at the table of power.

A combination of British realpolitik and religious enthusiasm for the aspirations of the Jews called forth the Balfour Declaration of November 2, 1917. This included playing to the gallery of Jews in the United States (so that they would support American entry into the war), in Alexander Kerensky's Russia (to support Russia's staying in the war), and even in the Axis countries (it was feared the Germans might publish a declaration of their own). It was also a ploy to keep the French out of Palestine, which the British wanted to control because of its position astride the trade routes to India.

The declaration, sent in the form of a letter from the British foreign minister, Lord Arthur James Balfour, to Lord James Rothschild, announced:

> His Majesty's Government view with favour the establishment in Palestine of a national home for the Jewish people, and will use their best endeavours to facilitate the achievement of this object, it being

> clearly understood that nothing shall be done which may prejudice the civil and religious rights of existing non-Jewish communities in Palestine, or the rights and political status enjoyed by Jews in any other country.

Despite what many think, however, the Balfour Declaration was never the source of legitimacy for Jewish claims to *Eretz Yisrael.* Morally, their history and obstinate refusal to give up their claim was; politically, their recent actions were. A somewhat watered-down version was adopted by the League of Nations when it formulated the British Mandate to control Palestine. Nor was the declaration an unequivocal endorsement of Zionism. The Jews were not promised sovereignty, but rather a national home; and whatever that meant, it was not to prejudice the civil and religious rights of the local non-Jews—in other words, it could not come at the expense of the Palestinians. Nor—and the significance of this has been forgotten—could it affect the political rights of Jews elsewhere. The success of Zionism, the declaration promised, could not serve European countries as an excuse to disenfranchise or expel their own Jews (though it could not prevent a charge of double loyalty). Lords Balfour and Rothschild may not have understood the Middle East, but they knew the Europeans well enough.

The Jews received the declaration with tremendous excitement. Its vagueness was no problem, precisely because Zionism at that point—and indeed, for a full generation to come—did not define itself as a movement to create Jewish sovereignty. A national homeland, even without a sovereign state, would have been a tremendous improvement, and at this stage the Zionists truly did not object to the balancing parts of the declaration. They were seeking a solution to severe Jewish predicaments, and while they were not exactly taking the aspirations of the local Arabs into account, neither were they hostile to them. Had there appeared an Arab movement seeking accommodation with the Jews along the lines of the Balfour Declaration, the Jews might very likely have been eager to cooperate. The idea that full sovereignty was an existential need of the Jews—indeed, a prerequisite for their continued physical and cultural existence—was not obvious in the aftermath of the Great War. Only later did the twentieth century force this understanding upon them.

When the British and French toppled the decaying Ottoman Empire, it was an extreme moment in the ebb and flow of a struggle between the Muslim world and Christian Europe that had been under way since the Muslim invasions were stopped in Iberia more than 1,200 years ago. As recently as 1683, there had been an Ottoman army at the gates of Vienna. In 1918, the entire Muslim world was under the direct or indirect control of Europe, and the caliphate—the seat of the broadly accepted leader of Islam—was no more. The shock for Muslims was intense, and current events may be part of the reaction to it. The events in Palestine were at the time but a small part of a larger picture; initially, even the small segment of the Palestinian population that was politically active tended to see their predicament as part of a pan-Arab struggle rather than a local clash between Jews and Arabs.

Palestinian spokesmen and their Western allies often cite the declaration as a prime example of European colonial encouragement of the Zionists against the Arabs. In the words of Edward Said, perhaps the most eloquent Palestinian spokesman: "It was the world that made the success of Zionism possible."[1] In reality, the story of European control in the region was brief, and except for North Africa it lasted a single generation at most; even calling it colonialism requires stretching the term, which is why countries like Iraq and Saudi Arabia are not members of the British Commonwealth. Zionism predated the European presence in Palestine and took advantage of it, but its very staying power and longevity belie the claim that it was part of an imperial European plan to divide the Arab world.

Leaving aside the relation of "the world" to the Jews in the 1930s and 1940s, which was hardly benevolent, such statements overlook the most significant aspect of British policy in Palestine: that whether it was pro-Zionist, anti-Zionist, or indifferent—and at various points it was all of these—it was never actively Zionist. At best, the British created convenient circumstances for the Zionists to operate in. Whether they would take optimal advantage of these circumstances was left to the Jews. In any case, there was very little they were doing during the years of the British Mandate that the Palestinians couldn't also have done, and if by its end the Jews were better poised to take control of their destiny, this was not the doing of the British, but the result of Zionist determination.

[1] Said, *The Question of Palestine,* p. 20.

The things the Jews were doing included setting up communal institutions, immigrating, and founding new settlements. On the communal institutions, more below. The immigration, however, was hardly the result of British policies.

World War I ended on November 11, 1918. In Eastern Europe, however, local skirmishes and wars went on for many months, even years. In what had been the Russian Empire, it took a brutal civil war for the Bolsheviks to bolster their control. In these wars, and especially in the Ukraine, masses of Jews were murdered. The lowest estimate I have found anywhere is 70,000 dead; most estimates are in the range of 200,000 to 250,000. The immigrants of the third aliyah (1919–1923) were mostly refugees fleeing the murderous hatred of their Russian, Ukrainian, and Polish neighbors. Yet the choice of destination was still theirs to make, as the United States had not yet shut its gates. The thirty-five thousand pioneers who came to Palestine were taking advantage of British willingness to let them enter, but their models were their predecessors of the second aliyah.

Yet fear for one's life and a utopian desire to rebuild an ancient homeland are not sufficient for success. A key factor is land—and it had to be acquired. Enter Yehoshua Hankin.

Hankin was born in the Ukraine in 1864. His family left in 1882, at the very beginning of the series of modern pogroms. He joined the most ideological settlers of the first aliyah at Gedera, until he married and moved to Jaffa. He found his calling in 1890, when he purchased the land on which Rehovot was founded, followed shortly by his purchase of the first plots for Hadera—all on the coastal plain. He was to spend the rest of his life purchasing land for the Zionist movement. After his death in 1945, he was given the most fitting of epitaphs, when a settlement in the Jezreel valley was named Kfar Yehoshua, "Yehoshua's Village."

In many ways, Hankin was a typical lieutenant to Ben-Gurion (although he was a generation older). Watching him in action, you get the sense of a deeply dedicated man, committed to building a Jewish national home on the ancestral land, making a significant contribution within a framework someone else had created, and sticking to what he did well. Without the dynamic revolutionaries around him, his efforts might have lacked their historic focus; without lots of committed lieutenants like him, the revolutionaries would have been stuck in barren debating clubs.

The need for someone like Hankin stemmed from the fact that the Jews could settle only on land that was purchased legally. Most of the land had been owned by the Turkish government, and now by the British, but neither had any intention of settling Jews on it. The Turks didn't want Jews settling at all. Initially, the British had no objections, but it was up to the Jews to acquire the land on their own. For that they needed buyers like Hankin, funds, and owners willing to sell.

The fifth Zionist congress in Basle in 1901 created the Jewish National Fund (JNF) with the purpose of collecting contributions from the Jews of the world with which to purchase as much land as possible. Yet the relative poverty of most of the Eastern European Jews who were the backers of early Zionism meant that the pennies had to be spent wisely. This meant buying consecutive tracts of land, wherever possible, on which to create agricultural settlements; these could be acquired mainly from absentee Arab landlords who were not earning much on their property because of its dubious quality.

The largest tracts available were the malaria-infested swamplands around the Sea of Galilee and to its north in the Hula valley (beneath the Golan Heights), along the coastal plain, and in the east-west region known as the Jezreel valley connecting the two. The hilly regions of the country, with their safer air, were either not for sale or not consecutive tracts. This made for an ironic outcome. The Zionists could purchase what seemed to be worthless land, yet should it prove redeemable, they might find themselves with much of the most fertile land in the country. It was precisely this challenge that was to animate the new wave of pioneering immigrants after 1918.

Hankin and his boss, Arthur Ruppin, head of the Zionist office in Jaffa, twisted the arm of the Zionist executive in Europe to force the purchase of sizable tracts in the Jezreel valley. Not being closely acquainted with those incredibly stubborn pioneers, one can easily understand the trepidation with which the notables of the executive parted with their funds for what probably looked liked a very poor deal. What remained was to drain the swamps, dig irrigation channels, and pave roads to make the area accessible, determine the suitable crops, and grow them, all the while not succumbing to malaria or just plain heat and sunlight.

The socialist-minded pioneers rose to the challenge through the creation of *Gdudei Ha' Avoda*, the Labor Battalions. The idea was to combine the invention of the kibbutz by the earlier pioneers and the ideologically motivated labor columns common in revolutionary postwar Eastern Europe. Whereas the original kibbutzim had been tiny affairs (the first, Degania, split once it grew beyond a few dozen members), the Gdudei Ha'Avoda were soon to have hundreds of members. Initially (1920) they regarded themselves as the proletarian army of the Zionist enterprise, out to prove that Jewish labor could shoulder any job. Their first big project was to pave a road north of Tiberius. They then took it upon themselves to prepare for agricultural settlement one of the large blocks recently purchased by Hankin in the eastern half of Jezreel. Some of them remained there for the rest of their long lives, eventually turning into the gnarled, rooted peasants they had dreamed of becoming.

Along the way, they had proven the correctness of much of Zionist thought. Hatred of Jews in Enlightened Europe was already proving more murderous than its religious predecessor had ever been, and within a generation it was to prove indescribably so. For all the price yet to be paid, Jews who came to Turkish or British *Eretz Yisrael* were quite simply saving their lives. They successfully changed the structure of Jewish society, moving into all walks of life. And they were rejuvenating the land beyond what A. D. Gordon or Yehoshua Hankin would ever have thought possible. The swamps metamorphosed into bountiful fields and orchards.

The names of settlements chosen in this wave of immigration told a richer story than those of forty years earlier: Ein Harod was the spring where God selected three hundred soldiers for Gideon when they cupped their hands to drink. Nearby Tel Yosef was named after Yosef Trumpeldor, the first, charismatic leader of the Gdud Ha'Avoda, who was killed at Tel Hai in 1920. Kfar Yehezkel, in a time-honored custom, was named after the brother of the philanthropist who donated the means to purchase its land. Geva was a modernized form of the Hebrew word for "hill," such as the one on which it stands. Beit Alfa was the Hebrew version of the Arabic name Beit Allifa, itself based on an earlier Hebrew name, Beit Ulpana. In a further ironic twist, this kibbutz, which belongs to the far-left and atheist wing of the kibbutz movement, is now famous for a magnificent mosaic floor, a relic of the synagogue of a wealthy Jewish community of the sixth century, which was found under one of its fields.

While the Jews were an ancient people struggling to find a new national existence, the Palestinians had never been a nation, but they already had

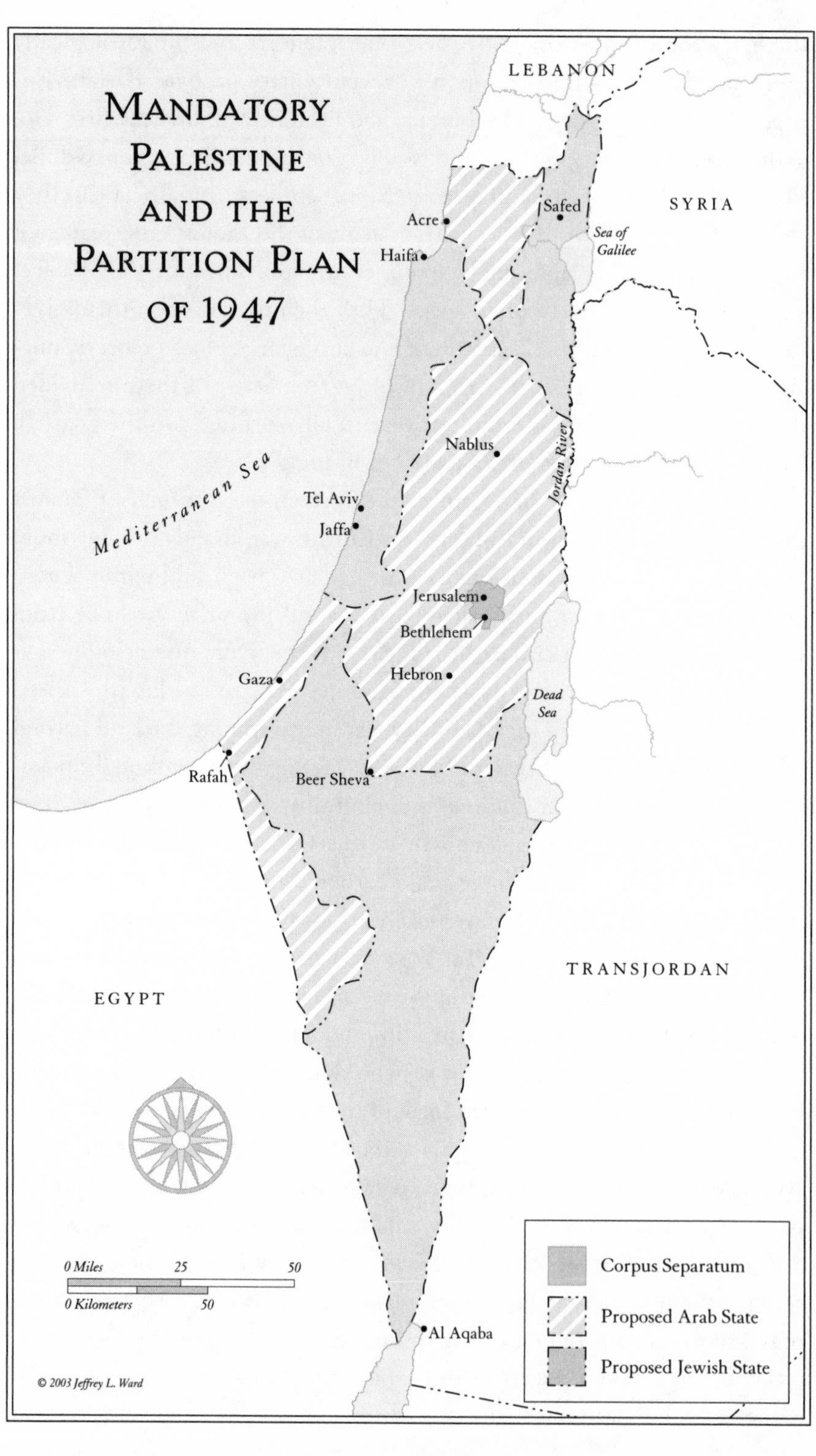

Mandatory Palestine and the Partition Plan of 1947
LEBANON
SYRIA
Safed
Acre
Haifa
Sea of Galilee
Nablus
Jordan River
Mediterranean Sea
Tel Aviv
Jaffa
Jerusalem
Bethlehem
Gaza
Hebron
Dead Sea
Rafah
Beer Sheva
TRANSJORDAN
EGYPT
0 Miles
25
50
0 Kilometers
50
Al Aqaba
Corpus Separatum
Proposed Arab State
Proposed Jewish State
© 2003 Jeffrey L. Ward

most of the essentials for becoming one: a common language and culture in what had recently been defined as a geopolitical unit. Now, just as their national aspirations were beginning to stir, they were faced with an unprecedented challenge.

People have being emigrating and changing the demographics of their new lands throughout human history. Within living memory, Europe has changed from white and Christian to something quite different, more multiethnic than ever before. In California, southern Texas, and other parts of the United States, English-speaking whites are now minorities. Of course, the whites had not exactly been the indigenous inhabitants since time immemorial, either.

Some migrations ensue peacefully, others with brutality. In most cases the tensions recede once the migration is completed. Sometimes they persist, though the longevity of the Irish rejection of English settlement, many centuries long, is unusual. Sometimes the locals resist the newcomers for generations, until the invaders give up and leave; perhaps the best example is the Arab rejection of European intrusion to the holy land in the Crusader era, which lasted almost two hundred years. Very rarely has a group migrated back to a land it had lost, and then only within living memory, like the return of the Jews to Judea in the Persian era or, just yesterday, the return of the Chechens from Siberia.[2]

In all of human history there has never been a case where a group migrated back to a land it had lost for longer than living memory; going back after two thousand years is in any case an impossibility for most groups, as only very rarely do nations live that long. Being a unique situation means that measuring its morality by universal criteria is impossible: what can you compare it to or measure it by? Moreover, if the Jews are a nation, how can it be moral to deny them a place of their own, like other nations? At most you can measure the morality of a nation's behavior, not its existence.

This was not the way the Arabs saw it. Hardly had the British begun to enable the Zionists to promote their goals when the local Arabs made their decision. Any kind of Jewish national homeland in Palestine was totally unacceptable and would be prevented by force.

Was this war? Not in the sense of warring states, since the parties

[2] Stalin deported the entire Chechen nation to Siberia during World War II, ostensibly out of fear that they might aid the German invaders. They were allowed back at the end of the 1950s, a few years after his death.

involved did not yet have that capability. The Arab nations surrounding British Palestine had not yet achieved independence, and the Palestinian Arabs were still unorganized in a way that resembled a national movement. Until the late 1940s, any military actions that took place in Palestine involved irregulars, generally local ones. Yet the decisiveness of their rejection was unmistakable.

In early 1920, the British, French, Zionists, and various Arab forces were maneuvering for positions, boundaries, and power bases in the Middle East. There were Arab attacks on at least eight Jewish settlements, most of them along the line between French and British dominions. Inside Palestine there were Arab demonstrations, strikes, petitions, and attacks on individual Jews. In March, an Arab mob assaulted some Jews in Jerusalem, while chanting *"Itbah al-Yahud!"* ("Slaughter the Jews!") and also, significantly, "Palestine is our land and the Jews are our dogs." A month later, reinforced by hundreds of men from other towns who were in Jerusalem for a Muslim holiday, the cry *"Itbah al-Yahud!"* was implemented literally, when Arab mobs spent three full days attacking Jews, both in the western center of town and in the Old City—ransacking homes, raping women, and demolishing synagogues. Most of the Jewish victims were of the Old Yishuv—descendants of Jewish families that had been around for generations or even centuries before the advent of Zionism; they were the least likely to be able to defend themselves. The number of casualties—six dead Jews and about two hundred injured—would have been higher had not the Haganah, the fledgling Zionist self-defense organization, managed to smuggle out some three hundred Jews who lived in the Old City. The British eventually quelled the violence, but not before killing some Arab rioters and wounding dozens more. Local Arab leaders accused the Jews of inciting the violence by cursing and blaspheming the Muslims and then killing Arab women and children.

In the immediate aftermath, the British authorities clamped down—on the Jews. Jewish leaders were arrested; even Chaim Weizmann's office was raided. Zeev Jabotinsky, leader of the local Haganah, and more than a dozen of his associates were sentenced to years of hard labor. Jewish immigration was halted. It was only the replacement of British military rule by a civilian one later that year that paved the way for renewed Jewish growth.

The story contains many of the elements that still plague Zionist-

Palestinian violence. The overarching position: Jews can be tolerated only as a second-class minority of individuals, never as a nation with claims of its own. The primary decision: Zionist aspirations were to be met with violence. The reason given: "The Jews are our dogs." Not the irritant of Jewish immigration, which had been going on for centuries, or the rise in its dimensions, which had been happening for some forty years, but the Jewish attempt to change the rules by ceasing to be subordinate *dhimmis* and to strive for a national home. The Palestinians rejected Jewish aspirations not because they were European colonialists and foreign invaders, but because they were familiar, second-class locals who had suddenly dared to overturn the natural order.

The violence, as always, was directed at those Jews whom it was easiest to kill. It was justified by totally specious accounts of its origins and outcomes: fairy tales. The fact that the violence came up against counterforce meant that there were casualties among the attackers, a fact that could be deftly twisted to show that they were actually the victims. And the external forces (here the British, later whoever felt the need to have an opinion), while acknowledging the Arab instigation of violence, felt that the underlying problems must be dealt with at the expense of the Jews.

Rejection of the Jewish right to exist as a nation; violence against unprotected Jews; lies to justify the violence; moral equivalence between murdered Jews and dead attackers. It could be practically any year from the 1920s onward. But how about *The Guardian* on January 3, 2001, as Palestinian violence against Israeli civilians was successfully bludgeoning Barak's government into making ever more desperate concessions. Under the title "Israel Simply Has No Right to Exist," Faisal Bodi, a British Muslim journalist, went back to the original sources. Citing God's biblical promise to Abraham, "unto thy seed have I given this land, from the river of Egypt unto the great river, the Euphrates," he expounded that whatever God meant, he must not have intended the land to be taken by force from its original inhabitants. Having discarded the primordial Jewish claim, he then rejected their modern one:

> When it signed the [Oslo] agreement, the PLO made the cardinal error of assuming that you could bury the hatchet by rewriting history. It accepted as a starting point that Israel had a right to exist. The trouble with this was that it also meant, by extension, an acceptance that

> the way Israel came into being was legitimate. As the latest troubles have shown, ordinary Palestinians are not prepared to follow their leaders in this feat of intellectual amnesia.

Actually, as noted above, the biblical story did contain quite a bit of violence, but Bodi, like most of Israel's critics, isn't so strong on his facts.

In May 1921, there was another outbreak of violence, this time centered on Jaffa, but with thousands of attackers also trying, largely unsuccessfully, to invade Petach Tikva, Hadera, and Rehovot. Forty-seven Jews died, most unarmed civilians who were murdered, while forty-eight Arabs were killed by the Jewish defenders and British police. But they had not been innocent civilians, nor were they murdered. There were additional riots and deaths in November that year. In 1922, the League of Nations adopted a watered-down version of the Balfour Declaration as the basis for the British Mandate; it carefully reassured the Arabs that the Jewish national home would be a limited affair. The Palestinians could fool themselves into thinking that provoking violence and murdering Jews might eventually bring the wished-for result, as the world would hurry to appease them.

The next large-scale violence was in 1929, and it too had characteristics that will be uncannily familiar: the rampaging murderers purported to be defending the Haram el-Sharif. Since 1928 there had been growing tension at the Western Wall, which included dropping stones and refuse from the Temple Mount onto Jews praying below, accompanied by malicious propaganda inciting Muslims to protect their holy places from the Jews who were scheming to occupy the Haram and desecrate it; for good measure, they threw in a description of the Jews as rapists and murderers of infants. Given the severity and insistence of the accusations, it should not have been surprising when on August 23, a Friday, thousands of Muslims listened to an inflammatory speech and then poured out of their prayers on the Mount to murder Jews. Over the next week or so, rampaging Arabs attacked Jews in numerous places, and a number of small settlements were temporarily abandoned. A total of 133 Jews died, most of them murdered, while only a small fraction of them were armed defenders killed while fighting back. One hundred sixteen Arabs died, some at the hands of Jewish defenders, most killed (not murdered) by British security forces.

The worst atrocities took place in the Old Yishuv communities, where the Jews were weakest. In Jerusalem's Old City, hundreds of Jews who had been living for generations in the Muslim Quarter were evacuated by the British, never to return. The worst violence, however, was in Hebron.

The Bible tells us that Hebron is where the Patriarchs are buried. The Book of Genesis goes out of its way to describe the negotiations leading to the purchase of the burial plot. A fifth-century commentary asks why all the details are given and suggests an interesting explanation: The Bible knew that in the future, the peoples of the world would reject the Jews' claim to the Patriarchs' graves in Hebron, to Joseph's grave in Nablus, and to the Temple Mount in Jerusalem, so it went out of its way to testify that these spots were all purchased legally.

There have been Jews in Hebron for about 2,100 of the past 3,200 years. There is no empirical way of determining who is really buried there, but the tradition identifying the graves of the Patriarchs is itself more than two thousand years old, as proven by the large building put up by Herod to mark the spot. It stands there still, one of the oldest buildings on the face of the globe, older than Christianity, far older than Islam. Herod was undoubtedly drawn to Hebron because of its pedigree, ancient even in his time. Hundreds of years after the Patriarchs, but a full thousand years before his own day, it had been the first capital of young King David. After the genocide of Hadrian, Jews were not allowed back into the town for 550 years. In the last thousand years, however, it was only in the Crusader period and the second half of the British Mandate that Jews did not live there—maybe 150 out of 1,000 years. In other words, the Jews of Hebron were not the Zionists, and the Zionists did not settle Hebron.

The Zionists were trying to build something new, and Hebron was very old. The Zionists were trying to return to productive agriculture, and Hebron was poor and urban. The Zionists regarded themselves as nonreligious, although in the time-honored tradition of putting behavior before belief, they were actually being very Jewish. Thus Hebron, ironically, was a local branch of much that they were revolting against. It sits up on the hills, far from those large tracts of malaria-infested swamplands the Zionists were eagerly purchasing.

In 1929, 630 years of consecutive Jewish settlement came to a violent end when the local Arabs vented their fury against the Zionists not on the Zionists themselves, who seemed at least partially capable of self-defense, but on the defenseless Jews of Hebron. Sixty-four (according to other sources, sixty-six) Jews were killed, from a community of about six hundred. There was nothing the Zionists could do to stop this. Once it was over, the British forced a group of Hebronite Arab men to bury the mutilated bodies of the murdered Jews, and they burst into song as they did so.

During the 1920s, then, the Palestinians made up their minds on the two crucial questions of war and justice. In response to the influx of Jews, they rejected the possibility of reaching any kind of accommodation, abetted, most likely, by their inability to see in the Jews anything other than a subject minority. Having decided on war, they had no compunctions regarding the manner of waging it. Incitement, lies, and above all murder of the weak: these were all decided upon decades before the Jews had the political or military power to oppress anyone or occupy land beyond what they had purchased legally. These twin decisions were to remain unchanged for decades; arguably, they have not changed to this day. The murder of non-Zionist Jews also demonstrated that distinctions between anti-Zionism and anti-Semitism, popular as they later became, were never sincere.

There was, however, one ray of comparative hope. Often when marauding Palestinians set out to murder Jews, there could be found some individuals who protected them. This was most famously true in Hebron, where the mob would gladly have killed all the Jews had not individual Arabs protected their neighbors. Someday, when peace is achieved between Israelis and Palestinians, these memories will be essential to the building of a mutual acceptance.

Deliberations on the Jewish side were to prove more moral, though at the beginning in the 1920s, there seems to have been very little dilemma. The decision to go to war—or, rather, the decision to respond to violence with force—was so obvious as to pass unopposed. The reality was that wherever Jews had a defensive capability, lives were saved; when they did not, Jewish civilians died horribly. The only question was to find the correct balance between reliance on the British and preparations for independent military capabilities. No other option existed short of abandoning the Zionist enterprise. This decision was certainly *jus ad bellum,* unless one denies the right of the Jews to exist at all, in which case there is nothing to discuss. *Jus in bello* was at this point not at issue, as the force being used was defensive even by the narrowest of definitions; Arabs dying at Jewish hands in the 1920s were engaged in attacking Jews when they died.

More interesting than the substance of these deliberations was their institutional context—for in spite of the fact that Jewish power was a novelty, it was deployed with the aplomb of a veteran nation-state. Well, almost.

The Jewish community in *Eretz Yisrael* was known as the Yishuv (literally, "the Settlement"). Its supreme communal organ was the Assembly, an elected body with universal suffrage of all Jews in the country. The Assembly in turn elected a National Council, Vaad Leumi, including representatives of all the Jewish groups and parties, and the Vaad appointed an executive of six to fourteen members. Eventually, the Assembly would be the body from which the Israeli Parliament, the Knesset, would emerge in 1949.

The League of Nations, in setting up the British Mandate, had envisioned a Jewish institution that would represent the Zionist movement in its dealings with the British. This was the Jewish Agency: an international, nongovernmental body, based in Jerusalem—the executive and representative of the World Zionist Organization. Although it was set up in 1922, it took until 1929 for the various factions to agree on its structure, since there were Jews in the Yishuv and abroad who did not regard themselves as political Zionists but wanted to participate in the efforts and demanded some representation.

Roughly speaking, the Vaad Leumi dealt with internal, communal issues, while the Jewish Agency dealt with external ones; both were national institutions. In the early 1920s, however, the most significant Jewish institution was the Histadrut. Nominally, this was the union of the Jewish workers. Yet given the broad goals of the pioneers who made up the backbone of the socialist camp of Zionism, it should come as no surprise that the union they established was actually an attempt to create an entire society. In its heyday, the Histadrut was a gigantic conglomerate that included, alongside the unions, some of the country's largest employers, such as the gigantic construction company Solel Boneh; the largest wholesaler of agricultural produce, Tnuva; the largest retailer, Hamashbir; a large construction company; a large bank; by far the largest health insurance and health service company; its own school system; the most influential daily newspaper, *Davar*; a publisher; and probably an additional dozen or so companies.

Jews being the talkative, argumentative people they are, it was only to be expected that these institutions and myriad smaller ones would be the source of endless squabbling and maneuvering for power and influence. One guide to the shifting basis of political power in Jewish Palestine is the career of David Ben-Gurion: he was the first head of the Histadrut until he switched over to the Jewish Agency, becoming its chairman in 1935, a move that indicated the eclipse of the union by the (future) state and the simultaneous wrestling of control of Zionism from Europe to the locals.

All of these organizations and institutions were voluntary. The Yishuv, not being a sovereign state or even an autonomous authority, lacked the power to coerce its members into compliance with its laws. Which goes partially to explain why the Haganah was set up by the Histadrut: in 1920, that was where the real power brokers were.

The creation of the Haganah reflected three crucial decisions. The first was not to trust the British with Jewish lives. During the Ottoman period, a few small organizations of Jews had trained themselves to guard the new settlements, the most famous being HaShomer. Yet these were tiny organizations, with local, almost pinpoint jurisdiction. Shomer means "guard," and that is about all they were. Haganah means "defense," and it was set up after the events of 1920 proved that while the British would try to preserve the peace, the protection of Jews was not their top priority. Also, as early as 1920, the founders of the Haganah suspected that the future might bring sharp divergences between British and Jewish interests, and they prepared accordingly.

This was the second decision: to maintain some parts of the Haganah underground, in the legal meaning of the term. The British knew the organization existed, but they didn't need to know everything about it, such as its purchases of arms abroad and eventually developing them on its own, its training practically all the adults in the settlements and eventually thousands from the cities, and so on.

The reality was that the Palestinian determination to combat Zionism by force, combined with British ineptitude in protecting the Jews, was forcing the Yishuv to develop a military capability that it would not have needed otherwise. None of the theorists of Zionism had ever said that military power was a Zionist goal. Yet once forced down that path, the Yishuv made a third decision, which from a moral perspective was perhaps the most important of all: that the armed wing of the movement would be subordinate to the elected civilian leadership. There would be exceptions, and small groups of secessionists who would occasionally operate outside the national institutions, but they would disappear as soon as the Yishuv became a sovereign state.

No one in Israel except history teachers can rattle off the details of each successive wave of immigration. On the contrary, while each was larger than its predecessor, the later ones lack the mythological hue of the first. A fifty-year-old Israeli whose parents came from Germany in 1938 won't identify herself as the daughter of fifth-aliyah immigrants; a thirty-year-old great-grandchild of a settler of the second aliyah actually might—rather like the descendants of the *Mayflower.* Moreover, although the creation of an urban middle class and the infrastructure to sustain it were crucial to the nation-building project, they lacked the larger-than-life heroism of the visionary laborers who had seen to it that malaria-infested swamps became rich breadbaskets. Yet from the mid-1920s, the main theme of the Zionist enterprise was to be the story of the cities, not the farms.

At the same time, the pioneering project continued, and grew significantly, even as its primary goal was changing. The utopian drive was receding, and realpolitik was taking its place.

As the Yishuv grew and flourished, the early Jewish naiveté regarding the local Arabs disappeared. The Arab rejection mirrored Jewish efforts, and the more established the Yishuv became, the greater and more violent became the rejection. The British responded with rational policies but wholly neglected to factor in the true motivating forces: the pent-up energy of the Jews, finally returning home after two thousand years; their rejection by a Muslim-dominated Arab world that in its 1,300-year existence had never been told that the Jews would one day be back; and the awesomely destructive power of European hatred of the Jews. Their eyes firmly shut to the historical immensity of the moment, British bureaucrats and politicians appointed commissions and tinkered with immigration quotas and regulations for the acquisition of land. The greatness of the

Zionists lay in their ability to translate their utopian goals into pragmatic, hard-nosed actions on the ground, such as defining borders by settlement.

At some unspecified moment in the 1920s, the Zionists understood that there would one day be some sort of partition and that the Jews would be allocated only those areas where they held a majority. The first such proposal, made by the British Peel Commission in 1936, noted where the Jews lived and suggested that this be made a Jewish state, minus Jerusalem with its Jewish majority, which was to remain British. The rest of Palestine would be an Arab state. The pattern that was to hold for the next sixty years had been firmly established, as was the form of the responses thereto: while the Jews agonized over the ministate being offered them, the Arabs solved their dilemma by rejecting it outright. Yet the point had been made: Borders have nothing to do with justice. They simply reflect patterns of settlement.

The Zionist policy of the time was deceptive in its modesty, as stated in the slogan "A *dunam* here and a *dunam* there" (a *dunam* is about one-quarter of an acre). Actually, the Zionist intention was to legally acquire as many *dunams* as possible, preferably consecutive ones, with an eye to strategic control of various areas. The funding came from the Jewish people, who in the interwar years were not exactly at the peak of their wealth; nor did they lack other, extremely urgent needs. The acquisition itself had to be done legally, there being no other option; in some cases, the legal acquisition didn't even promote Zionist goals, because the Arab tenants refused to move and there was no way to evict them. The essential act, therefore, was gaining not legal control but physical possession—by settlement. The various strands of Zionist ideology that had required that the Jews reclaim their status as a nation by reclaiming their ancestral land dovetailed precisely with the political needs of the moment.

Stubbornness and innovation dovetailed, too. From 1936 onward, the Arab resistance was consistently violent, while British bureaucratic hurdles to the creation of new settlements grew ever higher. The Yishuv responded with the invention of the Homa u'Migdal movement. According to a legal loophole left over from the Ottoman period, a settlement with a permanent structure and a plowed field could not be disbanded. So the prospective settlers set out at night with lumber and plowhorses, and within hours of arrival at the designated spot they had erected a building and plowed a field. Since the neighbors could reasonably be expected to try to prohibit this by force of arms, the structures to be erected included a stockade (*homa*) and a watchtower (*migdal*). British police would invariably arrive the next day, but the irrevocable facts were all there on the ground. Between 1936 and 1939, some fifty such settlements were founded; a similar number were erected between 1945 and 1948. The land had all been purchased legally, and the creation of the settlements themselves was legal. The suggested borders of the United Nations partition plan of 1947, allocating a significantly larger segment of British Palestine to the Jewish state than that envisioned in 1936, were proof of the success of these efforts.

This is not a history of the Palestinians, yet it is merely human to note that their story has been a tragic one. The 1920s and 1930s laid the foundations for this tragedy. There was no significant nation-building effort on their part, and this had nothing to do with the Zionists, who could not have impeded it even had they wanted to. The events of 1936–1939 were to cast the tragedy in stone.

Between spring 1936 and summer 1939, the Palestinians launched an uprising that was to seal their destiny. Unlike the pogroms of the 1920s, this uprising was a concerted effort that went on for years. As such, it affected Palestinian society in every nook and cranny. It was directed against both the Zionists and the British, who were seen as protecting the Jews. It included long strikes and boycotts, which were to prove counterproductive since they impoverished the peasants while forcing the Zionists to achieve economic autarchy. Meanwhile, the British were to make two diplomatic attempts to appease the Arabs. In 1937, the Peel Commission suggested partitioning the land so that almost all of it would become a Palestinian state and only a small segment would become a Jewish one. The Jews agonized but were inclined to accept. But for the Arabs—Palestinians and others—control by Jews over any sections of the land was totally unacceptable. The British also severely reduced the immigration quotas for Jews, precisely at the moment when the Jews of Europe most desperately needed somewhere to go. Then, in May 1939, after the revolt had been put down, the British published a white paper that effectively put an end to what remained of the Balfour program. A mere seventy-five thousand additional Jewish immigrants would be allowed in until 1944, and none thereafter without Arab consent. After ten years, if agreement could be reached among the three sides, the British would leave and a Palestinian state would be formed, with the Jews a minority in it. These terms were so harsh on the Zionists that for the first time there were no significant voices among them advocating acceptance. But the discussion was moot, as the Palestinians turned it down also.

The centerpiece of the revolt, however, was the violence. At first it was directed toward Jewish civilians in the towns, then later it spread to attacks on the roads and on British installations. Dozens of bombs went off in the first two months of the revolt. The British brought in massive reinforcements, which managed significantly to quell the uprising; this, together with their promise to send a commission of inquiry, brought a halt to the violence in the late fall. But after the Peel Commission made its recommendations, the uprising broke out anew in 1937. The longer it went on, the more sinister it became, from a Palestinian perspective: as the populace grew exhausted by the violence and the intransigence of the rebels, ever more of the victims were Palestinians, killed at the hands of their countrymen. Members and supporters of the hard-line Husseini clan murdered many members of the more moderate Nashashibi clan and its supporters, while in the countryside, gangs murdered peasants who didn't offer them full support. Thousands of educated, urban Palestinians left for other Arab countries. Palestinian society was not to recover for decades.

By the end of the revolt, thousands of Arabs, hundreds of Jews, and many dozens of British soldiers had died. Historians estimate that a majority of the Palestinian losses had been self-inflicted, which could mean up to two or three thousand. But the Palestinians had spurned any option short of the disappearance of Zionism, to be achieved by war and with no compunction as to its methods.

Compunction as to methods of waging war were to play a major role in the Zionist response to the uprising, but in order to follow their deliberations you must bear in mind the significance of the Sixth Commandment.

The Ten Commandments are among the best-known statements in history, even in our agnostic era. They contain one of the clearest distinctions between Judaism and the rest of humanity. The Sixth Commandment, as everybody knows, is "Thou shalt not kill." This is and always has been a source of endless hypocrisy, as no society has ever completely refrained over a sustained period from some sort of killing. The Commandment is posted on the wall of the church or the school, so clear that every child can understand it with ease, but it is not uniformly adhered to.

Jews are free of this hypocrisy, for they don't in fact have such a commandment. The original text does not say "*Lo taharog*" ("Thou shall not kill"), but rather "*Lo tirzach*" ("Thou shall not murder")—and therein lies a world of difference.

Judaism knows that killing is at times inevitable. It sets itself a far subtler goal, one that even adults must struggle to understand—but they are then required to abide by it, forever and always. The rub is that while killing is either done or not, murder is not defined, at least not in the Ten Commandments, yet Jews must tell one from the other.

What turns killing into murder is a combination of the perpetrator's intention and the actions of the victim. Murder must be the result of an intention to end life. Accidental death is never murder; the victim must not be engaged in an action that would justify death, such as assaulting the perpetrator to a degree that would justify killing in self-defense. Murder is defined not by the result—the ending of a life—but by the intention of the killer and the lack of it in the victim. The intention of the killer, it must be emphasized, is to be determined by him or her and not imputed by the friends of the victim—although in a court of law, the court may interpret the evidence to understand what the intention was.

This indefinable, subjective intention is fundamental to being civilized. It is also universal. The ethnic identities of the murderer and the victim are irrelevant. So are the material and social circumstances. Education, wealth, well-being, pent-up rage, frustration, despair, and the possible arrogance of the victim: all immaterial. Modern Hebrew has a trenchant way of saying this: Murder is murder is murder.

Not an easy proposition in our age of relativity, spin, propaganda, and conflicting postmodern narratives, but crucial nonetheless. Because a society that loses the ability to make adult distinctions will end up being childish, and children lack the ability to think in terms of universal morality. You might even say that they become adults by acquiring that ability—at least, that is the traditional Jewish understanding of adulthood.

The distinction between killing and murder is ultimately the theme of this book. It underlies the entire history of the conflict in the Middle East, but it is not a tool of propaganda invented for current political needs.

Rather, it has been at the center of Jewish understanding for thousands of years.

The Palestinian violence of 1936–1939 was to test harshly this understanding. The revolt called forth three new developments in the annals of Zionism at war. The first, somewhat surprising one was *havlaga,* "restraint." This was an attempt not to go to war at all, even when under attack. Since the British were fighting the rebels, the Jewish leadership felt it was in their best interest not to take part, insofar as this was possible, and for many months they refrained from any military action beyond static self-defense. Essentially, this was an attempt not to be drawn into a cycle of violence. Since many of the Arab attacks were on Jewish civilians, this required a degree of self-restraint that may have been rational but was hardly easy. It also failed, as the violence went on unabated.

Since moral restraint was not saving Jewish lives, people came to doubt its rationality. Eventually the policy dissipated. Mobile units were set up whose task was to patrol and intercept attackers. Some of these were formed in cooperation with the British, the most famous being the Special Night Squads, trained and commanded by the British captain Charles Orde Wingate. The experience and confidence gained in this second response to the Arab revolt was to prove valuable in the coming years.

The third development was a reaction to the failure of the *havlaga:* some of the Jews turned to terrorism. The preachers of moral equivalence often say that national independence movements always use terror at some point in their struggle. This is not an empirical, historical judgment, but a moral one. The facts are that some national movements use terror and others don't; for some, terror is the essence of the struggle, while for others it takes place only at the fringes, and so on. The implication of seeing terrorism in all national movements—including, for some, the American Revolution itself—is that it is normal, expected, and human to use immoral violence in the transcendent cause of nationhood and that once this goal is achieved it is equally normal to desist. As Edward Said reportedly answered, when asked to justify the murder of Israeli athletes at the Olympic Games in Munich: "This is history. These things happen."

Such a statement distorts the essence of morality, by claiming that such behavior is universal—which it isn't. It lumps all humans together in a way that is empirically false and also extremely deterministic. If everyone does something, there is no real freedom of choice. The essence of universal morality is that everybody can recognize and understand it, but that some individuals or groups decide not to. This leaves us with the moral decision to do right or wrong. It is what distinguishes us from animals, who merely follow their instincts.

We are often reminded of Jewish acts of terror committed prior to statehood. We are expected to agree that these acts of Jewish terrorism establish a moral equivalence between the parties and deprive us of the right to pass judgment on Palestinian terrorism as a tool of war. This is both a failure of moral intelligence and a distortion of the historical record.

At the end of 1937, some of the Jews of the Yishuv decided to do wrong. Faced with murderous Palestinian violence, and contemptuous of the policy of appeasement, a small group calling itself the Irgun Zevai Leumi (IZL) decided to respond with immoral violence of their own. The peak of this activity was in the summer of 1938, when they planted five large bombs in crowded Arab markets, murdering close to one hundred civilians. I have chosen the word *murder* carefully, for there is no other appropriate term for these actions, and the fact that their perpetrators regarded them as legitimate acts of retaliation for similar Arab atrocities is entirely irrelevant.

Whereas Arabs in general and Palestinians in particular required decades to start condemning Palestinian acts of murder, and still do so only by coupling "all actions of terror against civilians" so as to include alleged Israeli murders in their condemnations, the response of the Jewish community to these murderous attacks was immediate and unequivocal. The leadership of the Yishuv saw the actions as murder and fiercely condemned them. There was no cynical attempt to justify them as stemming from anger or despair or what have you. Lacking any legal method of coercion, the leadership could do little else, but significantly, the terrorists themselves, feeling rejected by their own, called a halt to their actions. They hadn't achieved their goal, and the Palestinian violence went on; as ever, there was no "cycle of violence."

In the summer of 1939, when the British essentially abandoned the pretense of basing their policy on the Balfour Declaration, the Yishuv would have launched a rebellion of its own—but didn't, recognizing Nazi Germany as the greater evil. This is best epitomized by the commander of the IZL, David Raziel, who was killed in 1941 while on a mission for the British. Only a small splinter group on the fringe of the IZL tried to fight the British even then, calling themselves Lohamei Herut Yisrael (LHI) or, less generously, the Stern Gang. In February 1942, British agents killed Avraham Stern, and the group ceased functioning for a few years.

Two parallel developments deserve to be mentioned. The first was the immigration of Arabs into Palestine during most of the years of British rule. Interestingly, while the British recorded the statistics of Jewish immigration, they seem not to have been counting the Arabs. Yet too many Arab villages near Jewish ones were growing too fast to be explained merely by natural population growth, and the doubling of the Arab population from below 600,000 in 1900 to well above 1.5 million in 1947 was too steep without significant immigration. An anecdotal illustration: One of the most important Palestinian heroes and role models, Sheikh 'Izz al-Din al-Qassam, a rabid preacher whose underground organization the Black Hand murdered at least eight Jews in the early 1930s before he was killed by the British, was himself Syrian. He arrived in Palestine in 1920, when he was already thirty-eight years old—so he wasn't a Palestinian at all. Not all Palestinians who claim to have been here "since time immemorial" really have been, and the ease with which this truth is omitted even by so important a Palestinian hero as al-Qassam is striking.

The second strand of the story was the predicament of the Jews of Europe. We now know that the Jews who didn't get out in the 1930s were mostly dead by 1945. Every single Jew who wanted to immigrate to Palestine but was denied the chance by the growing restrictions can be laid to the account of Palestinian violence and British appeasement; the number probably runs to the hundreds of thousands. Even this small fraction of Jewish dead exceeds all of the subsequent losses of Palestinian lives in their conflict with Zionism. This, Palestinian apologists might reasonably say, is hindsight. Yet what was obvious at the time was that there were violently antisemitic governments or political movements in almost all of the European countries in which there were significant Jewish communities; anti-Jewish legislation or agitation or both were the norm. The Palestinian decision at the time was to join this anti-Jewish camp at its violent edge. Let this be kept in mind when Palestinian propagandists decry their victimization by the victims of the Nazis.

Pattern of Settlements 1900–1948
LEBANON
SYRIA
Sea of Galilee
Haifa
Degania
Ein Harod
Tel Yossef
Kfar Yehezkel/Geva
Beit Alfa
Mediterranean Sea
Jordan River
Tel Aviv
Jaffa
Atarot
Old City
Jerusalem
Beit Ha'Arava
Etzion Block
GAZA
Kfar Darom
Dead Sea
Beer Sheva
TRANSJORDAN
EGYPT
Second Aliya
Third Aliya
Jewish Settlements destroyed in 1948
0 Miles 25 50
0 Kilometers 50
Eliat
Gulf of Aqaba
© 2003 Jeffrey L. Ward

CHAPTER

3

1948: Decisions About Genocide

For the Palestinians and their friends, the ultimate Zionist crime and the fountainhead of Palestinian grievances were the events of 1947–1949. Perry Anderson, editor of *New Left Review,* uses detached analytical language when describing the birth of the state of Israel to mask his distaste, yet ultimately his is a moral evaluation, not a reasonable statement of fact:

> In the course of the two waves of fighting between November 1947 and March 1949, but principally during the first, over half the Arab population was driven out of Palestine by Jewish attacks—some 700,000 persons. . . . The fear that drove [the Arabs to leave] was a function of the killings and expulsions of the war waged by the Zionist high commands, in which massacre, pillage and intimidation were instruments of policy to spread terror among the target population. The war of Jewish independence unleashed a massive operation of ethnic cleansing, on which Israel as a state has rested ever since. The expulsions were carried out in the typical conditions of *Nacht und Nebel*—under cover of military darkness—in which nearly all such crimes were committed in the twentieth century. ("Scurrying Toward Bethlehem," *New Left Review* 10 [July–August 2001])

This malicious and highly distorted version of events has become an article of faith among European and American leftists, whose horror about the Palestinian refugee problem outweighs any concern about the repeatedly proven genocidal intentions of the Arabs with respect to the Jews. It also contains an unusual twist. Most wars, once they are over, lose whatever moral ambiguity they may have had, and their results become accepted as "the way things are." Despite our official repudiation of the idea that might makes right, the result of an armed conflict is usually regarded as a judgment on the cause of the combatants, or at least as the new status quo. The war of 1948 is highly unusual in this regard. The Jews were the weaker party; their defeat was expected by most observers, and their eventual victory was unforeseeable; yet they are castigated for having won, and "the way things are" is now seen as a justification for further violence against them.

Anderson's tendentious reading of the history of Zionism is that in the name of justice, Israel and Palestine need to partition their land in a way far more beneficial to the Palestinians than any plan currently being discussed. He does not dwell on the Arab rejection of the original partition decided upon by the UN, since he would then have to describe their rejection of Israel's very existence, a position that in spite of his distaste, he doesn't go so far as to endorse. It doesn't take more than a few minutes of searching on the Internet, however, to find mainstream Palestinians who do, or at least imply that they do. Here is Zakaria Mohammed, poet and editor of *Al-Karmel,* the leading Palestinian literary journal, from his article "New Palestinian Historians?" in *Al-Ayyam* on November 4, 1999, while the Oslo peace process was still on track:

> The appearance of new Israeli historians resulted from a unique Israeli reality: the existence of an old and distorted official history, that was created by the Israeli system, namely the Zionist movement and later the state. The need for new Israeli historians derived from the existence of a history that cannot stand serious criticism. After all, what serious historian can believe that the 1948 war was a war of independence for the Jewish side? What serious historian can describe the Zionist movement as a movement of national liberation? Therefore, [any] true Israeli history has to be "new history," [because] the official and distorted history had to be amended or at least adjusted to reality. . . .

> The Palestinian views the new Israeli historian as a penitent rather than a "new historian." His history is no more than "a confession" before the "priest of history." This is an admission of sin and no more. The Palestinian historian [on the other hand] cannot be repentant because he has nothing to confess to the "priest of history."

Zakaria was one of 120 Palestinian intellectuals who in spring 2000 signed a communiqué to the Israeli public warning that the approaching peace talks would fail unless one of two scenarios was adopted:

> The first solution is based on the establishment of a Palestinian state, with complete sovereignty over the lands occupied by Israel in 1967 and Jerusalem as its capital, the right of return for Palestinian refugees, and the recognition by Israel of the historic injustice inflicted on the Palestinian people. The second solution is the establishment of one binational democratic state for the two peoples on the historic land of Palestine.

The practical consequences of these Palestinian positions were spelled out by the PLO's number two official, Abu Mazen, on November 23 and 24, 2000, in the London-based newspaper *Al-Hayat.* Explaining why the Camp David negotiations failed, he told his readers:

> The issue of the refugees was at least as important as the Jerusalem issue, and judging by the results, maybe even more important and difficult. We encountered, and will encounter in the future, fierce resistance on this subject from the Israeli government, because the bottom line is that [the return of refugees] means altering the demographic character that the Israelis hope to preserve. In addition, recognition by Israel of the existence of a refugee problem entails an acknowledgment of Israel's responsibility for this humanitarian tragedy. . . . Testimony by Israeli new historians [proves] that the main reason for the exile of the refugees was the premeditated massacres committed by the Zionist organizations in order to empty the land of its inhabitants. . . . It is noteworthy in this matter, and this is also what we clarified to the Israelis, that the Right of Return means a return to Israel and not to the Palestinian State. . . . When we talk about the

Right of Return, we talk about the return of refugees to Israel, because Israel was the one who deported them and it is in Israel that their property is found. . . .[1]

Abu Mazen is often described as a moderate and contrasted favorably with Arafat. In this passage, however, he is saying that the results of the war of 1948 must be annulled and that the future existence of a Jewish state is less important than the rectifying of a perceived injustice to the Palestinians. This is the history that Arabs teach their children. It is hard to see how any kind of accommodation can be reached when one side believes it has a monopoly of justice, feels itself to be totally wronged, and expects the other side to accept its own demise as the price for rectifying its "premeditated" evils. On a purely pragmatic level, such a position ensures ongoing war until the victimizing side disbands.

On both a factual and a moral plane, however, describing Israel as the villain and sole culprit of the events of 1948 takes quite a bit of willful blindness, manipulation, and deceit. It is frankly astonishing that at this juncture in history a case must be made for the justice of the Israeli War of Independence, yet that is the point we have reached after decades of anti-Zionist propaganda. Before examining the facts, however, one must start with the broader context within which the Palestinian refugee problem should be viewed.

Refugees are people who have left their homeland under duress. Some of them made the decision voluntarily, out of fear for their lives, their way of life, or their livelihood, and in the hope that things might turn out better for them elsewhere. Others were forcibly expelled and had no choice in the matter. The line between the two is not always clear, and it can be highly subjective.

Since the early 1950s, refugees have been assisted by the United Nations High Commissioner for Refugees (UNHCR)—unless they are Palestinians, in which case they fall under the jurisdiction of the United Nations Relief and Works Agency for Palestine Refugees in the Near East (UNRWA). According to UNHCR, the number of refugees around the world fluctuates dramatically but is consistently large: fifteen million in 1990, more than twenty-seven million in 1995, and more than twenty-two mil-

[1] Zakaria Mohammed and Abu Mazen, quoted from www.memri.org; the communiqué to the Israeli public was published by Amira Hass in *Haaretz,* March 13, 2000.

lion at the turn of the century, Palestinians not included. The highest tide of refugees was at the end of World War II, when there were an estimated forty million—excluding the Germans.

Germany has had its problems of identity for centuries. Part of the problem was the lack of clear borders, especially to the east. German speakers had been migrating eastward since the Middle Ages. By the late nineteenth century, when Germany appeared to be a clearly defined country, its eastern borders contained many non-Germans, while German communities farther to the east were to be found in other countries. Unlike the Jews, who have a vibrant national memory going back millennia, the common German identity began emerging only after the Middle Ages—in other words, millions had been settled in the east for centuries before they began defining themselves as Germans.

This was the source of much tension. It contributed to the outbreak of World War I, it was central to the continuation of the bloodshed on the German-Polish frontier after 1918, and it was one of the mainstays of Nazism. It was also one of the destabilizing elements that doomed the post–World War I arrangements. German demands to resolve the predicament of their compatriots to the east were what brought on World War II. No sooner had Hitler reached an agreement with Stalin in 1939 to carve up Poland than the SS launched a gigantic project of expulsion and repatriation, displacing entire communities of non-Germans to make room for ethnic Germans from the Soviet Union and elsewhere inside the borders of the enlarged Fatherland. Further into the war, German planners intended the deaths of millions of Ukrainians and other Slavs in order to clear the Lebensraum needed to make room for the Aryan master race.

As the Nazi tide was turned, everyone knew that the ethnic Germans of the east would have to go. The first to know this were the local Germans themselves, who left the lands of their fathers and forefathers and trekked westward with the retreating Wehrmacht. In the final months of World War II, this retreat turned into a tidal wave. At least ten million Germans poured into the rubble that was postwar Germany. The American scholar Rudolf Rummel has estimated that an additional million, probably more, died on the way or were murdered by the Czechs and Poles who had lived alongside them for centuries. In what had been eastern Germany but was now to become western Poland, the evictors and killers were not even bitter neighbors, they were newcomers: refugees in their own right who had been forced out of their homes in what had been eastern Poland but was becoming Soviet Ukraine, Belarus, or Lithuania, told to find new homesteads at the expense of the defeated Germans.

Though it is not often admitted, this enormous international project of ethnic cleansing was one of the causes of the unprecedented peace that has reigned since 1945, far outlasting the end of the cold war. Germans, Czechs, Poles, Lithuanians, and Ukrainians (but not Serbs, Croats, and Albanians) found themselves with borders that reflected not history but ethnic homogeneity, and they lived peacefully ever after, or at least until they began dismantling the nation-state in their new project of European unity. If human well-being is a goal to strive for, it is a sobering thought that brutal ethnic cleansing can greatly contribute to it.

This was understood even at the time. When in 1947 the British pulled out of India, the subcontinent was partitioned between Hindu India and Muslim Pakistan. An estimated sixteen million to eighteen million refugees changed sides so as not to remain as minorities in the wrong country; some five hundred thousand people died in the attendant violence.

At roughly the same time, millions of people in other areas were becoming refugees for political rather than ethnic reasons: more than two million Chinese left the mainland when it became Communist in 1949. In the 1950s, the Cuban revolution, the failed Hungarian revolution, and the Chinese conquest of Tibet each created more than a million refugees. The Korean War uprooted some nine million people. At least three and a half million East Germans escaped to West Germany during the first twelve years of that country's existence, until the construction of the Berlin Wall in 1961 closed the way. Things have gotten no better in the following decades, but it is the perspective of the early post–World War II years that must remain in focus for the moment, since they formed the historical context of events in the Middle East.

In 1944, it was becoming ever more obvious that Nazi Germany would eventually lose the war—and that it would be too late for most of the Jews. In mandatory Palestine, the severe restrictions on Jewish activities promulgated by the British in 1939 remained in place. The secessionists decided that they could and should renew their actions against the British, who were no longer in danger of being defeated by the greater evil of Nazism. Their relationship with the Haganah was rocky. In November 1944, LHI agents assassinated the British minister of state for the Middle East, Lord Moyne, an action that was seen by the leadership of the Yishuv as so destructive that the Haganah went so far as to hunt down IZL and LHI members and hand them over to the British. This policy was called the *saison,* or "hunting season." After the war, however, when the British barred entrance to Holocaust survivors desperate to start a new life, Haganah went to the opposite extreme and coordinated actions with the IZL and LHI against the British. This cooperation disintegrated after the IZL blew up the British headquarters in the King David Hotel in Jerusalem, killing dozens of civilians on all sides. Meanwhile, Jewish-Arab violence was spiraling out of control, the Truman administration was not supportive of British policies in Palestine, and in 1947, when the British left the Indian subcontinent, there seemed less and less reason to stay in Palestine.

A United Nations Special Committee on Palestine (UNSCOP) was set up, and its members spent the summer of 1947 learning and deliberating. Eventually they formulated a plan and sent it to the General Assembly. The proposal was to partition Palestine roughly according to demographics: the former swampy lowlands now inhabited largely by Jews would become a Jewish state, along with most of the empty Negev desert in the south; the entire central highlands, from the north all the way south to Beer Sheva, and the southern coast would become a Palestinian state. Jerusalem and Bethlehem would remain international, whatever that meant. In sum, the Jews would get about 55 percent of the land, most of it desert. Some five hundred thousand Jews lived there, as did four hundred thousand Palestinians, but with hundreds of thousands of Jewish displaced persons (DPs) waiting in camps in Europe, the balance was expected to tilt soon in favor of the Jews. More than one hundred thousand Jews lived outside of the proposed Jewish state, most of them in Jerusalem, but thousands in various settlements such as Atarot, the Etzion settlements, or Beit Ha'Arava to the north, south, and east of Jerusalem, or Kfar Darom, Yad Mordechai, Shavei Zion, and the town of Nahariya on the coast. All of these had been set up legally, of course, but they were too far from other Jewish settlements. Both states were intertwined, so that each of them had three separate blocks in a patchwork that vaguely resembled a checkerboard. The plan did not address the question of what would happen to those Jews and Arabs who ended up in the "wrong" country after partition.

If this was Western civilization's gesture of repentance for the Holocaust, it was quite stingy and not clearly viable; more than anything else, it simply acquiesced in what the Zionists had already created on their own in some sixty years of intense effort. Yet it was better than anything previously offered, the masses of Jews for whom the original enterprise had been undertaken were dead, and hundreds of thousands of remnants were stuck in European DP camps with no one willing to take them in—so the Zionist leadership accepted the proposal. The Palestinians and Arab states flatly rejected it, and their supporters today—if they deal with the historical facts at all—justify it as the rejection of Jewish colonialism.

On November 29, 1947, the General Assembly of the United Nations adopted the plan. Thirty-three nations voted for it, thirteen against, and ten, including Britain, abstained. It was the very last time the General Assembly would ever adopt a pro-Israel decision. The Jews danced deliriously in the streets all night; the next day, eight of them were murdered in three Palestinian attacks. Israel's War of Independence had begun, as had what the Palestinians would eventually call the *al-Naqba,* or "Catastrophe."

It was to be a war with four periods. The first half, from December 1947 until mid-May 1948, was between the Yishuv and the Palestinians; the Palestinians had the upper hand until the end of February but were defeated by mid-May. The British Mandate was terminated on May 15, 1948, a Saturday. David Ben-Gurion declared Israel's independence on the afternoon of Friday, May 14, and on May 15, as soon as the British were officially out of the way, Israel was invaded by the armies of Egypt, Transjordan, Syria, and Iraq. Here also the Arabs initially had the upper hand, although within a month it was apparent that they would not be victorious. The war went on intermittently until the end of 1948; armistice agreements were signed in 1949.

The Arab world was determined to prevent the creation of a Jewish state in any part of what they regarded as Arab territory or to allow any rule of Jews over Arabs. Zionism was no threat to Syria, Iraq, Transjordan, or Egypt, and it had just accepted a compromise with the Palestinians that would have allowed both sides to move forward toward bettering the lives of all their citizens. The consensual Arab decision to go to war was therefore a decision to destroy a stable and thriving Jewish community less than three years after the Nazis had been stopped. It was a reflection of a deeply felt conviction, stated openly, whereby in this part of the world only Arabs, preferably Muslims, can rule. There was nothing new about this position; their fathers and forefathers had lived by it for more than a thousand years. Nothing had happened in the modern era that might have changed their minds, and certainly not decisions by international forums or rules of war emanating from the West—which in any case had just spent six murderous years breaking them all. *Jus ad bellum* was Latin to Arab ears, and *jus in bello* equally so. If breaking the back of Zionism entailed conquering its territory and murdering its citizens, so be it.

The Palestinians at least had a case regarding *jus ad bellum,* since they could say they were defending their right to their own country. This position would have been weakened by the fact that they had never controlled any of the contested land: since the Arab conquest in the seventh century, there had never been anything remotely resembling an independent Palestine; indeed, to a certain degree, Palestinian nationalism originated as a response to Zionism. Yet it would be patronizing to take this line of reasoning much further. The only people who can determine the essence of a national movement are its members, and the Palestinians defined their territory by the lines drawn by British and other European diplomats in 1922. The Zionists were threatening these lines, and the Palestinians seemingly had the right to regard this as aggression and to defend themselves from it.

Assuming, of course, that *jus ad bellum* and *jus in bello* can really be separated. Sometimes, however, they can't.

The only way the Palestinians could have prevented the founding of the state of Israel was by killing its civilians, destroying their homes and communities, and somehow deporting hundreds of thousands of Jews. Earlier there might have been other options, such as allowing them peacefully to create a national home of limited sovereignty within a tolerant Arab entity; but in 1947, after the pogroms of the 1920s and the revolt of the 1930s, it was partition or destruction. The Palestinian decision, purposefully taken, clearly enunciated, and unflinchingly executed with all the force they could muster, in direct contravention of an international decision, was to destroy. Ultimately, it was a decision to commit genocide.

Once the Arabs had decided to respond to the partition plan with war, the Jews had a limited choice: They could fight for their lives or die. The war waged by the Jews in 1947–1948 was therefore indisputably just. There is no way to dispute this contention without abrogating the entire

Western system of ethics—which of course is precisely what Israel's enemies are content to do.

But was Israel's first war waged in a just way? This is a question that has concerned the Jews themselves as much as their critics and enemies—perhaps even more so. This need to account for their actions in a way that shows a decent respect for the opinions of mankind is one of the things that distinguishes the Jews from their enemies, who observe no morality at all in waging war and show no compunction in twisting the truth to their ends.

The following account of the 1948 war is based heavily on the research of Benny Morris; to the best of my knowledge, it is not broadly contested by Palestinian apologetics.[2] Despite the frequency with which his work is cited in support of the most extreme Palestinian views, even the revisionist Morris concedes that the 1948 war was a legitimate war of self-defense and Jewish independence, that no prior plan of ethnic cleansing was contemplated, that the Jewish atrocities were balanced by Arab ones, and that in any case these were dwarfed by genocidal Arab intentions which the Israelis thwarted.

The Palestinians, of whom there were at the time at least 1.2 million, perhaps significantly more, far outnumbered the Jews of the Yishuv, of whom there were about 600,000. Yet they were not efficiently organized. Indeed, with the exception of the small educated urban stratum, most of them did not yet identify themselves as a nation, their primary identification being with their family, clan, and village. They lacked a well-functioning national leadership and many of the institutions of a state. Even when they took up arms against the Yishuv, it was generally with local initiatives: the men of a number of villages would come together for a specific act of violence and then return to their fields. The Yishuv had been preparing itself for decades, and its many institutions seamlessly took over the running of the state from the departing British. The Yishuv was also fully aware of the degree of hatred borne by local Arabs and since the early 1920s had been preparing itself for the day when it would have to defend its existence.

Most significant of all were the frames of mind of the two communities.

2 Benny Morris, *The Birth of the Palestinian Refugee Problem, 1947–1949* (Cambridge, Eng.: Cambridge University Press, 1987), and *Righteous Victims: A History of the Zionist-Arab Conflict, 1881–1999* (New York: Alfred A. Knopf, 1999).

A not yet fully awakened Palestinian nationalism faced the oldest living nation in the world at its direst moment in millennia. This was to mean that many Palestinians would choose to move out of harm's way, while the Jews fought with a tenacity born of despair: they had no choice but victory. Most of the Jews of the Yishuv had just lost some or all of their family members; now their own lives were in immediate danger, and there was nowhere they could have gone, even had they wanted to.

The first significant group of people to remove themselves were in many ways the most important: the well-to-do, educated Palestinian town dwellers. No sooner had the partition plan been adopted by the UN, and skirmishing between the communities was intensifying, than they began moving their families out of harm's way, to Beirut, Cairo, Amman. Tens of thousands of Arabs from Haifa, Jaffa, and other towns left, settling elsewhere in relative comfort. To the extent that there was a leading group in Palestinian society, it had effectively beheaded itself, leaving the masses to fend for themselves.

In the early months of 1948, Palestinian fighters stepped up their attacks on Jewish settlements and travelers. The Jews retaliated, often attacking villages from which attacks on Jews had been launched. There were also some cases where Arab civilians were killed. Villagers began to leave their homes, usually to a nearby village, bringing with them the fear of war and the idea of avoiding it by moving—an infectious cycle of fear, escape, and widening fear. By March, many of those whose villages were slated to remain inside the Jewish state had fled, generally only a few miles deeper into the parts of the country that had been earmarked for the Palestinian state. The coastal plain, which was the demographic heartland of the projected Jewish state, and which already had a clear Jewish majority, was largely emptied of Arabs, tens of thousands having left.

This was not because the Jews were winning, because they weren't. They were losing. Arab attacks on Jewish settlements had been repulsed; Palestinians and Jewish secessionists had been planting bombs in each other's territories, and hundreds of people had been killed; but the Yishuv's main vulnerability were the roads. Most Arab villages were at least partially autarchic. The Jewish settlements, being economically and technologically more advanced, were integrated to a greater degree into a national economy. The roads were literal lifelines. In February and March, they were being successfully blocked, and outlying settlements were being starved—as were the one hundred thousand Jews in Jerusalem. Again and again, Jewish convoys trying to reach isolated settlements or Jerusalem were driven back with heavy losses. Jews who were captured were beaten to death, and captured bodies were mutilated. Things could be expected to get worse.

May was approaching, and everyone knew that once the British left, the Arab armies would invade. Many of the Palestinians who had left their homes with such alacrity had done so in the anticipation that by June they would be back and the Jews would be dead or gone. The leaders of the Yishuv and its semilegal armed forces, the Haganah, realized that waiting until the British departure was not possible. At the beginning of April, they began what they had called Plan D (Dalet): the concentration of units in a single area so as to achieve military superiority, using it to gain and consolidate control of strategic areas.

The Dalet plan is often cited by Palestinians as a major component in the perfidious Israeli conspiracy to expel them. Since it is the closest the Israelis came to programmatically expelling Palestinians, it is purported to be a plan of preconceived, systematic, and complete deportation. This quite overlooks the fact that it was activated only in the fifth month of a war initiated by the Palestinians themselves, and only four weeks before a much heralded invasion by regular Arab armies from the south, east, and north; had the Palestinians not started the war, or the Arab states not trumpeted their intention to invade, the Dalet plan would not have been necessary. Even Benny Morris states that the plan was strictly a military affair intended to create defensible lines before the invasion by forcing hostile Palestinian militias and their civilian supporters out of Jewish-held or adjacent territories that would be easier to defend.[3] It was also a dangerous gamble, as it called for depleting Haganah forces in some areas in order to achieve temporary numerical superiority in others. Luckily, it succeeded; faced with larger, better-organized units, the Palestinian forces disintegrated.

There was now a willingness on the part of the Israelis to expel Arab villagers where militarily necessary, but it was not yet happening on the ground, as the villagers in most cases didn't stay long enough to be ejected. Morris was unable to find documentation of an Arab order to evacuate the Palestinian population, but neither did he (or anyone else) have access to

[3] Morris, *The Birth of the Palestinian Refugee Problem, 1947–1949,* p. 62.

Arab archives. He does note the Arabs' tendency to move women and children away voluntarily from expected battle zones. Intended or not, however, the removal of their families weakened the resolve of the Palestinian men to stay and fight.

Three events in the first ten days of April had far-reaching consequences. The highest Palestinian military commander, Abdel Kader al-Husseini, was killed in battle, contributing greatly to Palestinian demoralization. The site of his death, the village of el-Kastel to the west of Jerusalem, changed hands a number of times, demonstrating to the commanders of the Haganah the need to raze strategic villages so they could not be retaken. The third event was the massacre at Deir Yassin.

The massacre at Deir Yassin is cited endlessly as proof of Jewish brutality and murderous intentions, with the larger aim of proving that both sides were equally bad, though the Israelis are thought to be worse because more powerful and therefore more successful in their evil intentions. This effort rests upon two highly tendentious assumptions. First, that the Israelis intended to be rid of the Palestinians once and for all; and second, that they intended to achieve this goal by murdering defenseless civilians until the survivors fled. Neither assumption stands up to close scrutiny.

The event itself was undeniably horrendous. On April 9, 1948, about 130 troops of IZL and LHI, supported to a limited extent by the Haganah, attacked the Arab village of Deir Yassin on the western edge of Jerusalem. It was a brutal fight, with about a quarter of the attackers killed or wounded, but when it was over, more than a hundred villagers were dead, mostly murdered noncombatants. Entire families were killed when grenades were thrown into their homes in house-to-house fighting. Others were mowed down while trying to escape. Some men may also have surrendered and been shot. If you look hard enough, you may be able to find some extenuating circumstances, but personally I find them unconvincing. Murder is murder is murder.

The leadership of the Yishuv was properly horrified, and a letter of unqualified apology was sent to King Abdullah of Jordan. More significant, however, was the internal Jewish response. Relations between the leadership of the Yishuv and the IZL were further strained, and this contributed to the *Altalena* military showdown in early summer, as described below. Yet for all its horror, the massacre was an aberration, not the centerpiece of Israel's policy.

The most far-reaching effect, however, was on the Palestinian populace. They fully knew that if they ever captured a Jewish settlement, it would be destroyed and its inhabitants tortured or killed; now they had apparent confirmation that the Jews would do the same. Four days later, a Jewish convoy of medical personnel was attacked on the road to Hadassah Hospital in Jerusalem. Seventy-three were murdered.

During the six weeks from the beginning of April to the end of the British Mandate in mid-May, the forces of the Yishuv gained control of swathes of territory that had been designated as Jewish in the partition plan, including the city of Haifa with its large Palestinian community. Jaffa, earmarked as a Palestinian enclave in the Jewish state, was also taken, as was the town of Acre. Most of the villagers fled, as did most of the town dwellers who had not previously left. In places where Arab peasants had refused to leave land that had been sold to Jews by absentee landlords, preventing Jewish settlers from taking possession, they were now forced off, but this was not a widespread phenomenon. Elsewhere, Haganah commanders saw the military advantages in the departure of hostile Palestinians from territories that would soon have to be defended from regular Arab armies and encouraged the villagers to leave.

The Jews in the cities, however, especially the civilian authorities, did not wish the Arabs to depart, fearing for the social and economic stability of the towns. Morris quotes various sources to demonstrate this: a report from British military intelligence in Haifa stated, on May 5, "The Jews have been making extensive efforts to prevent wholesale evacuation, but their propaganda appears to have had very little effect." *The Times* reported that "the Jews wish the Arabs to settle down again to normal routine, but the evacuation continues." An important factor in the Arab exodus was the propaganda of their own leaders, those who were still around, who spread horrific rumors: "Most widespread," *The Times* reported, "was a rumor that Arabs remaining in Haifa would be taken as hostages in the event of future attacks on other Jewish areas. And an effective piece of propaganda with implied threat of Arab retribution when the Arabs recapture the town, is that people remaining in Haifa acknowledged tacitly that they believe in the principle of the Jewish State." So the majority of the townspeople left. Yet while tens of thousands fled rather than live with the Jews, thousands more preferred to stay and brave whatever might come. They and their descendants are still there, in Haifa,

Jaffa, and Acre. There was a moral choice to be made—to live with the Jews or not—and as is often the case, the decisions made were irrevocable.

When the state of Israel was created in mid-May, perhaps three hundred thousand Palestinians had already fled. They had done so under duress and became refugees, but only a few had actually been evicted, and certainly not by any preconceived plan. Rather, the war was not turning out the way they themselves had expected. At the time, most of them would not have been overly worried. The combined might of the Arab states was about to be unleashed, and they looked forward to returning soon, not only to their own homes but to the empty homes and settlements of the Jews.

The comparative strength of the various Arab armies is not easy to determine at this date. The combined populations of the invading countries—Egypt, Transjordan, Syria, and Iraq (Lebanon decided mostly to stay out)—numbered in the tens of millions, while the Israelis numbered in the hundreds of thousands. As World War II had just demonstrated, larger nations can sustain greater losses and still find additional resources. Yet organization, commitment, and determination can also make a crucial difference.

In mid-May 1948, the Haganah was fielding up to thirty-five thousand fighters (including some women), and another three thousand Jews were armed by the IZL and LHI; the invading armies were about to commit thirty thousand. The Haganah had no heavy artillery and no combat aircraft; it had stolen or bought from departing British units three tanks and a handful of armored cars. On paper, the invaders had seventy-five combat aircraft, forty tanks, five hundred armored vehicles, and hundreds of field, antitank, and antiaircraft guns. However, the maintenance of the equipment and the Arab soldiers' training were poor, thus significantly reducing their effectiveness.

The UN Security Council laid an embargo on arms shipments to the Middle East, and this seems to have affected the Arab armies more than the Jews. The Haganah had been an underground organization throughout its existence and was used to procuring armaments through unusual channels, of which there were many in postwar Europe, starved for dollars but awash in military equipment. The most important was Czechoslovakia. No sooner were the British gone than these armaments began pouring in.

Most significant of all were the changes in manpower. Partly, the growth in size of the Israel Defense Forces (IDF), legally founded at the beginning of June, reflected the change from the semivoluntary Haganah to a recruiting national army. Far more significant was that the departure of the British meant that Israel could throw open its gates to masses of refugees from Europe, and many were inducted immediately upon arrival. As the war went on, the Arab armies grew to about 55,000, while the IDF reached 115,000 by early 1949.

If in March 1948 the Haganah first fielded a few battalions, by the end of the war the IDF was operating rudimentary divisions. Yet the significance of this is often misunderstood. The British had assumed that the Arabs would win, as did many other observers and of course many Arabs themselves. When the opposite occurred, it was not because the Arabs hadn't been serious in their intentions, but because the Jews had been grimly adamant in theirs. The Arab defeat, not moral considerations, saved them from committing genocide.

In the first weeks of fighting, from May 15 until the first cease-fire on June 11, Israel proved able to resist the invasions and more or less hold her ground. Although this may not have been obvious at the time, the war was essentially decided in these few weeks.

The invasion that is usually least discussed is that of the Arab Legion—the British-commanded army of what was then Transjordan. Its aim was the destruction of Palestine, not Israel. The opportunistic goal of King Abdullah—great-grandfather of the present king—was to conquer the West Bank of the Jordan and enlarge his own country at the expense of the Palestinians. There were clashes with the Israelis in Jerusalem and its environs, and on the road from the coastal plain, but as long as they didn't interfere with his army and stayed away from the areas he was interested in, he was not seeking a major fight.

The condition for this relative nonbelligerence was the dismantling of all Jewish settlements in Arab Legion–controlled territory. At Beit Ha'Arava, on the shore of the Dead Sea, Jewish settlers walked an officer of the Arab Legion through the settlement, pointing out the inventory they were leaving, then handed him the keys and left forever. Atarot, north of Jerusalem, fell in battle, as did the four settlements of the Etzion Block south of Jerusalem, where 240 defenders fell—dozens of them shot in cold blood by Palestinian irregulars after surrendering. The Jewish Quarter of

Jerusalem held out for a few weeks, but finally its hundreds of civilian inhabitants surrendered, ending almost seven hundred years of uninterrupted settlement. It was unthinkable, even to Abdullah—the only Arab leader willing to negotiate with the Zionists—that any Jews would remain in his territory.

A second invading army came from Iraq, which has no common border with Israel and needed to be supplied from afar. The initial force was five thousand men strong, soon to be reinforced to the strength of eighteen thousand. The Iraqis invaded Israel at Gesher, in the Jordan valley, but in spite of five days of fierce fighting, the settlement held. The Iraqis then tried to attack from the northern part of the Arab Legion–held West Bank. Additional fierce fighting followed, with many casualties on both sides, at the end of which the Iraqis decided to stick to Arab Legion–controlled territories.

The Syrians managed to muster only a small invasion force, which struck south of the Sea of Galilee. Here also, a number of days of fierce fighting convinced them that the campaign was not going to be the victorious stroll they had expected, and they retreated. They then tried again at a number of points, finally capturing the kibbutz of Mishmar Hayarden just before the cease-fire. They razed it, of course.

The most powerful invasion was the Egyptian one. Starting with more than six thousand troops, it built up to about fourteen thousand, backed by the largest air force in the region. Part of the force crossed the Negev and went up through Arab-held Hebron toward Jerusalem. Most of the Egyptian force moved up the coast from the Sinai toward Tel Aviv. Wary of leaving Jewish settlements in its rear, it attacked, conquered, and destroyed each one along the way. Many dozens of defenders were killed, but so were hundreds of attackers, and most of the aircraft were lost. An unforeseen chapter in the annals of Zionist settlement had been written. Although they vastly outnumbered and outgunned the defenders, the invaders managed to take only four Jewish settlements in almost four weeks of fighting; in doing so, they had lost so much time that the Israelis were able to set up defense lines ahead of the advancing army and even launched a counterattack. By the first truce, the Egyptian impetus had petered out. They continued to reinforce their units, but their attention turned to preventing Israeli control over the Negev.

During this stage of the war, there does not appear to have been any significant movement of Palestinian population. The Israelis were under attack, their settlements and towns were being shelled and occasionally bombed from the air, and if captured, they were razed. Every war has its de facto rules, and those were the rules of the 1948 war.

On June 11 a truce was declared that lasted a month, during which all sides reinforced their positions. The Israelis also dealt with the crucial constitutional issue of the secessionists.

States wield power externally, in relationship with other states, and internally, by holding the monopoly on its use. No sovereign country can allow autonomous groups to wield power outside of the accepted rules of political behavior. During the mandatory years, the institutions of the Yishuv, though democratic, were voluntary and could not coerce the secessionists to abide by the decisions of the majority. Within two weeks of attaining statehood, the IZL agreed to disband and join the newly created Israel Defense Forces. Three weeks later, this was put to the test when an IZL ship, the *Altalena,* arrived at the coast laden with arms. The IZL demanded that the arms be transferred to "its" battalions. Ben-Gurion was determined to demonstrate that there was only one military command structure and forced the issue. For two tense days Jewish soldiers faced one another and occasionally clashed; at least eighteen were killed, and finally the *Altalena* was shelled and sunk on the beach at Tel Aviv. The incident was to poison Israeli political discourse for decades, but Ben-Gurion had decisively won the day and thereby preserved the democratic integrity of the state. Israel would have only one military force, it was to be subordinate to the elected leadership, and it was to behave as an army, not as a terrorist organization.

The truce collapsed in July, and the IDF took the central-plain towns of Lydda and Ramla but failed in opening the main road to Jerusalem. In Lydda a tragic combination of chaos and mutual panic caused the newly arrived Israeli troops to fire on the populace, who seemed to be firing at them but probably were not. About two hundred civilians were killed, and tens of thousands of the townspeople were forced east into Arab Legion–controlled territory. After ten days of fighting, a second truce was agreed on.

As the Israelis grew stronger, their goal changed from defending their existence to achieving viable borders that might discourage additional invasions. However, although by late 1948 they had the power to do so, they never tried to conquer the entire country. Despite common assertions these days that the Jews have always harbored expansionist designs, what they wanted was a state for the Jews, not to displace the Palestinians.

The last significant stage of the war started in October 1948. In the south, Egyptian forces still cut off the Negev from the rest of the country, and contrary to the terms of the truce of July, they were besieging the Jewish settlements there in a bid to annex the entire Negev. In the third week of October, the IDF turned the tables, reconnecting to the settlements in the south while encircling and besieging the Egyptian forces; this operation included the taking of what was at the time the small town of Beer Sheva.

In the Galilee there was a raggedy Palestinian force with the impressive title of the Arab Liberation Army (ALA), commanded by an elderly Ottoman officer named Fawzi Quaqji. Numbering between three thousand and five thousand troops, the ALA had so far played no significant role in the war; now it chose the renewed fighting with the Egyptians as the moment to launch an attack on IDF positions in the Galilee. The initial attacks were successful, forcing the IDF to respond and to destroy the ALA. In the process, all remaining parts of the Galilee were captured. As the Arabs had done, the Israelis often shelled towns or villages before attacking them—though sometimes they didn't. As the Arabs had also done in the few cases when they took a settlement, the Israelis expelled the inhabitants—except when they didn't. There was an apparent relationship between the harshness of the Jews and the resistance of the locals or their previous behavior. Druze villages were usually left intact. Christian Arabs were often also not expelled, nor did they flee before the approaching Israeli forces. Muslims, especially those who had reason to fear retaliation for past behavior, either fled in advance or were expelled. Yet there was no consistent policy in this regard. There were cases in which different Israeli units reaching the same place had opposite policies, so that in some cases villagers fled from one unit, hid in the nearby hills, and returned when the next unit arrived. As this was happening, violence on both sides continued; at times Israeli units responded with considerable harshness after themselves sustaining losses, sometimes randomly killing local men.

Near the end of the fighting in the south late in October, an Israeli unit, apparently composed of new and poorly trained troops, took the village of Ad Dawayima in the Hebron foothills and massacred about a hundred of its inhabitants. Being an unusual case, the massacre caused intense public soul-searching; Natan Alterman, the most popular poet of the time, published a searing poem warning of the dire consequences of losing one's humanity. Had such massacres been the norm, as Perry Anderson and his ilk would have us believe, Alterman's poem would have made no sense. However, such cases were rare, and especially in the context of the world war that had just been fought, the IDF conducted its first campaign with what by any standard is unusual restraint. The isolated cases of mayhem that did occur were the result not of a policy, but of the chaos and tensions that are part of every war. I see no reason to claim that the IDF's record in 1948 was spotless, because it wasn't; it was merely better than that of any other army of its day.

At the end of December, the IDF again tried to dislodge the Egyptian forces that were still in the Negev. Some of the encircling IDF forces crossed the international border between the Negev and the Sinai. Having IDF forces inside Egypt was unacceptable to the British and the Americans, who bluntly demanded their immediate withdrawal; the outcome of the ensuing military and diplomatic maneuvers was the withdrawal of the IDF forces in return for Egyptian participation in armistice talks. Between January and July 1949, Israel negotiated and signed armistice agreements with Egypt, Lebanon, Jordan, and finally Syria, thus officially ending the first Israel-Arab war.

Some post-Zionists see these final months of the war as one of morally indefensible territorial aggrandizement, since the invasions had been stopped and the existential danger was past. Even as hindsight, this is not convincing. The Arab forces were still trying to chip away at what the IDF had achieved in months of bloody fighting, seeking ways to change the result of their failed war, and only after the decisive blows at the end of 1948 were they willing to begin armistice talks. Ultimately, this criticism of Israeli tactics is a reformulation of the basic post-Zionist discomfort with the Jews' willingness to use power to promote their essential interests.

About 6,000 Jews were killed in the war, equaling 1 percent of the Jewish population, making for a very costly victory and suggesting the scale of probable destruction had Israel lost. Palestinian loss of life was probably similar. The Egyptians admitted to some 1,400 dead, the Jordanians, Syrians, and Iraqis to several hundred each. But for the Palestinians it was a devastating defeat. More than half of them left or were forced out of their homes—about 700,000 refugees. Soon another group of refugees would join them in the misery of being uprooted.

There are today few living Jews whose families were not violently persecuted at some point in the twentieth century. Most were refugees at least once, and many in Eastern Europe were refugees three or four times, if they managed to live long enough. A vast majority of the six hundred thousand Jews of the Yishuv in 1947, those whom the Arabs intended to kill, were already refugees. They had fled the czarist pogroms, or the Petlyurian ones, or the vicious nationalist antisemites of Central Europe, or they had intuitively understood that they had to get out of a Europe threatened by Nazi dominance.

In 1947, hundreds of thousands were stranded in a Europe where they could no longer bear to remain, even had anyone offered the option. In blood-soaked Eastern Europe, hundreds, perhaps thousands, of returning survivors were murdered by their erstwhile neighbors: the last thing the usurpers of their homes wanted was to have them back. For a while in 1945 and 1946, the British had tried to prevent their coming to Palestine so as to mollify Arab displeasure, but by 1947 they merely wanted to wash their hands of the whole mess and leave the outcome to the locals.

Remote echoes of this story can be found in modern Palestinian propaganda, when they complain that the refugees of European persecution were fobbed off on them, thus forcing the hapless Palestinians to pay the price for the evil deeds of the Europeans. The Palestinians had thus become "the victims of the victims." This line of argument has exceptional potency with some Europeans, as it implies that the Palestinian suffering is ultimately of European making. There are various problems with this argument, such as the efforts of the mufti of Jerusalem, who spent the war in Berlin as a guest of the Führer, to have the SS kill Jews faster, and the conscious Palestinian attempt to finish what Hitler had started—another example of failed Arab intentions, allowing them later to bask in their righteousness. However, the most significant problem with the argument is that it denies the history of Jews from Muslim countries, for whom the Arabs themselves were responsible.

No sooner had Islam come into the world than it had to define its relationship to the Jews. Unlike Christianity, which started as an offshoot of a vibrant existing religion and defined itself against it, Jews in the Arabian Peninsula in the seventh century were a marginal group. Islam draws from Judeo-Christian roots, and in some ways it more resembles Judaism than Christianity does; the Arabs also claim descent from Abraham. From its origin it was further removed from Judaism than Christianity had initially been, and this dictated less inherent animosity. Hatred of the Jews was an essential and important component of Christianity for most of its existence; Islam preferred disdain.

As long as the Jews remained subservient to the powerful Muslims, they would be all right, at least until the Muslims had reason to harm them. They—and also the Christians—were called *dhimmi,* a Muslim legal term denoting second-class status. In some corners of the Muslim world, *dhimmis* were harshly discriminated against; in others, they enjoyed relative freedom and prosperity. But they never had equality, nor was it for them to determine how they would be treated. To the best of my knowledge, there was never a time when Muslims lived under Jewish sovereignty—where could such a thing have happened? Christian *dhimmi* had non-*dhimmi* co-religionists in other lands who were powerful and at times even ruled over Muslims; such a thing was inconceivable for Jews.

When such a possibility was finally proposed, in the twentieth century, it provoked generations of violent rejection. It took the Christian world more than 1,500 years of coexistence, two hundred years of Enlightenment, and the paroxysm of the Holocaust to bring itself even to begin dismantling its accepted lies about the Jews, in the early 1960s. But while Europe had been grappling with its relationship to the Jews for centuries, Islam faced its first serious conflict with Judaism only in the twentieth century. Any expectation that this conflict would be quickly and rationally resolved flies in the face of history.

The steep rise of Arab-Jewish tensions in British Palestine was accompanied by similar tensions elsewhere in the Arab world, abetted by the violent hatred that was climaxing in Europe. Attacks on Jews became common all over the Arab world; at times the number of the dead exceeded 100: Algeria in 1934, Iraq in 1941 (at least 150 dead), and Tripoli, Libya, with 130 victims in 1945. Each one of these events saw a Deir Yassin– or al-Dawayima-like number of dead, without the excuse of war, nor were the victims in any way a threat to their killers.

What happened next was one of the most astonishing events of the twentieth century, though you will find it in history books only if you know what you are looking for, and never in the anti-Israeli polemics of Perry Anderson or Edward Said.

Within a few short years of the founding of Israel, the Arab world emptied itself of its Jews. In some countries the process took a year or two, elsewhere it took a decade. The Jewish community of Yemen had been in place since the days of King Solomon, some 2,950 years ago, and may have had the longest unbroken history of any Jewish community. The next oldest, in Iraq, was at least 2,700 years old and had been the undisputed center of the Jewish world for perhaps 1,000 years. In the whole history of humanity, there are only a few communities that can boast of 2,700 years of creative existence, through war, conquest, destruction, famine, and pestilence. And then it was suddenly gone.

Of 130,000 Jews in Iraq, there remained a few hundred. Seventy-five thousand Jews left Egypt, more than 25,000 left Syria, 63,000 left Yemen and Aden, close to 40,000 left Libya, more than 100,000 left Tunisia, maybe 140,000 left Algeria, and 250,000 left Morocco. Only a few thousand had lived in Lebanon, but almost all of them left; they were joined by tens of thousands from Iran and Turkey, which were Muslim countries not at war with Israel. In all, close to 800,000 Jewish refugees were displaced from Muslim countries, the large majority of whom came to Israel, most of them in an intensive two- or three-year period. Numbers aside, however, something momentous and unexplained had happened. Even after the murder of six million Jews in Europe, there remained a few hundred thousands of them. The Muslim world, on the other hand, had rid itself entirely of its Jews in less than a decade, leaving tiny pockets in Baghdad, Damascus, and Cairo. And then all memory of this awesome convulsion disappeared from the world's consciousness, if it had ever been noticed in the first place.

How is the total collapse of these ancient communities to be explained? Were the relations between the Muslim majority and their Jewish *dhimmis* perhaps far worse than generally realized? Was the yearning for Zion among the Jews of Arab countries dramatically stronger than among their European brothers, and if so, why did a sizable minority of North African Jews prefer to go to France? Had they taken warning from the fate of Europe's Jews and feared the repetition of Auschwitz in the Arab lands?

What happened next was to complicate severely the history of the Arab-Israeli conflict for many generations: Israel gave the Jewish refugees homes, while the Arabs gave the Palestinians permanent camps.

The challenge facing Israel was greater by any measure. The absolute numbers of arriving refugees were larger than the roughly seven hundred thousand Arabs who had left. Proportionally the gap was immense, the absorbing population of Israelis being roughly equal to the population of refugees; the Palestinian refugees wound up in Arab states with a combined population more than fifty times their number. The war that had just been fought had taken place on Israeli territory, so that infrastructures that needed to be rebuilt were entirely an Israeli problem; while Israeli human losses had been high, with the exception of the Palestinians there had been no civilian Arab losses at all.

Israel rose to the challenge, though not with complete success: many of the serious ills of Israeli society fifty years later are rooted in the decisions and actions taken during those frantic few years. Yet within a decade, there were no refugees left, the tent camps had been dismantled, and the camps of temporary shelters were being dealt with; by the 1960s they were all gone (to be briefly rebuilt during the next mass influx in the early 1990s). Where refugees had been were now Israelis.

On a very hot Friday afternoon in August 2001, before an assembly of many hundred mourners, Arnold Roth stepped forward to say farewell to his fifteen-year-old daughter, Malki, who had been murdered the previous day in the center of Jerusalem for the crime of being Jewish. "I apologize in advance, for I can only do this in English," he told us, and then went on tell how, "with the exception of its final moments, the entire life of this child was an act of beauty."

A decade or so earlier, he and his wife had decided to move to Israel from Australia. Unlike most of the Jews who came here, there had been no real push to make them leave, only the pull of wanting to come. Yet at the worst moment of his life, he reverted to his mother tongue, forcing it to tell a tale of beauty where there could easily have been hate and despair.

The act of leaving your country—"the land of your birth and the house of your father"—can never be easy, even in the best of circumstances. Even when it is a voluntary act, it entails the loss of part of who we are and makes us smaller and weaker. It severs some of the moorings that give us assurance in an uncertain world. It transforms some of the things we have known since earliest childhood into useless information, while leaving us deprived of other knowledge that is essential for daily life. It need not be an unmitigated disaster, and often it opens new vistas for growth, but its scars will remain till the day of our death; these scars will divide us from our children, for whom the new land is their country, the land of their birth, and the house of *their* father.

The story of the Roth family underlines a basic paradox in the story of Israel: that it is the culmination of a dream while being simultaneously a haven for refugees. A large majority of its Jewish citizens arrived as refugees, generally destitute, uprooted from their lives. Yet unlike the dozens of way stations many of their ancestors had passed through, this one was perceived differently. It was the original home, the end of the wandering, a place their descendants would regard as their own forever. So much so that some descendants of refugees uprooted themselves one more time and came from countries there was no apparent need to leave, such as Australia or the United States.

This is a paradox that is central to the ability of Israel to absorb numbers of refugees proportionally greater than any other society. It is also the root of much of the internal tension that characterizes contemporary Israel: since this is truly home, each group demands the status of an owner, refusing to accept the subordinate position of the tenant that was often sufficient in the old country.

The outcome has done Israel a major disservice: she has been so obviously successful in integrating all those refugees and immigrants that it seems as though the process must not have been that painful after all—nothing to compare with the misery of the victims of Zionism, the Palestinians, who still suffer the pain of their uprooting.

Though the loss was common to Jews and Palestinians, it was equally so to Hindus, Poles, Pakistanis, Germans, Koreans, and millions of others. Defeated Germany, with an infrastructure that had been bombed back into the Middle Ages, inundated by millions of refugees, picked up its pieces and moved forward. So did everyone else. This, it appears, is normal.

The festering problem of the Palestinians is the exception, and great effort has been invested over decades to assure that it not be resolved except at Israel's expense.

The story of the Palestinian refugees has yet to be systematically and impartially told. Perhaps this cannot yet be done, since it will require access to many Arab archives, followed by an extended period of discussion and debate among scholars in an open society. Yet some of the story is clear.

According to the United Nations, Palestinian refugees are persons whose normal place of residence was Palestine between June 1946 and May 1948 and who lost both their homes and means of livelihood as a result of the 1948 Arab-Israeli conflict. To begin with, this is a strange definition. A young Arab from Amman or Baghdad who moved to Palestine as late as May 1946 and went home during the war is a Palestinian refugee forever, he and his sons and their sons and grandsons. Whoever promulgated this definition was aware that there were large numbers of such Arab migrants to Palestine, otherwise it would have made no sense to have such a narrow and precise formulation.

The reason for this definition is that there is a special UN organization whose sole purpose is to support them. This is the United Nations Relief and Works Agency in the Near East. During the war, various international agencies stepped in to assist the Palestinian refugees in their hour of need, including the International Red Cross, UNICEF, and others. In November 1949, when the war was over and Israel was coping with its tidal wave of refugees, the UN set up UNRWA to help the Palestinians. It is distinct from the United Nations High Commissioner for Refugees, which deals with all of humanity's other refugees. When it became operative in 1950, UNRWA took over the card files of the Red Cross, so as to identify its clients, and it has been keeping this record ever since.

A problematic record, truth be told. Since the relief agencies that UNRWA was replacing were distributing such basics as food and blankets to destitute masses near Arab cities, some of the local destitute turned up to be served and counted; when people died, there was no incentive for anyone to report it. By UNRWA's own figures, of the 950,000 refugees it "inherited," 90,000 were not bona fide refugees and were stricken from the rolls. Lacking the means to follow births and deaths, the UNRWA Web site to this day is wary of the reliability of its figures, merely stating that the numbers are what appear in its records.

UNRWA supports Palestinians in five geographic fields: Gaza, the West Bank, Jordan, Syria, and Lebanon. Each has its own characteristics.

Palestinians who fled to Egypt were not allowed into the country and were concentrated instead in the Gaza Strip, which was the area conquered from mandatory Palestine in 1948. In effect, they were dislocated within Palestine. Gaza was then controlled by Egypt, but not annexed. The Palestinians there, locals and refugees, were not given Egyptian citizenship, and their freedom of movement out of Gaza was curtailed. UNRWA knew of 198,000 refugees there in 1950. In 1967, the area was conquered by Israel, and since then there have been no Palestinian refugees in Egypt.

Palestinians in the West Bank and Jordan were given Jordanian citizenship. Thousands of them had been born in rural areas, had moved in the 1920s and 1930s to cities like Haifa and Jaffa, and in 1948 fled back to wherever they came from. Tens of thousands, perhaps even hundreds of thousands, hadn't moved more than twenty-five miles; given the size of the countries involved, it is hard to see how any of them could have moved more than a hundred miles. According to UNRWA, there were 506,000 of these in 1950 (East Bank and West Bank). When in 1967 Israel took over the West Bank, about 250,000 of them stayed put—in other words, stayed in Palestine—while tens of thousands fled to the East Bank, otherwise known as Jordan. In 1970, UNRWA recorded 506,000 of them (East Bank alone).

Refugees who fled to Syria in some cases did move farther than a hundred miles, even as far north as the Heirab camp near the city of Aleppo. Most, however, concentrated around Damascus. They are Syrian citizens, which means they enjoy less freedom than their cousins in Jordan—as all Syrians live under a harsher regime than Jordanians. UNRWA counted 82,000 of them in 1950.

In many ways, the most discriminated against are the refugees who fled to Lebanon. If they were Christians, they have long since integrated into Lebanese society or left the Middle East; this holds also for the Shiites, for whom northern Palestine and southern Lebanon were all the same unit until the Europeans started meddling in World War I. Most, however, were Sunni, and their arrival threatened to destabilize the uneasy ethnic balance in Lebanon. In an unfortunate attempt to stave this off, the Lebanese government never gave them citizenship, did its best to keep them in their camps, and barred them from many professions. The stereotype of the Palestinian refugees despairing in their camps, with no present and no future, is closer to reality in Lebanon than anywhere else. UNRWA had 127,000 of them in 1950.

There was one final group of Palestinians who were dislocated and moved ten or twenty miles down the road in 1948 and yet were dropped from UNRWA's rolls and responsibility in 1952: the refugees still inside Israel. There were 46,000 of them in 1952, and whatever problems they and their descendants may still have, they are not refugees but Israeli citizens.

That last group underlines the bizarreness of UNRWA's enterprise. Initially the refugees lived in tent camps outside the cities, just like their Jewish counterparts in Israel. UNRWA acquired plots of land on which to erect shantytowns, carefully calling the structures "shelters," even though by now some of them are five stories high and built of exactly the same materials as the residential structures across the road. The camps were not surrounded by barriers, and in time they merged into the surrounding towns. Look at aerial photos of Jenin, for example, and you will see that the "refugee camp" is simply a crowded quarter in the town, with no gate or discernible demarcation line.[4] Except for those in Lebanon, the more enterprising of the refugees eventually moved to better neighborhoods; some of the poorer locals, meanwhile, attracted by the cheap housing, moved in. None of the Arab states saw spectacular and sustained economic growth in this period, but progress was made, and soon UNRWA diverted most of its funds from existential basics to social needs, first and foremost education, but also health services and so on. What had been refugee camps evolved into lower-class residential neighborhoods—aesthetic eyesores, certainly, but bearing great resemblance, on a small scale, to Cairo, a city with no Palestinian refugees.

For many of these people, UNRWA became, more than anything else, an institutional framework for preserving their political identity as refugees—even if by now almost none of them have ever been in the villages and towns their grandparents left. Take the case of Jordan. In June 2002, UNRWA knew of 1,679,623 Palestinian refugees in Jordan, of whom only 293,215 still live in those neighborhoods that were once refugee camps, and the rest . . . are simply the Jordanians. College profes-

[4] See www.mfa.gov.il/mfa/go.asp?MFAH01160.

sors, truck drivers, lawyers, vegetable retailers, toy makers, teachers—and Jordanian citizens all. Having a United Nations organization dedicated to preserving their status as refugees makes about as much sense as having one that supports the descendants of the Irish in the United States, or a UN organization operating in French cities, supporting French citizens whose grandparents came from North Africa, and dedicated to maintaining their separate existence and identity.

It also bears mentioning that of the twenty-two thousand employees of UNRWA, 99 percent are Palestinians. (The top management is appointed by the UN.) The financing of this charade comes from the guilt-ridden West. For most of its existence, UNRWA's largest donor was the United States; from time to time, even the Israelis contributed. Recently the Americans have sharply reduced their contribution, and most of the present annual budget of $300 million comes from the European Union. Almost none of it comes from the Arab world, whose representatives state openly that since the West created the Palestinian problem, it is up to the West to deal with it.

Reporting to the United Nations, not some police-state leader with opaque finances, UNRWA has been admirably successful. In its primary field of education, the descendants of the Palestinian refugees have the highest level in the Arab world; they are the only Arab group outside Israel with educational parity between students of both genders. Somewhere along the way, they transformed themselves from destitute refugees into successful citizens of their host countries, while preserving the aggrieved mind-set of an unjustly wronged community to whom a great debt must be repaid; they have an international organization, funded by the international community, to prove the legitimacy of this claim. Later on we shall pick up the story at the point where the Palestinians moved toward sovereignty in the Palestinian Authority, but the bedrock of the story has been constant since 1949. The longevity of the Palestinian refugees' case stems not from their objective circumstances, but from a conscious decision not to allow the problem to fade, lest this mean peace with Israel.

Edward Said is probably the most influential of all Palestinian spokesmen. In *The Question of Palestine,* he makes much of Zionism as a colonial enterprise, launched by Europe against the defenseless Arabs; in this he is followed by legions of Israel's enemies. He then rushes past the events of 1947–1949 with the following unsatisfactory paragraph:

> It is true that such major events as the birth of a new state, which came about as the result of an almost unimaginably complex, many-sided struggle and a full-scale war, cannot be easily reduced to a simple formulation. I have no wish to do this, but neither do I wish to evade the outcome of the struggle, or the determining elements that went into the struggle, or even the policies produced in Israel ever since. The fact that matters for the Palestinian—and for the Zionist—is that a territory once full of Arabs emerged from the war (a) essentially emptied of its original residents and (b) made impossible for Palestinians to return to.[5]

Since he is loath to present a brief summary of the events, perhaps I should. After centuries of European persecution and the collapse of the anticipation that the Enlightenment would end it, a growing number of Jews decided to reconvene in their original homeland, hoping that might weaken the persecution and open a new chapter in their history. Most of them came from Eastern Europe and had nothing in common with either the goals or the methods of the imperial colonists of Western Europe. The international community condoned this effort and voted to partition mandatory Palestine between a Jewish and a Palestinian state. The Arab world embarked on a genocidal war to prevent this, and the same international community did nothing whatever to stop them. The Jews, fiercely aware that this was their last chance, stopped the aggressors and partitioned the land themselves along somewhat more viable lines. While about half of the Palestinians were displaced, most of them remained within the lines of mandatory Palestine, and 10–15 percent of them remained inside Israel, thence to become Israeli citizens. All of the Jews of the Arab world left their homes, effectively implementing an exchange of populations such as was standard elsewhere in the late 1940s.

Israel, having established her right to exist in a bloody war, was then forced to fight for the same right again and again. Moreover, the interna-

[5] Said, *The Question of Palestine,* pp. 100–101.

tional community never forced her enemies to abandon their hopes of destroying her, demonstrating how flimsy the connection can be between international decisions and morality. As we shall see, the Palestinians are still actively seeking the reversal of 1948, and Israel is still expected somehow to recompense the Palestinians for the crime of having won a war that was forced upon her and fairly won.

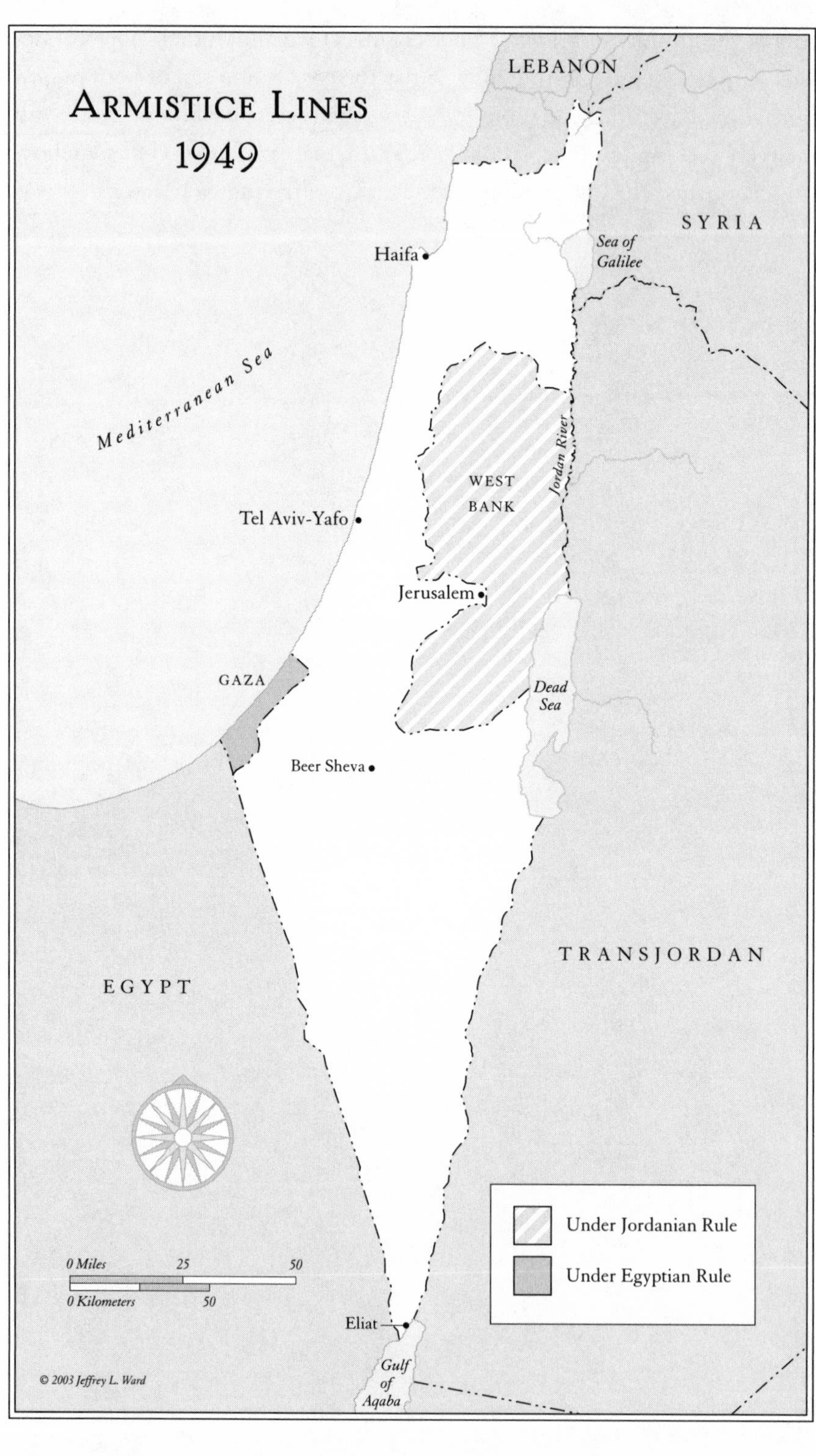
ARMISTICE LINES
1949
LEBANON
SYRIA
Sea of Galilee
Haifa
Mediterranean Sea
WEST BANK
Jordan River
Tel Aviv-Yafo
Jerusalem
GAZA
Dead Sea
Beer Sheva
TRANSJORDAN
EGYPT
Under Jordanian Rule
Under Egyptian Rule
0 Miles
25
50
0 Kilometers
50
Eliat
Gulf of Aqaba
© 2003 Jeffrey L. Ward

CHAPTER

4

1949–1967: The Decision to Persist

It is frequently asserted that both sides in the Arab-Jewish conflict have "squandered" opportunities for peace. Western commentators like to appear evenhanded at Israel's expense by making solemn pronouncements like "There is more than enough blame on both sides." This is another way of establishing moral equivalence between the parties. However, it is an outlook based on fantasy, not facts.

For the sake of argument, let us assume that a resolution to the conflict will be achieved only by the creation of an independent Palestine within the so-called 1967 borders—that is, the pre–Six-Day War lines, which included the partition of Jerusalem so that its historic center was under Arab sovereignty. Since these lines were drawn at the end of Israel's victorious War of Independence, in the armistice agreements of 1949, what impediment was there to implementing this option at the time? Certainly not any Israeli objections. Not only is there no evidence that Israel would have objected to the creation of a Palestinian state in the West Bank, there was nothing she could have done about it, since the project would have taken place beyond her borders.

But having purportedly gone to war in 1948 to save Palestine—and, implicitly, the Palestinians—from Zionism, the defeated aggressors seemed never to have entertained the thought of allowing the Palestinians to have their own state on the parts of Palestine not controlled by Israel. Nor did the international community demand this, in spite of the United Nations' decision of November 1947. During the armistice negotiations of 1949, pressure was put on Israel to return, at least partially, to the partition lines of 1947 and to repatriate many of the refugees. But the intention was to reach a settlement among Israel, Jordan, and Egypt. There was no serious mention of an independent Palestine. In any case, no peace agreement was concluded, and the Arab states remained legally at war with Israel.

It was as if all sides involved—Americans, Europeans, Arabs, and Israelis—were agreed that the issue had been one not of two nations claiming one land, but of the Arab rejection of a Jewish state in the middle of the Arab world. The Palestinians had been a useful club to threaten Israel. Having lost its value for the moment, it could be cast aside until the day when it might be taken up again.

And the Palestinian response to all this? In later decades, they were to prove tenacious fighters, never hesitant to use any brutality in the struggle for their "inalienable national right." But not in 1949, and not later, either, so long as the oppressive occupying forces were fellow Arabs. If there was a Palestinian national liberation movement at this period, it was weak and unimportant even in the eyes of most Palestinians and of no significance for the other Arab states.

If you believe that the longevity and intractability of the conflict in the Middle East is simply a result of the inability of Jews and Palestinians to agree on peacefully partitioning their mutually claimed land, why wasn't peace achieved in the early 1950s between Israel and the surrounding Arab states? Didn't anyone try?

They did try, fitfully. Offers, often secret, were made to negotiate with the Israelis, but their common theme was that Israel must pay for being recognized. She must give the Syrians half the Sea of Galilee, the Jordanians a territorial corridor to the Mediterranean, or the entire Negev (60 percent of her territory) to Egypt. Ostensibly, the Arab leaders making these offers could do so only if they yielded concrete gains, as their people were against any recognition of what was called "the Zionist entity." Actually, however, their ability to deliver on their promises was limited. The Syrian leader, Husni Zaim, lasted six months before being ousted and executed in 1950. Jordan's Abdullah was shot by a Palestinian assassin in front of the

Al-Aqsa Mosque in July 1951. Egypt's King Farouk was ousted in 1952, and King Faisal of Iraq, who in any case had made no offers to negotiate with Israel, was lynched in Baghdad in 1958. Agreements with such leaders could clearly not be counted on for long.

Once the tentative Arab offers stopped coming, none other than the Americans took up the idea that Israel should pay in territory for Western interests. In 1954, the Americans and the British tried to seal the Middle East from Soviet influence and hatched what was called the Alpha Plan. Israel would cede territory in return for Arab nonbelligerency, and the Soviets would lose a regional conflict that could be exploited. In 1956, another version, called Gamma, was floated. The Israelis never entertained the thought of participating in such plans.

Meanwhile, Arab rhetoric was unanimous in rejecting the existence of the Zionist entity (the word *Israel* was taboo). An Arab boycott against anyone doing business with Israel attempted to strangle her economically. Arab representatives refused to participate in any international activities where Israelis were present. The Egyptian army blockaded the Strait of Tiran, effectively throttling Israel's southern port of Eilat and her maritime connections with Asian markets. Clearly, there was still a long way to go before the Arab world resigned itself to Israel's existence, such recognition being a necessary condition for peace.

As usual, Israel's New Historians beg to differ. By their account, fleshed out in the 1990s, the Arab leadership's rejection of Israel wasn't really serious, and if only Israel—and especially her headstrong leader, Ben-Gurion—had been less obstinate, the entire structure of the conflict would have changed, and generations of warfare could have been avoided. Moving back from the 1949 borders should have been an acceptable price for peace. The foremost proponent of this thesis is the Israeli-born London-based author Avi Shlaim—for example, in his book *The Iron Wall: Israel and the Arab World.*

For such a view to be persuasive, it would have to be based upon copious Arab documentation of efforts to reach peace that were rebuffed by the Israelis—which, of course, it isn't. Instead, it is based mostly on a contentious reading of Israeli sources and castigation of Israeli actions. Morally too it is repugnant, assuming as it does that the Israelis, victims of Arab aggression in 1948, should have paid for their victory by rewarding the aggressors with territories to which they had no legal claim. Above all, the New Historians' thesis shows a complete misunderstanding of the historical situation. They take a legitimate position of the 1990s, transplant it to the 1950s, and then pontificate about Israel's missed opportunities.

In the 1990s, Israel was militarily and economically a regional superpower that had been at war for generations. A demand to "leave no stone unturned" in a quest for peace could perhaps have made sense at that point. In 1949, however, "peace" itself was not the goal. Existence was.

The Jews in the late 1940s were at their worst moment since the destruction of Jerusalem almost 1,900 years earlier. And not only the Jews of Europe, but also those of the Arab world. By a quirk of historical destiny, they had an opportunity for national renewal that was also unprecedented—but there was little reason to think that they would be able to take advantage of it and much reason to doubt.

The Israelis had a common language, but most of them didn't speak it. They had a common heritage, but little that had any bearing on creating a sovereign, democratic, industrial nation. Not only did they lack a tradition of civil society, many were still alive because they had known how to operate in the worst human jungle conceivable. Most were destitute. Few had education or training in fields essential to the running of a modern state; many were illiterate even in their mother tongues. There was only a rudimentary national infrastructure. Hundreds of thousands were living in shacks and tents. There was not enough food, no money with which to import it, and no export industry with which to acquire it. Nor were there obvious markets. The "old-timers" who had been in the country for ten or twenty years had just won a bitter war that had been fought in their towns and fields at great loss—and they were the lucky ones.

The General Assembly of the United Nations had already passed its last pro-Israel decision. Europe was still reeling from its own war and could be of no assistance to anyone. The United States was pro-Israel in a perfunctory, cool, and absentminded way. The cold war was raging, and the Soviets, after a brief flirtation, had written off Israel as useless, while seeking deeper ties with the Arabs. Most countries created in those years and the following few decades are still not particularly successful by Western standards, and the challenges facing them were minor compared with those the Israelis faced.

Thus Ben-Gurion and his colleagues can perhaps be excused for having priorities higher than making peace with the Arabs. Peace would have been nice, but the goal of Zionism was not to have peace. It was to ensure the existence of the Jews as a nation. Nothing could have been more moral.

One of the first and most urgent problems was to settle the immigrants. Hundreds of agricultural settlements were set up, mostly in areas where the Jewish population had been sparse. Sometimes empty Palestinian villages were used, often not. In the Hula valley, north of the Sea of Galilee, an ambitious project was undertaken to drain and settle the last swampy region. A few years later, a large water project was built, dubbed the National Carrier, to move water from the wet north to the arid south, thus pushing the arable perimeter of the country down into the Negev. Many new settlements were positioned on or near the borders, to consolidate Israeli control and prevent creeping changes and also to facilitate their protection. It was hoped that the settlements would produce badly needed food, bolster the economy, create employment, and recruit the new immigrants to the Zionist project.

For the pioneers of previous years, settlement had always been a primary tool of revolution, and there seemed no reason to change now. In their youth it had been the way to jump-start Zionism; now it seemed a fine way to create Zionists. For the hundreds of thousands of Jews pouring into the young state of Israel did not seem to the aged pioneers to be Zionists. They were lone refugees from Europe or large, unenlightened families from the Muslim world, but they weren't pioneering types, and had history left them alone, most of them wouldn't have come to Israel in the first place. What better way to mold them than by trucking them off with some hens and a cow to a remote hilltop, there to leave them with the promise that at the end of the week the truck would be back to collect the eggs and milk? Better than what *we* had, what with the malaria and everything.

This line of reasoning left much to be desired, but as noted earlier, these aged revolutionaries had never been particularly nice people. Arrogant and cruel, they had never shied away from their responsibilities; all their lives they had shouldered the heaviest loads themselves. Now these characteristics were hardened by the ultimate accolade: they were right. Never had a people needed such a bunch of characters as the Jews did in 1950.

The summer of 1945 found Germany battered and defenseless. The German state had ceased to exist, with young occupation officers serving as mayors, Allied military police preserving a semblance of law and order, and commerce based on a currency of cigarettes. The Red Army conquerors of Berlin raped tens of thousands of women. To the east, millions of Germans, those not being murdered, were forced from their homes. History's worst murderers lay powerless and awaited their fate.

Meanwhile, into their towns trekked hundreds of thousands of their victims: Jewish survivors of the ghettos, camps, and forests. If ever there could have been a justified taking of wrathful revenge, it was now. Starving in a ghetto in 1941, a young Jewish girl had written in her diary that she knew "there are also good Germans. They should be killed last." Now, it would have been easy to do, and with no danger of punishment for the avengers.

Here and there an individual Jew recognized an individual murderer and took his life, but if there were any cases of the killing of family members, they have disappeared from the memory of both sides. A small group of Jewish fighters from Palestine sought out and executed a few dozen carefully identified Nazi criminals. Another group, even smaller, made secret preparations to give truth to the ancient anti-Jewish canard and poison the wells. They talked and talked, but the water was never tampered with.

Like the story of the disappearing Jewish communities of the Muslim world, the remarkable absence of Jewish revenge for the Shoah never occurs to anyone. I have had occasion to request an explanation for this peculiar fact from many Germans of my own generation. In every case, the question has been met with befuddlement. It has never occurred to them that the most natural thing in the world would have been for the survivors of the death camps to have murdered or raped their own mothers, and they have never given the slightest thought to explaining why this did not happen.

The book that would explain this has yet to be written, but its thesis is already clear: Jews do not take revenge. When they were a persecuted minority they did not turn in rage on their tormentors, which apologists for Palestinian violence would have us believe to be a natural response to oppression, and when they finally acquired power they continued to refrain from policies of revenge. This will not go down easily with consumers of Western media, who are fed a steady diet of reports about the inescapable "cycle" of Israeli repression, Palestinian wrath, and Israeli revenge. From time to time, of course, some individual Jews do take revenge, but these are the exception, and most significant, their communities generally greet their actions with disapproval, as something "we don't do." Were there to be a cross-cultural scale of acceptable revenge, rated by the severity of provocations, the Jews would be found consistently at the bottom of the list of "just avengers." One doesn't have to take my word for it. The record of human history is open, the Jewish parts of it tend to be better documented than most, and the reader is invited to do his or her own investigation. And still I see the incredulity of those media-saturated readers, who see no reason to dredge up the history of medieval persecution of the Jews and their lack of response, when they daily see the opposite on the evening news.

The whole concept of a cycle of violence is simply a way for Westerners to express their view that the roots of the conflict are tribal and thereby wash their hands of it. In tribal society, where retributive justice is the basis of social order, an eye for an eye is the rule. And perhaps it is the case for Arab societies, where the modern state and civil society have not yet fully replaced the earlier tribal identities and allegiances. The Jews, however, got rid of this tribal conception of justice more than two thousand years ago and replaced it with an elaborate system of legal due process. The cycle of violence is a patronizing myth that obscures what Western observers should be able to recognize—namely, that Israeli actions in this conflict are not acts of revenge, but reprisals or, even better, deterrence.

The distinction is of great moral and practical significance. Revenge is motivated by hatred. A wrong has been done, or is perceived to have been done, and suffering has been caused. In return, the avenger sets out to inflict additional suffering on the perpetrator. The act of revenge must inflict pain that is similar in its dimensions to the initial pain or exceeds it; otherwise the emotional satisfaction and element of punishment will be lacking. Revenge rarely recognizes moral limits; indeed, almost by definition it may seek out the weak. *Webster's Dictionary* offers that it is "the act of returning evil for evil," and that's why it can start a cycle of unstoppable violence: each side is responding to the evil of the other. Reprisal is "the act or practice in international law of resorting to force short of war to produce redress of grievances." And deterrence is "the restraint and discouragement of crime by fear." Engaging in evil, combating evil, and deterring evil through international law: what a difference!

Telling one from the other is not nearly as hard as you might think, nor need it be subjective, any more than determining *jus in bello.* Indeed, reprisal and deterrence are aspects of just warfare, while revenge is an aspect of criminal warfare. With reprisal and deterrence, civilians and noncombatants are not to be killed. There must be some causal connection between the military target and the political goal. If successful, the reprisal or deterrence will cause a cessation of the initial evil, in which case its perpetrators will henceforth live in peace, without having suffered pain like what they themselves caused.

Revenge, in contrast, accepts no restraints; the dimensions of the evil it returns must be equal to or greater than those it answers. Listen to Winston Churchill and his cheering Londoners in 1941: "If tonight the people of London were asked to cast their votes whether a convention should be entered into to stop the bombing of all cities, the overwhelming majority would cry, 'No, we will mete out to the Germans the measure, and more than the measure, that they have meted out to us.' " In essence: Even if additional children die in London, we will continue until greater numbers die in Berlin.

Reprisal and deterrence pale in comparison. They lack the boundless urge to evil so powerful that one is willing to continue suffering so long as the enemy suffers more. By definition they must accept restraints; if not, they become merely feeble forms of revenge.

Most journalists and pundits don't know much about the Middle East in the 1950s. Those who do prefer not to dwell on a period when Israel was already living behind the lines that are now universally demanded of her, with the Palestinian fate quite beyond her jurisdiction. This is too bad, because there is much that is instructive to tell.

To begin with, Arab hatred and the preference for confronting Zionism with violence were still very much intact. The most significant indication of this was the ongoing murder of Jewish civilians. Initially, these killings occurred when Palestinian refugees attempted to return to their homes after 1949 and encountered Jewish refugees who had been settled in or near them. This must undoubtedly have been truly frustrating and infuriating, but perhaps not sufficient justification for murder. These are often described by apologists for the Palestinians as nonpolitical murders, and this may be accurate in that they were not organized actions by a politically motivated entity. Yet to call such killings nonpolitical disengages these events from the preceding thirty years, as though the whole conflict started when the Palestinians were forced off their ancestral homesteads in 1948. It also disregards a scarcely noticed aspect of these events—namely, that the dead civilians tended to be Jews, not Arabs.

As the time between the uprooting of the peasants and their attempted return grew from months to years, so the plausibility diminished that the infiltrators were merely mourning their lost homes. Yet rather than tapering off, the infiltrations multiplied and their violence grew. In 1949, there were 11 civilian casualties, 19 in 1950, 48 in 1951, and by 1956, some 270 Israeli civilians had been murdered, along with 447 wounded and an additional 258 soldiers killed. The infiltrators, now known as *fida'iyin* (fedayeen, or self-sacrifiers), were initially displaced Palestinian farmers, but by 1954–1955, they were mostly irregulars who were trained and armed by the Egyptians or the Jordanians, whose goal was to spread terror along Israel's borders; they were sent into Israel according to the calculations of their Egyptian or Jordanian overlords.

Faced with the challenge of protecting its civilians from violent death, the Israeli authorities sought an adequate response. Revenge would have been all too easy: train one's guns on the civilians on the other side of the border and shoot indiscriminately. This was never done, not even in 1952–1953, when ill-trained Israeli military units proved disastrously inept at preventing the violence. Until the end of 1956, various responses were tried. Some were successful on a local level—for example, a concentrated campaign of sniping in Jerusalem in December 1952 effectively put a stop to the Arab sniping that preceded it. All in all, however, Israel found no effective answer to the terrorism of the 1950s, until the all-out war of 1956 changed the balance of forces and bought close to a decade of relative quiet.

Yet the efforts had not been wasted, and lessons had been learned, especially from the disasters. Many of the basic characteristics of the Israeli way of waging war were formulated in this period of largely forgotten violence. Two in particular stand out for their long-term moral significance.

In the summer of 1953, a young reserve officer was called back to the army from his studies at Hebrew University. Major Ariel Sharon was given command of a new unit, called 101. Its task was to learn how to take the violence back to its source across the border, so as to convince the Jordanian and Egyptian authorities to restrain the irregular forces under their jurisdiction. The sheer belligerence implied by this decision has stuck to Sharon ever since: should Israel's enemies back their rejection with violence, they will be met with implacable force. Israelis have sometimes wondered about this strategy, many in the West have increasingly been alienated by it, and the Arabs have long understood that it can be used to camouflage their own violence. Sharon himself has come to personify this Israeli belligerence, to the degree that his actual deeds are obscured by the emotions he arouses—pride, suspicion, fear, or revulsion, depending on the observer.

On the night of October 14, 1953, a raid against the town of Kibiya, purportedly a jumping-off point for Arab raiders, ended in the deaths of sixty-nine civilians, men, women, and children—some were shot in cold blood, others had been hiding in buildings that were demolished after the raiders failed to clear them. This was clearly a war crime. The campaign to protect Israeli citizens was eminently justifiable, but not at the price of the lives of innocent Arab peasants and villagers.

The first official Israeli response was cowardly: Ben-Gurion claimed that uncontrolled militias had done the deed—this from the man who had sent his soldiers to disband the IZL by force. When the outcry continued, he disbanded Unit 101, though neither Sharon nor his men were tried or punished. The strategic response, however, was a moral decision to spare the lives of countless Arab civilians, as the IDF determined never again to choose nonmilitary targets. This choice was not as obvious in 1953 as it is today: a mere eight years earlier, the American and British bombing of German and Japanese civilians had been central to their strategy, and the French war crimes in Algeria still lay in the future, to mention only the leading democracies. The Israeli position was surprisingly progressive, and in the decades since, the resolve not to target civilians has been mostly adhered to.

The result in terms of military training and education, however, may have been the most significant of all. The IDF understood that protecting civilians from harm in the heat of battle might not always be an obvious priority and that soldiers must be trained accordingly. Twenty-some years later, when I was a trainee in a unit of young army recruits, our instructors hammered away at us that Kibiya must not be forgotten and that such a thing must never be repeated; neither they nor we had even been born at the time. Twenty-five years after that, when Ariel Sharon was elected prime minister and packs of foreign journalists went to Kibiya to interview the survivors of the massacre, not one of them mentioned this fact. By their account, Kibiya was a forgotten crime in Israel's past, instead of a central element in Israeli morality, a memory kept alive not by Arabs, but by Israelis themselves.

No Arab army teaches its recruits to avoid harming Jewish civilians or keeps alive the memory of anti-Jewish massacres as a negative object lesson. Yet it is the Jews who are considered immoral aggressors and the Arabs long-suffering victims of arrogant and unrestrained Israeli power.

Still, the record is not perfect, and more crimes would be committed against Arabs in the name of Israeli security. Israel's second war, the Sinai campaign, began on October 29, 1956. On the first afternoon, fearing that the war might spill over to the Jordanian front, an order was given to harshly enforce a curfew in the Israeli-Arab towns along the Jordanian border. The commander of one of the units of the border police, stationed at the town of Kfar Kassem, interpreted this in an extreme manner, and his troops shot forty-seven villagers in cold blood—workers returning from work without having heard about the curfew. It was a cold-blooded murder of innocent villagers, with no alleviating circumstances.

This time the killers were put on trial; two of the commanding officers were sentenced to many years in prison, although they were later pardoned, and this pardon was a blot on Israel's record. The long-term significance of the case, however, was in its legal and educational import. Henceforth Israeli soldiers were told that it was their legally binding duty to disobey what were called "categorically illegal orders."

Categorically illegal orders are a modern version of the Sixth Commandment, "Thou shalt not murder." Soldiers are expressly forbidden to murder, even if ordered to do so on the field of battle; if they do, they will be court-martialed. The order they were given will not be relevant to their defense, since their moral duty as human beings supersedes their duty as soldiers. Such a ruling can be applied only rarely: a merely "illegal order" must be obeyed; the "categorically illegal orders" must be disobeyed. The definition given by the court was hardly helpful, unless you came from a tradition that had been using the distinction between killing and murder for three thousand years: a categorically illegal act is one above which a black flag flutters.

With such a literary metaphor, eighteen- and twenty-year-old youths are armed and sent to battle. They must obey the orders of their commanders, under threat of court-martial, because otherwise an army cannot function; but they must not obey when they see the black flag, under threat of court-martial, because otherwise the society they defend with their lives may not be worthy of the sacrifice. This is the Israeli definition of *jus in bello*. It is not a philosophical construct for academic seminars, but a component of training for war. Israel's record prior to the murders at Kfar Kassem hadn't been bad; it was generally to improve from here on. The cold-blooded lining up of civilians to be shot has never repeated itself.

Unfortunately, the Israeli policy of measured reprisal failed, in that the attacks continued. By 1956, this failure had dovetailed with other developments and was pushing Israel to her second war.

Israel at the turn of the twenty-first century is the most powerful military force in her region; she probably has one of the more significant nuclear capabilities in the world; she builds and sends up her own military satellites. But in the 1950s, Israel was a tiny, insignificant state, lacking allies. Two illustrations suffice: Until 1954, there was only one full-fledged Israeli embassy anywhere in the world (in Washington), and even in 1956 there were but five (London, Paris, Moscow, and Buenos Aires). The first time an Israeli prime minister officially met an American president was in 1964, when Levi Eshkol met Lyndon Johnson.

Surrounded by hostile states that had recently tried to destroy her and from which murderous attacks against her citizens were a daily fact of life, Israel defined five conditions she would regard as casus belli: longstanding disruption of civilian life; blockading of the straits south of Eilat; a significant disruption of the balance of military power in the region; stationing of foreign (Arab) troops in Jordan; or the creation of a military alliance among Egypt, Syria, and Jordan.

By 1956, all five conditions had been met. The skirmishes along the borders of Gaza and the West Bank had escalated into a protracted low-level war, with rising numbers of casualties on all sides. The straits were blockaded, and then the air corridor above them was also closed, so that Israeli flights could not fly to Africa. The Soviet Union was selling ever more war matériel to the Egyptians; the Jordanians got rid of the British generals who commanded the Arab Legion so that it was now purely an Arab army. In October, Israel went to war against Egypt—joined, surprisingly, for reasons of their own, by France and Britain. The Israeli perception was that her neighbors were preparing a second attempt on her existence, and this had to be preempted before their power was too great to resist. Since most of the campaign (which lasted a week) took place in the open and largely uninhabited Sinai desert, there was little room for war crimes on either side. It was purely a clash of military forces. In addition to occupying the Sinai, Israel also conquered the densely inhabited Gaza Strip and destroyed the bases of the fedayeen there. But there seem to have been no war crimes here, either, not even in the Arab version of the campaign.

The United States swiftly forced the French, British, and Israelis to desist, and within a few months there remained no Israeli forces on the Egyptian side of the border. Yet the campaign had not been in vain. The seaway to Eilat was opened, large quantities of Egyptian military equipment were destroyed or captured, a United Nations Emergency Force (UNEF) was positioned along the border, and—perhaps most significant—the infiltrations into Israel stopped. The Egyptians (and the Jordanians) had been successfully deterred for the time being, so the tool of Palestinian fedayeen was cast aside. The next seven or eight years were the most peaceful Israel has ever had, with almost no terrorism—proving that, in some circumstances, an overwhelming military blow can indeed put an end to terrorism, at least for a number of years.

The basic rejection of Zionism and the determination to violently destroy Israel, which had been a constant in Arab policy since World War I, remained unchanged. In the 1960s, Soviet cold war strategists were using the Arab-Zionist conflict as a tool to enhance their penetration and influence in the Arab world. One method was to peddle cheap arms, military training, and political backing for the outrageous purpose of destroying a country and its citizens.

By 1964, at the latest, the Arabs were openly seeking ways to achieve their goals. Meeting in Cairo in 1964, the Arab League resolved to divert the waters of the Jordan River, critically reducing Israel's water supply, and declared that Israel must be destroyed. Since it was convenient for the Arab states, they again reached for the Palestinian tool with which to attack Israel, and they founded the Palestine Liberation Organization. Note that it was not the Palestinians themselves who decided to create the PLO after their defeat in 1948; the Arab League set it up in 1964 to attack Israel. For years, Palestinian independence had been off the Arab agenda; now it was back. Inventing the PLO was a prelude to war, not a result of it; the goal was to destroy Israel, not to rectify the misfortune of the Palestinians, which still could have been done by the Arab states irrespective of Israel.

The mid-1960s saw an escalation of violent clashes, many of them along the Syrian border, where Israel was thwarting Syrian efforts to divert the Jordan River and the Syrians were shelling civilian settlements. In spring 1967, the Soviets supplied the Egyptians with false intelligence reports claiming that Israel was amassing troops on the border. President Gamal Abdel Nasser responded by breaking the agreements of 1956 and deploying forces in the Sinai; this enabled him to block the Strait of Tiran south of Eilat. Nasser asked the UN to remove its buffer force, and U Thant, the secretary-general, complied with surprising alacrity. By mid-May, there were large Egyptian forces on the Israeli border, the Syrians were moving their forces forward, Israel had been cut off from the south, and within days, King Hussein of Jordan would put his forces at the disposal of the Egyptians. From Nasser down to the lowliest Arab media outlet, the message was clear and concise: Israel was about to be destroyed and her population pushed into the Mediterranean Sea. Israel mobilized all her reserve units, effectively halting most of her normal economic activity; all over the country, last-line trenches were being dug between apartment buildings.

For three weeks the diplomats talked frantically, but they were unable to convince the Egyptians to desist from what were effectively acts of war; the blocking of the Tiran Strait was a clear contravention of international law. The Americans tried to organize an international action to defuse the tension: a multilateral flotilla of civilian ships that would sail through the Strait of Tiran to Eilat, upholding international law and giving the Egyptians a pretext to back down. No other country was willing to join, and—mired in Vietnam—the Johnson administration was unwilling to act alone.

Twenty-two years after the Holocaust, there were solemn discussions in the Western media of evacuating the Israeli populace should their country be destroyed. That was the extent of the human solidarity and historical responsibility the international community could drum up for the Jews. No decisive action was taken, no threat against the Arabs to force them to relent.

On the morning of June 6, the Israelis struck, hours before the Egyptians intended to attack. It was a textbook example of a justified preemptive attack. Within hours the Egyptian air force was destroyed; by the next day, the Egyptian army was collapsing. The IDF took full advantage of the chaos and conquered the entire Sinai peninsula, opening the Strait of Tiran and reaching the eastern bank of the Suez Canal. This took five days.

The Jordanians could have stayed out of the war. On the first morning, Israel officially warned King Hussein not to join the Egyptians; if he wouldn't move, neither would they. Jordanian artillery shelled the residential neighborhoods of West Jerusalem and other Israeli towns, but still the IDF did not move. In the afternoon, Arab Legion units conquered the headquarters of the United Nations in the Middle East, which was (and still is) situated on top of the hill overlooking the City of David—the hill that had been the edge of Judean territory when David chose his capital. Conquering the headquarters of the UN was not a military achievement to write home about, except for the fact that the Israelis had never fortified their line in that direction: the way into West Jerusalem was now open. This was a threat Israel could not accept, and she responded forcefully. Within three days the Arab Legion, as the Jordanian army was called, was defeated, and its remaining units escaped to the East Bank of the river Jordan.

The Syrians, who had done more than anyone to heat up tensions in the Middle East before the war, chose to stay on the sidelines, severely shelling Israeli settlements but not attacking with ground forces. They presumably wanted to see which side would prove stronger before committing their forces to battle. On the fifth day of the war, having dealt with Egypt and Jordan, the Israelis attacked the Syrian positions on the Golan Heights.

The Syrian defenses collapsed, and by the next day Israel had taken the heights, putting an end to years of living under Syrian artillery. Lebanon alone of Israel's neighbors refrained from aggression, and no action was taken against her—a small, unnoticed, but significant story: Israel was fighting a defensive war, and she had no quarrel with anyone who was not attacking her.

Once again it is necessary to point out that the Six-Day War was forced upon Israel not because of settlements, military occupation, or denial of the rights of the Palestinians, but because her neighbors were unwilling to live alongside her, no matter what moral price they might have to pay. And once again, Israel saved the Arabs from the blot of genocide by winning the war. This time, however, the result was different: close to one million Arab civilians came under Israeli rule. About two hundred thousand of them, mainly from the West Bank, chose to leave; perhaps they knew how they would have behaved had the shoe been on the other foot. But they were not expelled, and there were no Deir Yassin–like massacres to put them to flight. The lessons of Kibiya and Kfar Kassem had been learned. It was a just war, justly waged.

For decades Israel had been a tiny country, surrounded by enemies eager to destroy her. With the brief exception of the six or seven years after the Sinai campaign, her borders were under attack and her citizens endangered. In the years prior to the Six-Day War, she had to fight even for her water supply. In the final weeks before the war, the Arab world had been agog with excitement about her impending destruction, and the rest of the international community had been indifferent, with lots of talk but no actions. The Holocaust survivors were mostly in their forties and fifties—the mainstay of Israeli society—and their children were soldiers. For a frightening three weeks, the specter of a second destruction had hovered over them with a horrifying sense of déjà vu.

Seven days later it was all over, and the fears seemed forever removed. Israeli society was swept off its feet by relief, and the exhilaration went on for months. Topping it all was the liberation of the Old City of Jerusalem. No other group in the history of mankind had dreamt a two-thousand-year dream; on June 10, 1967, the Jews saw the fulfillment of their oldest and most precious one. It was the most momentous day conceivable, the most important day in millennia, and Jews the world over, religious and secular, were acutely aware of this. Giddy with the greatness of the moment, the Israelis were not prescient enough to see the dark cloud around the sparkling silver lining.

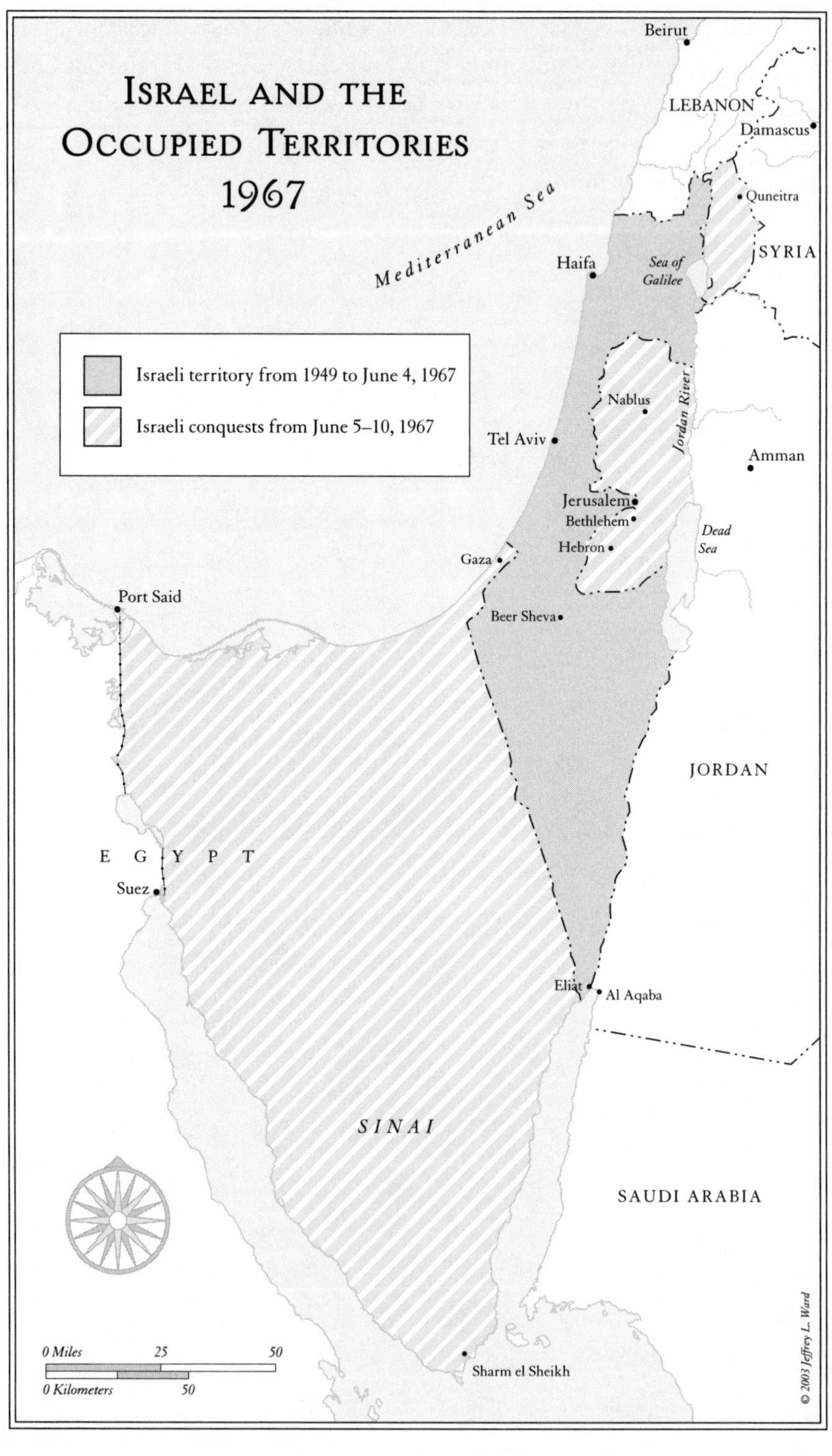

Israel and the Occupied Territories 1967
Israeli territory from 1949 to June 4, 1967
Israeli conquests from June 5–10, 1967
Beirut
LEBANON
Damascus
Quneitra
SYRIA
Mediterranean Sea
Haifa
Sea of Galilee
Nablus
Jordan River
Tel Aviv
Amman
Jerusalem
Bethlehem
Hebron
Dead Sea
Gaza
Port Said
Beer Sheva
JORDAN
E G Y P T
Suez
Eliat
Al Aqaba
SINAI
SAUDI ARABIA
Sharm el Sheikh
0 Miles 25 50
0 Kilometers 50
© 2003 Jeffrey L. Ward

CHAPTER

5

Contradictory Decisions: Making Peace and Building Settlements, 1967-1981

Many of Israel's critics, including some who are truly not her enemies, claim that the source of the conflict is clear, hence also its resolution. Israel occupies all of Palestine, frustrating Palestinian national aspirations. The Palestinians are fighting against illegal Jewish occupation. The Israeli settlement policy proves that she has no intention of ever allowing Palestinian aspirations. As the settlements multiply, Palestinian desperation grows, and with it their violence. As their violence grows, so does the repressive Israeli military occupation, creating a cycle of violence that is destroying any residues of trust between the warring parties and making peace ever harder to achieve. Israel is the powerful aggressor and must change her policies (or be forced to do so by the international community); the Palestinians are the aggrieved, weaker party, but if they were to be offered a just resolution to their predicament, they would make their peace with Israel. Resolving the Israeli-Palestinian conflict will also encourage the anti-Western sentiments common throughout the Arab world to subside and thus defuse the world's worst crisis zone.

Such is the current conventional wisdom in most of the world today. Most Israelis find this consensus extremely perplexing, and it is the source of the profound disconnect they feel between reality as they experience it and the story others tell about the conflict. Reducing the complexity and potency of the conflict to such a simplistic model, they feel, requires a willful decision to see only those elements of the story that fit the preconception, while ignoring what is really going on.

Until 1967, the only way Zionism could have appeased the Arabs enough to avoid war would have been by disappearing altogether. The Six-Day War could not change this. Only once an Arab decision to live in peace alongside Israel had been made would the terms of the peace become the mutual responsibility of Arabs and Israelis. But this clear state of affairs has been obscured by the Palestinian issue, which gave the Arabs a respectable cover for their enmity.

Before 1967, Zionism was never in a position to create, promote, or prevent Palestinian sovereignty, although Zionism obviously *would* have impinged upon the size and shape of such a state had the Palestinians created one. In fact, by conquering the territory of mandatory Palestine, Israel inadvertently removed the most significant obstructions to the creation of such a state, namely the domination of Egypt and Jordan, in which the rest of the world acquiesced. Israel suddenly held the key—and thus, along with the Palestinians themselves, the responsibility—to the creation of a sovereign Palestine.

As long as the Arab rejection of Israel remains implacable, the creation of a sovereign Palestine will not resolve the conflict, it will merely add one more state to the ranks of Israel's enemies; allowing the creation of such an enemy within mortar range of most of Israel's cities would be an astonishing and unprecedented case of political altruism, bordering on suicide. Yet should an Arab decision be made to accept Israel's existence, Israel's case for obstructing Palestinian statehood would be untenable. Should the Palestinians decide to live in peace alongside Israel, surely Palestinian sovereignty must ensue. The very principle by which Israel demands international recognition, that a nation that can define itself as worthy of sovereignty is therefore worthy of it, must of necessity hold also for the Palestinians.

Weakening one's defenses when surrounded by enemies who would destroy you is suicidal and therefore immoral. Subjugating another nation that is willing to live alongside you in peace is similarly immoral and, by unnecessarily prolonging the conflict, potentially suicidal. To complicate matters further, your own actions may influence the positions of your neighbors. Behave humanely and they may be weaned from their hatred;

behave spitefully and their willingness to accept you may be stunted and destroyed. Assuming, of course, that your behavior makes a difference. But what if it doesn't?

This is the fiendish conundrum that has faced Israelis ever since June 1967. The price for being wrong is immeasurable suffering on both sides. The leaders of the United States and the Soviet Union during the cold war had the power to make mistakes that would destroy the world; the president of the United States can still make wrong decisions that will affect us all. But it is hard to think of anyone else who faces stakes as high as those faced by the Israelis. Living in a democracy, your run-of-the-mill Israeli voter is routinely called upon to make decisions of an immediate potency that is unparalleled. And much of the world feels the need, and the right, to express an opinion.

Israel within her borders of 1949 was a mite less than eight thousand square miles, about the size of New Jersey. Now, after 1967, she was almost five times as large, or about the size of Kentucky. Yet before we consider the ultimate disposition of these territories, it is helpful to distinguish five different types.

By far the largest territory, comprising about three-quarters of the entire conquered area, was the Sinai peninsula. It is entirely desert and almost completely empty, with one small town, El Arish, on its northern coast and a few thousand Beduin scattered throughout the rest. It had strategic significance, abutting as it did on the Suez Canal, and under its sand was some oil—about one-quarter of Israel's annual consumption. It had been a part of Egypt since the Ottomans and British drew a line separating it from the Negev in 1906. For the Israelis, holding the southeastern edge from Eilat down to Sharm el-Sheikh ensured that the Strait of Tiran would remain open; two wars had already been fought over this. There were no Palestinians in the Sinai.

The Gaza Strip is adjacent to the Sinai; indeed, the town of Rafah is split between them. At 340 square kilometers (about 131 miles), it is small even by Israeli standards—roughly similar in size to Chicago and not much smaller than Hong Kong. The partition plan of 1947 allotted it to the Palestinian state, but it was conquered by the Egyptian army as it advanced toward Tel Aviv in May 1948. Refugees from southern Palestine were not allowed over the border into Egypt itself, being concentrated instead in the area controlled by the military. After the armistice with Israel in 1949, they stayed where they were, and the Egyptians set up a military government. None of the locals were given Egyptian citizenship. According to UNRWA, there were 300,000 refugees in 1967, but since there were fewer than 400,000 people in the entire Gaza Strip at the time, this number is dubious. The Israelis took a census and then did their best to keep precise records. According to their data, in the mid-1970s there were 420,000 people in Gaza: 53 percent of them (225,000) were refugees or their descendants; of these, 158,000 lived in refugee camps, 67,000 lived elsewhere, and 23,000 denizens of the camps were simply locals who had moved in. The Gazan economy had been heavily dependent on Egypt: the Egyptian military was the largest employer, and the agricultural produce was exported to Egypt.

Three times larger than Gaza, the 400-square-miles Golan Heights were conquered from Syria. Their strategic significance stems from their topography: Syrians on the heights threaten much of the Galilee, while Israelis there can threaten Damascus. At the northern end of the Golan, Mt. Hermon juts high above its surroundings, from which large swathes of Israel, Lebanon, and Syria can be spied upon. In 1967, thousands of peasants fled before the advancing Israeli army, but being Syrians, not Palestinians, they were not settled in camps and did not come under the jurisdiction of UNRWA; they were settled elsewhere in Syria.

There are four Druze towns under the shoulder of Mt. Hermon. The Druze are an offshoot of Islam who have become a separate religion, with their own ethnic identity. They are Arabic speaking and are concentrated in Lebanon, Israel, and southern Syria. Druze citizens of Israel serve in the army, and some have reached the upper echelons (there is currently one Druze two-star general). The Druze on the Golan stayed put when the Israelis arrived. They remain Syrian citizens and are not part of the Israeli-Palestinian conflict. Like the Sinai, the Golan was not part of mandatory Palestine, and its status will be decided between Israel and Syria.

There is also a curiosity connected to the Golan: the town of Ragar. It lies at the meeting point of the Golan, Lebanon, and Israel: over the shoulder of Mt. Hermon, geographically separate from Syria, but politically part of the Golan. At the end of the Six-Day War, a delegation of the townspeople made contact with an IDF unit, to ensure that they, also, came under Israeli control. Most of the townspeople have since acquired Israeli citizenship, and apparently many vote for the hard-line Likud. When Israel retreated to the international border with Lebanon, in 1999, it turned out that the northern houses of the town were in Lebanon; but the townspeople refused to be divided, so there are currently a few hundred Syrian Israelis living in Lebanon. The significance of the story is the way it contradicts everything one expects.

Most populous of all, the 2,000-square-miles West Bank was slated by the UN to become the heartland of Arab Palestine but was annexed in 1949 by Jordan. The annexation was recognized only by Pakistan and Britain. This means that Jordanian building projects there were as illegal as those of the Israelis after them. It also means that demands made between 1967 and the late 1980s that Israel return the area to Jordan made no legal sense.

Jordan's treatment of the population in the West Bank mirrored Egypt's in Gaza: everyone was given citizenship, there were no restrictions of movement, and Jordanian rule was no harsher than on the East Bank. Between 180,000 and 300,000 Palestinians fled the West Bank in 1967, depending on whom you ask. The Israelis kept open the bridges over the Jordan River, enabling movement of population between East and West Banks. The population in the early 1970s was about 600,000. According to UNRWA, in 1970, 273,000 were refugees; the Israelis counted about 100,000 refugees, 70,000 of whom were in camps. Since the population of the camps was counted precisely, the difference between UNRWA and Israeli figures underlines the fact that the definition of refugees was largely political. UNRWA was not claiming that the population of the camps was four times what the Israelis were claiming. In any case, all of these people were living in mandatory Palestine.

Small and landlocked, the West Bank is at the heart of the Jewish-Arab conflict, a conflict with far-reaching strategic implications. The strategic value of the West Bank lies in its proximity to most of the population of Israel. Hostile Arab troops in the West Bank can easily make normal life impossible for almost all Israelis, with primitive and highly mobile weapons such as mortars and Katyusha rockets.

In the Middle East, not a single inch of contemporary border existed in 1900. The British and the Ottomans determined the Negev-Sinai border.

The British and French drew the borders between mandatory Palestine and its northern neighbors in 1922. The borders between Palestine, Transjordan, and Iraq were unilaterally drawn by the British at about the same time. The Arab states inherited these lines from the departing colonial powers but had no qualms about violating them when invading Israel and Palestine in 1948. They were also very careful to recognize the armistice lines with Israel of 1949 not as international borders, but simply as the lines each side held at the end of hostilities (with minor mutually agreed modifications). No one else regarded them as necessarily final either until 1964, when Lyndon Johnson declared that peace in the Middle East should respect the existing lines. Even that statement did not reflect any broad international consensus.

Still, accidental as the lines may have been, each of them had at least some form of consensual origin. There was one area where no such agreement had ever existed: Jerusalem.

The United Nations partition plan had called for an international administration in Jerusalem and Bethlehem. Instead, in 1949 the Israelis and Jordanians divided the area between them, with most of it going to Jordan. When Israel declared her half to be her capital, this was not recognized by most countries, calling forth the unique fiction whereby Tel Aviv is referred to as Israel's capital by the international community, although the seat of government is in Jerusalem. But while the rest of the territories occupied by Israel in 1967 had a recognizable claimant—Egypt, Syria, or eventually Palestine—there was no legal claimant to Jerusalem or Bethlehem.

The Israelis were not interested in Bethlehem, which was henceforth regarded as part of the West Bank. Jerusalem, however, interested them very much. No sooner were the hostilities over than the government drew a line around the city and annexed it officially. The line was more or less defined by strategic necessity, so that the hills overlooking the town would all be within the perimeter; in addition, a finger of territory jutted north, past the destroyed pre-1948 Jewish neighborhood of Atarot to the small airport north of it. There were about seventy thousand Arabs within these lines, making up about a third of the population of the city. These were given the option of Israeli citizenship, and most have a hybrid legal status that gives them the advantages of citizenship (free movement, social security, national health insurance, and so on) without the right to vote or be elected to the Knesset. They can vote in municipal elections, but most do not. The annexation, of course, was not accepted by anyone outside of Israel.

If the Arab-Jewish conflict were in fact, as it appears, merely a political struggle for independence from Israeli occupation, the status of Jerusalem would be a minor detail. On the other hand, as long as Jerusalem stands at the very center of the conflict, you can be reasonably certain that Palestinian statehood is merely a cover for something much more ancient and intractable.

It was Hadrian's legacy to empty Jerusalem of its Jews and to continue its urban life as if they were never there. Having razed it completely, he rebuilt it as a Roman military city, naming it Aelia Capitolina. Such cities had a standard structure. They were square. They had two intersecting main roads, one east-west, the other north-south. They didn't have indestructible artificial mountains to interfere with the symmetry, and although this one did, it was marginalized by building the city in such a way that the thing was on the edge of town, and nothing of importance was built on or near it. Moreover, it just so happened that in order to achieve a square form, the southern parts of the previous town could be left outside the walls, in effect being cut out of the city and its history: if it's not inside the walls, it must never have been. The spring, the tunnel and pool, and, on the hill to the west, an ancient marker that tradition said was the grave of King David—all these were out.

Hadrian's spite soon spent itself. The unruly Jews were gone, but an offshoot of their religion was to take over the Roman Empire, which became officially Christian in the fourth century. Between 330 and 638 C.E. Jerusalem was an important town in the Byzantine Empire. The population grew and spread north and south of the square Hadrian had forced it into. The multitudes of Christian pilgrims were interested in the sites of the life and death of Jesus, not in the ruins of the Jewish Temple. It had more than twenty churches; some, such as the Church of the Holy Sepulchre, stand till this day, albeit extensively rebuilt. Yet for all its prosperous tourist trade and religious monuments, Byzantine Jerusalem was not an important cultural center.

Omar bin al-Khattab conquered Jerusalem in 638 C.E., ending the

Byzantine era and beginning the Arab one. An early Muslim story tells that he was incensed to find Jerusalem full of churches, while the Temple Mount was abandoned and covered with garbage. He had the place cleaned up and built a large wooden mosque above some ruins he found there. The first Muslim gesture in Jerusalem was supportive of the Jewish tradition and critical of the Christians.

From the mid–seventh century, Jerusalem was controlled by the Umayyad dynasty, whose capital was in Damascus. The Umayyads did not control Arabia and had a political incentive to play up the religious significance of Jerusalem; this led them to identify the Koran's story of Muhammad's flight to heaven with Jerusalem. But of course, the fact that Jerusalem (Al-Quds) has been the third most holy spot on earth for Muslims for 1,400 years is far more significant than the details of the original decision.

The most impressive and long-lasting achievement of the Umayyads was the construction of the Mosque of Omar, also called the Dome of the Rock (completed in 691 C.E.). This beautiful eight-sided tile-walled building with the golden-leafed dome is actually not a standard mosque at all; instead, it is a marker over the rock at the peak of the mountain from which, according to tradition, the Prophet rose to heaven. Intriguingly, the Muslims have accepted the Jewish tradition that identified the spot as the place where Abraham almost sacrificed his son, with one major difference: The son, according to the Muslims, was not Isaac but his older brother, Ishmael. The structure itself has withstood everything that fourteen centuries have thrown at it, whether earthquakes, wars and conquests, or simply 1,300 winters and summers; it is unusual among the surviving ancient structures of humanity in that it still serves the purpose for which it was built.

Across the plateau stands the Al-Aqsa Mosque. It was first built in 705 C.E and repeatedly rebuilt. From the Muslim perspective, it is Al-Aqsa that is the most important site.

Israeli archaeologists who dug in the Old City following the Six-Day War have discovered some of the most important findings from this era: the Umayyad palaces. These were five large and impressive palaces built to the south of the Temple Mount, or, as the Muslims were now calling it, the Haram el-Sharif. One of them was the palace of the caliph when he stayed in Jerusalem and was connected directly to Al-Aqsa. Historians knew nothing of them, as their remains had been covered for centuries, and they are a Jewish contribution to the Muslim heritage in Jerusalem.

In 1099, the Christians returned. As they approached Jerusalem, the Jews joined their Muslim neighbors in the attempt to repulse them. Their task was to defend the wall of the city near where most of them lived, in the northeastern part of town—the section now known as the Muslim Quarter. But the Christian hordes were too powerful and broke into the city, massacring everyone in their way; a contemporary account written by one of the invaders tells proudly that the blood of the "infidels" was ankle deep. Their clothes soaked in blood, the pilgrim warriors convened on the Church of the Holy Sepulchre and praised their God for being on their side.

Then one blistering hot day in the summer of 1187, the army of Saladin annihilated the combined military forces of the Crusaders at Hittin, a hill above the Sea of Galilee. Once it was over, it transpired that all the Crusader knights in the country had been at Hittin: like a pricked bubble, the kingdom of Jerusalem disintegrated and disappeared. Saladin entered Jerusalem as a hero.

Upon entering Jerusalem, he called on the Jews to return. In 1190, a group of hundreds of Jews from England and France settled in Jerusalem. The alliances and affinities of the day were such that European Jews were of the camp of Muslim Arabs, against Catholic Europe. Saladin's entourage also included the founder of the Husseini family, who settled in Jerusalem and whose descendants were to be implacable enemies of Zionism, led first by Haj Amin al-Husseini and later by another scion of the family, Yasser Arafat.

In 1260, there was an invasion of Tatars, for whom Jerusalem held no significance one way or the other, and they simply razed it. Peace came after 1267, when the Mamelukes, whose base was in Egypt, conquered the land. Their reign was to last more than two hundred years and would include many impressive building projects that stand till this day, characterized by their penchant for using stones of alternating colors. Along with the Mamelukes came Nachmanides.

The Ramban (Rabbi Moshe ben Nachman) was already in his seventies and perhaps the greatest Jewish scholar of his day. He had lived most of his life in Gerona, until he was forced by King James I of Aragon to represent the Jews in the Barcelona Disputation (1263)—where Dominican scholars, headed by Pablo Christiani, a converted Jew, intended to prove the truth of Catholicism and the falsity of Judaism. There are, of course, different versions as to the outcome of the disputation, but the king aborted it before completion. Faced with violence, Nachmanides left Spain and traveled to Judea. Crossing the entire Mediterranean was in those days a very dangerous enterprise; doing so as an old man was even more so. He arrived safely in Jerusalem immediately after the Mameluke conquest and found the city in ruins.

Among the ruins were two lone Jews. Together they repaired one of the Crusader ruins on the hill facing the Temple Mount. It was an elongated structure, sunken beneath street level, with an entrance from the west end and no windows. This became the Ramban Synagogue and the anchor of a budding Jewish community. This part of Jerusalem—the southeastern corner of the Old City—is called the Jewish Quarter. This was not a European-style ghetto to which Jews were confined, but rather the part of town in which they preferred to congregate; non-Jews lived there also, and some Jews lived elsewhere.

The Ottoman Turks arrived in 1517 and stayed precisely four hundred years. Sultan Suleiman rebuilt the walls on the foundations of Hadrian's line, and that is where they still stand. They were an anachronism even as they were being built, since early cannon were already in use and these walls could not have withstood them. Nor were they meant to: they were ornamental, perhaps a sign of respect for a town that had known better days.

The Jewish community of Jerusalem was no longer endangered, but it grew slowly. In 1837, there was a strong earthquake in the Galilee, and the town of Safed was severely damaged. Many of its Jews fled south, and by settling in Jerusalem, they tipped its demographic balance. For the first time since Hadrian, Jews were once again the majority in Jerusalem.

The battles of 1948 left the Jewish Quarter empty of Jews and severely damaged. For the next nineteen years, no effort was made to rebuild it. In July 1967, I was taken to visit the place it once had been. We entered a dank ruin and clambered up what had once been a stairwell: three or four stories, but it seemed more. At the top we found ourselves in an abandoned room with no paint on the walls and no glass in the windows. We were at the edge of the Armenian Quarter, looking down at a field of rubble. It was a searing image, rather like the pictures you have seen of Warsaw after the Germans left.

The first day ordinary civilians were allowed to visit the Western Wall, the lines were literally miles long and stretched back through the Old City, across what had been the border and into West Jerusalem. Within months, archaeologists were encouraged to embark upon ambitious digs in and around the Old City; most ambitious of all, the Jewish Quarter was systematically excavated and reconstructed. One of the earliest buildings to be renovated was a ruined Crusader structure. It was an elongated building, sunken beneath street level, with an entrance from the west end and no windows. (Windows have since been added on one side, opening onto a submerged courtyard.) You can go there any day of the year at the hours of prayer, for it is once again what it was: the Ramban Synagogue.

For three thousand years, Jews have tried to live in Jerusalem and generally succeeded. But its central importance was in the staying power it gave to the Jews who were elsewhere. They have been mentioning Jerusalem three times a day for the past 1,900 years, or 640,000 days. During the centuries when the Jews were unwanted aliens on the margins of Gentile society, they comforted themselves that someday they would return to Jerusalem. Culturally separate from their environment, they shared this daily dream with all other Jews, creating a cultural community that was stronger than time or geography. The unparalleled phenomenon of a people living without a homeland for almost two thousand years without disappearing happened because they never forgot for a moment that they did have a homeland, and the homeland had a capital, and they were determined to persevere no matter what until they returned to the normal mode of national existence. Jews face Jerusalem when they pray, which means that wherever they are they must orient themselves: if they are to the west of Jerusalem, they must identify the east. Even today, if you're ever on an airliner with Orthodox Jews, you can observe, as they prepare for the daily service, how they peer out the window, consult the map of the route, and carefully determine the correct direction. Jerusalem is not an idea, it's a very concrete place. Muslims, of course, can easily empathize with all this, since they do the same—toward Mecca, not Jerusalem.

Zionism, being the creation of pragmatic atheists, was not at first particularly interested in Jerusalem. It was too urban, but especially, it was too burdened by religion and messianic aspirations, and the early Zionists told themselves that these were anachronisms. Yet they would not be able to ignore Jerusalem or build their project only outside its walls. It was no coincidence that the first mass murder committed in the conflict took place in Jerusalem in 1920; nor was it a fluke that the riots of 1929 were about the Temple Mount. Had the Arabs not provoked the war of 1967, Israel would never have gone to war to take the Old City. But they did provoke the war, and their loss of Jerusalem was the price of that fateful decision.

The first action the Israelis took in Jerusalem was to raze the small Arab neighborhood at the foot of the Western Wall, so as to enable hundreds of thousands of Jews to visit the sole remnant of the Temple complex. The second thing they did was to return civilian control of the Temple Mount itself to the Muslim *waqf* (religious endowment). This was a sign of respect that no one in the world could have forced upon them, nor had anyone called for it; in retrospect, it was probably misguided. Certainly no credit was given for it, as if it were the most natural thing in the world for a nation that has just won a defensive war to hand over the holiest place in the world to the enemies who have just tried to destroy it.

Outside the walls, Israel set about building Jewish neighborhoods on the empty hills around Arab East Jerusalem. Here and there Arab houses stood on these hills, and they stand there still as Arab enclaves in Jewish neighborhoods. By Israeli reckoning, these neighborhoods are not settlements at all, since no one else had any superior legal claim to the city. Within a decade there would be a Jewish majority even in the eastern half of the city, and there still is—so calling it "Arab East Jerusalem" is a tendentious political statement, not a description of any legal or demographic reality, although there are, of course, Arab neighborhoods.

There now begins the long history of lies and misrepresentations regarding the Israeli occupation. The Six-Day War was not premediated by the Israelis, and its outcome was even less so. No one reasonable disputes this. Once it had happened, it was not immediately clear what the implications would be, although the warning of maverick philosopher Yeshayahu Leibowitz that Israel would one day rue her control over the Palestinians has proven prescient. But even he had no practical suggestion to make. In 1967, there were no Arabs stumbling over their feet in a mad rush to make peace with Israel in return for the territories.

While Israel had no intention of relinquishing her newly acquired control of Jerusalem, all the other areas were initially open for discussion, if only a partner for discussion could found. Indeed, on June 19, 1967, a mere week after the war, the government decided that the territories were negotiable in return for peace. So much for Israel's imperialist ambitions or her lust for Arab land. The American government was informed of the decision, but it was not made public at the time, because no sane negotiator embarks upon negotiations by showing all his cards.

The Arab states responded at a summit in September in Khartoum by agreeing unanimously on three nos: no to recognition, no to negotiations, no to peace. In November, the United Nations Security Council adopted Resolution 242, which called for a just and lasting peace based on

> withdrawal of Israeli armed forces from territories occupied in the recent conflict; termination of all claims or states of belligerency and respect for and acknowledgement of the sovereignty, territorial integrity and political independence of every State in the area and their right to live in peace within secure and recognized boundaries free from threats or acts of force.

The territorial issue was left vague, so that the Arabs could say that the intention was a withdrawal from all of the territories, while Israel could say that a partial withdrawal would suffice. Palestine was not mentioned, since in 1967 the Palestinians were still a minor factor in the Arab-Israeli conflict. Israel accepted the resolution and accepts it still: she will pay for peace with territories taken in 1967. The innumerable strident demands that Israel respect the resolution, or that the United States force her to do so, are beside the point, since the resolution calls also for recognition of Israel's sovereignty, territorial integrity, and political independence. There must be two sides accepting the resolution, and the Arab side must accept Israel's right to exist.

The PLO rejected the entire resolution, as its official goal was the destruction of Israel. At the beginning of July 1968, the Palestinian National Council adopted a constitution, known as the Palestinian Charter. This is a bloodcurdling document, clearly stating the Palestinian rejection of Israel's existence and their choice of means to achieve this: violence, and only violence.

Article 2: Palestine, with the boundaries it had during the British Mandate, is an indivisible territorial unit.

Article 9: Armed struggle is the only way to liberate Palestine. Thus it is the overall strategy, not merely a tactical phase. . . .

Article 10: Commando action constitutes the nucleus of the Palestinian popular liberation war. This requires its escalation, comprehensiveness, and the mobilization of all the Palestinian popular and educational efforts and their organization and involvement in the armed Palestinian revolution. . . .

Article 15: The liberation of Palestine, from an Arab viewpoint, is a national (qawmi) duty, and it attempts to repel the Zionist and imperialist aggression against the Arab homeland, and aims at the elimination of Zionism in Palestine. . . .

Article 19: The partition of Palestine in 1947 and the establishment of the state of Israel are entirely illegal, regardless of the passage of time, because they were contrary to the will of the Palestinian people and to their natural right in their homeland, and inconsistent with the principles embodied in the Charter of the United Nations, particularly the right to self-determination.

Article 21: The Arab Palestinian people, expressing themselves by the armed Palestinian revolution, reject all solutions which are substitutes for the total liberation of Palestine. . . .

The underlying structure of the conflict did not begin to change before the early 1970s. In the meantime, in spite of Israel's overwhelming victory, and consistent with the Arab public decisions in its aftermath, the violence against Israel continued. The Lebanese continued not to participate; the Syrians, having lost the Golan Heights, were not in a position to easily attack Israeli civilians, although they occasionally hit military targets on the Golan. But at this stage, their role in the conflict was comparatively minor. The Jordanians often shelled the town of Beit Shean and its outlying agricultural settlements; more significant, Jordan was becoming the main base of the military units of the PLO.

The PLO was founded in 1964 and began to attack Israeli targets in 1965. Its leader, Yasser Arafat, escaped from Israeli security forces in the West Bank and moved to Jordan, where he began a long career of successfully promoting the Palestinian cause while violently destabilizing whatever country he lived in.

From 1968 onward, the PLO engaged in three types of activity: attacks on Israeli targets, military and civilian, along the border; infiltration into the West Bank in order to activate terrorist cells; and—a novelty at the time—exporting the conflict to Europe, initially by attacking airliners. Bombs went off in places like the central bus station in Tel Aviv, the central open-air market in Jerusalem, or the cafeteria on the campus of Hebrew University. The terrorists who planted a land mine north of Eilat that exploded under a school bus, killing three and wounding sixteen, may have wanted to kill Israelis, but not specifically children; when a school bus was ambushed in May 1970 near Avivim on the Lebanese border, killing twelve and wounding twenty-four, the attackers knew precisely what they were doing.

Most significant in terms of its cost, both human and material, was the war of attrition officially launched by the Egyptians in early 1969, although it had been under way for many months. This was mainly a static war between the two armies on either side of the closed Suez Canal. Its main tool was artillery, along with occasional commando raids, and as time went on, it was increasingly a war of air forces in which the traditional Israeli tactical advantages of speed and mobility were effectively canceled out.

None of these parallel campaigns of 1968–1970 were instigated by the Israelis, nor is it clear what Israel could have done to prevent them, short of the strategy adopted. This was to take the war to its initiators in the hope that attrition might prove a two-edged sword, while making thousands of tiny, incremental improvements in the campaign against terror: putting a fence around the university, paving agricultural roads in border areas, positioning more policemen in the markets, training the public to be observant and forever on their guard.

Almost nine hundred Israelis died in this two-year period, but by

August 1970, following an escalating bombing campaign deep in Egyptian territory, the Egyptians had had enough and were willing to accept a cease-fire. No sooner had they done so than Jordan's King Hussein determined to put an end to the activity of the PLO in and from his territory.

The price of military activity against Israel across the river Jordan was that civilian life on the eastern bank had also been totally disrupted; moreover, by 1970, there were growing indications that the military presence of the PLO was threatening the stability of the Hashemite crown. Jordan was awash with PLO military units that answered only to Arafat, and although their ultimate enemy was Israel, there were multiplying clashes with Jordanian forces. The events of September 1970 ended the Jordanian tolerance of the PLO.

Hussein dealt with the PLO with extreme harshness, killing thousands in two weeks in what was to become known as Black September. Hundreds of PLO fighters fled . . . to Israel, crossing the Jordan and surrendering themselves in the reasonable expectation that their fate at the hands of the alleged archenemy would be better than at the hands of the avowed Arab brothers. The Syrians decided to take advantage of the turmoil to impose their own hegemony, and columns of Syrian armor invaded Jordan from the north; the United States thereupon asked Israel to mobilize in order to convince the Syrians to desist. The sight of massing Israeli forces focused the Syrian minds, and they pulled back, leaving Hussein with an unexpected debt to Israel. A few days later, Gamal Nasser died of a sudden heart attack, to be replaced as president by Anwar al-Sadat.

In the Gaza Strip, local terrorist cells remained highly active for another few months, although most of their victims were dozens of Palestinians murdered for alleged cooperation with Israel or simply for working there. At the beginning of January 1971, two Israeli children were murdered, and the CO of the southern command, General Ariel Sharon, embarked on a fiercely efficient large-scale crackdown. About one hundred Palestinians were killed in ten months and hundreds of others arrested. Gaza was to remain virtually free of violence for more than ten years.

The upshot seemed to be that perseverance and a willingness to sustain casualties while adapting to a new form of warfare would eventually bring the hoped-for respite. Yet this sentiment hardened Israeli resolve perhaps more than was healthy. The diplomatic pretext that enabled the Egyptians to cease their war of attrition had been the plan presented by William

Rogers, the American secretary of state, which called for the evacuation by the Israelis of territories held since 1967 in return for recognition and peace. Following the upheavals of fall 1970, the United Nations sent an envoy, Dr. Gunnar Jarring, to negotiate between Egypt and Israel. After months of shuttle diplomacy, Jarring felt that the Egyptians might be ready to reach an agreement, while the Israelis were too hesitant to take advantage of the moment. The archives are not yet open, so this cannot be substantiated, but the events of the rest of the decade were to pose a brutal question: Could the Arab pattern of reflexive rejection of Israel have been broken at this point, and did the Israelis therefore fail to take advantage of a historic opportunity for change?

Rational decisions are influenced by a combination of past experience and one's view of the situation at hand. The Israelis at the end of the 1960s had never enjoyed universal acceptance of either their borders or their capital, they had repeatedly been attacked by neighbors who made a fetish of refusing to recognize their right to exist, and the war was even now continuing on most fronts. Perhaps they can therefore be excused for assuming that what had worked so far might still be a good idea. And what had worked quite well since the inception of Zionism was the definition of territorial interests through settlement.

So, rightly or wrongly, Israel began building settlements in the newly occupied territories. In order to understand this controversial policy, it is important to note that these were not the settlements of the 1980s and 1990s, set up by right-wing governments as the centerpiece of their partisan agenda. They were mostly agricultural, they were set up by center-left Labor-dominated governments, very few of the settlers were religious, and they were built in five strategic areas: between Gaza and Sinai, on the southeast of Sinai across from the Strait of Tiran, on the Golan, in the Jordan valley between the West Bank and the East Bank, and in Jerusalem. They were not set up in the broad expanses of Sinai or along the Suez Canal, signifying the Israeli recognition that even though the war was still going on, someday it would be over and most of Sinai would be open to negotiations. Nor, for the same reason, were they set up in the heavily populated areas of the West Bank and Gaza. Yet intentions count for little in the long run, and the changing demographics led to an imperceptible hardening of Israel's mood and a growing reluctance to use the negotiating chips acquired in 1967. A constituency was slowly growing that had an interest in not testing to see whether the Arabs were changing their minds about Israel.

There were also two fateful exceptions to the pattern of settlement. One was the Etzion Block, south of Bethlehem, where four Jewish settlements had been destroyed in 1948, many of the men gunned down after surrendering. In 1968, a group of their children moved back. It is hard to think of anything more just than orphaned sons rebuilding the villages in which their fathers had been killed. The second exception was Hebron, where a group of settlers forced the government to allow them to settle in 1968.

If Zionism's goal was to create a refuge from persecution, there was no need for Hebron to be in it. Yet Zionism had always been more than merely a search for a safe haven; indeed, its tremendous power stemmed precisely from the combination of modern impulses in the ancient homeland—and what could be more ancient than Hebron? Then again, Zionism had seen itself as a constructive movement building something for the Jews, not taking something from the Arabs, and certainly not dominating them against their will. On the other hand, Jews had been expelled from Hebron—more precisely, massacred—and the survivors expelled. Faced with this conundrum, the government acquiesced in the creation of Kiryat Arba, a Jewish town on a hill above Hebron.

It was not as if there were a Palestinian partner with whom one could discuss this, since the Palestinian attitude was moving from violent rejection to total intransigence.

August 1970 ended the war of attrition between Israel and Egypt, and September saw the end of Jordan as a significant military base for the PLO. For all its drama, however, it did very little toward resolving the conflict with the Palestinians. Having been thrown out of Jordan, the PLO went to Lebanon, where it was eventually to reappear as a more lethal enemy than ever before. In the meantime, lacking a convenient border across which to attack Israel, it attacked where it was easy to do, in Europe. Initially, the easiest way was to hijack airplanes. An El Al airplane was hijacked from Rome in July 1968. It was flown to Algeria, and the crew and Israeli passengers were held for thirty-nine days before being liberated in return for some Palestinian terrorists. The Israelis learned from the experience, and no Israeli airliner has ever been hijacked since.

If Israeli planes were hard to hijack, they could still be attacked from outside, where the locals and not the Israelis were in charge of security. In

February 1969, Palestinian terrorists attacked an El Al liner on the runway at Zurich Airport. The pilot was killed. An Israeli security man, Mordechai Rachamim, jumped off the plane and attacked the attackers, killing one. A similar incident took place in Munich a year later; this time, Arye Katzenstein, a passenger, threw himself on a grenade and was killed instantly but saved the lives of many of his fellow passengers. The Europeans took note of the pattern and began to escort every El Al liner across the tarmac with armored personnel carriers, and the attacks ceased.

Also in February 1970, Palestinian terrorists blew up a Swissair plane flying from Zurich to Tel Aviv; all of the forty-seven passengers and crew were killed. The Hashemite campaign against the PLO was triggered by the hijacking by Palestinians of three Western airliners (TWA, Swissair, and Pan Am) en route to Israel. Once the international arena became the main area of activity open to the Palestinians, however, they sharply escalated their activities. The chosen instrument was a new organization set up so as to give the PLO leadership deniability: Black September.

Although its name indicated anger at the Jordanians, and its first public act was the assassination of Wasfi Tal, the Jordanian prime minister, Black September's primary goal was to carry out acts of terror against Israeli and Jewish targets abroad—the more grandiose the better. The logic was the perverse but realistic assumption that killing Jews before the international public eye would promote the Palestinian cause; presumably the public would tell itself that the predicament of the perpetrators must be very deep if they were willing to go to such lengths. The logic was to bear itself out magnificently.

Between 1971 and 1973, Black September carried out dozens of terrorist attacks—sixty of them in 1973 alone. Outstanding among them was the kidnapping of a Sabena airliner to Lod Airport in May 1972: in this case, Israeli commandos liberated the passengers, although one of them died in the cross fire. (The commander of that mission was Ehud Barak, and one of his men was Benjamin Netanyahu.) Two weeks later, three Japanese Red Army terrorists who had been "loaned" to Black September reached Lod on an Air France airliner with suitcases full of weapons; once in the crowded terminal, they opened fire in all directions, killing twenty-seven and wounding seventy-one.

The most spectacular terror act of all, prior to September 11, 2001, was staged in front of the world's largest concentration of cameras: at the

Olympic Games in Munich in September 1972. Two of the Israeli team members were murdered as the terrorists broke into their dormitory; nine others were held hostage and died in a bungled German rescue attempt late that night. Three of the terrorists were captured alive, but less than two months later they were free men, after their colleagues hijacked a Lufthansa airliner. Visitors at the museum of the Olympic Games in Lillehammer, Norway, are informed that after the attack, the games resumed: "even the Israelis wanted it so." In reality, Israelis and Palestinians both took notice that the world hurried back to its games as soon as the shooting was over.

Israel's response to Black September included some sophisticated attacks of her own, with the essential and time-honored distinction that whereas the Palestinians were aiming almost exclusively at civilians, the Israelis took pains not to hit civilians and generally succeeded. The most spectacular of these responses was in April 1973, when Israeli commandos infiltrated Beirut and killed three key PLO men in their apartments. Throughout 1973, the Israeli pressure against the Black September leadership mounted, causing them to spend ever more time on survival and ever less time on terror. In the fall of that year, the organization disappeared. Almost none of the organizers of the attack on the Olympic team survived into the 1980s. Yet what could be construed as a military success in the war against terror was soon to prove a political disaster in the fight for world opinion. In the aftermath of the Yom Kippur War and the Arab oil embargo, the Israelis were to learn that much of the blame was to be laid at their doorstep for the crime of denying justice to the Palestinians.

The beginning of the Yom Kippur War is, for Israelis, one of those events that one never forgets. As with the assassinations of John F. Kennedy or Itzhak Rabin, everyone who was there at the time can recall the precise details of how they heard, where they were, and what they did. It was truly a before/after event. Before, Israeli society had been secure, even hubristic, in its feeling of invincibility. Surrounded by a world of hatred, Israel perceived the ancient patterns of persecution to have been smashed, the forces of destruction awed by defeat. Individual Jews were still being attacked and murdered, as before, but even in the war against terror, Israel was scoring as many blows as she was receiving, and what more could a Jew expect? After, the hubris was gone, the awareness of national mortality was back, the feeling of invincibility was pulverized. Worst of all, confidence in the leadership had evaporated. Adolescence was over.

Egyptian and Syrian forces attacked on October 6, 1973. The Israelis, secure in their false assumption that no Arab army would dare to attack, failed to see what was coming and began to mobilize only in the last few hours before the attack. For a few precarious, casualty-laden days, the outcome was not clear. The determination of the attackers was unexpected, their equipment was better than foreseen, and the chaos on the Israeli side was indisputable. Two retired generals—previous chief of staff Haim Bar-Lev and Ariel Sharon—were hurriedly reenlisted, an unprecedented measure not calibrated to enforce confidence in the abilities of the system. On both the Golan and in the Sinai, the attackers had breached Israeli lines, and the fighting was taking place on what had been Israeli-held territory. In an unguarded moment of tension, Defense Minister Moshe Dayan mumbled something about the possible destruction of "the Third Temple."

By the second week, both sides were being sustained by massive airlifts of munitions from their respective superpowers. Eventually the military pendulum swung back in Israel's favor, and strictly militarily, the outcome was impressive. The Syrians were thrown back from the Golan and were soon defending the approaches to Damascus; the Egyptians managed to hold on to their bridgeheads east of the Suez Canal, but following an audacious counterattack engineered by Sharon, they were in acute danger of being encircled and cut off by Israeli forces west of the canal. Yet these military aspects were only a part of the picture. Rumors filtered back from the front about mismanaged and costly battles, the two most famous being at the "Chinese Ranch" in the Sinai and Mt. Hermon at the northern peak of the Golan. The appearance of Israeli invincibility had been smashed, and the Arabs could claim to have fought Israel to a draw.

Perhaps more than any other, this war could be depicted in morally neutral terms. For Israel, it was a just war in that once the aggression began, there was no option but to fight back; the Arabs could claim that they were trying to retake territory that was legally theirs; and for Egypt, a case could be made that war was necessary since previous diplomatic efforts had led nowhere. Most of the fighting had taken place in areas empty of civilians, so that none of the combatants engaged in war crimes, except perhaps the Syrians who tortured the POWs they caught.

In lieu of open archives, historians cannot yet say if Egypt had truly been ripe for peace prior to the 1973 war, only to be rebuffed by Israel. The semivictory of 1973 made their position clearer. Israeli invincibility had been destroyed, opening the way for a peace between equals. On the Israeli side, the shock of the Yom Kippur War was to have social and political implications that would reverberate at least until the 1990s. Regarding the conflict with the Arabs, an ominous question now loomed: Could all this have been avoided? Can the next one be avoided? Beneath the surface, there were the beginnings of two widely diverging understandings of the situation: those who saw no change in the implacable Arab rejection of Israel's right to exist and those who were willing to postulate that there was such a change. Since the government of Golda Meir had just catastrophically misread the Arabs' military intentions, a growing number of Israelis began to wonder if it was also misreading their strategic intentions.

If 1973 gave both Israel and Egypt an impetus to lay aside their swords, 1974–1975 did the opposite for Israel and the Palestinians. First there was the Arab oil embargo, which sent the Europeans scurrying to appeasement at Israel's expense, agreeing that Israel's intransigence was the root of the conflict. It began to dawn on Israelis the extent to which the Palestinian terror had succeeded. Then Henry Kissinger launched his shuttle diplomacy between Cairo, Damascus, and Jerusalem, forcing the combatants to disengage their forces by moving Israeli troops back and away from the front lines of October—hardly a sign of Israeli aggression; perhaps even a sign that they might be willing to pay for peace with land. Rather than test this with a peace initiative of their own, the Palestinians redoubled their efforts to murder Israeli civilians, mainly from Lebanon, where they had in the meantime rebuilt much of what had been destroyed in Jordan. There were close to one hundred dead in attacks on Kiryat Shemona, Nahariya, Beit Shean, Tel Aviv, and Jerusalem, almost all of them civilians.

Most traumatic for Israel was the attack on the town of Maalot, a few miles south of the Lebanese border, on May 15—the day Palestinians commemorate their Catastrophe of 1948. A squad of terrorists entered a private apartment in the predawn hours and murdered a husband and wife and their four-year-old son. The five-year-old daughter was the last to be shot, but she miraculously survived and never forgot the smile on the terrorist's face as he shot her. Then the terrorists turned to a local school, in which a large group of children were sleeping as part of a three-day outing. Some of them managed to escape, but dozens were held hostage. Later in the day, the army tried to liberate them, but this time the terrorists managed to kill twenty-four of their hostages before being killed. A famous photo showed a soldier evacuating one of the wounded girls: his sister.

The attack caused bitter soul-searching. How to explain that some of the teachers had been among those who managed to escape as the terrorists launched their attack? Had the decision to take out the terrorists been wise? Many terrorist squads were being caught before reaching their designated targets, but how had this one penetrated so far into Israel?

Undoubtedly encouraged by their bloody successes, the Palestinian National Council convened in Cairo on June 9 and adopted a new political program, commonly referred to as "the Phased Plan." Wary, perhaps, of the possibility that Egypt might soon be negotiating with Israel, the Palestinian leadership reaffirmed its goal to completely replace Israel and its rejection of Resolution 242 ("The Council therefore refuses to have anything to do with this resolution at any level, Arab or international, including the Geneva Conference"). Yet acknowledging the changing international circumstances ("in the light of a study of the new political circumstances that have come into existence in the period between the Council's last and present sessions"), the council allowed for alternative tactics to be used, if necessary, with the understanding that "any step taken toward liberation is a step toward the realization of the Liberation Organization's strategy of establishing the democratic Palestinian state specified in the resolutions of previous Palestinian National Councils." In order to determine the correct approach at any given time, "the leadership of the revolution will determine the tactics which will serve and make possible the realization of these objectives." Having said that, Palestinian terrorists continued in their attempts to murder Israeli citizens; the only reason there were fewer casualties was that Israel beefed up her defensive measures along the Lebanese border, and most of the terrorists who attempted to cross were killed.

The events of the mid-1970s called forth two opposing views in Israel as to the essence of the situation. A growing group on the Left felt that the Arab world was beginning to accept Israel's existence and that this trend must be encouraged by signs of willingness to purchase peace with the territories held since 1967. These were the people who would coalesce into the Peace Now movement in 1978. A growing group on the Right inferred from the Palestinians' categorical and obstinate refusal to accept Israel that the historic task for the Jews was to incorporate into their state the entire biblical homeland. These were the people who burst upon the scene in the dark summer of 1974 under the title Gush Emunim.

The name means "Block of the Loyal" (or "Group of the Loyal"), and they were a new breed of Jews. Unlike most previous Zionists, they were Orthodox; unlike most Orthodox, they were deeply involved in Zionism. Their spiritual mentor was Rabbi Avraham HaCohen Kook, a maverick scholar who had been the chief rabbi in the 1930s. Breaking with the mainstream orthodoxy of his time, he found tremendous religious significance in the atheist pioneers. In a complicated combination of mysticism and pragmatism, he saw them as the harbingers of the redemption; the Jews who felt themselves farthest from God were finally undertaking *tikkun olam,* a correcting of the world. After his death, this school of thought was further developed by his son, Rabbi Zvi Yehuda Kook. Many of Zvi Yehuda's disciples were young Orthodox men who were fully part of the modern world, who had been reared in a post-Holocaust world where Israel was a reality, not an aspiration, and who had no feelings of inferiority toward the secular world or toward the Orthodox. They had been combat soldiers in 1967 and in 1973 and fervently felt that God was demonstrating His will. The period 1948 through 1967 had been stages of the redemption, but 1973 had been the result of a faltering, and now the Jews must do what was expected of them and continue moving forward. This meant settling the biblical heart of the land, which the Zionists had heretofore been skirting because it was where most of the Palestinians lived: the highlands of the West Bank.

In order to achieve this, the government had to be forced to do what it didn't intend and allow Jews to settle in areas densely inhabited by Palestinians. From 1974 onward, members of the Gush put growing pressure on the government: demonstrating, setting up unauthorized settlements, circumventing the army, and then negotiating their terms of surrender. They were uncannily adept at making the most out of the quarter measures the government was willing to concede so as to make the problem disappear, understanding that incremental successes were far better than inaction. It was slow going, but they were not to be put off.

In May 1977, Menachem Begin's Likud Party won the elections. Begin was the first Israeli leader not to come from the political Left. As a young man in interwar Poland, he had been a follower of Zeev Jabotinsky, leader of the right-wing Revisionist Party; Begin was the head of its Betar youth movement. Shortly after the Nazi invasion, he escaped to the Soviet Union and eventually made his way to mandatory Palestine in 1942. In Palestine he quickly took over the IZL and commanded it until 1948; Ben-Gurion's bloody resolve to subordinate the IZL at the *Altalena* incident was directed against Begin. Begin was a memeber of the Knesset from its founding, but as long as Ben-Gurion had any say in the matter, he was consigned to the outer fringes of the opposition, never to be allowed into a coalition. While his ideology was firmly nationalist, his education and bearing were far more European and metropolitan than the gruff farmer-revolutionaries of the labor camp. He was by far the best orator Israel ever had, though his opponents called his talent demagogy. His election signified a coming of age of the Israeli electorate, no longer willing to elect Labor simply because Ben-Gurion had created the state, or else it signified a growing chauvinism, based on Israel's ability to withstand decades of conflict without breaking. It depends on whom you ask.

Begin immediately set about doing what both new trends in Israeli society—the doves and the hawks—had hoped for. He made peace with Egypt, paying the full price, and he encouraged a vast expansion of the ideological settlements. Most likely, the two were connected in his mind.

Within weeks of assuming power, he and Sadat were discussing a possible visit to Israel by the Egyptian president, and in November he came. Sadat's gesture was an outstanding act of political bravery and farsighted statesmanship. It was also the first indication that there existed in Israel a potential for an alternative behavior that, when activated, would override everything else. Put simply, Israelis were hardened fighters, committed to living by their sword, but they were unable to withstand an assault of goodwill.

Sadat's breathtaking visit to Israel changed the landscape overnight. He said nothing that had not been said previously—every inch of the Sinai must be returned to Egyptian sovereignty, all of the Israeli settlements there must be dismantled, the Palestinian problem must be settled by the creation of an independent Palestine alongside Israel, and so on—but the context was dramatically changed. He left no doubt that he accepted Israel and respected her sovereignty, since he was speaking from the podium of the Knesset. He declared unequivocally, in a statement that was to be broadcast thousands of times over the coming months and years, so that every minute inflection of his voice was to be etched on the minds of his Israeli audience—"No more war! No more bloodshed!"—and backed up the seriousness of his intention by remaining unmoved as the regimes of the entire Arab world severed relations with him and his country.

It took more than a year of tough negotiations, but the upshot was a foregone conclusion: All of the Egyptians' demands were accepted, and peace was signed. Sadat had hoped that his gesture would carry the other frontline Arab regimes in its wake, thus creating a comprehensive peace in the Middle East, but this did not happen. Without such actions from his fellow Arabs, Israel was not confronted with the need to make concessions on other fronts. Yet future events were to indicate that the pattern would repeat itself when required: a majority of Israelis would respond to clear and unequivocal peace gestures by rising to the challenge and accepting the terms, including the dismantling of settlements.

The terms of the Egyptian-Israeli peace treaty stipulated a gradual withdrawal from the Sinai, in such a way that the final stage, which included the dismantling of the settlements west of Gaza and near the Tiran Strait, would take place only after the next elections. When the time came, only one party (Techiya—"Renewal") ran on a platform opposing the peace treaty, and it garnered a mere 3 percent of the votes.

There is actually nothing surprising about this. David Ben-Gurion once famously said that Jews are paranoids who are being persecuted. The Arabs had attempted to commit genocide in 1948 and have been killing Jewish civilians as a form of politics since World War I, declaring repeatedly that Jewish sovereignty in the Middle East is unacceptable. Many Israelis saw—and see—no need to gamble on the assumption that perhaps they have changed their minds, until presented with compelling evidence. Such evidence, however, will be accepted and acted upon. Quite reasonable, if you think about it, even if it puts the onus for the longevity of the conflict on the Arabs.

What would Begin have done if the Palestinians had followed in Sadat's footsteps and signified their wish for a mutually negotiated settlement? It's an irrelevant question, as the thought never crossed the minds of their leaders and spokesmen. Faced with the ongoing violent rejection of Israel's right to exist, Begin was able to indulge his heart's desire and give free rein to the settlers of Gush Emunim. They, for their part, saw themselves as the vanguard of Zionism.

First, the drive. Gush Emunim intended to fuse an ideology—in their case, a religious one—with a mode of operation, in order to create what the Zionists had made possible but had not completed: a modern Judaism on its ancient homeland. They criticized secular Israeli society for its willingness to be merely a Middle Eastern branch of Western society, disconnected from Jewish tradition; they criticized the traditional Orthodox society for its passivity in the face of modernity, for its attempts to ward off change by insulation.

Second, the social method. Gush Emunim copied the centrality of settlements from the success of early Zionism. Then as now, a majority of the Jews had not been settlers, but the leading elite had. Leaving the confusion of the towns for the clarity of the villages, the early settlers had distilled their thoughts and actions; this had allowed them to concentrate on what was most important and thus pull everyone else after them. The leaders of Gush Emunim repeated endlessly that they were the modern pioneers, in a calculated attempt to expropriate the heroic and mythological baggage that came with the term.

Third, the geographic method. As the pioneers had settled large consecutive tracts of useless swampland, so Gush Emunim took over the barren hilltops in a calculated attempt to place their outposts so that the entire territory would be encompassed.

Fourth, the legal method. Unlike the 1920s, when each *dunam* had to be acquired from its previous owner, the settlers of Gush Emunim had potential access to the roughly one-third of the territory that is owned not by private individuals, but by the government. There was a legal nicety here, whereby there was no internationally acknowledged government. After the Six-Day War, no one recognized the Israeli occupation, but the government claimed that until decided otherwise, the Israelis were the government, just as previously it had been the Egyptians or Jordanians. If their actions had not been illegal, how could the Israeli ones be?

Contrary to what your newspaper may tell you, the settlements are built not on the ancestral fields or orchards of the Palestinians, but on rocky and windy hilltops that support no one. This was not always the case, and in the early stages, Gush Emunim indeed tried to use the power of the government to take over private land; the Israeli Supreme Court put a stop to this in 1979. One entire settlement was even dismantled because it sat on private Arab land. In fairness, however, it must be said that the roads to the settlements often do require confiscation of private land.

Fifth, being the toughest of the tough. This was to prove harder for the settlers of Gush Emunim than for the early pioneers. There was no malaria to die from. Setting up a new settlement entailed spending a year or three in a tiny prefab living unit, but invariably this was replaced by large, spacious homes with red-shingled roofs, private gardens, and a room for each child even when there were six of them, as there often were. Ironically, it was the Palestinians who were to present the settlers with the means to prove that they were the direct spiritual descendants of the pioneers of yore, by making life extremely dangerous. The more violence was directed against the settlers, the more plausibly they could cast themselves as stoic visionaries determined to pay any price to attain their goal. As they never tire of saying, they are doing this for the rest of us by absorbing the violent ire of the Palestinians, and for all of our descendants by assuring the Jewish possession of the ancestral homeland. These declarations always have the preaching tone proper for the leaders of a faltering flock.

And the names of the settlements, what did they tell? Shiloh is the early site of the tabernacle in Joshua's day. Beit El is where Jacob the Patriarch spent the night fleeing from the wrath of Esau and where he dreamt of the ladder to heaven. Elazar is named after a Hasmonean general of that name, who died in battle on the same spot when he stabbed an elephant in its soft underbelly and was buried by it almost 2,200 years ago. And Hebron has always been Hebron for the Jews, no matter what anybody else called it.

The sixth point of resemblance to the early pioneers—hard as it will be to believe—is the benign patronizing of the local Arabs. The settlers of Gush Emunim know that the success of their policy clashes with the national aspirations of the Palestinians, since it leaves no territory the Palestinians can call their own. They accept this but point to the hundreds of national groups the world over that will never have their own nation-states, some of whom are considerably larger than the Palestinians. Their position is clear: The historic claim of the Jews to the single sliver of land that was their ancestral home is greater than that of the Palestinians, who are part of the Arab world and its dozens of national states, but who never had their own national state.

Having said this, we should add that the settlers are not antagonistic to the Palestinians as individuals. Initially, they were eager to be good neighbors. Once the issue of privately owned land had been decided in the Palestinians' favor, the settlers abided by it. If it were up to the settlers, their Palestinian neighbors would enjoy rising prosperity and all the trappings of modernity and technology. There is nothing racist about their position—nor is there any hatred. The settlers tend to be highly educated, upper-middle-class people—civilized people, and as such they behaved.

I know that sentence will not pass most CNN-sated readers unchallenged. Even some of my friends from the Israeli Left will cringe upon reading it and will launch into a diatribe about the entire settlers project being a violent rape of Palestinian rights. Which is a debatable point, but not a relevant one, as the statement refers not to the settlers' politics, but to their actual behavior when faced with violence—and faced with it they are.

The settlers have been under physical attack for decades. During the *intifada* of the late 1980s, they fitted their cars with reinforced windows as protection against rocks and fire bombs. These days the reinforced windows are useless, as the Palestinians are using guns. They travel as little as possible, at times only in convoys. The roads they use every day have become death traps. All of them can tell of being attacked; many have seen friends or acquaintances gunned down. They aren't shooting back, however, even though their men are armed and well trained.

There is a tiny minority among them that engages in reprehensible acts, and they deserve to be mentioned. In a few identifiable corners of the West Bank, there are concentrations of brutal chauvinists of the worst kind. One is at the settlement of Tapuach, south of Nablus, which contains some violent thugs who are a blemish on the face of Israel; others can be found in the small Jewish section of Hebron. In the early 1980s, an organization from the very heart of the settler community started revenging Palestinian violence with murders of their own. The Israeli authorities managed to arrest them on the eve of blowing up a bus; three innocent students had already been murdered, and a number of prominent Palestinians had been wounded.

Baruch Goldstein came from Kiryat Arba, on the hill above Hebron. Early in the morning of the Jewish holiday of Purim in 1994, he armed himself to the teeth, entered the mosque inside the Herodian structure at the center of town, and commenced shooting the men as they prayed. He shot them in their backs. Twenty-nine of them died before the others managed to overpower and kill him—an act of self-defense, surely. The background to his act is irrelevant, and there are no neutralizing words that can be used to soften what he had done: it was the worst cold-blooded mass murder by an individual in Israel's history, before or since.

The two-hundred-thousand-plus settlers condemn the violence of these men as much as the rest of us. They are not about to descend to a Balkan-style interethnic conflict. No matter what you have been told, their moral level is as high as that of any of their detractors, if not higher. Unlike their critics, moreover, they have been tested by fire. Faced with the human urge to retaliate against murderous violence that threatens their homes and children, they have stuck to their values.

All of which goes to explain the ostensible success of the settlers. While they have always been a minority in Israel, they played on powerful motifs that could not easily be shrugged off without casting a shadow on much of what Zionism had achieved. Moreover, for quite a number of years their operations could not in any real way be considered a major source of provocation, since the Palestinians were demanding the destruction of Tel Aviv and Kiryat Arba in equal measure. Governments of the Right that were asked to choose between Jewish claims to Shiloh and Palestinian ones to Haifa had no compunction in making their choice; governments of the Left told themselves that the whole settler project would be disbanded whenever the Palestinians decided to emulate Sadat, and until then, why clash with the basically positive settlers in the name of justice for the murderous Palestinians? The far Left, often not in power and thus free to say whatever it wanted without having to take responsibility for the results, tried valiantly to explain that this was insane, but again, they were in no way assisted in their efforts by the Palestinians they claimed to represent.

The supreme irony is that the settlers, of all people, may have contributed more than anyone else to the eventual change in the Palestinian position. Given the encroaching Israeli takeover of the West Bank, they were faced in the 1980s with a harsher choice than ever: no longer a choice between part of Palestine now or all of it after the destruction of Zionism, but the opposite. Part of Palestine now or none of it ever. And while the Palestinians pondered that, the settlers were forging an ever growing constituency inside Israel that was eager to reach out to the Palestinians, if only to save the soul of Israel herself.

Zionism has always seen itself as a constructive, positive, and hopeful movement. It has been and remains willing to invest considerable efforts in achieving its goals and has been undaunted by seemingly insurmountable obstructions. Its purpose was to better the conditions and prospects of the Jews by bringing them back to their land. It never saw itself as a destructive movement, and certainly not as the oppressor of anyone else. It has not been a religious movement, and it has always been pragmatic.

The outcome of the Six-Day War presented Israel with the possibility of possessing the entire ancestral homeland at the price of withholding independence from the Palestinians. This extreme dilemma tore at the heart of the Zionist enterprise, defining the main political agenda for twenty-five years. Ultimately, the question the settlers posed to the rest of us was, Do we really need Hebron? Perhaps, given the right conditions, might we even be better off without?

The Palestinians didn't like the settlements from the beginning. Sprinkling them on the hilltops meant bringing in police forces to cope with demonstrations and military forces to guard them, years before the outbreak of the first *intifada*. It meant constant bad press for something many Israelis weren't in favor of themselves. The hard core of the settlers needed no prodding, but settling two hundred thousand people meant offering financial incentives, cheap mortgages, lower income tax tariffs; it meant paving hundreds of miles of roads: all these had to be paid for, at the expense of whatever else.

The worst, in some of our eyes, were the moral costs. The occupation itself predated the settlements by about a decade, and as long as the Arab countries refused to countenance peace with Israel, it was inevitable. Such clarity was power. From 1977 or so, that clarity was replaced by growing murkiness. Egypt broke the taboo on living in peace with Israel, and as this had happened once, it might happen again. But the onus of its not happening slipped slowly onto both sides, as the settlements multiplied; once the PLO declared its willingness to accept Israel's existence, in 1988, the onus of not testing its sincerity was increasingly on Israel.

There was an ever growing tension between being a democracy inside the 1967 lines and a nondemocratic ruler beyond them. Due process, equality before the law, even simple freedom, all existed inside the lines but were curtailed outside them. As the level of violence mounted slowly over the years, so did the repression. It was never bloody repression along the lines, say, of France in Algeria in the 1950s, but neither was it anything to be proud of, and a growing number of Israelis moved from discomfort to distaste and from distaste to revulsion. As they did so, a chasm opened between them and the settlers, who seemed to be transforming what had once been an unfortunate necessity into an ideologically justified condition of permanence.

Between the two camps stood the great majority of Israelis, who were skeptical about the possibility of making peace with the Palestinians but had no existential need to rule over them should an alternative appear. This is the camp that has been tilting elections back and forth since the mid-1980s, testing the alternatives. They agreed with the settlers that divesting control over the Palestinians merely for moral reasons was an elaborate form of suicide; they agreed with the peace camp that Zionism was not about denying statehood to the Palestinians, it was about creating the best state possible for the Jews. Underline the word *possible*.

By implication, their answer to the Hebron question was No. Hebron, for all its antiquity, is not essential to the fulfillment of Zionism.

While the schism in Israeli society induced by the settlements lay at the heart of Zionism, it grew slowly. The growing military involvement in Lebanon created a parallel rift on the morality of waging war, and it climaxed much sooner.

CHAPTER

6

THE 1980S: WRONG DECISIONS

A common Hebrew adage says that people who do nothing make no mistakes. The idea is that anyone who makes decisions and acts upon them will have to live with their consequences; staying on the sidelines will save you from the danger of doing wrong, but at the cost of never doing right.

Zionism is the decision of the Jews to make choices that influence their national existence and living with the consequences. Mistakes were indeed made from time to time, and some have been mentioned already. The surprising thing was how few really significant ones were made: as a century of Zionist activity was marked in about 1980, the movement had succeeded beyond anyone's reasonable expectations. The centenary, however, was also to be marked by grievous miscalculations that would tarnish Israel's record. Initially they were simple miscalculations, but as time went on they were based on a basic misreading of Israel's role and her ability to influence the direction of events in the Middle East.

The underlying theme was the ongoing Palestinian refusal to accept Israel and their insistence on murdering Israeli civilians. By 1976, the Israelis had effectively sealed the border with Lebanon, forcing the terrorists to circumvent it, often by sea. In March 1978, two squads landed on the coast and committed the worst single terrorist event to date. They murdered the first person they saw, an American tourist, then hijacked a bus of families returning home from a holiday on the main road between Haifa and Tel Aviv. Shooting and throwing grenades as they went, the hijackers raced toward Tel Aviv. The bus was stopped at the northern entrance to town, and in the ensuing battle thirty-five Israelis were killed and dozens wounded.

Previous Israeli policy had been to put pressure on the country harboring terrorists. This worked in Egypt in 1957, in Jordan in 1970, and to a lesser extent in Lebanon in the early 1970s. By 1978, however, the Lebanese state was disintegrating in a protracted and brutal civil war in which the Palestinians were playing a destabilizing role. The writ of the central government was worthless, with Maronite Christians, Druze, Sunnis, Shiites, and Palestinians all controlling their own fiefdoms and warring with the others. In the eastern Bekaa valley, the PLO was running training camps for terrorists from as far away as Japan, Italy, and Germany—an early version of the Taliban's Afghanistan. The most powerful player was Syria, which had historically regarded Lebanon as rightfully part of its territory; its president, Hafez al-Assad, most famously demonstrated his opinion of human rights in early 1982, when he quelled a rebellion of the Islamic Brotherhood by killing some twenty thousand of his own citizens in the northern town of El-Hama.

Following the attack on the bus, Israel embarked on a lethal path of intervention in Lebanon, which provided her worst moments. The first step down this path was not understood as such at the time.

In March 1978, Israel occupied a swathe of southern Lebanon, carefully avoiding the Palestinian refugee camps on the coast. Most of the PLO fighters in the occupied area escaped ahead of the advancing columns, though some remained to fight. A few hundred were killed. Had it ever crossed the minds of the Israelis to take revenge rather than preempt additional acts of terror, they would have bombed the refugee camps and left the fighters alone. After the raid, Israel turned over a narrow strip of land along the border to a local, mainly Christian militia that called itself the Southern Lebanon Army (SLA); the United Nations stationed an interim force in Lebanon (UNIFIL) between the PLO forces, which rapidly returned to the villages they had been ejected from, and the Israelis.

The mini invasion of March 1978 had basically achieved nothing. The PLO continued its attacks on Israel and added a new element: Soviet-made Katyusha rockets, which were shot over the heads of UNIFIL, the SLA, and the border.

Since they were to play a constant role in the conflict for many years, it should be explained that Katyusha rockets are small, cheap, easily operable, highly mobile, and not particularly accurate, but with a range of a few dozen miles; their payload is large enough to destroy a small structure upon impact and to kill people if it hits close enough. It is not a weapon of mass destruction, but it is a weapon of massive threat, since there is no effective defense against it. Two men with knapsacks on their backs can walk through the night to a hilltop, shoot off a couple of rockets, and walk home to bed. If they repeat this nightly for a week, each time choosing a different hill, they can effectively shut down normal life in the entire target region.

As the civil war in Lebanon continued, Israel was drawn ever more into its byzantine complexities. Without the Israeli public being fully aware of the change, the Israeli decision makers began to think in terms of intervening in the Lebanese civil war. In essence, they were evolving from using a defensive strategy punctuated by occasional offensive tactics to acting like a regional power that uses force to achieve a wider range of goals. While Israel has the reputation of a trigger-happy country, especially compared with the extreme reluctance to use force common to Europe, in reality she had always limited her use of force to straightforward defensive goals, her militant image stemming from the great frequency with which she has had to defend herself.

The assumption underpinning the new doctrine was that the Christian Phalange forces might prove a valuable ally, pitted as they were against Israel's own enemies, the PLO and the Syrians. This assumption was to prove devastatingly false, but by the time this became clear, it was too late. Initially, the Israelis armed and trained the Phalanges. By 1981, the Phalanges were doing their best to provoke the Syrians to a degree of brutality that would pull the Israelis into the fighting. PLO artillery and Katyushas were killing Israeli civilians in northern Israel, and Israeli aircraft were killing larger numbers of civilians near PLO targets in Lebanon, including Beirut; the Syrian and Israeli air forces were eyeing each other and waiting for the moment to act. The deterioration toward war was halted by the diplomatic efforts of the American emissary Philip

Habib, who managed to negotiate a cease-fire between Israel and the PLO.

Responding to PLO attacks on Israeli citizens was self-defense, hence *jus ad bellum.* Taking sides in the Lebanese civil war, where all sides routinely slaughtered civilians by the hundreds, was less justifiable, and resorting to inaccurate bombing of military targets in the middle of civilian neighborhoods was simply indefensible. While it was by no means a policy of indiscriminate murder as a way of waging war, it was dangerously close. Further, the Israeli media failed to clearly report that this was what was happening, or if it was reported, the general public did not pick it up.

The 1980s saw the nadir of Israeli behavior. While the response to Sadat's gesture proved that she would rise to a sincere Arab effort at peace, the reverse was not attempted: making a Sadat-like gesture to the Arabs. As long as the underlying structure of the conflict had been total Arab rejection of Zionism and the intention to destroy it, such a gesture could be written off as naive. Post-Sadat, however, the Israelis could have asked themselves if the rejection might be less total than previously supposed. This was the policy advocated by the Israeli peace camp, which since 1978 had been publicly represented by the Peace Now organization and voiced in the Knesset by the opposition parties of the Left. It was not the policy of Menachem Begin and his government. Begin himself and many of his voters regarded the West Bank (now officially relabeled "Judea and Samaria") as the historic heart of the promised land and could not conceive of relinquishing Jewish control over it; a broader part of the electorate took the continued violent rejectionism of the PLO seriously and preferred to wait for it to change before making offers.

The treaty with Egypt had stipulated Israeli-Palestinian negotiations over autonomy in the West Bank and Gaza, but since neither the Israelis nor the Palestinians had any interest in their success, nothing came of them. Neither side had anything remotely acceptable to say to the other. And so Begin's government embarked on its policy of building settlements throughout the territories. The elections of summer 1981 were the closest Israel had ever seen, and Begin's victory had more to do with internal social issues than anything else: in effect, he was pitting the non-European half of the populace against the European half.

The run-up to the clashes of summer 1981 had elements of a proxy war with Syria, and in Lebanon the true price of the Israeli policy was soon to be demonstrated.

Arafat's PLO remained committed to the destruction of Israel, with terrorism against civilians its method of choice. Yet in Lebanon it had also become an important player in the multisided civil war that had been raging since the 1970s. The agreement of summer 1981 stipulated quiet along the border with Israel, but in the Palestinian reading of that agreement, terror actions elsewhere in the world were permitted. Since the bases from which such actions were launched were all in southern Lebanon, from the Israeli perspective the PLO was in effect claiming freedom of action and immunity from response.

Begin's idea was to massively invade Lebanon, overpowering anyone who got in the way, clearing the PLO out of its bases in the south, and connecting with the Phalange, whose main territorial base was north of Beirut. This would enable the accession to the Lebanese presidency of Bashir Gemayel, the leader of the Phalange, who seemed friendly to Israel. He was then expected to make peace with Israel and, with her backing, put an end to the civil war and reassert Lebanese independence from Syria. The Israelis would end up with the PLO gone and peace with Lebanon; the Phalange would end up in control of Lebanon, the civil war would be won, and Syria would revert from hegemonic power to a mere neighbor. The code name for this plan was Big Pines.

What the Israelis overlooked was that the rules of engagement in Lebanon included duplicity, changing sides whenever convenient, and, most significant, mass murder of noncombatants. At least thirty thousand Lebanese died in their war, uncounted thousands of them civilians. Joining such a fray meant playing by its rules. It also meant embarking on a "war of choice," as Begin was to call it at the brief moment when it seemed to have succeeded. Not a war of self-defense, as in 1948, 1967, and 1973, or a justified preemptive one as in 1956, but a calculated gamble on the chance of making life in a nasty neighborhood more bearable. Had it succeeded, it would undoubtedly have gone down well in the history books—but it didn't.

The Israeli government that sent the IDF into Lebanon in June 1982 had the backing of exactly half of the Knesset. Since votes of no confidence need a simple majority to pass, this constituted the narrowest of possible majorities. There was never a decision taken in the government to embark on Big Pines. On the contrary, when it was presented to the government in May 1982 by Defense Minister Ariel Sharon and Chief of Staff Rafael Eitan, it was rejected. What was eventually authorized, and initially backed by a large part of the electorate, was a limited campaign against the PLO bases in the south. This plan was called Little Pines, and it called for the IDF to destroy the PLO installations forty kilometers north of the border, roughly the range of Katyusha rockets. Yet Little Pines proved impossible to contain in a situation where the military and political leadership were itching to go beyond it.

In the initial stages, the IDF maintained its observance of the codes of war. Fights with armed men trained to kill civilians in a war of destruction are not hard to justify. Even when attacking PLO units entrenched inside refugee camps, the Israelis took great precautions not to hurt civilians. Lebanese civilians, who felt the entire campaign was not their business one way or the other, watched the action from the rooftops. On the Syrian front, in eastern Lebanon, the IDF provoked a fight and got it. The Syrian antiaircraft formations that had been such a bone of contention were destroyed in a dazzling operation, while on the ground the IDF armored columns did not manage to achieve their goal of cutting the Beirut-Damascus road—but thereafter, the significant acts of the war were all in the west.

By July, Israeli troops were encamped on the hills above Beirut. For the next two months, Israeli pressure was exerted in all directions to force the PLO to evacuate the city. The centerpiece of this effort was a series of incessant attacks on encircled and besieged West Beirut by Phalange proxies who smuggled car bombs into the city and cut off the water supply, by artillery, by slow block-by-block advances of troops, and by aerial bombardments. These, which were screened on televisions across the world, left no room for doubt that the Israelis were killing civilians by the hundreds. Tense and highly charged demonstrations took place in Israel, both for and against the fighting. One of the high points was the very public resignation of Colonel Eli Geva, commander of a brigade of paratroopers, who refused to lead his men into an attack on West Beirut. Even some of Begin's coalition partners indicated that such an attack would bring down the government.

Begin and Sharon refused to back down, convinced that if enough pressure was exerted, their goals would be achieved. For a moment events seemed to have vindicated them, when in late August the PLO withdrew from Beirut. Arafat and other leaders went to Tunisia, the only country willing to accept them, and thousands of PLO rank and file were sent north or into Syria. The evacuation took place under the auspices of American and French troops, stationed in Beirut to assure the Palestinians that the Israelis would not harm them during the withdrawal. While the PLO were evacuating, the Lebanese Parliament convened and chose the young Phalange leader Bashir Gemayal as president of Lebanon. This was the moment when Begin, feeling that the campaign had been vindicated, spoke of the "war of choice."

Three weeks later, the tables were turned. The Syrians arranged the assassination of Gemayel. The Israelis, citing fear of mass revenge actions, moved into West Beirut, then inexplicably allowed Phalange forces into the Sabra and Shatila refugee camps. The Phalangists immediately began murdering Palestinian civilians in revenge for having destroyed the old order in Lebanon and for Palestinian atrocities against them in the civil war. The Palestinians portrayed it as a genocidal murder by Israelis, and the number of dead civilians was claimed to be six thousand in a conscious play on Begin's custom of justifying Israeli actions by the six million of the Holocaust. This was propaganda—but the truth was awful enough. According to an official Lebanese inquiry, nearly five hundred civilians had been murdered; the Israelis estimated the number to be closer to eight hundred. The festering frustration in parts of Israeli society exploded. There was an avalanche of protest, culminating in that gigantic demonstration mentioned in the first chapter. So great was the animosity toward the war and its unacceptable—and unattainable—goals that a process began that was to bring the troops back more or less to their starting point, not many miles north of the international border.

The Lebanon war was a catastrophe—strategic, political, and moral. Rather than putting an end to the civil war, it strengthened Syrian control, which did, however, lead to a winding down of the war. The military infrastructure of the PLO was largely destroyed—another contribution to peace in Lebanon—but anyone who had expected this to lead to the disappearance of the PLO itself was sorely disappointed. Shorn of an autonomous military base near Israel, the PLO hesitantly embarked on a new course of action, which in the 1990s was to achieve the opposite of what Begin, Sharon, and Eitan had intended. The Israeli presence in southern Lebanon contributed greatly to the creation of a new anti-Israeli force, the Hizbollah. This militant Shiite group was funded, armed, and trained by the new Islamist regime in Iran, which of course did not depend on any actions of Israel. But the prolonged IDF presence gave Hizbollah a cause for the masses to rally to: freeing the homeland from an occupier.

Those of us who are politically minded know that a majority of the people around us care somewhat less than we do about many of the issues that animate us. And there is at least one individual—a friend, brother-in-law, or colleague—who epitomizes for us the middle-of-the-road majority that is to our left, or right, or whatever. Yoram was like that for me. We met as twenty-year-old instructors at the armored corps academy and served together for many years as reservists. Yoram's parents had been lower-middle-class in Poland and left in the interwar period in search of a better life. In Israel they were middle-class, and by now Yoram, who is a hard worker, is comfortably upper-middle-class. No academic qualifications to mention, but a solid businessman. Like his parents, he is politically centrist and always votes at elections, but never for the staunch ideologues. He is conspicuous for two things: for standing almost seven feet tall and for being constitutionally incapable of taking the army seriously. Since the army always takes itself very seriously, having a joker like him around is salutary.

Of course, Yoram was for the peace treaty with Egypt and its concomitant price. Before the invasion of Lebanon, he was probably wary of what our government was going to get us into. Once it had started, however, at least for those first days, he was quite jovial about how Sharon and Begin weren't going to be wimps. Even then, however, he was full of humorous gibes for our fellow reservists from the settlers' camp, warning them not to start dreaming of setting up any settlements in Lebanon, which he wouldn't tolerate. It never crossed his mind to participate in the gigantic rally after Sabra and Shatila. People like Yoram get up early in the morning and go to work and have no time for histrionics that go on until late at night. Yet the war in Lebanon did affect him. His attitude toward the Palestinians remained skeptical, but his willingness to throw Israeli military power into the breach was severely limited. Look at all the chaos our nonwimp leaders stirred up, he would have said, and what good did it do anyone?

Indeed, most significant for many Israelis was the internal political fallout. Israeli war crimes in Lebanon had been minor compared to those of the other participants, and they paled against the darker moments in the history of most warring nations of the twentieth century—but they were certainly far worse than anything Israel herself had previously done. It had been largely an unnecessary war, waged wrongly, and many Israelis came away from it with a deep feeling of defilement. Yet many others felt that precisely this moral fastidiousness had caused the failure; given the nastiness of the neighborhood, they felt, the best way to survive was by being top dog—and being acknowledged as such.

The rot was to prove deeper than most Israelis had thought. On the evening of April 11, 1984, four terrorists hijacked a bus on line three hundred from Tel Aviv to Ashdod. It was eventually stopped and stormed north of Gaza; two of the terrorists were killed in the clash, as was one of the passengers, a young woman. On the face of it, another small terrorist incident in a series of thousands that are, always have been, and most likely will continue to be part and parcel of life in the Jewish state. What made it unusual was that someone slipped and thereby revealed a frightening cesspool.

By the time the bus was stormed, there were journalists on the scene. A few snapshots were made of two General Security Service (GSS) men hauling two live terrorists away from the bus. The next morning, the official story was that all four terrorists had been killed as the bus was being stormed, and a small group of journalists and their editors had proof this was false. Israeli journalists, not BBC.

The GSS (also known as Shin Bet) is in charge of internal security, making it vaguely the counterpart of the FBI. More than any other organization, it has the task of protecting Israeli citizens from terrorism, and over the decades it has saved the lives of countless innocent people, enabling them to live their lives undisrupted. Its members are highly trained, highly committed individuals. As far as outsiders can know such things, they are mainstream people, even an elite; extremists are weeded out, if they ever get in in the first place.

Israel being a small place where most people know most other people, the GSS and its political overlords knew of the danger immediately, and pressure was brought to bear to plug the leak. The editors were warned of the dire consequences of harming the GSS in general, and the photographed agents in particular, should the story break. They were reminded that the dead terrorists had been cold-blooded murderers, or would have been had they not been stopped—which was, of course, true. One can also assume that veiled threats of one sort or another were floated. Nevertheless, the editors at one newspaper went public, though they did smudge the faces of the GSS agents in the published photos.

The furor was to continue unabated for almost four years. Initially, there was widespread fury at the paper for publishing the story. Then there were questions as to the event itself. Then there was an extremely ugly cover-up attempt by the GSS, whose centerpiece was the indictment of Brigadier General Yitzhak Mordechai, who had been on the scene and was tried but acquitted. The awareness that the GSS had framed a general set in motion the creation of a governmental commission of inquiry, headed by Chief Justice Haim Landau. The findings of the commission were mind-boggling: it appeared that for years the GSS had been running a double system whereby the strict truth was told within the service and lies were told to the rest of the world. The commission found that GSS agents had routinely lied in court to achieve convictions. The ensuing uproar threatened the service's very existence, which was a luxury that the country could ill afford, so a scandalous presidential pardon was concocted whereby the top brass lost their jobs but were not brought to trial. On the other hand, they were also forbidden—by later judicial decisions—from ever again holding public positions.

On balance, Israeli democracy came through intact, though not with flying colors. The procedures of the GSS were unforgivable. The press had proved a worthy watchdog, initially in the face of tremendous pressure and no small measure of public animosity. The government was primarily pragmatic.

Yet to complete the complexity of the story, two additional facts: Precisely as the storm was breaking, the GSS had a major success, one of historic importance, when its agents broke a ring of terrorists among the settlers that had already murdered a number of Palestinians and intended to do much worse. In that story, the GSS was the hero, the judiciary handed down reasonable verdicts, and the politicians bore the burden of infamy when they secured the early release of the convicts, within a few short years. The second fact is truly bizarre. It is the story of Yossi Genossar, one of the pardoned GSS officials. During the *intifada,* he was to lose a son. Then, in the 1990s, as an Israeli businessman with manifold contacts with the Palestinians, he was to be crucial in some of the negotiations with them, at times being the only Israeli who enjoyed the trust of the top Palestinian negotiators—who of course knew precisely who he was.

In December 1987, on two consecutive days, the *intifada* erupted, and Hamas was founded. At the time, no one took notice of the juxtaposition; seen from the perspective of September 11, 2001, however, it was absolutely devastating.

In a way, the *intifada* can be construed as a positive development, even from an Israeli perspective, as it forced clarity upon a murky situation. At least in its initial stages, it was what it called itself: a shaking off. The Palestinian populace living under Israeli occupation took its destiny in its own hands, independent of the gang of professional terrorists trailing around the Middle East behind Yasser Arafat, committed to terrorism as the sole means for the destruction of Israel and showing little interest in the day-to-day lives of the Palestinians themselves. In the early 1970s, Golda Meir had foolishly stated that "there is no Palestinian people," as if this were something for an outsider to say one way or the other. Even at the time, the very structure of her sentence belied its content: the *intifada* was to be the final nail in the coffin of her thesis. By running a widespread and sustained rebellion against the Israeli occupier, in which a broad section of society—including women, unusual for an Arab society—actively participated, the community that called itself Palestinian proved its existence as a nation in a way that could not be overlooked even by its most committed adversaries. In doing so, it forced Israeli society to face the price of continued occupation and required us to decide if this was a price worth paying for continued control of the entire land. Sensing this sea change in the terms of engagement, the PLO itself redefined its role, its strategy, and its tactics.

Some of the central elements of the *intifada* did not contravene any code of war. General strikes, large demonstrations, refusals to pay taxes or to purchase Israeli products even when no alternative existed: for the first time in decades, their tactics could not be brushed aside as criminal actions designed to prosecute a hopeless and irrational war against Zionism itself. The one widespread practice that still involved attempted murder of civilians was the stoning of civilian vehicles, which indeed could have lethal effects. Irrespective of one's opinion of the settlers, they were civilians; they had been taking possession of land, not killing people; and as Israel had demonstrated in 1981, settlements can be dismantled. Dead civilians cannot be resurrected.

There were, of course, considerably more dead civilians on the Palestinians' side. The IDF had long since learned to fight wars against other armies with the barest minimum of civilian casualties. It had even proven capable of fighting armed militias in southern Lebanese refugee camps without harming the civilian population. The *intifada* presented a new kind of challenge, one that would require a new period of learning. At times, success or failure hinged on the subjective perspective of young and confused soldiers confronted by large numbers of angry rioters armed with primitive weapons and murder blazing in their eyes. The training, equipment, and procedures necessary to extricate oneself from such a situation without harming anyone are not innate. They must be developed and imparted in advance. As time went on, the IDF got better at the task, and fewer civilians got hurt; but never was a truly satisfactory level of casualties achieved, and anyway, what would such a level have been? A populace willing to confront an army cannot be so coddled as to totally eliminate casualties, if they are determined to have the confrontation. What remains are politics and a contest of wills: Which side will falter first? Who will decide that the price of conflict is too high?

The root of the Israeli conundrum was precisely Israel's inability to use her full force to deal with the challenge. When in spring 1982 Syrian president Assad was faced with an *intifada*-like uprising of Islamists in the city of El-Hama, he called in the air force, killed twenty thousand of his own citizens, and enjoyed the resulting quiet until his death many years later. Israel had the military might to put down the *intifada* with brute force, but she never considered this option; even the few Israelis who might have conceived of such a policy had seen in the previous few years that their society would never allow it. So they muddled through the years of the *intifada,* forcing elderly men to remove roadblocks built by their sons or young men to climb poles to remove Palestinian flags hung there by their brothers. Exceptionally harsh cases of brutality were court-martialed, but most were not. Tens of thousands of Palestinians went through prison, undoubtedly reinforcing their national commitment; no public figure of their generation will get far unless he can cite a stint in an Israeli prison. Except for the settlers, Israeli civilians refrained from traveling through the occupied territories, thus deepening the divide between them and the general populace, but, more significant, psychologically dividing the land into "ours" and "theirs" years before such a division happened by negotiation. Yet the Israeli resolve did not break, since at this stage there was no viable alternative.

Outside Palestine, and primarily in Tunisia, the PLO changed its spots, though it remained a leopard. The mainstay of Arab rejectionism had for decades been the Soviet Union, which was now visibly disintegrating. The Arab world had decided to welcome Egypt back into the fold, acquiescing in its relations with Israel. And the populace suffering under Israel was clearly fed up with the decades of futile rhetoric that had brought nothing. In July 1988, King Hussein of Jordan renounced his claim to sovereignty over the West Bank, leaving Israelis and Palestinians to sort out their partition alone. In November, a mere forty-one years late, the PLO officially accepted the United Nations' partition plan of 1947. In December, searching for a formulation that would allow official contacts with the United States, Arafat renounced "all types of terrorism, including individual, collective, and state." He also explained that the PLO had accepted UN Resolutions 242 and 338 as a basis for negotiation with Israel. In the eyes of the Americans, and some Israelis, there was now, finally, a Palestinian partner with whom one could negotiate.

But let us not forget Hamas.

Before publishing my opinions on Nazi Germany, I learned German and spent years reading tens of thousands of pages of historical documents. I lack the training to say anything original about Islam and Islamism. Yet a few well-known facts should be noted.

The rise of radical Islam is part of the story of the Arab encounter with the outside world. While it may reflect the tension with enlightened Western liberalism, its proponents prefer to see their own culture as superior and at war with what they perceive as decadence. Moreover, some of its key figures were highly educated men who had already managed to acquire the best there was to offer outside but spurned it. It was they who were doing the rejecting. Sayyid Qutb, for example, perhaps the single most important Islamic thinker in the Arab world from the 1950s, was a highly acclaimed literary critic; he turned away from the West during a two-year sojourn in the United States, between 1948 and 1950, filled with revulsion for the freedoms he saw there. Among his closest associates there were engineers, lawyers, and academics.

The Muslim Brotherhood was founded in Egypt in 1928. When the Palestinians rose in the mid-1930s, the Brotherhood supported them fervently, and in 1948, thousands joined the Egyptian force invading Israel. In 1956, hundreds petitioned Nasser to let them out of the prison camps, where he was holding them in order to again fight the Jewish infidels, promising to return to jail once the campaign was over. But as the Soviet influence in the Arab world deepened, they began to have second thoughts. By 1967, some of their leaders refused to support Nasser in his second attempt to destroy Israel, stating that they could see no real difference between his atheist regime and the Jewish infidel one.

In 1979, one of their clan (of the Shiite branch) took over Iran and set up an Islamic republic. Ten years later, the atheistic Soviet superpower that had been so dominant in their part of the world collapsed. Those who see human history as the result of materialistic forces shaping human behavior overlook at their peril the tremendous power of ideas and the emotion they both build on and promote. For the Islamists, the demise of the Soviet bloc was a vindication of what they were preaching and also a tremendous windfall, as their major rival in the Arab world was suddenly discredited and gone.

The influence of their ideas and organizations was growing all over the Muslim world, assisted by generous funding from Saudi Arabia. It would have been incredible if this phenomenon had skipped Palestine, one of the major theaters of action in their campaign against the infidels.

The Palestinian branch of the Muslim Brotherhood was founded in the 1960s and grew significantly in the 1970s. Initially it was ignored by the Israelis and later temporarily encouraged by the military government as a counterweight to the PLO, the known enemy. Its teachings were explicitly antisemitic, but this was ignored. Its leader was Sheikh Ahmad Yassin, and it was his decision to use the organization to create a new political and military structure the day after the *intifada* broke out, thus showing a far more astute understanding of the event than anyone else. Physically he is a severely incapacitated invalid, a fact that would deflect Israeli attention from him for many months.

Hamas means fire, ardor, fervor, zeal, or fanaticism. It is an acronym for Harakat al-Muqawamah al-Islamiyya ("the Islamic Resistance Movement"). Its covenant, published in August 1988, is a long and wordy document replete with quotations from traditional Muslim sources. Since a sizable minority of Palestinians support Hamas, and most of Israel's critics refuse to take it seriously, it is important to note some excerpts from this horrific document:

> **Article Eleven:** The Islamic Resistance Movement believes that the land of Palestine is an Islamic *waqf* consecrated for future Muslim generations until Judgment Day. It, or any part of it, should not be squandered: it, or any part of it, should not be given up. Neither a single Arab country nor all Arab countries, neither any king or president, nor all the kings and presidents, neither any organization nor all of them, be they Palestinian or Arab, possess the right to do that. Palestine is an Islamic *waqf,* land consecrated for Muslim generations until Judgment Day.

> **Article Thirteen:** Initiatives, and so-called peaceful solutions and international conferences, are in contradiction to the principles of the Islamic Resistance Movement. Abusing any part of Palestine is abuse directed against part of religion. . . . There is no solution for the Palestinian question except through Jihad. Initiatives, proposals, and international conferences are all a waste of time and vain endeavors.

> **Article Twenty-two:** For a long time, the enemies have been planning, skillfully and with precision, for the achievement of what they have attained. They took into consideration the causes affecting the current of events. They strived to amass great and substantive material wealth, which they devoted to the realization of their dream. With their money, they took control of the world media, news agencies, the press, publishing houses, broadcasting stations, and others. With their money they stirred revolutions in various parts of the world with the purpose of achieving their interests and reaping the fruit therein. They were behind the French Revolution, the Communist revolution, and most of the revolutions we heard and hear about, here and there. With their money they formed secret societies, such as Freemasons, Rotary Clubs, the Lions, and others in different parts of the world for the purpose of sabotaging societies and achieving Zionist interests. With their

> money they were able to control imperialistic countries and instigate them to colonize many countries in order to enable them to exploit their resources and spread corruption there.
>
> You may speak as much as you want about regional and world wars. They were behind World War I, when they were able to destroy the Islamic Caliphate, making financial gains and controlling resources. They obtained the Balfour Declaration, formed the League of Nations through which they could rule the world. They were behind World War II, through which they made huge financial gains by trading in armaments, and paved the way for the establishment of their state. It was they who instigated the replacement of the League of Nations with the United Nations and the Security Council to enable them to rule the world through them. There is no war going on anywhere, without having their finger in it.
>
> **Article Thirty-two:** After Palestine, the Zionists aspire to expand from the Nile to the Euphrates. When they will have digested the region they overtook, they will aspire to further expansion, and so on. Their plan is embodied in *The Protocols of the Elders of Zion,* and their present conduct is the best proof of what we are saying.

This is the charter of one of the most important political movements the Palestinian nation has. Pretending that its members don't really mean what they say, or that they say it only out of frustration at Israeli actions, is patronizing and foolish. If any party in a democratic society adopted a platform remotely like it, they'd be drummed out of town; if they garnered the support of a third of the populace, their neighbors would all be frantically rearming. And if they then moved from words to deeds?

Hamas, along with the smaller Islamic Jihad, carried out most of the terror acts of the *intifada* at a time when the PLO was wondering if they might be counterproductive. Being new to the task, they initially carried out small-scale attacks by individuals against other individuals (stabbings, kidnapping, and murder); from the outset, and true to their ideology, they never distinguished between the occupied territories and Israel proper, since the distinction has no meaning for them. Their main base was in Gaza, where they enjoyed substantial popular support from the first; in the

West Bank this took longer to achieve. Their very existence should have posed a severe question but for some reason didn't: Were the Palestinian people ever going to accept any sort of Jewish entity? Were the *intifada* and the many changes it wrought a dialectical advance toward a resolution of the conflict, perhaps a final act of mutual attrition and exhaustion, to be followed by sober reconciliation—or were they merely a new stage in an irresolvable conflict?

These unasked questions should have been glaringly obvious even at the time, because of the essential difference between this new generation of Palestinian extremists and their purported Israeli counterparts. Outsiders routinely view the religious extremists on both sides with distaste, and with "a plague on both their houses" mentality they write off the entire conflict as the irrational antics of religious fanatics. Yet this seemingly rational and enlightened perspective totally disregards the fact that murderous violence against civilians is the hallmark of the Palestinian extremists; the hallmark of the settlers is the creation of settlements. Even a child, you would think, could see the moral difference.

Benny Morris has written that Hamas emerged in 1987 "like a butterfly from the cocoon [of the Muslim Brotherhood]." On a far larger scale, this was happening all over the Middle East. For decades the Soviet Union and the cold war had seemed to motivate and perpetuate the Middle East conflict. When the cold war was won by the West, we were told that the conflict might wind down, if only it were managed wisely. Yet what if this was not true, and out of the cocoon of Soviet support for anti-Western, antidemocratic, and antienlightened regimes would soon appear the full-blown rejection of these values and their political incarnations? Islam, after all, is 1,400 years old, while communism lasted 70 and the cold war less than 50. Why assume that communism motivated Islam, rather than that Islam, or a radical strain of it, manipulated communism? In such a scenario, would there be anything the Israelis could ever do that would satisfy their enemies, short of simply disappearing? Would there be anything the West could do, short of fighting for its life? This was the question not asked on December 10, 1987.

CHAPTER

7

A Society Worth Fighting For

People who dislike Israel love calling her a racist state. Type the words *Israel* and *racism* into Google, and you'll get 240,000 results. Among the first hundred or so you will find Sherri Muzher, a Palestinian American activist, lawyer, and freelance journalist, summing up the United Nations Conference Against Racism at Durban, South Africa, in September 2001:

> How could anyone claim that Israel is not a racist state? It is even called the Jewish state of Israel. It is a state for one religion and the founders of Zionism simply intended for such a homogeneous state. . . . Nobody wants to be called a racist, particularly those who were forced to wear patches to identify them in Nazi Germany. But the policies Israel pursues are exactly this. If it doesn't like the well-deserved label, then it should stop its racist practices.[1]

In a similar vein, Ghassan Khatib, minister of labor in the Palestinian Authority Cabinet, wrote an article titled "Israel Is a Racist State" on the Web site of the Palestine Solidarity Campaign:

[1] www.serendipity.li/more/muzher.htm

> Finally somebody has had the courage to call Israel what it truly is: a racist state. But the official United Nations conference on racism convened in Durban, South Africa, was very hesitant to apply international law to the Israeli case. Still, Palestinians are encouraged by the recommendations of the non-government international forum in Durban because, for the first time since the beginning of the Intifada, somebody has dared to point out the Israeli atrocities and its violation of international humanitarian laws.[2]

In late 2000, Phyllis Bennis, a scholar at the left-wing Institute for Policy Studies in Washington, D.C., explained:

> Within Israel there are really four levels of citizenship, the first three being various levels of Jewish participation in Israeli society, which are thoroughly racialized. At the top of the pyramid are the Ashkenazi, the white European Jews. At the level of power the huge contingent of recent Russian immigrants—now about 20 percent of Israeli Jews—are being assimilated into the European-Ashkenazi sector, though they are retaining a very distinct cultural identity. The next level down, which is now probably the largest component of the Jewish population, is the Mizrachi or Sephardic Jews, who are from the Arab countries. At the bottom of the Jewish pyramid are the Ethiopian Jews, who are black. You can go into the poorest parts of Jewish West Jerusalem and find that it's predominantly Ethiopian. This social and economic stratification took shape throughout the last 50 years as different groups of Jews from different parts of the world came, for very different reasons, to Israel. So while the divisions reflected national origins, they play out in a profoundly racialized way.[3]

In September 2002, Nelson Mandela gave an interview to *Newsweek,* castigating George W. Bush and Tony Blair for racism in their campaign to disarm Iraq: "Neither Bush nor Tony Blair has provided any evidence

[2] www.palestinecampaign.org/archives.

[3] Max Elbaum interviews Phyllis Bennis for *Colorlines*, http//www.arc.org/C_Lines/CL Archive/story_web00_04.html.

that such weapons exist. But what we know is that Israel has weapons of mass destruction. Nobody talks about that. Why should there be one standard for one country, especially because it is black, and another one for another country, Israel, that is white."

If you listen to these people carefully, you will notice that while their terminology is the same—they are castigating Israel as racist—they really mean quite different things. Sherri Muzher alludes to the original meaning of the term: the idea that humanity is—and should continue to be—divided into races and that they should not intermingle. This nineteenth-century notion evolved in the twentieth century into the idea that the different races had varying value, some being creative and positive, others destructive and negative. This idea was at the heart of the Nazi worldview and was a primary motivating force for their behavior and actions. Once they were defeated, everyone agreed that they had been awful, and to identify anyone with them became the ultimate insult. As Muzher says: "Nobody wants to be called a racist, particularly those who were forced to wear patches to identify them in Nazi Germany." (A deft bit of propaganda if ever there was one, since the Nazi crime was not forcing Jews to wear patches but to murder them systematically.)

Phyllis Bennis is not blaming Israel for Auschwitz-like genocide. For her, the meaning of racism is derived from the crimes of slavery and segregation committed against American blacks. That the slur is all the more potent for its Nazi echoes is fine, but the content of her accusations is American. Mandela too could be expected to use the term in its American sense—but he doesn't. Rather, he sees racism not in terms of restrictions on the freedom of individuals because of their group, but as a crime of the rich countries of the Northern Hemisphere exploiting those of the south. Ultimately, he uses the potent word as a corollary of European colonialism. Intriguingly, this means that the crime is less the depriving of equality or freedom than the depriving of independence: whether or not Iraqi citizens enjoy freedom is of less significance to him than whether they are independent of colonial rule, even if that independence takes the form of a bloody dictatorship. Coincidentally or not, this plays directly to the gallery of Western European public opinion, where colonialism is regarded, these days, as the ultimate sin.

What would a truly racist Israel look like, according to each of these three meanings of the term? There is, of course, a precedent for the worst, full-blown type of racism. Hitler wanted to get rid of the Jews, and he was willing to plunge humanity into the worst war ever in order to create the conditions for mass murder. Millions of his countrymen were eager to help, and almost none of them did anything to interfere. It took them about four years to murder six million Jews, along with millions of Russians, Slavs, Gypsies, and other "subhuman" peoples. They were at their most efficient from April to November 1942, 250 days in which they murdered some two and a half million Jews. They never showed any restraint, slowed down only when they began to run out of Jews to kill, and stopped only when the Allies bombed them to bits and abolished their country.

The genocidal regime in Rwanda in 1994 seems to have been roughly similar in its extreme racism, but no other recent examples come to mind, and certainly nothing that has happened in the Middle East. In an entire century of conflict between Palestinians and Jews, the combined number of dead *on both sides* is less than one week's worth of Jews in 1942. In the bloody first two years of Ariel Sharon's premiership, until early 2003, about 1,600 Palestinians died, most of them combatants and more than 100 of them suicide killers; also, about 600 Israelis, overwhelmingly civilians, were killed—a three-hour job for the Nazis. Any analogy of Israel to Nazi Germany and its machinery of death is obscene.

Previous chapters have dealt with the second accusation, whereby Israel's racism lies in its colonialism. The only (flimsy) resemblance between European colonialism and Zionism is that some of the Zionists—perhaps half—came from Europe; even these were mostly destitute refugees, often from Europe's periphery, and almost none from the colonizing nations of Western Europe. Their goal was to set up a state in which they would be the majority, not the ruling caste, and to create a society that reflected the values and culture of the Jews. In order to find any similar colonial movements, one must go back to the eighteenth-century Americas or, at a stretch, to nineteenth-century Australia. These are not the historical phenomena by which Europeans are so embarrassed when they castigate colonialism.

There remains the third meaning of the term, whereby Israel is held to be racist for her discriminatory policies against her own weaker ethnic groups. This is racism of the American type and also reflects the American understanding of South African apartheid (though it is not, as noted above, that of Mandela himself). This accusation has two variants: that

Israel is racist from top to bottom, and that Israel is "merely" racist against her Arab citizens. The description by Phyllis Bennis, were it in any way true, is what a thoroughly racist Israel would look like, and many of Israel's Jewish critics, including the post-Zionists, have adopted this tendentious view. An Israel that is "merely" racist against Arabs, and not against the weaker ethnic Jewish groups, would look roughly like apartheid South Africa.

Anyone who describes Israel as a racist state intends to be offensive and is well aware that for Jews there can hardly be a more infuriating accusation. The defender of Israel, however, cannot merely point to the lack of Nazi-like policies, because the accusation isn't really about Nazism. In order to refute the accusation, one must therefore address what it is really about, not what makes it so infuriating.

First, the accusation of multilayered racism. Far from being a monolithic society of "whites," Israel is a raucous cacophony of groups. There are at least six of them, subdivided but nonetheless identifiable as the "tribes" of modern Israel. These include traditional Ashkenazi elites, the descendants of Muslim-country immigrants, the settlers (discussed above), the ultra-Orthodox, the Russians, and the Israeli Arabs.

Baruch Kimmerling, a sociologist from the tribe of the traditional elites, recently suggested an Israeli definition of WASP: Ashkenazi, secular old-timers, socialist in the sense of European social democracy, which is vaguely similar to what Americans would call liberals. Basically, the descendants of the predominantly Ashkenazi immigrations up to World War II. The survivors of the Holocaust and their children also belong in this group, with qualification. Some of them were the same type of people as those who got here before the war, but many others were simply refugees. Had one spoken of Israeli tribes in the 1950s, they certainly would have been a separate one. By the 1990s, however, they had long since assimilated into the elite by the power of their own determination. Their children are indistinguishable from the rest.

I shall call this group the mainstream, not because they are, but because for many years they were, in terms of being the loudest voice. The educated professionals, academics, journalists, writers, poets and artists, industrialists, and many of the wealthy classes are more likely than not to belong to this group. Its founding fathers came from a milieu that was either Orthodox or had been until recently; when they rebelled against what they saw as an antiquated religion, their rebellion was grounded in personal acquaintance. Yet it was to have implications they may not fully have thought through, since it was both cultural and geographic. If they ever thought of their future children when they rebelled, they expected them to be like themselves—creators by choice of a new agenda. Had they continued to live in Europe, this trick could conceivably have been pulled off. Raising their children, when the time came, in a different land meant that the children could not resemble their elders. Not only had the choice to rebel against tradition been made for them before birth, even the ability to know what the tradition had been was gone. The parents were apostates, but their children were ignoramuses. After the Nazis there wasn't even an old country to which one could return to learn about it.

Their children, grandchildren, and by now even the great-grandchildren have no regrets about their abandonment of traditional Jewish life. In a very tough century, they felt themselves to be on the side of the winners. They identified with the triumphal West, which still felt good about itself: democratic, affluent, welfare state on the European model, rational, free inquiry, and so on. Had one asked them what was intrinsically Jewish about all this, they would have responded that most of Israel's citizens were Jewish, that they spoke the language of the Jews, and celebrated the holidays of the Jews in the land of the Jews—wasn't that enough? The French live in France, the Norwegians in Norway, and the Jews, finally, live in Israel. Why must one torture oneself with endless soul-searching? The Norwegians don't. Had one persisted in asking if this was worth dying for, as Jews throughout the centuries had at times been called upon to do, they would have shrugged and said that as long as one was persecuted one must persevere, as they must do in the face of Arab rejectionism; eventually, however, peace would reign, and Israel would indeed become the Jewish branch of the West. One could then say that the Messiah had more or less arrived. Even better, one could say that the Jews had finally regained normalcy. Now do you mind if we go skiing in Switzerland?

All of which was fine as long as the only threats were external military ones. For decades and generations, the sons and daughters of this tribe bore the brunt of the wars, initially almost alone, and they did not waver, nor have they wavered till this day. They can still say, with satisfaction, that they built and maintain the Jewish state. Except that since the 1980s, new elements have appeared to threaten the stability of the equation.

The left-center political camp most of them prefer lost power in 1977, partly because enough of them changed sides. Sick of the smugness of the Labor Party and its endless electoral victories, they were also reeling from the implications of the Yom Kippur War and a series of cases of high-level corruption. In 1982, the "wrong" government sent them to the "wrong" war. As the economic level of Israel rose, more of them built ever strengthening bonds with people elsewhere. Israelis of all groups traveled more often, but the educated secular ones built professional bonds, which brought them into contact with non-Israelis beyond the ski slopes and the department stores. This was happening just as international criticism of Israel was rising for its control over the Palestinians. When the *intifada* started, Israel seemed to have lost her synchronization with the rest of the world. Then, in the 1990s, the tribalism inside Israel seemed to spin out of control, and the local WASPs feared that their enterprise was being hijacked. And if they tell you there was no panic in their reaction, they are not being honest with themselves.

The peace process offered salvation. It would resolve the anomaly of a Western democracy occupying someone else's land and thus enable Israel to reenter the right club. It was being driven by the Labor Party and its camp—the camp of choice for Israel's WASPs. By its success, it would ensure additional electoral victories, which would then allow them to reorganize much of what had gone wrong in the previous twenty years. All this would bring about a mass migration of other Israelis into their ranks, they would once more be truly the mainstream, and history would be back on track. The process even had a Norwegian name.

Unanswered—indeed, unasked—was the question of whether the Palestinians understood that theirs was to be the task of putting Zionism back on course. The supporters of the Oslo process truly wished for peace and genuinely thought that Palestinian independence and sovereignty on terms compatible with Israel's basic needs were goals worth striving for. But what if the Palestinians intended to achieve their goals at a price beyond anything Israel could ever afford to pay? This possibility, and the many indications that it must be taken seriously, could not be acknowledged by most of the political Left between 1993 and October 2000. Some have yet to do so.

A perfect summary of this position appeared as a short article in *Haaretz* in November 2001. Dr. Eyal Gross, a professor of constitutional law at Tel

Aviv University, published a scathing critique of Israel's policies toward the Palestinians. His punch line, meant to be devastating, was that Israel is defending its ethnos, not its demos—that it cared for the ethnic group of Jews more than for the civil group of citizens.

No one in any of the other Jewish tribes would be troubled by the possibility that Israel is out to protect the Jewish ethnic group. On the contrary, they would regard that as the reason she exists.

Near the end of his fine book *From Beirut to Jerusalem,* Thomas Friedman summed things up with the story of his grocer Sasson, a Jew who hailed originally from Iraq. Sasson was not politically active beyond voting in elections, and Friedman saw in him the key to Israel's political decisions. While Sasson probably voted for the Right, he was no extremist, and if offered a fair deal that would end up giving the Palestinians their independence and Sasson his security, he'd probably go for it.

Undeniably, 1492 is a date every child recognizes: Columbus discovered America. The same year, the Jews were expelled from Spain in the largest catastrophe to befall the Jews for centuries in either direction. The Jewish community in Muslim Spain was the richest and most influential since the heyday of Babylonian Jewry. Both the Bar Kochba catastrophe and the Shoah were worse, but the destruction of Spanish Jewry by the triumphant Christians ranks as a blow so severe that it was to reverberate until the twentieth century. Among the hundreds of thousands of expellees, some made their way to *Eretz Yisrael,* and their descendants are here still. Their communities in Safed, Tiberius, Hebron, and of course Jerusalem grew slowly over the centuries. Only in the nineteenth century was there any significant Jewish immigration from Europe, so that when the proto-Zionists began arriving, the majority of the Old Yishuv, the existing Jewish community, were Sephardim—Hebrew for Spaniards, though it is often used imprecisely to mean Jews from Muslim societies. I shall call them Oriental Jews, English for the Israeli term *edot hamizrach.* They are today the largest group in Israel.

In the Diaspora there was often a correlation between the cultural level of the hosts and the importance of the local Jewish communities. When Muslim culture was more advanced than Christian, the significant Jewish communities were in Muslim lands; as the pendulum swung toward Europe, the importance of the Jewish communities there rose. By and large, the Muslim-based Jewish communities were less extreme than their European cousins: the persecution of Jews under the Muslims was not as severe as in Christendom; but neither was the legal emancipation of the Jews in Muslim societies ever so complete as in Europe. There were no major schisms in Oriental Jewry such as the Hasidim-Mitnagdim controversy of the eighteenth century, which tore apart communities and families in a struggle to define the correct way to live a Jewish life; nor could one observe the large numbers of young Jews thronging to utopian ideologies, as in the nineteenth to twentieth centuries. The Enlightenment reached the Muslim lands and their Jews in a limited, censored version. Political Zionism was brought to these Jews, not coinvented by them. All of these causes were to prove a major handicap when hundreds of thousands were ejected from their homes after 1948. Already Israel defined itself as Western, and many of these refugees lacked the tools for success in a modern society.

The European immigrants had mostly been young—including the ideologists of the mid-1920s, many refugees from Europe in the 1930s, and most Holocaust survivors. No matter what their individual circumstances, these young immigrants had broken with their elders prior to arriving and were thus free to develop a new leadership. The masses of refugees from the Arab countries, on the other hand, came with their entire families—and then watched as their elders and leaders failed to adapt to the new conditions and lost their authority.

The mainstream, especially its nail-hard leaders, had no time for such traumas. Ben-Gurion's historic decision to face the incredible challenge of absorbing more refugees than there were citizens in his fledgling state contained a streak of characteristic cruelty: such tasks cannot be done "nicely." The avalanche of refugees were dumped unceremoniously wherever the harried bureaucrats put them—some empty Arab homes on a hilltop, a cluster of tin shacks on the border, or a tent camp in the mud. They were told to learn Hebrew and to forget everything they had ever learned that was not needed for the moment. They were lectured about the genius of Israeli socialism and sternly admonished to vote for Ben-Gurion come election time. There was no respect for their cultural baggage and no patience for their emotional needs. A few hundreds of thousands were Holocaust survivors—they at least had an immediate cultural empathy with the

Zionist bureaucrats. The Oriental Jews lacked this familiarity, and this exacerbated their predicament and prolonged their disjointedness.

Faced with such a challenge, they had no way to "do it right"; what was important was to succeed. And succeed they did. By the late 1960s, the last huts had been dismantled and everybody had a real roof over their heads. No one had starved. Many of the adults would never regain the position and status they had enjoyed in the old country, but their children were growing ever more successful in the new one. The early 1970s saw an explosion of frustration, centered on a group of angry young men calling themselves "the Black Panthers," alluding to the black militants in the United States, playing quite purposefully on the idea that ethnic discrimination equals racism. The allusion was calculated to offend, and it did. Their violent demonstrations were intended to shock, and they did. Golda Meir met with their representatives and said simply "They're not nice." Yet the reality was that the generation of the Black Panthers were already entering the middle classes; indeed, within ten or fifteen years, they would largely *be* the middle class. In 1977, they found their political voice, in the unlikely form of Menachem Begin.

Begin had the same background as most of the mainstream Zionist leaders: Eastern Europe. As commander of the IZL in the mid-1940s, he seems to have formed an empathy for the particular perspective of those of his men who were Oriental, for their feeling of being steamrolled and thrust aside by the imperious drive of the leaders of the Yishuv. Begin's feeling of being sidelined was reinforced continuously over the next thirty years as Ben-Gurion and his successors managed to keep him away from political power. He briefly joined a national unity government on the eve of the Six-Day War but left in 1970 when the government accepted the Rogers Plan in spite of his objections.

In May 1977, he finally won an election. Internationally, his government is remembered for making peace with Egypt, for founding most of the settlements, and for going to war in Lebanon. To his voters, however, he was the one who gave them the feeling that they were equal citizens, as good as anyone else. His party, the Likud, welcomed Oriental Jews and presided over their massive entrance to the political arena at all levels. His rhetoric contained far more traditional Jewish content than that of his predecessors, which pleased voters who had never felt comfortable with the agnosticism and even atheism of the socialists. The record of his government was mixed, even in the field of social legislation and policies, but broad sections of the electorate felt he was on their side, and through him, Israel was becoming more of a country in which they could feel at home.

In the fifteen years between 1977 and 1992, in which the Likud dominated the government or shared it with Labor, Oriental Jews took their rightful place in the establishment. In 2003, the Israeli president is from Iran, as was the previous chief of staff. Since the 1990s, about half of the government ministers have been Oriental Jews. Only the position of prime minister remained to be taken: for all its rhetoric, even the Likud has never had an Oriental candidate for the top position. (Labor did briefly, in 2002, but replaced him before the elections of 2003.) Outside the military and the public administration, the imbalances persist mainly in areas where higher education matters. Most university professors are Ashkenazi, as are most Supreme Court justices, but long-term trends indicate that this will be rectified in time. The rate of intermarriages is reasonable, so that eventually the issue will disappear. But not just yet.

Shas, the party of many Oriental Jews, first appeared in the municipal politics of Jerusalem in the early 1980s. In the elections of 1999, it was the third largest party, only two seats behind the Likud, although it lost many of its voters in 2003. It was described as a party of protest, which is true, but the agenda of that protest deserves to be defined. While many Oriental Jews have done quite well, they are still overrepresented in the weaker segments of society, especially the geographic periphery. Yet that is not where Shas appeared, nor were the predicaments of the periphery the primary interest of its founders. Instead their agenda was cultural.

Go at random to any two synagogues, one Ashkenazi and one Oriental. Listen carefully to the sermons given by the rabbis, and you will be struck by the difference. The body of literature they quote from is the same; very likely, the points each one wishes to make are similar. Yet there is a significant difference in the way they express themselves. The Ashkenazi rabbi will probably be rational and analytical. The Oriental rabbi is more likely to illustrate his point with human interest anecdotes. Both methods are conductive to creative thought, but they're not quite the same. Shas started out as an internal squabble among the yeshivas of Jerusalem, demanding that the Oriental method not be subordinated to the Ashkenazi one. Not that the two can't live amicably alongside each other—but they should do so as equals.

Once the issue appeared on the scene, it suddenly became obvious that it had implications for a far wider public than the original five blocks of Jerusalem where it started. Thomas Friedman didn't tell us whether his grocer Sasson was Orthodox or not, because in the early 1980s it didn't seem to be an issue. Yet one can assume that Sasson went to the synagogue from time to time, even without being Orthodox in the strict sense. Had a close member of his family died, he would have mourned in the traditional way, including three daily visits to the synagogue. In these and many other small things, he would have been close to the tradition of his fathers, and he would have expected the same of his children. He would have been as respectful as anyone else of human life and dignity, including that of his enemies, but he wouldn't have expressed this in the form of universal laws or intellectual constructs, which he would find distasteful. Stirring speeches about human rights and so on would leave him cold, no matter whom they came from. Rather, he would have spoken in terms of "live and let live"—backed up, however, by swift retribution if he and his were attacked.

He would also have assumed the worst about the Arabs in general and the Palestinians in particular, having lived under them for centuries, although as Friedman noted, he wouldn't have been averse to living alongside them—once they had decided to leave him alone. Meanwhile, he might well have been interested in refashioning his own society, away from the cold rational universalism represented by the mainstream toward a more traditional Jewish way of life. Interestingly, there are no reliable statistics about the socioeconomic status of third-generation immigrants by land of origin, so the only thing one has to go on is anecdotal evidence. But I would guess that Sasson probably has quite a few grandchildren, themselves already young adults. A few have undoubtedly climbed the social ladder and could easily be among the high-tech innovators whose success is tied to the NASDAQ. They may even have left Sasson's cultural camp for assimilation into the mainstream. Some of their siblings or cousins are still solidly middle-class, and Sasson's profile largely fits them, too. One or two may have reverted to an active orthodoxy of the Oriental kind. The line between the Likud and Shas voters among them is blurred and flexible. It is safe to assume that all of them voted for Sharon in 2001, but many may be hankering for the return of Benjamin Netanyahu: like Begin, an Ashkenazi with the background of the Western elites who, with his silver tongue, nevertheless says what he feels without the slightest hint of inferiority.

When peace comes, someday, they will be willing to pay the price, though not perhaps the full price deemed reasonable by the West. Their appreciation of the importance of Jewish tradition and its claims will be greater than that of the mainstream. The Israel they dream of is democratic, modern, wealthy—and decidedly Jewish. They'll have no objections to the legal laws of marriage remaining heavily influenced by religious law, for example.

People in the Israeli mainstream generally congratulate themselves on their intelligence, education, and ability to analyze their condition rationally. In the 1980s, they often referred to themselves as the "camp of the sane," surrounded, please understand, by crazies, especially the nationalistic ones who were winning elections, building settlements, and refusing to understand that Israeli compassion was the key to peace. The arrogance of such people is misplaced, and nowhere are their pretensions more striking than in relation to the ultra-Orthodox.

The ultra-Orthodox pride themselves on being the direct successors of the medieval Jews, whose high levels of literacy and education were far above their surroundings. In reality, they are as modern as everyone else, in their own way, but they are still above all a community of highly educated people. The body of knowledge they concentrate on is largely not that recognized by Western universities, but their honing of the mind is no less sternly disciplined, and they can turn with ease to the fields of knowledge that interest the broader public; the rest of the world cannot reciprocate.

A few years ago, one of them grew fed up with the incessant chatter about the excessive ultra-Orthodox tapping of the public purse. Though he lacked any academic education in economics or accounting, he spent two years deciphering all the relevant sources in the public domain, and pretty soon he was *the* expert on the subject. Even the officials of the treasury admit that Roitman understands everything they do.

Today's ultra-Orthodox communities call themselves *haredim,* those who "are in fear of the Word of God." Contrary to what they claim, however, they are largely a creation of the nineteenth century. Or rather, their way of life is an adaptation of an older tradition to the dramatically changed circumstances of modernity. For centuries their forebears had been cooped up in very narrow confines, especially in Europe, and had learned to make a virtue of necessity. When the Enlightenment at last unlocked the gates of the ghettos, the Jews had forgotten how to live in unfettered freedom. The *haredim* are the descendants of those who decided to preserve the ghetto's restrictions of their own free will.

This freely made decision to reject freedom was something quite new, and it would demand tremendous, never-ending efforts. Their chosen strategy was not to change, to freeze things as they were, down to the level of their clothing: they thus continued to wear the fashion they were wearing at the moment the decision was made. Since the rest of the world moved onward, this effectively created a distinct Orthodox uniform. This in turn made it easier for them to force compliance on their entire community. It is not clothing, however, that makes the man, but the content and form of his life. So the community set out to fill the lives of its members to such a degree that the attractions of the outside world would hold no danger.

A major obstacle promised to be the military service that is compulsory for all Israeli citizens. In the state's early days, the *haredim* convinced Ben-Gurion to exempt their best students from military service, on the grounds that its profane way of life was inimical to the holy way of Torah. Ben-Gurion, atheist that he was, recognized the cultural importance of their enterprise. He probably also saw in them a remnant of the world into which he himself had been born, which after Auschwitz seemed on the verge of extinction. This act of misplaced sentimentality was to have unforeseen consequences. The rabbis now had a double incentive to multiply the number of yeshiva students. In order to keep them out of the military, they had to spend all their time at a yeshiva and were not allowed to work. This was the main condition for their political party, Agudat Yisrael, to join Begin's first coalition: that funds be allocated to the support of yeshiva students.

The *haredim* had initially been anti-Zionist, as Zionism seemed to preempt the intentions and actions of God. The Holocaust destroyed the center of the *haredi* world, and for the next thirty years the survivors concentrated on building new centers, primarily in Israel and the United States. Israel's wars interested them to the extent that their own communities were affected, but the price of peace was not important to them. They had no problem with returning Sinai to Egypt and foresaw no problem in transferring holy sites to the Palestinians. The whole thing is temporary one way or the other: someday God will fulfill His promises to the Jews. This flexibility gave the *haredim* great political power in the 1980s, when Left and Right seemed almost balanced, leaving them in the position of political kingmakers. They would demand a high price for their support. First, religious legislation, such as that forbidding El Al to fly on the Sabbath, or severely restricting medical autopsies, which are seen as desecrating the holiness of the dead. Second, additional funds to support the yeshivas, which were growing by leaps and bounds.

Although prepared to support either side, the *haredim* preferred to do business with the Right, which was perceived as more traditional and less atheistic. This appearance of impartiality was burst in 1990, when Shimon Peres and the political leader of Shas, the brilliant young Arye Deri, connived to topple the national unity government of Yitzhak Shamir in order to set up a narrower one based on Labor and Shas. With a dozen parties and a number of turncoats, the arithmetic was fiendishly complicated, but at the end of the turmoil the Ashkenazi rabbis had decreed that their two parties would not join the atheists; by default, the Oriental *haredim* of Shas had to follow suit. Kingmakers no longer, the *haredim* had placed themselves firmly in the camp of the Right.

This was no vague Sasson-like preference for the traditionalists of the Likud combined with skepticism of the Arabs; it was a return to a full-blown rejection of the pragmatism of social Zionism. But this time, from the opposite side: no longer a rejection of its ideology with an indifference to its outcome, but a rejection of its ideology with the determination to hold on to all of its yields. The *haredim* had moved from the outer periphery of the Zionist enterprise to its very center—and had done so without ever bearing the brunt of military and reserve service. Moreover, even their participation in the country's economic burden was minimal, as those tens of thousands of men in their yeshivas were not working. Once they were old enough not to go into the army, they left the yeshivas but lacked the training to be as productive as their literacy and intelligence could have enabled them to be.

The ultra-Orthodox have an exceedingly high birthrate and a very low level of income. They live in small and cramped quarters—in poverty.

Yossi Beilin, a leader of the mainstream tribe, one of the architects of Oslo, and a spokesman for rationalism and Western values, recently referred to their rapid expansion as a blight. Numerous children growing up in poverty are stunted, robbed of their potential, whether they are Palestinians or ultra-Orthodox. To which anyone in the know could respond only with disdain. Ask the police, who invest exactly no funds at all in preventive measures to combat crime in the ultra-Orthodox neighborhoods, knowing that there is no need. The strength of this community stems not from funds, but from the power of will.

As eighty years ago, so now, the rabbis and the atheists glare at each other over their radically different plans for the Jews. Bound together by the murderers who would kill them all, they are held apart by their widely divergent cultural language. Yet someday, should there be peace, Israel could have a smaller army, and the *haredim* could stay out of it without hiding in their yeshivas for years on end. They would join the labor market, probably with great success. The walls of the ghetto would finally disappear, and the various strands of Jews may start to talk with one another rather than shout.

Into this heated atmosphere who should stumble but the Russians. As the Soviet Union began to crumble, Jews were finally allowed to leave after decades of obstinate refusal, and by 1990 the floodgates were open. The pinnacle of surrealism was reached in January 1991, as the Americans and their allies prepared for war in the Persian Gulf.

Earlier that year, in July, Saddam Hussein had abolished Kuwait. President George H. W. Bush had mobilized the world, and in response Saddam assured his people and the world that he would "make the fire burn half of Israel" (why only half, we wondered). Israelis had all been supplied with gas masks. Hotels emptied, foreign businessmen left, and a mood of encroaching dread loomed over the streets. Meanwhile, an airlift of Soviet and El Al planes was daily bringing in three thousand new immigrants. It was the ultimate expression of Zionism at its best: the world going haywire and the Jews building their state.

By the mid-1990s, a million new immigrants had arrived—since there had been just over five million people in Israel before, this meant an addition of more than 15 percent. Yet it was never quite clear why they were coming: some not fully defined combination of wanting to get out of the Soviet Union, not wanting to see how post-Communist Russia (or Ukraine or Belarus) would turn out, the unaccustomed ease of getting to a quasi-Western country if you could demonstrate a degree of Jewishness, hope for a better standard of living, rejoining long-lost cousins, and so on. No one pretended that Zionism was a major motive for most of these immigrants, but neither could they have told themselves that they were moving to a Middle Eastern version of Cincinnati. As they got off the planes, they were handed citizenship papers and gas masks.

They brought unusual baggage: pianos and violins and books by the shipload. Ten years later, there must be a dozen Russian-language bookstores in Jerusalem alone, with signs in Russian (*"Knygi"*). And pork stores, also with Russian-only signs. At one point, there were thirteen different Russian-language newspapers. There is a Russian radio station and a theater troupe of Russians (who perform in Hebrew). The orchestras were swamped with applicants, and a few new ones were founded. There were some other interesting results, such as having the highest ratio of engineers to population in the world, but this was not relevant to the main issue: How would these immigrants change our communal identity?

The mainstream originally spoke Yiddish, Russian, Polish, German, Romanian, Hungarian, Czech, and probably a dozen other languages; today they all speak Hebrew. The Oriental Jews likewise spoke a multitude of Arab dialects, Ladino, Persian, Turkish, Greek, and so on. The *haredim,* or at least some of the Ashkenazi ones, are unusual in that they have preserved Yiddish as a living language, but alongside Hebrew, which they also speak: their control of its depths is probably unequaled by any other group.

The magnitude of the problem was starkly demonstrated when in October 2001 a Russian airliner was accidentally shot down by the Ukrainians en route from Tel Aviv. All sixty-six passengers were immigrants to Israel or their relatives. Normally, the radio stations would have switched to a program of mourning and stayed there for three days—but they didn't. Unlike the suicide attack on the Dolphinarium discotheque, which was an attack on Israel in which most of the dead were also immigrants, this was neither an attack, nor did it occur in Israel, nor were the victims recognized by anyone except their families. So a large festival planned for that afternoon in the center of Tel Aviv continued untroubled.

It is still a mere ten years after the peak of the immigrant tidal wave. The dense social connections that exist among Israelis have yet to envelop the immigrants, and their very numbers slow this from happening. Yet there are deeper, long-term patterns that leave room for cautious optimism.

Many of the immigrants came in three-generation units: grandparents, parents, and children. The grandparents will never really learn Hebrew and never integrate into the society as equals. Yet many of them fit the national ethos: they fought in World War II, or helped liberate the camps, or their brother-in-law made aliyah in 1936 and was a Haganah commander in Jerusalem or the CEO of a famous export firm. Throughout the history of Israel, they were always there—stuck behind the Iron Curtain, perhaps, but still part of the story.

The middle-aged immigrants may also never attain the ability to speak and discuss in Hebrew as they can in Russian, and thus they will remain slightly diminished in our eyes. We will never appreciate the depth of their thought or the edge of their humor. So they prefer to huddle in a milieu where they can be fully themselves. None of this is stopping them from influencing events, and nowhere is this more obvious than in politics. Theirs was the first group of immigrants to field important political parties upon arrival. They are spread all over the political spectrum but lean to the right—except when they don't. They played a key role in electing Yitzhak Rabin in 1992, out of frustration at the inability of Shamir's Likud government to deal with their needs. They regarded the peace process with a healthier combination of hope and skepticism than did many of us who were committed to it beyond what reality justified. Being less committed to past patterns of voting, some of them swung to the right, assisting Netanyahu to win in 1996, then swung to the left in 1999, for Barak. Unexpected but true: these new voters with no previous experience of democracy are adding volatility to Israeli democracy, breaking down entrenched voting patterns. You cannot marginalize a group that routinely swings elections.

And the children? They serve in the army. If one were to seek a single explanation for the cohesion of Israeli society and its ability to integrate masses of newcomers, this might be it. The central fact about military service is its universality; even today, when the distance between ideal and reality is growing, the essence has not changed significantly. With the exception of the ultra-Orthodox and the Israeli Arabs, every male either serves in the army or has a good reason not to; to a lesser extent, this is true also of the women.

Men serve three years, usually at age eighteen. Everyone starts with basic training, followed by professional training; depending on the unit, these courses take six to eight months. In most cases, officers will be chosen from rank-and-file soldiers who have proven their abilities and will be trained for an additional six months or so. Upon commission, they will sign on for an additional year of service. The pay for the entire three years is meager, allowing soldiers to buy cigarettes, candy bars, and shampoo at the canteen, but not much else. They can expect to be engaged in life-threatening activities throughout their service, even when not at war, operating lethal equipment of immense destructive power while sleeping short hours under harsh conditions. By the time they have completed their service, they can expect their country to have spent more on their training than many will earn in their lifetimes; in return, they will have been given responsibility such as many of their peers in other societies will never have. They will have operated complex tools, pushed their bodies far beyond what they thought they could take, and learned to cooperate with their pals on numerous levels; many will have been required to train others and guide them toward the same unexpected abilities.

They will also have wasted time, learned things they never needed to know, and dedicated precious months to ridiculous tasks such as painting tree trunks (white). They will have been transferred from place to place on the whim of some bored bureaucrat. They will undoubtedly have repeatedly spent hot, sweaty hours in the sun toiling at some ridiculous task, only to do it again the next day because someone forgot to pay attention at a meeting. They will have been solemnly told that what they are doing is of the highest significance, only to find out later that it needed to be done the opposite way. They will have risen before dawn in order to hurry up and wait.

During basic training, they will exert themselves and strive for perfection even at tasks that seem to have no intrinsic value, such as removing all dust from their equipment while living in a tent in a dusty field. Obviously an idiotic task, but it comes from the sergeant and so must be done. Yet the system will also demand that they understand exactly what is happening around them and how they fit in. Even before they complete their first level of training, they will be required to be able to think for themselves.

They will never be sent into action unless they know in advance—as far as possible—not only their own role, but the roles of their companions and immediate superiors. Only thus will they be able successfully to extricate themselves if things go badly wrong.

A few will have been ground down and rejected or ejected. A very few will be scarred for life. Most will have learned the ropes in a large, not always intelligent system. More important, they will have formed friendships of an intensity and depth previously unsuspected. They will have learned the remarkable power of humor to battle stupidity yet will also have learned its limits. They may also be breathtakingly unaware of their own class and socioeconomic baggage, since these play a very limited role at this intensive period in their lives.

At the age of twenty-one or twenty-two, without an academic education, they come out well qualified to face much of what the next few decades will throw at them. Coming from a hierarchal system that encourages its members to think for themselves, they are capable of functioning within other hierarchies without being awed by them. They will hold the opinions they choose to hold, not those put forward by their superiors, and while respecting the achievements of others, they are not likely to regard anyone as their superior at all.

And if they were unlucky enough to have served during the *intifada* or as part of an oppressive occupational force, they will have had to remember that black flag from Kfar Kassem while executing the policy of a democratically elected government. This is a challenge none of their peers in Western societies will have been asked to assume: the excruciatingly fine calibration of defending their country and its decisions while respecting the dignity and well-being of civilians who are not part of the same democratic discussion and who wish them gone. Some will have failed, most will have done their best, and almost all will be aware that the superficial platitudes that satisfy their untried peers in calmer countries have little to do with reality.

All of this holds for young women as well as for men—though perhaps the women will have suffered more of the nonsense and less of the satisfaction. In recent years, even that will be less true, as since the 1980s the military has been integrating women into many of its units.

Foreign journalists may wonder at the fact that Israel's military never threatened her democratic institutions, never encroached on the authority of her elected officials, and never embarked on a policy of its own. At times they think they are seeing such signs and tell their readers that the IDF is getting out of control or that the generals are dictating policy. Yet for the military to interfere in the running of a country, it must be a separate, clearly identified segment of society. The IDF never became that. On the contrary, it is a citizen army that contributed immensely to the cohesion of Israeli society. Throughout Israel's history, it has been forcing people of divergent walks to sleep in the same tents. It has forced them to work together and treat one another as equals no matter what their background; it has offered upward mobility to anyone qualified to achieve it, and it has forced them to face the intricacies of reality together. It is a "people's army" in the literal sense.

The Russians do face Israeli society with a challenge of a new type: that of integrating non-Jews. Coincidentally, the far smaller immigration of black-skinned Jews from Ethiopia contributes to the problem.

If Israel were really a racist society, in any of the meanings described above, she would never have welcomed more than one hundred thousand black-skinned immigrants. The Jewish community in Ethiopia has been basically out of touch with the rest of the Jewish world since before the creation of the Talmud—before the forging of rabbinic Judaism. Yet sometime in the early 1980s, when it became clear that there was such a Jewish community and that its members were determined to come to Israel, it was decided to bring them.

The story of their immigration deserves a separate account; some of it contains harrowing tribulations as they smuggled themselves across the desert to the collection points. Twice, in the 1980s and in 1991, Israel ran large-scale airlifts, dubbed Operations Moses and Solomon. Yet bringing them in was only the beginning, since most of them came from a very primitive region in northern Ethiopia and had no experience of life in an industrial society. Their cultural and professional skills could hardly have been less adapted for the task, and for all the good intentions of the Israeli authorities, there was the usual quota of mistakes and stupidities. Twenty years later, their integration has been only a qualified success: by and large they are a functioning part of society; most, however, have integrated into the lower socioeconomic rungs, and comparatively few have made it up from there. Yet given the original gap and past experience, it is reasonable to expect the process to succeed.

Along with the Jews of Ethiopia came relatives who were not Jewish. Likewise with the Russians. Since the late 1980s, an estimated two hundred thousand immigrants have arrived who according to halacha (Jewish law) are not Jewish. Yet they have learned Hebrew, live according to the Jewish calendar, and serve in the army—in short, they are indistinguishable from their neighbors. Their sheer numbers are challenging the way Israelis understand themselves, by forcing urgency on one of Israel's central questions: Who are the Jews?

The Orthodox establishment has a clear answer: A Jew is anyone who was born to a Jewish mother or who has converted. The affiliation of the people overseeing the conversions has been moot for decades, as the Orthodox establishment is not willing to share this privilege with non-Orthodox rabbis, and the non-Orthodox lobby in Israel is very small. (Most non-Orthodox prefer secularism to Reform or Conservative Judaism.) Those two hundred thousand immigrants, however, may be making that issue irrelevant, since they are creating a new reality, one in which there are many Israelis who are culturally Jewish but not religiously so. Zionism intended to create a Hebrew-speaking sovereign society for Jews, as the United Kingdom is a society of English-speaking British. If the Hebrew-speaking Israelis are Jews, are these people not also?

There is another group of non-Jewish immigrants. These are the foreign workers who have made Israel their permanent residence and are raising families here: Nigerians, Colombians, Filipinos, Romanians, and others. At present estimate, there are perhaps six thousand children of such families who were born in Israel, speak Hebrew, and consider themselves Israelis. One of them died at the Dolphinarium, along with her Russian-Israeli teenager friends.

The founding fathers of Zionism, with their manifold hues, would have appreciated the dialetic. By creating a Jewish state, they changed the terms of Jewish existence. Once the terms were changed, the issues changed accordingly. Will one outcome of Zionism eventually be a redefining of Judaism to include anyone who wishes to partake in the Jewish national project? It is too early to say. Yet the mere possibility underlines the degree to which the claim that "Israel is racist" is an unfounded slander.

For her Jewish citizens of all stripes and colors, including possibly even for her neither-Jewish-nor-Arab citizens, Israel is a country of immigrants, with all the problems and advantages that come with that description. Once the immigrants make their new country their own, she is truly their own. The pervading loyalty that most Israelis feel to their country, their pride in her, and their obstinacy in defending her in the face of never-ending challenges speak to this better than any theoretical treatise.

But what about the Arabs? If Israel is not the multilayered racist society some people claim, perhaps she is nevertheless an apartheid state of Jews discriminating against Arabs?

The meaning of this accusation should be briefly fleshed out. At the heart of both the American racism against blacks and the South African apartheid system were legal measures of segregation. Intended or not—and they were mostly intended—these measures discriminated against blacks, severely limited their freedom and life options, and were, of course, humiliating. While purporting merely to separate blacks from whites, in reality the separation was hierarchical, with power and wealth going to whites, degradation and poverty going to blacks. Indeed, this was the original motivation for the laws and the social system they created: to roll back the emancipation of the blacks in late-nineteenth-century America (the "Jim Crow" laws from the 1880s) and to roll back the migration of blacks from the countryside to the cities in South Africa (the apartheid laws from the 1940s). Underlying, motivating, and preserving both systems was a deep-seated and all-pervading prejudice, hatred, or fear felt by whites against blacks.

Many Palestinian speakers and some of their allies describe the entire Zionist project in terms of apartheid, because its result will be that parts of the disputed territory will become Jewish and other parts Arab, and this will be less than the Palestinians would have gotten had the Zionists never come or should they simply disappear. Proponents of this position are effectively saying that the very existence of a Jewish state is immoral and unacceptable. The accusation being dealt with here, however, is less extreme and centers not on the Palestinians in the West Bank and Gaza, who will be the citizens of a sovereign Palestine once their war with Israel is resolved, but rather on the Arab citizens of Israel. There are about one and a quarter million of them—almost one-fifth of the population. Most are descended from Palestinians who didn't leave in 1948; at least one hundred thousand have come back since then, usually reuniting with family members who never left.

The situation of Israeli Arabs is much better than that of blacks under either Jim Crow or South African apartheid, although there is much that Israeli Jews could be doing better. And, at least since the collapse of the peace process, there are some significant things the Israeli Arabs could be doing better, too.

There are no Jim Crow or apartheid laws against the Arabs. Legally, Arabs enjoy full equality with Jews. Israel is a democracy, and everyone is equal before the law. The very fact that Israel must defend herself by explaining this is a sign of how successful her detractors have been in pressing their insidious case. Israel's Arabs vote and can be elected and are the only Arabs in the Middle East who participate in fully democratic elections. Following the elections of 2003, they have three political parties, but there is nothing to stop them from uniting into one; if they did, it would be the third largest party in the country. So far they have preferred to split their votes, while many of them vote for the same parties as the rest of us: Meretz, Labor, and Likud all sponsor Arab candidates, and believe it or not, in 1999 even Shas garnered one of its seventeen MKs from Arab votes (meaning that more than thirty thousand Arabs voted for Shas). Moreover, as few outsiders realize, Israel has two official languages, Hebrew and Arabic—an Arab MK, for example, can make his speeches in the Knesset in Arabic. In addition, the Israeli Arabs' standard of living is considerably higher than in most Arab countries, which isn't surprising since Israel is richer than its neighbors. They have their own press, their representatives regularly participate in political discussions, and they are habitually interviewed in the Israeli media, where they are uninhibited in telling Israeli Jews what they think.

Unfortunately, this positive litany cannot be taken much further, and much of the picture is negative. Arabs are the poorest, least-educated segment of Israeli society. Unemployment is always higher among them than any other group. While there are no anti-Arab laws on the books, nor could there be without the Supreme Court striking them down, there are laws that are slanted against them. An important example is the ability to acquire land, which is crucial for a segment of society that is still disproportionately rural. Most land in Israel is owned not by individuals, but by the Jewish National Fund which allocates plots to individuals for forty-nine or ninety-nine years. The officials of the JNF can make life hard for anyone without there being clear discrimination, and in the case of Arabs, this bureaucratic practice is so entrenched that even the courts have begun to intervene. A second example are the laws that allocate higher governmental financial support, such as government-funded mortgages or child support, to families where at least one parent served in the military. You would think this hurts the ultra-Orthodox and the immigrants as much as the Arabs, but there are other laws that recompense *haredim* or immigrants, while there aren't such laws for Arabs. (As this is being written, the Supreme Court is deliberating the entire concept of connecting financial support to military service.)

The infrastructure in Arab towns is worse, on all levels, than that of the Jews. Even the fact that they have towns took years to be officially noticed: the legal distinction between an urban and a rural community entails a significant difference in funding, and small towns are eager to be recognized as cities. With the exception of Nazareth, which Israel inherited as an Arab city, no Arab "village" was accorded that status into the 1980s. In mixed cities such as Tel Aviv–Jaffa, Haifa, and Acre, the Arab neighborhoods are among the poorest. Their schools are more crowded, the streets less often paved, the municipal services of poorer quality. Aren't segregated neighborhoods and townships just what Jim Crow and apartheid were all about?

The clear and resounding answer is that these segregated townships prove nothing of the sort. Rural Jews and Palestinians have not shared villages in centuries, if ever. There were no Jews in Um el Fahem, Kfar Kassem, or Arabeh, ever, and the last Jewish family in Peki'in left generations ago. Nowadays, Um el Fahem, Kfar Kassem, and Arabeh have grown to be midsize towns and are no longer rural, but there are still no Jews there, nor are there any who want to move there. The same, merely reversed, is true of Petach Tikva, Zichron Yaacov, or Rishon LeZion, Jewish agricultural villages that have grown to be cities. The situation in the larger cities is a bit less decisive, but in Jaffa, Haifa, and Acre, to name the three most important mixed cities (Jerusalem is a case unto itself), the different communities tend to concentrate in their own neighborhoods.

The reason for this division, which is not segregation, is simple: Jews and Arabs have different cultures, and most people on both sides have no wish to change this. Arabs speak Arabic and send their children to Arab schools; their holidays are different, as is their preferred music and at least partly also the television stations they watch and the literature they read. Individual Arabs sometimes move into Jewish neighborhoods in larger cities—I have an Arab neighbor two doors down from me—but they are the exception that prove the rule. I also know of a case where a Jewish woman moved with her two children to an Arab town, where she was welcomed as an individual; but it was also made clear to her that she must not be the harbinger of a movement of Jews into the town.

Living in separate areas does not mean living without contact. Both communities enjoy full freedom of movement, and some activities are done together. Transportation, commerce, theaters and culture, vacations—in these and many other activities, there are no divisions between Arabs and Jews, unless they be voluntary, in that rural Arabs are unlikely to be interested in concerts of the philharmonic (but neither are most ultra-Orthodox Jews).

The question therefore is not whether the Jews and Arab citizens of Israel will one day assimilate and mix to the degree that their communal identities are blurred, as may be happening in middle-class America and perhaps one day will be conceivable in South Africa. That is not the goal in Israel, nor is it something to strive for. Rather, the question is whether the two communities can learn to live in peaceful coexistence, with mutual respect and partnership in sharing their country. And the question behind that is whether there is racial (or ethnic) prejudice against Arabs.

The answer, unfortunately, is yes. The cultural differences themselves need not be negative, but they are reinforced, all too often, by mistrust and animosity. Put simply, many Israeli Jews don't like Arabs. Modern Hebrew mostly has nothing special to say about Arabs, but there are some denigrating sayings, such as *avoda aravit* ("Arab work"), which means unprofessional or low-quality work. Arabs are frequently employed in menial jobs, creating and reinforcing a Jewish prejudice that Arabs have less dignity and can be expected to do tasks a self-respecting Jew would not. Once on the job, they are often treated as second-class people who can be ordered around and reprimanded in a way a Jew could not. Even here, however, the picture is not monolithic, and just about every Arab worker, including the non-Israeli ones, has a story about an Israeli employer who went out of his way to be fair—alongside the story of an exploitative employer who insulted and wounded his dignity.

Since Jews are the majority in Israel, these social norms make a difference. Because of their lower level of education, Arabs generally have lower-paying jobs and lower status. Yet even those who do complete a higher education have fewer options to choose from. The chance that a young Arab straight out of a university will land a good job in a Jewish company is not high, for example. Social contacts between Jews and Arabs are not very common, except in two corners of society: the non-Zionist far Left and the underworld. Elsewhere there are sometimes fine collegial relations among professionals, but these are not often full-fledged social contacts.

To this glum picture, however, must be added the fact that Arabs have never, anywhere, regarded Jews as their equals, unless it be beyond the perimeters of the Arab world. Ashkenazi Jews have no tradition of relating to Arabs one way or the other, but Oriental Jews remember centuries of Arab disdain (tempered by Westernized tolerance in some places in the last century before Zionism). Now that the power structures have been changed so dramatically, not all Jews rise to the challenge of not doing to the other what you would not like done to you.

In the 1990s, as the Israeli-Palestinian conflict seemed to be winding down, internal Arab-Jewish relations also seemed to be improving. A growing number of Arab commercial centers, restaurants, and bed-and-breakfast establishments derived most of their business from Jewish customers, and with wealthy Arab tourists from Jordan and the Gulf states in West Jerusalem's largest mall, the local Arabs weren't noticed anymore. Yet this improvement merely underlined how much mending there remained to be done.

The explanation for this is complex, beginning with the Arabs' cultural inability to cope with the modern world. Most Arab societies have not yet figured out how to combine their way of life with the benefits that democracy and free markets can offer. I cannot say why this is so, but its power as a justification for the backwardness of the Arab section of Israeli society is quite limited: even if there is an objective problem, it is the task of the state to deal with it. Second, the Arab minority in Israel is of the same nationality as the enemies of Israel. This also should not be relevant, as there is no intrinsic correlation between national identity and funding for sewage projects. In the real world of politics, however, it isn't so simple. Israeli governments are always built on coalitions of various parties. One party—usually the largest, but sometimes the leading party of the largest camp—offers incentives to other parties to join and support it, until it has created a majority. More will be offered to whoever can afford not to join, unless he is so politically distant as not to be worth talking to. The Arab parties have traditionally been seen as closer to Labor than to Likud, by virtue of their policies vis-à-vis the Palestinians; in practice, this has meant that Likud never tried to entice the Arabs to vote for them in large numbers, and Labor never had to pay for their support. This may perhaps be similar to the position of black voters in America, who were for a long time taken for granted by the Democrats and not wooed by the Republicans.

Even serving in the army does not completely break down the barriers. Arab citizens of Israel are not expected to serve in the army. But some do. For which a word of explanation is in order.

A minority of Arabic speakers in Israel are Druze, who decided in early 1948 that Israel was going to win the war and threw in their lot with her. They served in the IDF alongside the Jews; the Druze town of Beit Jahn in the upper Galilee has the unfortunate distinction of having the highest ratio of fallen soldiers to population in the country. There is even one branch of the army that cannot exist without Druze soldiers: the scouts. These are men who are trained from earliest childhood to graze their livestock and to read nature as the open book that it no longer is to urban mankind. The army relies heavily on their abilities to patrol borders and track down anyone who penetrates the fences. There is at least one scout on every jeep patrolling the fences, and there are many fences, so we're talking about a sizable number of men. They are all either Druze or Beduin volunteers, and this partially explains their high casualty ratio.

Jewish politicians of all parties regularly speechify about our blood ties to the Druze, our common fate, mutual responsibility, and so on, but they rarely back their speeches with funds. The Druze are a bit better off than the Arabs, but the conditions of both are a scandal and indicate a deep problem: that Israel is engaged in an ideological project that can include non-Zionist *haredim* and Zionist non-Jews, but not patriotic Druze.

The language gap cannot be overestimated, because language is culture, and culture is what the whole Zionist project is about: creating a place for the Jews to live on their own terms, not as a conditional favor from their neighbors. The Arabs may speak Hebrew, but as a second language, and this is neither temporary nor generational. They do not sing our songs. They celebrate different holidays, have different historical memories, heroes, and goals that spring from them. They are not part of the Zionist ethos, and their quarrels with us are not intrafamilial squabbles. The Arabs in Israel are not only permanently members of another culture, they are members of the majority culture in the Middle East and would gladly swamp us if they could. Two hundred thousand Russian non-Jews have decided to join us, but they and their children are loosening their ties to Russia in order to join the Jews. Israel's Arabs remain Arabs and have no intention of becoming Jews, not even culturally.

Until September 2000, then, you had the following: legal equality with some hitches in implementation that were, however, being slowly rectified by the courts; economic inequality that was acknowledged by all and generally bemoaned but was nonetheless persistent; and social prejudice that was perhaps beginning to mend but was still quite potent enough to influence the economic sphere, if not the legal one. And then everything got worse.

A large majority of Israelis regarded as perfidious the Palestinian decision to respond with violence to Barak's offers in the summer of 2000. The Arab Israelis, on the other hand, spent the first week or so of Palestinian violence rioting in its support. No one in Israel had ever expected the Israeli Arabs to be Zionists, and everyone knew that they see themselves as Palestinian in nationality while being Israeli in citizenship, so their taking the side of the Palestinians in itself would not have been problematic. However, the Palestinians weren't merely rejecting an Israeli offer, they were demolishing the entire conceptual framework of the peace process by using violence to promote their positions—and the Israeli Arabs were supporting them with the largest and most violent riots in years. Reeling from the impact of the Palestinian explosion, the Israeli authorities made all the possible mistakes in facing their own Arab citizens.

The police used live ammunition in an attempt to stop the rioters and immediately began killing people. Israeli political culture is often raucous, but no one ever shoots Jewish rioters who are shutting down major traffic arteries. Offhand, I can't remember Jewish rioters ever torching gas stations and uprooting lampposts, but those are not capital offenses. During the first days of the violence, thirteen Arab demonstrators were killed, with no casualties on the Israeli side—unlike the Israeli soldiers on the West Bank and Gaza, who were in real danger from the firearms of the rioters, the Israeli police faced no such danger from the rioting Israeli

Arabs.[4] After a week or so, mobs of Jews also began to form, in upper Nazareth and in Hadera, and there was a day or two of clashes between mobs from both sides. Once we realized how deep was the precipice on which we were perched, the violence subsided, and throughout the coming years of violent *intifada* it did not flare up again.

It took Barak's government months to decide to do the right thing and set up a judicial commission of inquiry, headed by Theodore Orr, a justice of the Supreme Court. As this is being written, the Orr Commission is still deliberating, although observers of its proceedings expect its findings to be scathing against the police and their political overlords.

No matter what the commission's findings, however, the massive Israeli-Arab support for Palestinian violence had most Israeli Jews asking themselves what, exactly, their Arab fellow citizens thought the issue was and how many of them supported extreme Palestinian positions that don't accept the existence of Israel at all. These concerns were strengthened during the *intifada.* Political support for the Palestinian struggle aside, Israeli-Arab active participation in acts of terror against Israelis has always been minuscule. Yet since September 2000, there have been repeated cases where Israeli Arabs have supported Palestinian terrorists. Among a population of more than a million citizens, this participation is still tiny, but it's worrying. More worrying still have been the statements of some Israeli Arab leaders, including men who command the support of tens of thousands. Sheikh Raad Salach, a leader of the Islamic movement, has made inflammatory statements, including the baseless but familiar canard that Israel intends to destroy the mosques on the Haram el-Sharif, and MK Azmi Bishara has made statements supportive of the Palestinian war against Israel. In the elections of 2003, his party grew from two to three MKs, still small but not insignificant. A democracy must ensure its members' freedom of speech, and attempts by right-wing politicians to block a number of Arab MKs from running for election were struck down by the Supreme Court; but clearly some of the sentiments popular in some circles of Israeli Arabs are not conducive to peaceful coexistence.

An illustration of the problem was reported in *Haaretz* in January 2003. It dealt with the relations within the staff of the Association of Civil Rights in Israel (ACRI), a high-profile organization with a few dozen employees,

4 There was one Jewish casualty, a driver whose car was stoned—but this actually happened miles away from the areas where the clashes were taking place.

Jews and Arabs, many of them lawyers, all of them highly educated, and by definition unusually attuned to Palestinian grievances. *Haaretz* told of severe tensions between the Jews and the Arabs, to the extent that the chairperson of ACRI and some of the employees had been forced out or left. Readers were left with the impression that even in such an untypical group, where the Jews are far to the left of the mainstream, their Arab colleagues expect of them a renunciation of Israeli policies to a degree that the Jews cannot offer. If such a group cannot live together, we asked ourselves, who can?

The Arab Israelis represent an existential challenge to Zionism. The Jews deserve a country of their own in which to create the society that best reflects their communal will. Yet that country must also offer full freedom and equality to the Arabs who live in it. This will eventually be achieved by maintaining a large Jewish majority that democratically preserves the Jewish character of the state and, indeed, enacts it, while having a set of laws and a constitution that clearly upholds the full equality of the minority of Arabs and protects them from any kind of discrimination. Most European nation-states with growing Muslim minorities have yet to figure out how to do this, even without a war with neighboring Arab countries, but European failures cannot exonerate Israel, and we must continue to strive for such a just society.

The sorts of changes that are needed include a significant diversion of public funds into the infrastructure of Arab towns and educational systems. There has never been an official affirmative action policy in Israel, for any group, so that it is not clear if such a policy would be the right thing for the Arabs. But the professional structure of their segment of society does need to be changed dramatically so that their preponderance in agriculture and low-skilled jobs can be reduced.

Most problematic of all will be the task of educating both communities to better accept each other, because, unlike the situation in the United States or in South Africa, the discriminated group truly does threaten the discriminating one, or at least can easily be perceived as doing so. After all, Israel is at war with much of the Arab world, including the Palestinians, and Israel's Arabs are Palestinian by nationality, even while they are Israelis by citizenship.

Only once such a program of reform is under way will we be justified in demanding reciprocal acceptance from our Arab fellow citizens—but then, the onus of acceptance will also be on them. If their country treats them fairly, they will not be able simply to proclaim their allegiance to their nation against their country. They—and we—will have to find a way to work out these tensions. For ultimately this is not the story of a Jewish majority arbitrarily discriminating against a minority. It is the story of the larger Arab world, which has yet to allow the Jews to live peacefully in its midst. Israel's Arabs are caught in the middle.

Yet the story has an optimistic aspect. One of the most important indicators of human well-being is the death rate of children. In 1944, the last year of British rule for which there are data, the death rates for children up to the age of five for Jews and Muslims in Palestine were 4.5 and 21 percent, respectively. In 2001, after fifty-three years of Israel being responsible for all her citizens, the figures were 0.25 percent for Jews and 0.5 percent for Muslims. This is the lowest rate of death for children anywhere in the Middle East; in oil-wealthy Kuwait, by way of comparison, the rate was 1.2 percent.[5] The large gap in 1944 was not the creation of the Zionists, it was a reflection of the degree of modernity in the two communities. The tremendous improvement reflects advances in modern medicine and infrastructures that Israel offers her citizens. The dramatically improved ratio between the two communities indicates that far from the sphere of identity politics, Israel must be doing something right. No racist country could cite such figures, and should peace ever be achieved, the foundations of a better coexistence are already in place.

[5] Amnon Rubinstein in *Haaretz,* January 15, 2003.

CHAPTER

8

The 1990s: Deluded Decisions

When did the Oslo peace process finally end?

In June 2002, President George W. Bush gave a speech outlining a road map for peace. Essentially, it called for a peaceful and democratic Palestine alongside Israel. Connecting democracy to sovereignty infuriated many Palestinians, as the Oslo process had never made such a demand; Bush's speech could thus be seen as an official rejection of the Oslo process. But then, by June 2002 there wasn't much left of it anyway.

In April 2002, the IDF finally invaded most of the Palestinian towns on the West Bank, effectively abolishing Palestinian self-rule in an attempt to stem attacks on Israeli civilians. Since this Palestinian near sovereignty had been the main achievement of the Oslo process, the Israeli action was clearly rolling it back. But then, by April 2002 there wasn't much left of it anyway.

In February 2001, the Israelis booted Ehud Barak out of office and replaced him with Ariel Sharon by the widest margin in Israeli history. Sharon was elected to put an end to the negotiations that had been going on for months parallel to a wave of violence that had already cost the lives of hundreds. Since these negotiations had been the essence of the Oslo process, Sharon's election could be understood as an Israeli repudiation of it. But then, by February 2001 there wasn't much left of it anyway.

In September 2000, armed Palestinian men opened fire at Israeli troops at many places in the Gaza and West Bank. Since the *basis* of the Oslo process was that the Palestinians renounced violence and the Israelis began to transfer territory, this Palestinian violence could be understood as a repudiation of the process. But then, by September 2000 there was good reason to believe that the peace process had already ended, smashed by the differing positions of both sides as to what it was meant to achieve. Appearances aside, by September 2000 there wasn't much left of it anyway.

In July 2000, Barak made the Palestinians an offer that demonstrated the Israeli understanding of a just peace: Israel would hand over to sovereign Palestinian rule almost all the territories occupied since 1967, Jerusalem would be shared, and a formula would be developed to address the Palestinian human misery produced by the 1948 war and its aftermath, including the right of a limited number to return to their original homes or towns in Israel. In return, Israel expected the Palestinians to declare that the conflict was legally over. Barak had reserved a few concessions for the final round, but essentially he had offered almost everything Israel could afford to offer if she was to remain a Jewish state.

The Palestinians did not respond and made no counteroffer on which basis negotiations could continue. Moreover, upon returning home empty-handed, Arafat and his aides were greeted as heroes who had not caved in to the combined American-Israeli pressure. Though most of us refused to acknowledge it at the time, this should have opened our eyes to the fact that the Oslo process may have been brain-dead from its very birth.

You didn't need to know Arabic or follow the Palestinian and Arab press to learn how badly most Israelis had been deceiving themselves; Palestinians and their Western apologists were venting their venom in mainstream European media outlets. Take Tim Llewellyn, former BBC Middle East correspondent. Writing in *The Observer* on October 15, 2000, he framed the problem in terms of fifty-two years of Palestinian dispossession and castigated the Israelis for being duplicitous throughout the years of the peace process. They weren't really withdrawing from the territories, they had never stopped building settlements, they were ethnically cleansing Jerusalem and imposing apartheid laws while forcing Arafat to act as a quisling who arrests Palestinian activists at the whim of the Israelis. But all this, he told his readers, was minor. The real Israeli crime was that she expected the Palestinians to declare an end to the conflict:

> The Palestinians found out this summer that Israel wanted yet more concessions: their legal rights to proper, effective self-determination traded for a clean bill of health for Israel. For an ephemeral state, Arafat was to sign up to dropping the whole Palestinian case against Israel. For the administration of a sticking plaster, a deep and angry wound was to be forgotten: the exodus from Palestine; the horrors of massacre and exile; the right of return; all recognised by and enshrined in international law and United Nations resolutions.

Moreover, Llewellyn argued, the Israelis had the temerity to want some continued connection to East Jerusalem. What Llewellyn seems to overlook is that his demand for the creation of a Palestinian state without a formal end to the conflict amounts to the creation of a state that is still at war with Israel, hence a mortal danger to her survival. This, of course, can never be accepted by Israelis.

The frightening truth may be that while a large majority of the Palestinians have reconciled themselves to their inability to destroy Israel militarily, they still do not accept her right to exist as a Jewish state. Instead they intend to submerge her demographically, by returning millions of "refugees" to her borders, cheered on by many Europeans and some Americans. The symbols of this demand are the holy places in Jerusalem, which they insist Israel give up even before her demise, regarding any non-Muslim control there as an obscenity.

The fatal flaw at the heart of the Oslo process was that its Israeli propagators were unwilling or unable to entertain this thought. Faced with mounting evidence that it must be taken seriously, they scrupulously looked away, preferring to right Israel's wrongs and patronizingly assuming that if they did so, the Palestinians would reciprocate. This blindness stemmed from the seemingly rational assumption that the conflict was about practical injustices, not wishes and fantasies or irrational concepts such as religious destiny or historical purpose. Who in their right mind would kill or die for those?

Notwithstanding the paranoid delusions of many Palestinians and their sympathizers, the initiators of the process from the Israeli side—people like Shimon Peres and Yossi Beilin—were not evil, nor did they behave in a devious manner. They approached the situation with the intellectual tools of enlightened democrats, including the attempt to see every event from more than one perspective, to internalize the viewpoints of the enemy so as better to appreciate their actions. They could easily see where Israel was behaving wrongly or unjustly, by ruling militarily over disenfranchised Palestinians, and surmised that these injustices must be the motivating forces of conflict. In their rush to remove Israel's injustices, they convinced themselves that they would defuse Palestinian hatred; in their yearning for normalcy and peace, they convinced themselves that the Palestinians wanted the same things but lacked the tools to achieve them. Yet for all their intelligence and education, they were unable, or perhaps unwilling, to see that at the heart of their enterprise lay a simple logical fallacy: that if one side is wrong, the other must inevitably be right.

Israel may or may not have misread the sincerity of Egyptian peace feelers in the early 1970s. She certainly misread the Lebanese political map ten years later, allowing herself to be drawn into policies that were both strategically wrong and morally repugnant. All the while, the Palestinian occupation was festering, the repression necessary to maintain it was growing, and when the occupied populace finally rose up against it, the delusion that it might somehow be sustained was blown away. By the end of the 1980s, the commonly accepted wisdom about the Israeli-Palestinian conflict was that it was "about" the Israeli occupation and the settlements, not the Arab refusal of Israel's right to exist. Since Israel was the mighty occupier, she alone held the key to the conflict by ending the occupation and withdrawing the settlements. By refusing to do this, she was not only acting against her own interests, she was morally unjust.

The misadventures of the 1980s strengthened the assumption that if only Israel had been more forthcoming, things would have been dramatically different; perhaps even peace could have been achieved. In the mid-1980s, the cold war began to wind down, and soon oppressive regimes from Prague and Warsaw to Managua and Manila were falling, to be replaced by democratically elected governments. Even the Soviet Empire would crumble, holding out the hope of freedom to Lithuanians, Ukrainians, and Uzbeks. The vile apartheid regime in South Africa fell, and for a moment the rest of Africa seemed to be swept by the wave of democracy. Where once had stood European colonial empires, the young Asian Tigers were testing their strength. Even in Northern Ireland there were glimmerings of hope. Francis Fukuyama proclaimed optimistically that with the ultimate victory of enlightened democracy, the bloody warring chapter of human history was drawing to a close.

Apparently only Israel refused to partake in the wave of democratization, stubbornly depriving the Palestinians of their right to self-determination. For Israelis used to disregarding the rest of the world, this wasn't so bad; but for the Western-educated elites with their manifold ties to Europe and the United States, it was all most embarrassing. And as heirs to the Zionist tradition of actively forcing reality rather than waiting for a remote messianic future, they set out to rectify Israeli wrongs, despite the fact that no one in the Arab world had embraced the end of history and never asking whether the Palestinians might still cherish the goal that they had obstinately held out for generations: the destruction of Israel itself.

The first *intifada* ended officially in September 1993 when Yitzhak Rabin and Yasser Arafat signed a Declaration of Principles (DOP) on the White House lawn. But the *intifada* itself had already been losing steam for some time. Despite its heroic aura in the eyes of the world's media, the *intifada* had brought no tangible improvement in the lives of Palestinians; the longer it went on, the more Israelis learned to live with it. It may perhaps have prepared some minds to accept a final arbitration of their differences, but the road to this result must run through practical negotiations to achieve precisely defined agreements that would then have to be implemented. This began in 1993 with the process known as the Oslo Accords and failed spectacularly in 2000.

Oslo's failure could have been predicted, as some unnoticed pundits said at the time. One reason could have been that one or both sides came to the process without clean hands. According to some right-wing Israelis, the Palestinians had merely changed tactics and, using the strategy defined in the 1974 "Phased Plan," had decided to strengthen their position via negotiations, only to return at some future date to violence. Some Palestinians meanwhile saw the entire enterprise as a Machiavellian ploy to exchange direct and costly Israeli control over the Palestinians with cheaper but equally effective indirect control. In reality, however, the failure of the Oslo process was the result of more mundane causes than calculated perfidy.

Sometimes, to a limited degree, reality can be forced from its likely path by an unusual individual. A generation after Sadat, there are still no significant indications that the people of Egypt have accepted Israel as a neighbor and illustrations galore that most of them would welcome her disappearance. But since Egypt is an authoritarian state, the people were not consulted, and given the hundreds of miles of empty desert between the two countries, there wasn't much the legendary man in the street could do about it. Israelis and Palestinians don't have that luxury. Their conflict and its eventual resolution *will* impinge upon their everyday lives; moreover, the man in the street will have quite a lot to say about the success or failure of their efforts. Peace will come only when both peoples are interested in it, and *on similar, mutually acceptable terms.* The task of the leaders is therefore not to force peace on an unwilling populace, but to guide them firmly toward this possibility.

Until the late 1980s, the intractability of the conflict stemmed not from the resistance of extremists, but from the fact that the moderates on both sides could not agree. It was not the settlers and the Muslim Brotherhood who were unable to reach an agreement, it was Israel's doves and their Palestinian counterparts. The feeling that this was no longer so had grown parallel to the *intifada,* as Israeli members of the peace camp found a growing common language with moderate Palestinians, and the would-be Israeli peacemakers wished to take advantage of it. However, the tactic they chose was problematic.

Their assumption, based on the Egyptian precedent, was that once a true peace offer was on the table, a large majority of Israelis would support it. The problem was that as long as the PLO seemed determined to destroy Israel, a sizable majority saw no point in offering concessions. The best way to break the deadlock would be to appear before the electorate with an agreement that had already been negotiated, swinging the skeptics into the arms of the peacemakers and leaving the settlers isolated, at which point, it was assumed, the settlers and their political backers would bow to the democratic will.

There could have been other ways to achieve the same goal. Sadat broke the deadlock by his dramatic gesture and by reassuring skeptics in Israel that the war was over. Since the terms in the Palestinian case would inevitably be harsher for many Israelis than withdrawal from Sinai, one might perhaps have demanded of Arafat that he also make a dramatic gesture prior to the negotiations, one that would change the very structure of the conflict at the beginning of the process rather than its end.

In hindsight, this preference for sleight of hand over public political drama may have contributed to the failure of the process and the deaths of many innocents on both sides. Therefore the reasons for the choice are important. I see four possible explanations. First, the peacemakers had a bad conscience about Israel's treatment of the Palestinians and did not feel they could demand gestures from them. Second, the peacemakers were less sensitive than a majority of Israelis to the emotional price of relinquishing Jewish control of the biblical heartland. Third, they were anxious to dismantle Israeli control over the Palestinians and saw this as an Israeli gain, not a concession for which some payment must be made. Finally, and most disquieting, they may have sought a dramatic gesture but failed to achieve it and went on without it anyway. This fourth possibility lies at the heart of the matter, because of the basic demand of Israeli-Arab peacemaking: that Israel must weaken its military defenses and evacuate conquered territories in return for Arab assurances. In the Egyptian case, these assurances were given in advance and in sincerity; the result was that in return for weakening her military defenses, Israel received a strategic benefit of far greater magnitude. And what of the Oslo process?

In May 1992, the Labor Party under Yitzhak Rabin narrowly won the elections, thus returning to power a government that had already promised to exchange land for peace. For a while, nothing seemed to happen except for a wave of Hamas-instigated murders, which ended when the government deported 412 Hamas leaders to Lebanon. The international community condemned this, of course, as contrary to international law, but since it caused an immediate cessation of the murders, it was worth it, and anyway, the deportees were home within a year. Against this backdrop, Israelis and Palestinians, meeting in Norway, began the unofficial talks that were to lead to the historic breakthrough.

Initially, the talks were not only unofficial, they bordered on the treasonous. In democracies, elected officials or their representatives carry out the nation's foreign policy; these talks started without the relevant officials even knowing about them; as they progressed, they were sanctioned by ever higher-ranking officials, although the story later told was that Rabin heard about them from the General Security Service before being notified officially by his foreign minister, Shimon Peres. But he did not interfere and was eventually convinced to endorse them. In August 1993, information began leaking to the public, and shortly thereafter the sleight-of-hand tactic was used with what appeared at the time as wild success. The DOP was hailed, inaccurately even at the time, as the end of the conflict.

The Oslo Accords were trumpeted as a historic compromise on both sides. But what, precisely, were these compromises? Amid the congratulatory speeches, this was left fatally vague. Unlike the Egyptian precedent, in which no changes were made on the ground until both sides had signed an agreement outlining the final status, the DOP foresaw a "process" of mutual concessions, assuming that as it moved forward the hardest issues would become easier to deal with as the erstwhile enemies built mutual confidence from the successes achieved on the way. Perhaps it could have worked; but it didn't. And then it turned out that no "Plan B" had been considered. Moreover, the potential for failure seems to have been there from the outset in the widely divergent understanding of what each side had agreed to undertake.

Both sides agreed that the conflict would be resolved by the partition of the land and the immediate creation of an autonomous Palestinian administrative entity; they also agreed on a five-year time frame in which the rest of the issues would be decided. In order to enable the creation of the Palestinian Authority, Israel would begin to evacuate mutually determined sections of territory, starting with most of the Gaza Strip and the area around Jericho.

The Palestinians told themselves that they would end up with an independent state in the pre-1967 borders, including East Jerusalem as their capital; that Israel would recognize her responsibility (blame?) for the creation and duration of the refugee problem; and that a pragmatic solution would be found that would include the right of many of them to return to their homes. It was also clear to them that the settlers would leave. At most, a few small border corrections between the states could be envisioned, and they would, of course, be reciprocal. Since sovereign Palestine would cover only 22 percent of mandatory Palestine, the Palestinians regarded this as a historic compromise; no additional concessions were foreseen, and the purpose of the remaining negotiations was merely to work out the technicalities. In light of the tremendous compromise they were making, one gets the impression that they came away from the agreement with strong feelings of victimhood intact: this was a pragmatic agreement with an enemy who had proven too strong to be vanquished.

Israelis meanwhile told themselves that the war with the Palestinians was now over and that terrorism would cease. The dream of Jewish control over the land of the Bible was also over, and much of the biblical heartland would be transferred to the Palestinians. Not expressly articulated but acknowledged by all was the fact that many of the settlements would either be disbanded or end up under Palestinian sovereignty, which meant much the same thing. Jerusalem would be dealt with in a way that would preserve the Jewish connection to it, although this was hazy: no one expected the Jewish neighborhoods built since 1967 to be involved. The contours of the final status, including the borders, would be hammered out in negotiations over the coming years. Most Israelis seemed to have understood that the result of all this would be a sovereign Palestinian state, not a series of second-class Bantustans, as some in the press have alleged. The refugee issue was widely assumed to have been shelved, and even hardened peace activists assured themselves that the Palestinians understood that there could be no massive "right of return," since the point of partition is that each people would have its own state.

Some of the differences in understanding could have proven to be minor had the process moved forward satisfactorily. Had terrorism ceased and the two entities begun to work together on their joint future, most Israelis would have acquiesced in borders close to those of 1967. Some of the issues, however, seemed so intractable—notably Jerusalem and the right of return—that the audacity of starting the process without knowing in advance how they might be resolved seems incredible. We must have been desperate for peace, if we were so blithely willing to overlook the danger.

And a mortal danger it was, as the process sprang to life with a time bomb built into it in the form of the inherent imbalance of the entire enterprise. Only one side was called upon to take a life-endangering gamble: the Israelis. But why should this have been the case? By 1993, the *intifada* was exhausted and posed no major threat. The fiasco of Palestinian support for Iraq in the Gulf War of 1991 had severely reduced international, and even Arab, patience with the PLO. True, Israel's global image was that of an oppressive occupier, but worse things have befallen the Jews. The collapse of the Soviet Union had further deprived the Arab states of their main military backer and supplier, while inundating Israel with more than a million new immigrants, many highly educated and all of them highly motivated to build better lives.

In this optimistic scenario, the Israelis now agreed to sanction a Palestinian entity of growing independence, size, and military power. The

Palestinians for their part had nominally relinquished their claim to the entire land, which they could never have achieved anyway, and in return were handed control over part of the land, which they also could never have achieved on their own. For Israel, allowing the Palestinians to build a protostate meant granting them powers they could never have gained militarily, while voluntarily accepting restrictions that only a military defeat could have forced upon them. Tens of thousands of armed Palestinians were granted entrance to areas previously controlled by Israel, and Israeli forces were banned from returning. The most awesome military power in the region was purposefully weakening its defenses and actively enhancing the military capabilities of a sworn enemy, in the hope that the enemy would become a peaceful neighbor. In return, the Palestinians had to swear before the world that they would never revert to warfare, come what may.

In September 1993, Yasser Arafat gave his word in writing that the Palestinians would never return to violence as a means to achieve their political goals. In the years prior to the Oslo Accords, Palestinians killed about 30 Israelis annually. In the fifteen weeks between the ceremony and the end of the year, there were 14 fatal attacks on Israelis, with 21 dead. Despite Arafat's promise, 1994 was the bloodiest year for Israelis since 1948; 1995 was not much better; and both were exceeded by 1996, when 81 Israelis were killed—equal to the entire decade of the 1980s. During the twenty-six months between Oslo and the election of Netanyahu, before the upswing in the settlers' activity, almost 170 Israelis were killed.

The Israeli response to the skyrocketing Palestinian terrorism was not what might have been expected. Moreover, it was very different from what *The Guardian* tells you nowadays. As a matter of fact, if there is an accepted wisdom about Israel's behavior in the 1990s, it is basically the opposite of what really happened.

Since sometime in the 1980s, every poll of Israeli public opinion told the same story: A large majority—about two-thirds of Israelis—knew that there would one day be a sovereign Palestine in the West Bank and Gaza. Many thought it would be a bad idea but were nonetheless convinced of its inevitability. As time went on, the outright supporters of partition for peace slowly grew, and Rabin's election in 1992 was a clear indication that they were gaining the upper hand in the internal debate about the viability of "Greater Israel." A slim majority not only accepted the inevitability of partition, but was willing to vote for it.

The DOP was signed in midterm, so the electorate was not consulted, but the polls indicated widespread support. Its opponents managed to field a few gigantic protest rallies with hundreds of thousands of demonstrators, but most of them seemed to be settlers or the mostly national-religious hinterland from which the settlers came. The other segments of Israeli society all seemed either to be in favor of the process or unwilling to do much to protest it.

Then Rabin made his fatal mistake. Correctly reading the mood of most of the electorate and feeling that he was backed by a solid majority, he allowed himself repeatedly to snub the opposition in his customary blunt language ("They can spin around like propellers for all I care," was one of his gentler comments). Stubbornly refusing even to contemplate the possibility that the process might not succeed, he ignored the dramatic rise in Palestinian terror or, worse, pretended it had no significance and even invented a callous term for the dead, calling them "victims of peace." As the terror spiraled, the public mood began to change, Rabin's popularity slid, and populist politicians of the opposition headed by Benjamin Netanyahu began to feel wind in their sails. By the summer of 1995, the Israeli government was building bridges to the Palestinians, despite the terror, while severing contact with a growing segment of its own society. The internal rift was as deep as it had been in 1982–1983, with the opposite party in power. The crescendo came on November 5, 1995, when Yigal Amir assassinated Yitzhak Rabin.

The assassination was the act of a small clique of fanatics, embedded, however, in a wider context of dissatisfaction with Rabin's policies. The world understood this to mean that Israeli support for the peace process was flimsy at best and would later portray Israel as not being ready for peace. The Israeli Left, rocked to its core by the depth of the animosity, sanctified the peace process with Rabin's blood; there was now no chance whatsoever that Palestinian behavior would be tested empirically. Most interesting of all, however, was the response of the Right.

On the eve of the assassination, Netanyahu and Rabin had been evenly balanced in popularity. The morning after, deeply tainted by association with the camp of the murderer, Netanyahu was totally unelectable to anything. Six months later, he was prime minister.

Horrified by the depths into which we were descending, the political Right stopped pressing its case and gave up the argument. There were no more large demonstrations against the peace process until the last days of Barak's term, more than five years later. The leaders of the settlers stated openly that they dared not oppose the government, lest the demons on their fringe again spin out of control. More significant, however, were the actions of Netanyahu. As the elections of spring 1996 approached, he held a well-publicized series of seminars within the leadership of the Likud, debating the party's relationship to the facts created by Rabin's government. At the end of this process, he had forced his hard-line Likud Party to accept that the Oslo process could not be rolled back. The centerpiece of Likud's identity had been insistence on the Jewish right to all of *Eretz Yisrael;* Netanyhu publicly broke that and approached the elections as the party that would continue the peace process with circumspection and skepticism rather than with the wild abandon of Labor.

This line took on potent plausibility when in February and March, Hamas launched a bloody series of five suicide murders in eight days, leaving dozens of Israeli noncombatants dead in Tel Aviv, Ashkelon, and especially in Jerusalem. Peres, seeing his chance of reelection slipping from near certain to not at all, screamed at Arafat that the violence had to cease, and it immediately did. But this built very little confidence in either Peres or Arafat: if they could stop the violence so easily, why had Arafat allowed it to happen at all, and why hadn't Peres shouted sooner? Yet while many of Netanyahu's voters hoped he'd find a way to stop the process, he garnered a narrow majority only by assuring voters of the center that he wouldn't.

Once elected, he proved a disastrous prime minister. Instead of the hard-liner portrayed by the international press, he seemed to have no consistent line at all, on any subject. Whatever position he took, he could be counted on to take a different one shortly thereafter. He antagonized his allies, alienated his associates and aides, frustrated his supporters, and exasperated those of us who had voted against him but would have been willing to be pleasantly surprised.

This lack of direction wreaked havoc also on the peace process, not because he demolished it intentionally, but because he continually jolted it back and forth. He started by assuring everyone that he would slow the process but never stop it, demanding of the Palestinians what he called "reciprocity"—meaning essentially that they live up to their commitments, a demand that Rabin and Peres had woefully neglected. Yet he failed to convince the Palestinians (or anyone else) that reciprocity was anything other than a sham with which to trip up the process itself. In October 1996, Ehud Olmert, Jerusalem's mayor, abruptly opened a new tourist site: a tunnel through the archaeological excavations along the *outside* of the Temple Mount. The Palestinians reacted in their customary manner. Convincing themselves that the Jews were attacking the Haram el-Sharif, they called for a vehement repulsion of the Zionist aggression. The novelty was that this time they were armed, since they had promised the Israelis at Oslo that violence was a thing of the past and had thereupon been allowed to arm. There were violent mass demonstrations in most of the Palestinian towns; on the edges of their enclaves, where Israeli troops could be found, armed men fired at them from among the demonstrators. Fifteen Israeli soldiers and seventy Palestinians were killed in two days. Bill Clinton hurriedly hauled Netanyahu and Arafat to the White House, where they were joined by the ailing King Hussein of Jordan. Netanyahu dropped all demands for reciprocity and handed the Palestinians the single city they did not yet control, Hebron. From then on, more than 90 percent of the Palestinian population was no longer living under Israeli rule, a point to keep in mind when Israel's critics talk about decades of brutal occupation.

The sight of a prime minister from the Likud relinquishing control over the oldest Jewish settlement in the world (only a sliver remained under Israeli control), immediately after the Palestinians had violently reneged on their irrevocable commitment to negotiate their differences, should have convinced everyone of the depth of Israel's commitment to the peace process. But it didn't. We of the peace camp remained furious at Netanyahu for gambling with it; the rest of the world shrugged its shoulders and muttered that since we should never have been there to begin with, there was nothing very commendable in our leaving. And the Palestinians took note: violence can stampede even a Likud prime minister into concessions.

Following this inauspicious beginning, Netanyahu spent the next two and a half years talking tough and negotiating ineptly, pretending to be a hard-liner while handing over additional territory to the Palestinians while also accelerating the construction of the settlements. No one knew what he really intended or if he himself had any idea where he was going. Yet with all of his erratic inconsistencies, one thing did happen: The Palestinian terror dropped and by his last year had basically ceased. The Palestinians seemed to have felt that faced by an unpredictable Netanyahu, it was against their interests to give him any excuse to slow the process.

Intended or not, this lull in the terror seemed to convince the Israeli electorate that the Palestinians were willing to live up to their part of the bargain; this was crucial when in late 1998 Netanyahu's coalition collapsed, and in May 1999, Barak was voted in by a landslide. The Israeli electorate had resoundingly voted for an apparently coolheaded leader to take them through the final stages of the peace process, fully understanding that the time for dithering was over and the ultimate decisions must be made.

Hardly more than a year later, the peace process was dead and the Palestinians were launching their insane war on our civilians.

There were, it now seems, five major causes for the collapse of the peace process.

First, the Palestinians were to pay for their growing sovereignty with the cessation of terror. This should have been noncontroversial, since the terror itself was purportedly aimed at forcing the Israelis to relinquish their occupation, and now it was ending. Arafat demanded the right to bring thousands, then tens of thousands, of armed men into the PA in order to break the backs of Hamas, Islamic Jihad, and other violent rejectionists. For Israelis reared on the memory of the *Altalena,* this made perfect sense. But the breaking of the rejectionists' military capabilities never happened, or rather, it was done halfheartedly and never effectively, which amounts to the same thing. Arafat is not Ben-Gurion.

Second, the Palestinians were to educate and encourage their people to live in peace alongside the Israelis. Actually this demand was mutual, except that the Israelis had never taught their children that Palestinians are the scum of the earth, that they are descended from pigs and monkeys, or that it is the will of God they be destroyed. The Palestinians had been inculcating their children with precisely such hatred toward the Israelis (and Jews in general) for many years, they continued doing so throughout the years of the peace process, and they are doing so today. So does most of the Arab world. The most powerful examples are the video clips screened endlessly on Palestinian television that show the heavenly rewards showered on heroic children who have confronted the evil occupiers: these must be seen to be believed. I have never heard of anything similar in any other national conflict.

One result of such incitement is that after a while, the inciters and their audience don't even see it anymore: the lies become truth in their eyes. In August 2001, an Arab-Israeli journalist, Said Kashua, was invited to the

Palestinian TV station in Ramallah to see for himself that there is no incitement to hatred on Palestinian television. His host was Zael Abu Rakti, head of the station's news division. Abu Rakti took Kashua to the studio, where he moderated a live intellectual talk show whose participants included the mufti of Jerusalem, Sheikh Akrama Sabri; Dr. Ibrahim Elfaneh, an archaeologist; and Dr. Taysir Jebarah, dean of Al-Quds University. The mufti spoke of Israeli plans to destroy the mosques on the Haram el-Sharif. The archaeologist showed charts detailing these plans. The dean explained that there is nothing Jewish about the Western Wall and never was. All agreed, of course, that there had never been anything Jewish on the Haram and certainly not any Temple. The panelists also agreed that an old Muslim law forbids Jews to enter Jerusalem. A suggestion was made to call on Israeli Arabs to set fire to fields by throwing burning cigarettes from their car windows. After the show, Abu Rakti proudly announced to his guest: "You see? No incitement at all!"

As long as the peace process was alive, its supporters refused to see these facts. Instead we dismissed them with the assurance that as soon as peace came the incitement would end, that no one really took such things seriously, and that our interlocutor was simply proving his desire to damage the peace process, perhaps so as to preserve Israeli settlements. We further told ourselves that nit-picking wouldn't help and that for the larger goal of peace, it was necessary to disregard the occasional Palestinian lapse.

The third cause of Oslo's failure was that daily life for the Palestinians got worse, not better. Having spent decades in the shadow of Israel, which offers Western freedom and a rising standard of living, they must have expected that once the Israeli occupation was gone, its style of life would arrive. Instead, the opposite occurred as the PA developed into a typical third-world kleptocracy run by and for the benefit of Arafat's corrupt inner circle. Partly this was the result of a steeply rising level of terror against Israel precisely at the moment when its military options were being reduced. Previously the military government had used all sorts of ugly tricks, such as bribery, administrative arrests, bureaucratic chicanery, the use of turncoat informers, and other reprehensible tools of oppression. Only after the Israelis were gone did these tactics—frequently denounced on all sides—appear to have been useful and responsible. By 1995, Israeli forces were out of the Palestinian cities and most large towns. When Palestinians took advantage of this to set up an infrastructure of terror, Israel was left with blunter tools, including roadblocks between the Palestinian enclaves and the prevention of Palestinian workers from commuting to jobs in Israel. This created mass unemployment, frustration, additional terror, and so on: precisely what the terrorists hoped for. Still, during Netanyahu's tenure the attacks decreased significantly, antiterror measures were greatly lightened, and Palestinian freedom of movement and economic activity grew.

The fourth cause for the failure of the peace process was the continuing growth of Jewish settlements in the occupied territories. This was the one issue that clearly *was* Israel's responsibility, and her failure to do the right thing in this regard gave the Palestinians an excuse not to deal with their own failures. Between 1993 and 2000, the population of the settlements grew by some 30–40 percent. Given the fact that Israel was scheduled to evacuate most of the territories, this was indeed puzzling and raised justifiable questions about Israeli sincerity. There were two major explanations for the continuation of settlements. One was that much of the ongoing building was taking place precisely in the small parts of the West Bank that many Israelis did not intend to give up: the area around Jerusalem and the first hills above the country's narrow coastal waist. Second, Israeli politicians assumed that they could pacify the settlers by allowing them to build, secure in the knowledge that when the time came a majority of the electorate would back the dismantling, as they had in the case of the Sinai.

The fifth failure was Israel's slow and stingy withdrawal. The DOP unwisely stipulated that throughout the process Israeli forces would be withdrawing, until at the end the terms of final status would be agreed upon, coinciding with completion of the phased Israeli withdrawal. But there was no agreement on what these lines might be. Meanwhile, as the terror and incitement continued, many Israelis felt they were being asked to give up strategic assets in return for nothing. Moreover, they feared a trap, whereby Israel would divest her territorial bargaining chips and then have to pay for the end of the conflict by severing her bond to Jerusalem and accepting the right of return. The Palestinians, meanwhile, understood this stinginess as having a strategic significance of its own: that Israel intended to allow them only a truncated collection of cantons, which they referred to propagandistically as "Bantustans." Perhaps they also feared that if Israel held on to territorial negotiation chips, she would persist in rejecting the right of return and on preserving some affiliation with the holy sites in Jerusalem.

Blame therefore can indeed be assigned to both sides—but not equally. The crucial distinction between the Palestinian failures and the Israeli ones lay in their irrevocability. Murdered civilians are dead forever. Poisoned minds take decades to clean, if not generations. In contrast, settlements can be dismantled in months and territories not vacated in interim agreements can be included in the final status agreement. Moreover, the willingness to give up these territories can be tested empirically, so that cultural perspectives, subjective interpretations, and wishful thinking have nothing to do with the issue.

This is what Ehud Barak offered at Camp David in July 2000. Palestinian representatives and their myriad apologists have told how Barak was cold, devious, impetuous, scheming, unreliable, untrustworthy, and so forth—all of which may or may not have been true, and none of which is of any particular relevance. The only thing that mattered was that he had offered to rectify, in one fell swoop, the two failures Israel had made in the preceding seven years, on top of which he offered the Palestinians a final status agreement that was closer to anything they had ever been offered by an elected Israeli leader. True, he did not offer them everything they wanted, but neither did he threaten them with violence should they reject his offer.

Had the Palestinians been sincere, the best thing they could have done would have been to reciprocate by dealing with their own serious failures and continued to negotiate. The differences between the sides were minor by all accounts, since Barak was offering to dismantle the settlements in the Gaza and most of those in the West Bank and had agreed to discuss swapping land in return for the concentrations of settlers he wished not to remove. He was offering the Palestinians contiguous territories in the West Bank and all of Gaza, not "Bantustans," as Israel's critics charged in a conscious (and quite maliciously inaccurate) attempt to equate Israel with apartheid South Africa. He agreed to share Jerusalem and even indicated his willingness to seek agreement on the issue of refugees, although he was never going to let masses of them return to Israel proper. His offers needed ratification by the Israeli electorate, but public opinion polls were unanimous in indicating that this could be achieved, on one condition: that the Palestinians join in declaring that with this agreement, the conflict was now over. This was the Israeli demand that so angered Tim Llewelyn, as we saw above. But far from being an unreasonable demand, it was the point of the whole process. Reaching a mutually acceptable resolution while remaining at war or holding out for more concessions would have been insane.

It was the time-honored paradigm: the Arabs get territory and the Jews get words. Instead, the Jews got war, the Palestinians got even more misery, and peace became a remote and irrelevant dream.

If the Palestinian goal in the Oslo process was what its Israeli initiators said it was when they garnered the support of the electorate, the violent rejection of Barak's offers from Camp David through Taba is inexplicable, irrational, and deeply frustrating. "We were trying to give them what they want and deserve," the plaintive cry went up in the Israeli peace camp, "but they refuse to take it. Don't they understand that if they continue this way, Israelis will begin to wonder if they want more than we can offer them? What will happen to the peace process then?" What indeed.

The Middle East Media Research Institute (MEMRI) and its Web site (www.memri.org), which translates Arabic media reports into English, presents compelling evidence that long before Sharon's visit to the Temple Mount—indeed, long before the disastrous negotiations at Camp David in July 2000—important Palestinian figures were quite openly setting goals (in Arabic) that no Israeli government could ever accept and telling their public that should these goals not be achieved through negotiation, they would be pursued by other means. By 1998 at the latest, some of Arafat's closest aides—not fringe figures, but people like Abu Ala, Nabil Sha'at, Marwan Barghouti, and others—were saying candidly that the basis for the final settlement must be the partition plan of 1947. Palestinian minister of labor Rafiq al-Natsheh, interviewed on the PA TV on February 19, 1999, gave an accurate prediction of what transpired eighteen months later:

> The peace we hoped for is the liberation of the land and the establishment of a state. . . . If these principles are not implemented, obviously we will continue our political and non-political struggle, until our national goals are achieved. . . . We will not agree to conclude the fulfillment of our national goals before the Refugee Problem is solved, whatever the price may be. We will not conclude the fulfillment of our national goals before Jerusalem becomes the sole and eternal capital of the Palestinian State . . . this goes for the settlements and before that to

> the prisoners. . . . All these matters will be, again, subject to struggle in the phase after the declaration of the state. . . . If forced on us, due to familiar conditions, that not all that we wanted was written and that not all that we wanted was committed—does that mean we gave up our principles? The land is ours, the authority is ours, and Jerusalem is ours. We will not achieve our goals before the return of the refugees, and before Jerusalem becomes the capital of the Palestinian State on our land.

Is there is an essential difference between this statement and the position of the Palestinian leadership in the 1920s or 1930s? "The land is ours, the authority is ours, and Jerusalem is ours." He didn't add, "The Jews are our dogs," but then he was a government minister, not a genocidal mullah inciting a mob.

Palestinian apologists and die-hard members of Israel's peace camp customarily deflect criticism for such statements by finding equally repugnant statements on the Jewish side; having satisfied themselves that words are not important because everyone uses bad ones, they press ahead with their agenda. Yet it is hard to conceive of a high Israeli official publicly announcing that once an agreement has been made it will be breached, and if one is not made, the existing agreements will be torn up. MEMRI quotes many such statements.

The apologists are right, however, that the facts on the ground are also important, and none are more damning than those regarding the so-called refugees. Between 1993 and 2000, the PA was purportedly in a process of reconciliation with Israel, and it also controlled many of those infamous refugee camps. Its treatment of them during this period is instructive.

In the 1970s, Israel launched a bold initiative to resettle the hundreds of thousands of people then living in squalor in the refugee camps she controlled. Near the city of Gaza she built a model neighborhood—Sheikh Raduan—and tried to convince people to move into it, but with only partial success. Elsewhere, the project never got off the ground. The residents of the camps didn't want to leave them, perhaps for fear they would be dismantled and a potent symbol lost, as indeed the Israelis hoped.

These so-called refugees, most of them in fact descendants of refugees, came under Palestinian rule in 1993. According to UNRWA's not particularly reliable figures, the PA inherited 1.2 million refugees (683,560 in

Gaza and 517,412 in the West Bank); at the time, 1,288,917 Jordanian citizens registered with UNRWA, 337,308 Syrian, and 346,164 in Lebanon. Also according to UNRWA, the refugees constituted 75 percent of the population in Gaza, 34 percent in the West Bank, and 33 percent in Jordan. In other words, half of the population ruled by the PA regarded themselves as refugees, as well as almost 2 million Syrians, Lebanese, and Jordanians.

If both sides had in fact agreed that there would be a Jewish state within the 1967 borders and a Palestinian one in the West Bank and Gaza, you would expect this to show in the subsequent actions taken by the PA. Massive Sheikh Raduan–like building projects, perhaps, or the dismantling of UNRWA, at least in its relations with the 39 percent who were already living in what was soon to be an independent Palestinian state. You would not have expected seven years to pass without the slightest change or amelioration in those camps.

Peter Hanson is the commissioner-general of UNRWA, and every November he makes an annual report to the Special Political and Decolonization Committee at UN headquarters in New York. In 1996, he told of the Peace Implementation Program (PIP) through which UNRWA was upgrading its infrastructures. In the West Bank and Gaza, a total of $177 million had been invested, along with $34 million in Jordan, Syria, and Lebanon. There was a problem, however:

> I would like to share with you our exasperation at the interpretation given in some refugee circles to our PIP activities: this "expansion" in services is perceived as part of a conspiracy to settle refugees in host countries. Simultaneously, there are allegations of a "reduction" in services, which is attributed to the same cause, i.e. a resettlement plan. I mention this in passing, to show that our work is never easy and each word or act on our part is open to the most inaccurate interpretation.

If adding funds in 1996 suggested to the Palestinians a conspiracy to rob them of their unique status, the next year there was a shortfall of funds. No matter: in November 1997, when the PA should already have been deeply involved in the massive project of creating a better society, Hanson reported the following:

> Since 1950, successive generations of Palestine refugees have had an "organic" relationship with the agency which was created specially and only for them. Anything which affects the Agency has an impact on the Palestine refugees, and vice versa. No other operational agency has this "twinning" between itself and its beneficiary group. The Agency's ongoing financial crisis has made refugees very nervous all over the area of operations. They are convinced that the lack of adequate financing is part of a conspiracy to phase out UNRWA before a solution is found to their problem.
>
> And for them, UNRWA is a symbol of the commitment and obligation of the international community towards them as long as the refugee question remains. The end of UNRWA prior to that resolution is viewed by them as an abandonment of their cause. This is why for the Palestine refugees any diminution in support or services is seen as diluting that international commitment. To this day, I am mobbed by requests to reinstate the general food distribution which was cancelled in the early 1980s.

The refrain was repeated in 1998, and in 1999, following the election of Barak and his commitment to the peace process, Hanson returned to Palestinian fears of a conspiracy:

> The establishment of a new Israeli government, the re-started peace process, and the Sharm al-Sheikh accord have made the refugee issue the most prominent one in the minds of the refugees. Conferences, workshops, and seminars on the refugee issue are multiplying. There have also been rumours and media reports throughout the year, that UNRWA was about to be wound up, or closed down, and that the Agency's financial crisis was due to a "conspiracy" by the international community to "close the refugee file" and to force the refugees to settle where they are.

As'ad Abd al-Rahman was at the time the chairman of the PLO's Refugee Department. On February 28, 1999, he held a press conference in Ramallah, detailing the position of the PLO regarding the resolution of the refugee issue in the final status agreements with Israel. MEMRI published excerpts from two Palestinian newspaper reports on the event (*Al-Hayat al-Jadida* and *Al-Ayyam,* March 1, 1999):

> Abd Al-Rahman rejected the possibility of solving the refugee problem by absorbing the refugees in the future Palestinian State in the West Bank and the Gaza Strip. "The refugees will not be satisfied with citizenship in the Palestinian State after its establishment," said Abd Al-Rahman. He added that the Palestinian State will be one of the states hosting the refugees, who insist on returning to their homes and homeland, in accordance with [UN Security Council's] Resolution 194. Abd Al-Rahman further claimed that the Palestinian Authority, like Lebanon, Syria, and Jordan, is a host of refugees, and it will maintain this status, after the declaration of an independent Palestinian state.
>
> Abd Al-Rahman added that for the Palestinian leadership no other scenario is conceivable but the realization of UN Security Council Resolution 194 that stipulated their right for return and compensation. The Palestinian side in the multilateral negotiations on the Refugee Problem only presents methods for the implementation of Resolution 194 as "the one and only solution we believe in." We are not willing to discuss any alternatives, Al-Rahman added.
>
> Abd Al-Rahman presented the PLO Refugee Department's position and stated that the department faced two main missions. The first mission is "to protect the political rights of the refugees to return to their homes, and to receive compensation for 50 years of suffering and loss of revenues from their property." The other mission is to alleviate the suffering of the refugees in the camps.
>
> Abd Al-Rahman estimated that eighty percent of the Palestinian refugees insist on implementing their right of return and compensation, a fact that foiled all the attempts over the years to solve their problem through citizenship in the hosting countries.

Incredible as it may seem, the PA's idea of peace with Israel included the notion that more than two million Jordanian and Syrian citizens, as well as hundreds of thousands of third- and fourth-generation disenfranchised Lebanese, and also about *half* of the population of the PA itself, must all have the right to move to Israel, even after a sovereign Palestinian state has been created. This position essentially envisions a reversal of the Arab defeat of 1948 or, to be more precise, a replay of that aggression through negotiated means. It disregards all of the mistakes made by the Palestinians and simply turns the clock back on them, as though they bore no responsibility for anything that happened then or since. It also places responsibility for compensating the refugees completely on Israel, to the neglect of the Arab countries whose invasions led to their original displacement and military occupation by Israel. Ultimately, it bespeaks a continuing Palestinian rejection of Zionism while paying lip service to Israel's existence.

One could, of course, brush this aside as mere rhetoric, or a hard-line negotiating tactic, although to do so overlooks the deadly reality that the PA was doing nothing to tell its citizens that it was time to start building a better reality rather than dreaming about what could not be attained without apocalyptic struggles. But in the end, the pretense that the Palestinians merely wished to end the occupation in order to get on with their lives could be maintained only until the day an Israeli leader offered them precisely that, and this is why the Palestinians rejected Barak's offers at Camp David, Clinton's framework suggestions in December 2000, and the Israeli positions at Taba in January 2001. The Palestinian strategy was not inexplicable, nor was it irrational. It was simply perfidious. In Palestinian eyes, the Oslo process had yielded the utmost that could be expected. It was time to move on to the next stage: bludgeoning Israel with violence until she made further concessions and ultimately surrendered her sovereignty.

CHAPTER

9

The Jerusalem Intifada: Resolve, Fortitude, and Morality

The Arabic word *intifada* means "shaking off," rather as a dog shakes off rainwater when coming in from a storm. The word was first used at the end of 1987, when the Palestinians told themselves that they were shaking off Israeli domination; to an extent, the description was accurate. In September 2000, they didn't need to shake off Israeli domination, since the Israelis had just offered to leave on their own and since summer 1995, more than 95 percent of the Palestinians were living in the Palestinian Authority and not under Israeli occupation. The Palestinians said this themselves, when they dubbed the violence "the Al-Aqsa *intifada*": not Israeli domination, but Israel's control over the Haram el-Sharif. Over the next years, they then launched more murderous attacks on the Jewish civilians of Jerusalem than at any other place in the country, constantly underlining that what was at stake was not the margins of the conflict or the last 5 percent of the West Bank. What is contested is the very heart of the conflict.

For as long as the Arabs have been Muslims, Jerusalem—Al-Quds—has been a holy city, the Haram el-Sharif has had two mosques, and (with the exception of the Crusader kingdom of Jerusalem and the British Mandate) it has been under their control. That the Jews might also lay claim to this mountain is simply inconceivable to them. For Jews the importance of Jerusalem can be stated in the simplest words: The dream that gave them their unique longevity was one day to return to Jerusalem. June 7, 1967, was therefore the most momentous day in two thousand years, for that was the day on which the dream came true. No other group in human history ever nurtured a dream for two thousand years and then saw it come true.

The violence since September 2000 should be called by its true name: the Jerusalem *intifada*: the Arabic word *intifada,* as it was launched by the Palestinians and will drag on as long as they insist on continuing it; Jerusalem, the city, the mountain at her center, and either side's relationship to it, epitomize the entire conflict. Until both sides find a way to accept the relationship of the other side to Jerusalem and specifically to that mountain, there will be no peace. Before that happens, each side will have to explain to itself what their relationship is and how it can contain the claims of the other. This process has not even started. It cannot be done by outsiders, such as the Europeans, or the United Nations, or even the president of the United States.

Can the Jews make a political decision to relinquish control over the historic sections of Jerusalem and the Temple Mount and continue to exist as a nation? This question must be carefully thought through, for its implications will reverberate for as long as there are Jews. If after preserving the dream for two thousand years we achieved it only to abandon it now, Judaism will be forever changed. Maybe its spirit will break and it will crumble; perhaps it will adapt and continue, all the wiser for the decision. Future generations may damn us for throwing away their heritage for the bauble of momentary peace; equally possible, they may bless us for farsightedly setting an ancient people on a path to renewed vitality—and then again, they may bless us or damn us for insisting to hold on to it. No one alive today will ever know.

Relinquishing control over Jerusalem would be the most momentous decision taken by the Jews since Rabbi Yochanan left the city to set up his yeshiva in Yavne, thereby transforming Judaism from a religion with a physical center to one with the dream of a physical center. What other decisions even approach it in magnitude? The Jewish embrace of the Enlightenment did not commit anyone but the individuals involved and their descendants. The decision to launch Zionism was also not taken in a way that committed the entire people—the consensus that the Jews need a state was forced upon them by Nazism, by European indifference to the Jews' fate, and by the Arab regimes after 1948. A decision to evacuate the heart of Jerusalem, on the other hand, will be irrevocable, in that it will be committed by the first and only Jewish political entity in 1,900 years. Future generations of Jews will not be able to write it out of their preferred version of history.

It was therefore an act of supreme hubris when in July 2000 Ehud Barak convened the sixteen men he had brought with him to Camp David and debated how much of Jerusalem to offer to the Palestinians. He didn't have a mandate to do so—far from it, he had been elected on a platform that called for Israeli control of the entire city. Nor had the Palestinians made any great concessions in the preceding days that might justify such a breathtaking gesture.

And as hubris it ended in disaster. For the Palestinians, the compromise offered by Barak wasn't remotely satisfactory. The very idea that the Jews might have a claim to their Haram el-Sharif was preposterous in their eyes. They then demonstrated that they had absolutely no patience even for any internal Jewish discussion of the matter, or for any Israeli anguish over the looming loss. In Palestinian eyes, not only did the Israelis need to hand over their most holy site, they were expected to do so as a thief might return stolen goods. Most of the international community agreed with the Palestinians wholeheartedly on this point and still does.

In the United States, the civil rights movement demanded of American society that it redefine itself. This caused years of national soul-searching, yet eventually the discussion was truly over, and all but some marginal diehards accepted the outcome. The issue of abortions has proven harder to close, and pro-lifers still face pro-choicers at its margins. A Jewish decision to relinquish control over Jerusalem is more significant to the Jews than civil rights or abortion, yet once Barak and his sixteen anonymous and unelected colleagues had abruptly made it, the entire world took it on board as an accomplished, irrevocable fact. Only Ariel Sharon, the leader of the opposition, still dared question it.

Ariel Sharon's visit to the Temple Mount on September 28, 2000, the day after David Biri was killed at Netzarim, may have been foolish and provocative, but it was totally legitimate. Barak's offer to divide Jerusalem had been presented to the Palestinians, not to the sovereign Israeli electorate, and Sharon by his action was attempting to jump-start the debate that such a decision requires. Barak, although still prime minister, had lost most of his coalition parties and seemed on the verge of falling from power, and it is the duty of opposition leaders in parliamentary democracies to seek to replace the prime minister. Barak's offer to the Palestinians had severely weakened Israel's negotiating position without achieving the slightest concession, and Sharon's action was a protest against what could be portrayed as inept negotiating. There was even an internal Likud reason for the visit, as Sharon wished to bolster his position as head of the party against a resurgent Netanyahu—although not pretty, such are the bricks and mortar of democracy. And of course, Sharon was also announcing to the Palestinians that not all Israelis agreed with their prime minister in his haste to renounce the Jewish claim to the Temple Mount. After all, the Palestinians had not accepted Barak's proposals, nor had they even been willing to discuss them, and Sharon was making it clear that not all Jews thought that the obvious next step would be to make additional concessions.

The essence of mutual acceptance is that each side recognizes the needs of the other, even if it will not always grant them. Sharon, even while making his multifaceted demonstration, offered a partial gesture of such recognition when he stayed away from the two mosques, essentially saying that while the sovereignty over the mountain should be Jewish, he accepted the sanctity of the mosques; this has been the Israeli policy since 1967.

The Palestinian response to the visit demonstrated that such considerations were all irrelevant. Since in their eyes the Jews have no legitimate claim to the Temple Mount—indeed, they are foreign usurpers—any Jewish action that said otherwise was a casus belli, to be rejected with disdain, fury, and violence. These were the people we thought we could make peace with.

The previous time there had been an Israeli symbolic act near the Temple Mount had been in 1996, when the Palestinians broke their commitment to refrain from violence and thereby forced the Israeli prime minister to make concessions he hadn't intended to make. Since early 2000, the Israeli intelligence services had been warning that new violence was incipient, even going so far as to pinpoint September as the likely date of its outburst. The attack near Netzarim was the first lethal incident. Sharon's visit must have seemed like a perfect way to start a rerun of 1996, but its instigators failed to take into account two developments. The first was political. While many of us in the peace camp were willing to blame Netanyahu for whatever went wrong in 1996, we were not so quick to blame Barak after his offers at Camp David and their rejection by the Palestinians.

The second difference was military. If October 1996 was a Palestinian trial run for September 2000, so was it also for the commanders of the IDF. They understood that the inconceivable was actually quite likely: in spite of all the solemn agreements, the Palestinians could be expected to again train their guns on their partners in peace. The generals set out to ensure that next time, their soldiers wouldn't get killed. They instituted special procedures, equipment, and training, and sure enough, when the Palestinians returned to violence in fall 2000, there were only a few Israeli casualties. Yet in the bizarre logic of the conflict, this simply proved to the rest of the world that the Israelis were the aggressors, a vicious and brutal colonial power gunning down harmless demonstrators. If the Palestinians hoped to change the structure of their relationship with Israel, rather than merely force some marginal concession, they couldn't have dreamed for more.

This chapter was written in the third year of the Jerusalem *intifada*. One can only hope that its worst novelties have been seen and that what remains will simply be more of the same, with an eventual dwindling of violence.

There were, roughly speaking, four stages to these unfolding events: the initial days, the months of Palestinian escalation, the campaign of the suicide murders, and, eventually, the large-scale Israeli responses. Each can be observed from four perspectives: that of the Palestinians, the Israelis, the Arab world, and the major Western media. At each stage, one may ask what they all thought was happening, how they responded, and what ideas and expectations informed these responses.

Stage One: The Initial Days

Starting on September 27, 2000, with the Palestinian attack on the IDF post near Netzarim that killed David Biri, the uneventful visit of Ariel

Sharon to the Temple Mount the next day, and the explosion of widespread violence from September 29, the first stage of the Jerusalem *intifada* lasted about a month. It was characterized by large demonstrations of Palestinian men and youth at IDF checkpoints. These generally took place outside of the Palestinian towns, from which the IDF had long since withdrawn, so that the demonstrators had to purposefully go to the flashpoints. Often they alerted the local or international press, yet the presence of the press never caused them to hide the fact that firearms were being used by both sides. Nor did this prevent the media from presenting it as a one-sided conflict. Such was the case at Netzarim, where twelve-year-old Muhammad al-Durrah was killed. The confrontation occurred outside of town, the cameras were invited in advance, the shooting was initiated by the Palestinians, and they could have stopped it whenever they wanted or simply paused it to evacuate the child. Lacking an autopsy, we will never know whose rifle fired the deadly shot, but the range and angle lend credence to the possibility that it was a Palestinian gun. (But as we have since learned to our horror, the Palestinians are willing to sacrifice their children if it leads to the deaths of Israelis.)

By the end of October, about a hundred Palestinians had been killed by the IDF, thirteen Israeli Arabs and one Israeli Jew had died in internal clashes, and twelve Israelis had been killed by Palestinians. Most of the Israelis were travelers and other noncombatants; only four were killed in action. Two were lynched. While these numbers were lopsided, and while the number of dead Palestinians could perhaps have been kept even lower, the numbers on both sides were higher and more balanced than they had ever been in the first *intifada*. This time, it was a shooting conflict from the first.

The Israeli Left predictably blamed the initial Israeli response to the demonstrations for fanning the fires. According to this theory, had Sharon not fanned the flames by visiting the Temple Mount, and had there been no Palestinian casualties in those first days, their justified fury would have spent itself and the peace process could have stayed on track. Leaving aside the amazing proposition that Israeli soldiers should have been shot at from close quarters without returning fire, this also assumed that there was no Palestinian motive for violence other than frustration at the lack of progress in the negotiations.

It is difficult to say what the Palestinians thought they were doing and why, but some provisional comments can be made. The Israelis at Camp

David had just made a substantial offer, to which the Palestinians had not responded. The post–Camp David negotiations were slowly restarting. The distance between the Palestinian demands and what the Israelis had already offered seemed narrow (if one takes their English-language declarations at face value). At this point, then, no matter how you look at it, the Palestinians decided to break the basic rule that negotiations were to replace violence. Did they do so absentmindedly? Unintentionally? Or did they hope for a replay of the events of 1996, when violence had stampeded the Israelis into weakening their stance? Most likely it was none of these, but rather the strategic decision cited above: The negotiations had yielded their utmost, and it was time to discard them, taking what had been gained in the process and returning to violence to achieve what was not being offered in negotiations—not the last 3–4 percent of the West Bank, but an unlimited right of return and the liberation of Jerusalem from Jewish hands.

The immediate Palestinian demand was that an international force be sent to protect them from the aggressive Israelis. This was in effect a demand to free them of the Israelis without the reciprocal payment of officially ending the conflict. It would have paved the way to an independent Palestine that was still at war with Israel and could still freely demand the right of return as the price for peace.

Not surprisingly, the Arab world vocally backed the Palestinians. More surprising to Israelis was the response of the West. If there was any abhorrence of the Palestinian turn to violence, it was muted, while the castigation of Israel for killing "unarmed demonstrators" was nearly universal. The best that anyone could muster was a condemnation of the so-called cycle of violence. This is a bogus notion that assumes the only reason the violence wasn't stopping was that each side insisted on having the last shot. But even that nominally evenhanded condemnation tended to be slanted against Israel, because, as Jacques Chirac explained to Ehud Barak, Israel, being the stronger side, must be the first to stop. Bill Clinton flew to the Middle East in person and at the Egyptian resort of Sharm el-Sheikh tried to bang together the heads of Barak and Arafat. A cease-fire was agreed upon, and Israel was to redeploy her forces to where they had been on September 27, but the Palestinian violence did not cease. Most pundits blamed both sides, as if Barak, having gambled his political life on the peaceful resolution of the conflict, was secretly eager to break a commitment he had just made to the president of the United States, while Arafat, who had returned to his people as a hero for not giving in at Camp David, was horrified by the violence but couldn't stop it because of Israeli actions. The sole remnant of this meeting was the decision to set up an international committee of investigation into the causes of the violence. Chaired by ex-senator George Mitchell, it convened in December.

The Israelis were stunned. We had spent the summer steeling ourselves to finally dismantle the settlements and putting on a brave face about the division of Jerusalem, telling ourselves that living at peace with our neighbors was worth relinquishing the dreams of centuries; even many of the settlers began to prepare for the move. August had been less hopeful than July, but September had seen the renewal of negotiations, and all of us knew the price that would have to be paid. And then it all exploded: seven years of assuring ourselves that we were moving into the postconflict stage of Zionism and preparing to enjoy our acceptance into the club of normal nations, gone in the fifty-two-second sequence on the evening news showing the death of a terrified Palestinian child. Once again we were cast as the evil, anachronistic colonial vestige, denying the basic rights of the helpless and downtrodden Palestinians, out of some inexplicable racist drive to conquer and control them or an insatiable thirst for their land. Only this time, unlike in 1996, we couldn't blame ourselves, nor could we blame our evil leaders. Barak was prime minister, not Netanyahu, and instead of stubborn demands for reciprocity, all he had wanted was a proclamation that the conflict was over.

Later, supporters of the hard Right would tell us they'd known all along this would happen. In October 2000, however, even most of the Right was stunned by the perfidy of the Palestinians and the support they so easily collected from so much of the world. As our hopes crashed down around us, we turned inward and united around the truth that was obvious to us, though seemingly no one else: Our war is just.

STAGE TWO: PALESTINIAN ESCALATION

November was a bloody month for both sides, but from December onward, the numbers of casualties on both sides decreased. One significant development was the steep drop and eventual disappearance of those

Palestinian demonstrations. Perhaps the public had tired of what had never really been a spontaneous outburst of anger. More likely, the arms bearers were setting in for the long haul. Either way, once the IDF outposts ceased to come under attack, the "victims" of Israeli "aggression" stopped dying.

The number of Israeli casualties grew as settlers were gunned down on the roads, then sank as the army figured out partial solutions such as lethal ambushes of Palestinian attackers. A second significant development was that the PA let out of its jails the terrorists it had been holding since the tremendous Israeli pressure of 1996. Thus was inagurated a policy of encouraging those with the know-how to blow up Israeli citizens. The first attacks were bombs placed in vehicles and smuggled into Israeli towns; some were discovered, and even those that exploded rarely killed more than a few citizens. Worse was to come.

Whether the Palestinians had stumbled into violence or premeditated it, this second stage demonstrated clearly that they had no intention of relinquishing it without something to show for their efforts. If one can believe their public statements, they were convinced they were fighting a war of liberation against a tenacious and brutal occupier who could be ousted only by force, as if the recent Camp David conference had never occurred. If they were surprised by the reaction of Israelis, which was quite different from that in 1996, they weren't saying so and seemed to believe that all that was needed to win was some additional pressure. But while the Israeli response may have been a disappointment, that of the international community must have been a comfort, since no one was telling them that they had destroyed all that had been built, and many in Europe supported their demands for an international peacekeeping force.

The Arab world, while backing the Palestinians with rhetoric, was not as helpful as they hoped. The Egyptians and Jordanians made it clear that they were not going to war to assist the new *intifada,* nor were they willing to sever relations with Israel. There were many gestures and few real actions.

The world at large deplored the violence and repeatedly called upon the two sides to behave. The popularity of the "cycle of violence" myth grew greatly in this period, with an interesting twist: Whatever Israel did, literally any military action it took, was deplored as an overreaction and cited as strengthening the Palestinian hatred, adding fuel to the flames, and accelerating the cycle of violence. Israeli noncombatant deaths consistently outnumbered those of combatants, but no action we took in our own defense was considered legitimate. Perhaps the Palestinians' distressing failure to achieve full sovereignty within the framework of the Oslo Accords was so disturbing to world opinion that nothing else could really matter until they achieved it: not their own crimes, not Israeli attempts to ensure their own security. That is the most charitable explanation one can offer, but it is not the only one.

The Israeli response was complex. The military was groping for ways to protect Israeli lives while adhering to Jewish codes of behavior. These codes acknowledged that one cannot use force without causing pain, nor can you combat people who would kill you merely by gestures or words. Faced with an adversary who is willing to kill, there is no choice but to resort to some sort of power, and the use of such power is rarely pleasant to observe. Yet it is not impossible to define a hierarchy of acceptable use of power. Murder—and revenge—is always forbidden. Killing should be avoided whenever possible, though in war people will die, and the decision to fight means accepting that. It is, however, essential to do your best to limit the killing to combatants. Other actions, such as destruction of property or the imposing of other hardships, should be avoided, unless they replace killing, since material damage can be repaired, while the dead are dead forever.

Measures taken by the Israeli military included threatening but basically theatrical actions, such as the rocketing of empty Palestinian police stations from helicopters, and practical measures to reduce the ability of terrorists to reach Israeli citizens. These included banning Palestinian men from working in Israel—which caused both great unemployment and growing poverty. As the attacks continued, each Palestinian town was encircled by tanks and roadblocks, and severe limitations were placed on freedom of movement for ordinary Palestinians. The Israeli security forces insisted that these measures were foiling homicidal attacks; yet they were also quite obviously causing great hardship for the Palestinian populace. It was a lose-lose situation for everyone involved. But was there any choice?

This is what the government now set out to test. In a stark contradiction of its own policy, whereby there could be no political negotiations as long as the violence went on, talks were resumed. Bill Clinton's days in the White House were numbered, and soon there would be elections in Israel, so a last-ditch attempt was made to reach an agreement. Near the end of December, the president literally dictated his terms to delegations from both sides. Take it or leave it, the delegates were instructed. The terms represented a step toward the Palestinians, with close to 100 percent of the West Bank going to the Palestinians, as opposed to some 90–95 percent offered by Barak, and Jerusalem to be fully divided by ethnic neighborhoods. The Palestinians rejected the terms without the slightest pause in the violence. Feeling perhaps that there was nothing to lose, the Israeli negotiators made additional concessions, well beyond anything that had been mandated by elections. These offers were made in January, at the Red Sea resort town of Taba, even while the murder of Israeli citizens continued. Had they been interested in reaching a negotiated settlement, all the Palestinians had to do was to halt their violence for three weeks while declaring that an agreement was in the offing, and the Israeli electorate would have been forced to express its opinion at the polls. But they didn't.

STAGE THREE: THE SUICIDE MURDERERS

The first suicide attack came on December 22, 2000, and was aimed at a group of soldiers at Mechola in the northern Jordan valley. Three were wounded, and the attacker died. It was one day before Bill Clinton presented his final ideas for peace, three weeks before the talks at Taba, and more than six weeks before the election of Ariel Sharon. There were three additional attacks before Sharon took office—and many more thereafter.

The suicide attacks were often lethal, precisely because they were guided and activated by the most precise targeting device ever developed: the bombers themselves, who tried to insert themselves in crowded places before detonating. Overwhelmingly they chose civilian sites: restaurants, buses, hotels, supermarkets, discotheques. In 1994–1996, we had tried to discern a pattern and told ourselves that early mornings were the most dangerous hour, as the murderers liked to spend their last night praying. But this pattern didn't hold. The murderers struck at all hours of the day or night, anywhere. All they needed was a group of Israelis to aim at. Initially, it seemed there was a standard profile to the killers—angry young men, marginalized in their own society. But this too proved to be unfounded. They came in all shapes and sizes: teenagers and grandfathers, poor and educated, unemployed and leaders of men, and, soon enough, women. In one case, a seventeen-year-old girl went to school in the morning, left in the middle of the day, and blew herself up in the early afternoon at a Jerusalem supermarket. One night someone sent three thirteen-year-old boys to kill and be killed at a settlement in Gaza. They were identified and shot as they crawled into the settlement and recognized as children only after their deaths. Another time someone sent two brothers, aged twelve and eight (!). The eight-year-old was sheltered from the ensuing pandemonium by one of the Israeli families on the settlement, until they realized who they had and handed him to the guards.

Early on, the murderers had slunk away from their families, lest their mothers, at least, restrain them. By late 2001, that was outdated. Bereaved fathers announced in the presence of their remaining sons that they prayed for the younger children to emulate their brothers. There were documented cases where mothers danced before videocameras, exhorting their sons not to falter as they set out to kill the Jews and ascend directly to heaven. These tapes were broadcast repeatedly, to great acclaim.

Slowly it dawned on us that this was not a radical form of negotiation or the despairing cry of a downtrodden people gasping under its yoke. This was something entirely new: a whole society insanely in love with death. There is no political goal to be served by such insanity. From time to time, human beings surprise themselves by inventing new forms of evil, and this was clearly one of them. Search as we might in the history books, we could not find a precedent for the suicidal drive of the Palestinians, straining against all barriers in their determination to die with as many Jews as possible and supported by their entire society.

And on September 11, 2001, the entire world learned that this phenomenon could be exported. The enemies of the Jews, it turned out—not for the first time, we noted with bitter satisfaction—were the enemies of humanity itself.

One way to explain this Palestinian ferocity might be to claim that the oppression they were suffering was unprecedented. If they were suffering more than anyone else ever had, you could see how their reaction might go beyond any previous reaction. To claim that the Israeli oppression was unprecedented in its severity is patently absurd, yet such a claim was routinely made by the Western-educated Palestinian spokespeople, in impeccable English. Listen to Hanan Ashrawi, representing the Palestinians at the World Conference Against Racism, Durban, South Africa, on August 28, 2001:

> Rarely has the human mind devised such varied, diverse, and comprehensive means of wholesale brutalization and persecution. . . . Sisters and brothers, never before has an occupation army imposed such a total and suffocating siege on a captive civilian population, then proceeded to shell their homes, bomb their infrastructure, assassinate their activists and leaders, destroy their crops and trees, murder their civilians at will, steal their lands, and then demand that they acquiesce like lambs to the slaughter.

It wasn't the fundamentalist—and, to Western eyes, outlandish—extremists of Hamas broadcasting these fables, it was the moderate Palestinians, those with long records of constructive discussions with their Israeli counterparts. Unfounded as these accusations were, you have to wonder if the Palestinians really believed them; true belief, as we know, is a powerful factor in history.

Another reason to overturn the natural order of things, whereby parents protect their children from death and leave strangers unmolested, would be if the natural order was already overturned. When future scholars analyze the Palestinian orgy of death, they might note that for many Muslims, the idea of a non-Muslim reign over territory in the heart of the Muslim world, Dar el-Salaam, is against the proper order. Christians reconquering Iberia was bad enough, but Jews blocking the road to Mecca is a disturbance of a different order. What was discussed at Camp David and Taba, unlike what preceded it, was an end to the conflict and therefore a permanent acquiescence in the Jews' sovereign presence.

There is also the fact that the hatred of Jews in today's Muslim world has reached an intensity to rival that of the Nazis. And not only in Gaza, but in Pakistan, where Jews have never lived, and in the Muslim suburbs of Paris. To put the onus for this on the Israeli settlers of the West Bank seems as convincing as saying that the Holocaust happened because Rosa Luxembourg was Jewish. Most Germans in 1933 never thought to participate in genocide—yet when the time came, they did, directly or indirectly.

In the interval they spent eight years inculcating themselves with state-sponsored hate. And it took precisely eight years of state-sponsored hate to do the trick in Palestine, starting in 1993 and reaching fruition in 2001.

The response of Israeli citizens to the repeated attempts on their lives and the attacks on the fabric of their society was stoic. We gave thought to every little activity that makes up daily life, such as taking a bus, doing errands, commuting to work, or shopping in the neighborhood supermarket. Nonessential activities were dropped, postponed, or modified. Yet we basically continued the patterns of daily life. At least nineteen Israelis have been murdered on the road to my neighborhood in Jerusalem, in so many attacks that I've lost count, but no one stopped taking the road, nor was there any noticeable movement of families away from the neighborhood.

As time went on, our security services got a bit better at forecasting suicide murders, and incredible as it may seem, we learned to treat them rather like weather forecasts: "Okay, kids, if you must go downtown, today is a good day because the alerts are down from 'extra high in Jerusalem' to merely 'high in general.' " Or when one of the kids was visiting a friend in Beit Shemesh: "Don't leave her house until they've caught the terrorists they're looking for to the south of you."

In the early 1990s, when the Palestinians initiated this heinous form of warfare, we told ourselves that there was no defense against it. By 2002, we were proving otherwise. Living in a state of high awareness, with police or armed citizens within a stone's throw at any moment, began to make a difference. In more and more cases, ordinary citizens noticed suspicious individuals, or a wire sticking out from a shirt, and sprang into action. A young Israeli Arab figured out who the man waiting with him at the bus stop was, coolly asked him if he could borrow his cell phone for a moment, then used it to call the police, who arrived immediately. Bus drivers kicked suicide murderers off the steps of their bus and slammed the door; pedestrians grabbed their arms before they could detonate and gave time for everyone else to run; in some cases, when murderers pinned to the ground seemed about to free themselves, they were simply shot. In early November, a potential murderer was shot from close range while struggling, but a second bullet set off his explosive vest, killing three of the men who had been trying to restrain him. That evening, the first shooter was interviewed from his hospital bed, and he refined the standard procedure: "Listen, guys, if someone's holding a struggling suicide murderer, the first guy to be in firing position shouts that he's ready, and everyone else waits; then, only one shot, and only to the head. Otherwise, look what happens."

Contrary to what you might expect, there have been no cases of mistaken identity: no innocent Arabs pounced on and shot while walking down the street. Israelis are quite careful with the weapons they carry. Moreover, it's a small country, and everybody either knows everybody else or their brother-in-law, or went to high school with their best friend's sister. I don't know anybody who lived through this onslaught who didn't have some connection to one of the victims. Yet quite early on, we developed the ability to filter the news: "An attack in downtown Netanya? Do I know anyone likely to be there at this time of day? No? Well, then, back to work." For those hit, it was devastating and will never heal; for the rest of us, it was disruptive and threatening, but not earth-shattering. Israeli society was never remotely near crumbling.

This should have been obvious even to the Palestinians, the pointlessness of their enterprise making it even more irrational and bizarre. If they were trying, in some macabre way, to talk to us, they were using the wrong vocabulary. The violence of fall 2000 could have been seen as an extreme tactic in the negotiations over the final few territories that Barak had not offered to evacuate; but ultimately the never-ending series of suicide murders of civilians took on a life of its own. No matter what interpretation you gave it, it was a crude attempt to force Israel to her knees; should it succeed, this tactic would be used again and again, both in Israel and elsewhere. Israel's response thus became a test case for mankind. Not crumbling, while admirable in itself, would not be enough.

The almost complete absence of vigilante actions among Israelis was also admirable and far from expected. Nothing would have been easier than to respond to attacks on innocent civilians with spontaneous reprisals and counterattacks. Much of human history would indicate that such a response is quite normal. Even the alleged Palestinian justification for their own crimes—that they were suffering grievously—could as easily have justified wrathful counterattacks by Israelis whose neighbors and families were being murdered in restaurants and on buses and street corners. That didn't happen. Yet this restraint, while important for our souls, was not solving the problem. Nor, for that matter, were the escalating actions of the IDF, which was now ferociously blockading all the Palestinian towns, alternately occupying, evacuating, and reoccupying them. The security forces said that they were intercepting more attackers than were getting through, but that was cold comfort.

And what of the ostensible bystanders? As the murders continued and lost any semblance of rational justification, many Americans parted from the Europeans in their view of what was happening; this trend was greatly reinforced after the attacks of September 11, but this new sobriety was somehow lost on most Europeans. Throughout these events, there were observers who insisted that no acceptable use of power could ever stem the violence and that the only conceivable response would be to grant the suffering culprits a better life, as if such depravity could come only from extreme deprivation. In the context of the Jerusalem *intifada,* this was tantamount to a demand that the Israelis offer the Palestinians even more than had been offered at Taba. Admittedly, this might not satisfy them; such a move might whet their appetite even further, since it would prove that the Israelis were breaking under the pressure. It might even lead to the eventual submergence of the Jewish state under a wave of Arab "returnees." But what alternative was there?

STAGE FOUR: THE LARGE-SCALE ISRAELI RESPONSES

More than one hundred Israelis were killed in March 2002, as the suicide attacks reached a climactic frenzy. By the end of the month, two successful attacks were being committed every day. The worst of them all was committed at the Park Hotel in Netanya, when a murderer blew himself up in the midst of a seder celebration, killing 29 and wounding 140. The Egyptians and Syrians had struck on the symbolic day of Yom Kippur; now the Palestinians had defiled Passover. Restraint was no longer an option.

Restraint? I hear the eyes of readers popping. What restraint? There were already more than a thousand dead Palestinians in March 2002.

Something strange had happened to the Israeli military planners over the years: Their resolve to win had wavered. This may go back as far as 1973. The IDF had roundly won the Yom Kippur War, but at a high price; the initial Arab successes and the presence of Egyptian armies on previously Israel-held territories at the end of hostilities granted a modicum of plausibility to the Arab view that there had been a draw. This most likely made it easier for Sadat to launch his dramatic peace overture. Perhaps there were advantages to vagueness as a military outcome.

In Lebanon, the Israeli army beat the vastly inferior military forces of the PLO but failed to achieve any tangible political goal. Perhaps, we asked ourselves, once our own existence was secure there was nothing further to be gained through military action? The first *intifada* certainly strengthened this feeling, while the accepted wisdom gleaned from Desert Storm in 1991 was that in some circumstances, Israel stood to gain from total abstention from fighting, even when her own cities were under attack. The entire structure of the Oslo process was predicated on the assumption that diplomacy was the sole method to achieve political goals. Even the post-1996 military planners were touched by this encroaching defeatism: the goal, should hostilities break out, would be not to destroy the enemy's capability, but to limit it as much as possible. Contain the damage, don't destroy the enemy's army.

By the time the Jerusalem *intifada* broke out, Israeli defense planners, political leaders, and voters had built a new tactical consensus: Israel must maintain the might to defend herself against destruction, and this power would be put to use in case of full-scale military aggression; lesser aggression would be headed off by reminding the aggressors of our ability, not by really using it. We would discourage them, we would frighten them with our awesome capabilities, and we would shoot to kill when under fire ourselves. But in a nutshell, we would browbeat them, not beat them.

More than three-quarters of Israeli casualties were noncombatants. In contrast, and despite Palestinian claims of a civilian "Holocaust," well over half of the dead Palestinians were combatants, and more than 95 percent of those were male. (For detailed statistics, see the analysis by Don Radlauer at www.ict.org.il.) Having learned the lessons of Lebanon and the first *intifada,* the Israelis were doing their best to wage war justly. At no point did Israeli forces ever target civilians intentionally. Sometimes civilians were hit, and in some cases apologies were made, including by the prime minister himself. However, most of these civilians had been caught in the cross fire between combatants of both sides and could therefore have been killed even by their own people. Palestinian police stations were reduced to rubble, but very few policemen were hit; in many cases, the Israeli aircraft hovered above the targets for ten or twenty minutes, ensuring that everyone had time to get out. When twenty-one Israelis, mostly teenage girls, were murdered in front of a discotheque in Tel Aviv, Israel did not respond at all, hoping against all evidence that Arafat would call off the violence in the face of international abhorrence. Six weeks later, when fifteen Israelis were murdered in a pizzeria in Jerusalem, the awesome Israeli response was to close down some Palestinian offices in East Jerusalem.

All this changed the day after the seder massacre. The Palestinians had finally gone too far even by the unique standards of the Middle East. What followed was the collapse of a much beloved conception whereby popular terror cannot be beaten but only appeased. For the first time in twenty years, the IDF was told not to send a message but to vanquish its foe. Strict limitations were set, such as that Arafat himself was not to be touched no matter how direct his involvement in terror and that holy sites of all religions were to be respected, even if murderers hiding inside them could not be arrested. Growing American pressure also meant that the time allowed for the operation was limited. Above all, the orders were to hit the armed men, not the civilian population openly sheltering them.

So the soldiers did what they are trained to do: they faced, fought, and defeated the enemy. No B-52s dropping bombs from on high: they fought them eyeball to eyeball and inch by bloody inch. And they defeated them. In Ramallah and Bethlehem the battles were short, in Tulkarm and Kalkilya there were hardly any. But in Nablus there was a fierce battle, and in Jenin there was one of the toughest battles in decades.

Jenin proudly called itself "the Capital of *Shahids,*" (martyrs) and in the days before the IDF arrived, its terrorists booby-trapped dozens of buildings with hundreds of mines. According to the Geneva Conventions, it is forbidden to fight from within a civilian population, but people who glory in murder don't care about international law, unless it is to accuse their opponents of breaking it. Most of the mines were set off during the battle, causing major destruction, and in the final stages, IDF bulldozers razed the last buildings from which the Palestinian fighters were refusing to budge. Some of their leaders, who had sent dozens of suicide murderers to their deaths, surrendered. According to Human Rights Watch, fifty-two Palestinians died in the battle, twenty-two of them civilians—fewer than the number of dead civilians at the seder table in Netanya. Twenty-three Israeli soldiers were killed. The IDF could easily have destroyed that section of the Jenin refugee camp from the air, sparing most of the soldiers while killing more civilians, but this is not the Israeli way of war. In essence, twenty-three Israeli soldiers died so that the Palestinian terrorists would be defeated with as few civilian deaths as possible.

Operation Defensive Shield, as it was called, was greeted by the Europeans with a howl of protest such as had not been heard since the massacre at Sabra and Shatila in 1982. The howl was accompanied by the greatest concentration of attacks on Jewish targets in Europe since the Holocaust. The focus of the protest was initially the Israeli siege of Arafat, who had himself photographed with a candle on his table, although the lights were on in the room. After a few days, interest centered on the events in Jenin, yet there was scant relation between the accusations hurled at Israel and the reality on the ground. In Washington there seemed to be uncertainty, not to say confusion, regarding the Israeli operation, but the aggregate line seemed to be qualified support tempered by the expectation that it be completed as soon as possible.

The campaign broke the rhythm of the suicide bombers' campaign, but it did not bring calm. Once every week or so, an attacker would successfully reach his target, and by late May, the attacks were being launched almost daily. When twenty-seven Israelis were murdered on two consecutive days in Jerusalem in mid-June, the IDF was sent back into the West Bank towns it had evacuated under American pressure, this time to remain indefinitely. On the same day, President George W. Bush gave a much awaited speech on the Middle East, connecting Palestinian sovereignty with democracy.

The passing of the initiative from the Palestinians to the Israelis, accompanied, as most people eventually had to admit, by a surprisingly low rate of civilian casualties on the Palestinian side and a dramatic drop in civilian deaths among Israelis, seemed to give everyone pause. As long as Israeli citizens were being massacred, international discussion had centered on the dire need to return to the negotiating table. Now, with the PA visibly in shambles, it turned to the need to resurrect the peace process in a healthier form that would be less corrupt and less prone to use murder as an instrument of policy. The American administration introduced the new vocabulary, but many Europeans hesitantly joined, and soon even the Palestinians were mouthing plans to reform their security agencies and (someday) hold elections. President Bush then stated unequivocally that the road to an independent Palestine led through the creation of a benign democracy. This was too much for the Europeans, but the parameters of discussion had been irrevocably changed.

Nazi Germany lost World War II by early 1943, but the war went on for an additional twenty-eight months, with millions of dead. The Palestinians lost the Jerusalem *intifada* in the summer of 2002, though as I write the murders continue. Just this week, a terrorist shot two small children in their beds, after shooting their mother. Military pressure has significantly lowered the intensity of terror attacks, making life in Israel more bearable, though Israelis still live with a level of fear unprecedented anywhere else. There is, however, a steep human price to this, and it is being paid by the Palestinian populace.

Hundreds of roadblocks all over the West Bank make traveling almost impossible. The IDF routinely takes over Palestinian towns and villages, entering homes and making arrests. The cities of the northern West Bank—Tulkarm, Kalkilya, and Ramallah—have repeatedly been entered by large IDF forces, who set curfews and disrupt what is left of normal life. In Jenin and Nablus, the IDF presence has become essentially permanent, and the curfews sometimes last longer than the breaks between them.

Contrary to what you are told, the IDF is not targeting Palestinian civilians, although there have been cases of civilians hit in cross fire and of civilians killed after being falsely identified as combatants—but not many. The number of Palestinian men who have been arrested is in the thousands, but most of the truly innocent don't stay long, and the battering given to the terrorist organizations indicates that many of the right people are being arrested. The real tragedy of Palestinian life is that their society has been pulverized. Unemployment is stratospheric, poverty all-encompassing, and freedom of any sort nonexistent. There is no life-endangering hunger, but there is horrifying misery. This was never what Zionism was supposed to be about.

Yet to paraphrase the shrill demands of the Europeans and others: What is the alternative? Sometime in 2001, the West Bank town of Jericho dropped out of the *intifada,* and there has been no fighting there, no IDF invasions, no curfews. In late summer 2002, the populace of Bethlehem had had enough (and at least a third of the local armed men were dead, arrested, or exiled), and it too dropped out of the *intifada* for a few months, until some terrorists took advantage of the lull to launch a suicide murderer from there. There never was such a thing as a cycle of violence, but the Israelis are proving that they are willing to have a cycle of normality: towns that wish to live in peace with Israel are welcome to do so. Jenin and Nablus are the opposite. Every time the IDF declares them subdued and starts moving out, Israeli civilians are shot, bombed, or burned to death in Kfar Saba, Karkur, or Kibbutz Metzer.

These atavistic murders serve no conceivable goal. Israel has demonstrated that she will not flinch in face of the murder of her citizens, nor will she be bludgeoned into taking any action she would otherwise refuse. On the contrary, as long as the murders go on, no electable politician will even think of negotiating with the Palestinians, and those who would like to do so will not win elections. The murders merely provoke additional military measures, and the main victims of these are Palestinians. One is therefore compelled to look elsewhere to understand what motivates the murderers: to Nazi Germany in its final stages, for example, where all was obviously lost yet the murder of Jews went on until the last moment. Military power played a crucial role in the war against the suicide murders, but the danger has not passed in the Middle East or in the larger war on terror. The massive use of suicide attacks has now been added to the permanent arsenal of those who hate democracy. Humanity, or the segment of it that wishes to base its existence on law rather than brute power, has been put on warning: it must devise some weapons of defense.

International law in the form its knee-jerk advocates cite when enumerating all the things that a moral society may not do to protect itself seems not to be an adequate defense. Yet a careful use of international agreements can still allow an adequate defense to be developed. First is the doctrine of double effect. Developed by Catholic thinkers in the Middle Ages, it states that soldiers engaged in legitimate acts of war, who have no intention to hurt civilians, do not bear moral responsibility for civilian deaths as long as there is a reasonable proportion between the military goal they achieved and the damage they caused. This is a far cry from contemporary calls for war to be waged with no civilian casualties whatsoever (a call that is always directed at Israelis and Americans, not terrorists). Michael Walzer, however, feeling uncomfortable with the rather considerable leeway inherent in this doctrine, suggests it be amended to require a conscious effort not to kill civilians, again in proportion to the ends. Bombing legitimate military targets while causing unintended civilian injuries is morally acceptable only when the planners have taken a degree of risk to reduce this damage, perhaps by precision bombing rather than blanket bombing. Sending a team of commandos to achieve the same end, while it would cause no civilian casualties, would probably be too high a risk.

Walzer wrote *Just and Unjust Wars* in the pre–smart bomb era, yet his thesis is clear and reasonable. It takes into account the reality that once you are at war, there will be objectives that must be achieved even at the cost of civilian lives, and it tries to put reasonable restrictions on the power of soldiers while enabling them to do so. In World War II, there were attempts to stop the Nazis from producing atomic weapons; try as they might, the British planners could succeed only at the price of killing dozens of innocent Norwegians. Surely the potential price of failure justified these actions. Although an extreme case, it demonstrates the fallacy of labeling any and all killing of civilians as criminal actions.

The IDF generally fights well within the parameters of Walzer's upgraded doctrine of double effect, and Jenin was a dramatic example: the battle underlined the inadequacy of much of the current international discourse when faced with the antihuman willingness to slaughter civilians by suicide bombers. A far more complicated case was the assassination in July 2002 of master terrorist Salah Shehade, founder and commander of the military arm of Hamas. The Israeli air force assassinated Shehade by dropping a one-ton precision bomb onto his house in Gaza; the bomb hit its target, but the blast killed fifteen civilians, many of them children, who were sleeping peacefully in the adjacent buildings. Shehade's wife and daughter were also killed. This was the closest the IDF came to a war crime in the entire *intifada,* so it deserves careful scrutiny.

Shehade was a master murderer; there was no feasible way to arrest him and bring him to trial, and the longer he lived, the more massacres he generated. Killing him was a perfectly legitimate act of war. There had been seven previous cases, we were told, when the IDF had him in its crosshairs but had refrained from killing him for fear of killing his family or other civilians, even though this had allowed him to continue killing Israeli citizens. This kind of moral restraint goes far beyond Walzer's requirement. The real moral problem was posed by the weapon that was chosen. Surely the professionals of the IDF should have foreseen that dropping so big a bomb in a crowded area would kill a lot of neighbors.

Minister of Defense Benjamin Ben-Eliezer explained that Shehade had been killed at that moment in order to thwart a mega-attack of unprecedented scope; therefore, by implication, killing fifteen Palestinian civilians had potentially saved the lives of hundreds of Israelis. But I admit that even this explanation left me unconvinced. If the Israelis knew about the impending attack, could it not have been aborted in some other way? The depressing conclusion seems to be that this case, while isolated, was not defensible. Yet the deliberations show that a society under attack can still hold discussions on morality, striving to balance the protection of its own civilians with a reluctance to harm the enemy's. This is not a statement the Palestinians can make.

There is a second way of grappling with the moral and legal problems generated by the absolute need to defeat an aggressor who had put no limits on his own depravity. This is the ancient Jewish doctrine of violating the law in order to defend it.

Every legal system must have a source of authority, otherwise people wouldn't live by its rules. In Judaism, the ultimate authority is God, and Jews who abide by the halachic precepts do so because they accept that it is God's will. On the other hand, every legal system must also have the ability to adapt to the changing contours of human existence, whether external or internal, objective or subjective. That's why legislation is a never-ending process. Clearly, there must be a relationship between the legislators and the source of authority, to ensure the new legislation's legitimacy. Democratic parliaments renew their relationship with the source of authority through elections.

Judaism is not a democracy, but its sages long ago realized that without the ability to adapt its laws, it would atrophy and die. So they transferred the practical legislative authority to themselves and their successors, with the condition that the decisions be made using agreed-upon tools. The biblical source for this is Deuteronomy, chapter 30, verses 11–14: "The law is not in the heavens." The Talmud tells of a dramatic case in which the majority of sages were of one opinion, but the one who disagreed with them strengthened his position by performing miracles. This proved that his position was the one God intended—but to no avail. The majority rejected God's interference, noting that once He had given them the power to decide, it was no longer His but theirs.

Being a culture that is comfortable with ambivalence, Judaism has a far more radical option, for times of unusual need. It is based on a verse in Psalms: "It is time to do for God." (Psalm 119, verse 126) The second half of the Hebrew verse can be read as "for they have violated your Law," but also as "by violating the Law"—and the second possibility was preferred already by the Mishnah, more than 2,200 years ago, when mooting the possibility that conditions will sometimes be so extreme that the law can be saved only by violating it. (Intriguingly, I have not found a single translation of the Bible into English that offers the version preferred by the Mishnah.) This option is not to be taken lightly, but it is there as a legitimate tool. In order to defend God's name, it is sometimes permissible to desecrate His law.

The laws of democratic societies emanate from human beings, so they surely must incorporate similar concepts—and they do. The sovereign, ultimately, is the people, or to be more accurate, the contemporary generation. If the need and the communal determination are strong enough, the will of the living generation can override the constitutional decisions of its ancestors. Should the current generation be faced with a previously unimagined threat, their ultimate need is to meet it. As long as the existing tools are sufficient, they must be used. Should they need to be modified and adapted, so be it. But should conventional methods prove insufficient, the society must consider the unacceptable rather than accept its own destruction.

Warfare by suicide murder against civilians is one of the greatest threats one can conceive of—indeed, until recently, it was not even conceivable. No sanction will discourage the aggressors, since they accept the ultimate sanction in advance; indeed, they rejoice in it. Defensive barriers must be built—physical and others—and manned with unwavering resolve for as long as it takes, most likely decades. Sometimes the defenses will momentarily fail, and innocents will die; at other times the attackers will find a previously unnoticed weak point, and again innocents will die. Yet if the saving of innocent lives demands lesser injustices to the perpetrators or their societies, even these must not be ruled out. What could be more immoral than the conscious abandon of innocent lives to be murdered in order to preserve a legal system that was created prior to the danger or that cannot face the brutal challenge thrust upon it?

Restricting the freedom of movement of entire communities is immoral. Refraining from these restrictions when there is unequivocal proof that this will lead to the murder of innocents is worse, because movement restricted can later be granted, while dead innocents will never live again.

Demolishing the homes of civilians merely because a family member has committed a crime is immoral. If, however, empiric evidence can be gleaned whereby potential suicide murderers are willing to die but will refrain from killing out of fear that their mothers will become homeless, it would be immoral to leave the Palestinian mothers untouched in their homes while Israeli children die on their school buses. Accidentally killing noncombatants in the cross fire of battles being fought in the middle of cities is immoral, unless, as the story of 2001 unequivocally proved, refraining from fighting in the Palestinian cities inevitably means the Palestinians will use the safe havens of their cities to plan, prepare, and launch ever more murderous attacks on Jewish noncombatants. These concrete examples and others like them demonstrate the moral considerations that Israelis, unlike their Western detractors, have been dealing with since the Palestinians proudly decided to use suicide murder as their primary weapon. The deliberations are legitimate (indeed, essential), and they dare not become mere routine—but neither can they be brushed off as immoral and needlessly cruel. Innocent people are being murdered, and the obligation of civilized society is to protect them.

Israelis are told that rather than meet legitimate protests with repression, we must understand and address the "root cause" of the problem. At the moment, the root cause for the violence is the Palestinian refusal to make peace with a sovereign Jewish state; this is abetted by the most widespread and virulent hatred of Jews the world has seen since Nazism, encompassing most of the Arab world and tolerated by wide swathes of the West, particularly Europe. It is precisely this understanding that makes it imperative that Israel employ her power wisely, so that as few innocents as possible will die and the concomitant Palestinian suffering will be as limited as possible, so that Palestinian society may someday replace its murderous hallucination of a *Judenrein* Palestine with an attainable dream of peaceful life alongside Jewish Israel.

Israel's enemies, and even many of her friends, damn us for being violent and castigate us for our brutality. They would do better to open any history of the twentieth century. Nailing people by their ears to fences; ramming heated metal rods into live bodies; cutting open abdomens or, preferably, wombs; throwing infants into the air and catching them on bayonets; slaughtering families; freezing to death or boiling—enough! Most of these abominations, and worse, have been done to Jews in the twentieth century, but we haven't done these things to other people. Faced with generation upon generation of warfare against an enemy who gloats in murder and dances over Jewish blood, we have mostly done our best not to return evil for evil. Our record is far from perfect, but it is better than anyone else's.

Which brings us back to the beginning. Jews do not murder, they are not wantonly brutal, nor do they seek revenge. Of course, some do commit these crimes, because individuals are flawed and fallible. But when Jews do murder, or torture, or take revenge, they are frowned upon, not celebrated. Through centuries of oppression, often cooped up in closely confined ghettos with no hope of ever being set free, their movements severely restricted and their well-being totally dependent on the whims of a local duke or bishop, they never thought to teach their children to nurse fantasies of murderous revenge. Rather, they turned inward and found solace in their ancient traditions and literature and their expectation for a better future. It is exceedingly unpolitically correct to say, but it is an empiric fact: Jews, both persecuted and sovereign, generally behave in a more moral way than their enemies and their detractors ever did. The Israeli moral superiority over the Palestinians is the source of their strength and what will give them the fortitude to continue, no matter what the price, for as long as it takes—until someday the Palestinians decide to make peace with a Jewish Israel.

CHAPTER

IO

Future Decisions: Living at War and Making Peace

Some months ago, I had occasion to make one of those emergency room visits that parenting seems to require. Not far from us was a young Arab couple whose three-year-old daughter was clearly in worse condition than my teenage one. The father hardly spoke Hebrew, and the mother not at all. The doctor, a young woman whose native tongue was Russian, called the nurse, who had a reasonable smattering of Arabic she had picked up on the job. She quickly realized, however, that this case needed full command of Arabic, so the Russian doctor called down the top doctor of the night shift. Ten minutes later he appeared, in the green uniform of a surgeon: an Israeli Arab.

The hospitals of Jewish Jerusalem have almost as many Palestinian patients as Israelis. War or no war, the Palestinians know good medicine and do not hesitate to use it. Whatever they may think of us, they trust us with their lives in times of medical distress, secure in the knowledge that we will do our best for them. Even journalists who can find nothing positive to say about us often inadvertently admit this, when describing how Palestinians were detained by evil Israeli soldiers at a roadblock on their way to the hospital; they merely forget to mention that the hospital may have been a Jewish one. So perhaps Jews and Palestinians can live peacefully side by side?

Being born Palestinian or Jew does not determine the moral decisions one will make. Yet the group into which one is born does have an impact. Some groups encourage their members to hold human life—their own and those of others—in higher or lower esteem. This is a fact of history, not a subjective interpretation. Another factual truth is that since World War I, Jews and Palestinians have not respected the lives of their adversaries to an equal degree. Purposeful killing of defenseless Jewish civilians has been a constant in Palestinian policy, and at times it has been the centerpiece of that policy. Jews only rarely murdered defenseless Palestinians, and when they did they were condemned by their own community. No Jew ever walked into a Palestinian child's bedroom and intentionally killed her. Palestinian murderers have done so again and again.

This is not a theoretical discussion. It goes to the heart of the conflict, where there exists an inherent moral imbalance. At every stage, Palestinian power over Jews would have had much direr consequences for the Jews than Jewish power over Palestinians has ever had. Even at their harshest, in 1948, the Jews ejected about one-third of the Palestinians, watched while another third left, and allowed a third to stay, giving them equal legal rights and unequal social conditions. This, at a moment when the Palestinians were announcing very clearly their intention to destroy Jewish life in the land, backed by all the force they were able to muster. Since 1967, Israel has controlled a sizable segment of the Palestinian people, and her behavior in that role leaves much to criticize. Yet only a fool or worse would argue that if the situation were ever reversed, the Jews would merely be forced to watch the Palestinians build towns on the sand dunes near Ashdod or in the hills west of Jerusalem. Should the Palestinians ever gain control over the Jews, Palestine will become as *Judenrein* as most of Europe is today: a small community here or there and ghosts on every street.

Put as starkly as possible: Israel blocks the national aspirations of the Palestinians (or used to), but Palestine threatens the very existence of the Jews. This is the permanent backdrop to the crucial question: Can Palestinians and Jews live together peacefully?

All wars end sooner or later, and the survivors live in peace. It can take a while—generations, sometimes centuries—but eventually every war plays itself out, or is decisively won, or simply winds down. Indeed, most wars do not outlast their initiators, so that the Israeli-Palestinian conflict at eighty-plus is already one of the world's oldest. Eventually, one can hope, even this war will end and its survivors will live in peace.

But while wars may end, the hatreds that inspire them don't necessarily die. Europeans hated Jews enough to murder them periodically from the third century until the twentieth and in broad swathes of the continent the killing ceased only after almost all the Jews were dead. The Jews may be gone, but the hatred remains. The crucial question today is whether the conflict in the Middle East is a long war or a permanent hatred.

Let's assume optimistically that it's merely a long war. As this is being written, in May 2003, peace negotiations are once again being mooted, encouraged by an American administration that has just deposed of Saddam Hussein's brutal regime in Iraq. These negotiations will be severely handicapped by events since October 2000. The disillusion of Palestinians with Israel in general and with the misnamed peace process in particular is intense, they say. For Israelis, or the majority of us who are not die-hard proponents of negotiations at any price, the bottom has been knocked out of the basic assumptions of the Oslo process. Transferring power to the Palestinians so that both sides can learn to respect each other hasn't worked; the Palestinians have demonstrated beyond any reasonable doubt that their promise to adhere to their agreements is worthless, even when given solemnly and in writing before the entire world. Moreover, it took the rest of the world less than one newscast to forget that such a commitment had ever existed. Given the basic structure of the conflict, whereby Israel must weaken her position on the ground in return for promises of good behavior, many of us cannot imagine how we might again go about negotiating. What assurances can they give that would convince us to allow them more territory or sovereignty, now that we know how much damage they can do with what they have?

However, let us assume for the sake of argument that enough mutual trust can be created so as to allow meaningful negotiations to resume. We might also posit a situation where a friendly president of the United States were to order both sides back to the negotiating table. What then would have to happen in order for good intentions to overpower generations of hostility and bloodshed? In the following paragraphs, I will try to spell out what each side will have to give and what cannot be given. First what Israel must give: territory and respect.

Peace between Israel and Palestine will require that Israel leave practically all of the territory taken in 1967 in the Gaza Strip and the West Bank. Not because there is anything inherently holy about the lines of June 1967, but because the Palestinians need a territory on which to live their national life, and the line of 1967 has been accorded international recognition. Most potential changes to that boundary do not give Israel any advantages worth fighting for, should there ever be the option of not fighting. There can be small changes in the line, such as incorporating settlements that straddle it, but their significance is minimal. Conceivably, both sides could agree on minor exchanges of territory, so as to leave large blocks of settlements inside Israel while compensating the Palestinians for them. But this should not be a sticking point: true peace without the settlements would be preferable to almost any alternative, if only someone would offer it to us.

The essence of this requirement is that Israel must abdicate her claim to the biblical heartland. It is a decision to lay greater value on the future than the past and to accept that Israel's role in Jewish history is to allow the Jews to develop a normal national existence, not to recompense for what they lost in the wars against the Romans; it can enable the Jews to fulfill their prophetic visions of social justice, truth, and morality, not the geographic ones of hills and valleys. The symbolic expression of this forward-looking choice will be Israel's relinquishing of control over the second most holy place in the Jewish world, Hebron, where the Patriarchs are buried.

Second, Israel needs to show her respect for the Palestinians. This means that the Palestinians must be regarded as neighbors, not tenants. They are here because this is their home. Israel does not grant them an independent state in her magnanimity, she simply does the right thing and gets out of the way of their building a normal society. Moreover, she can and should accept the historical truth, which is that she had a hand in the suffering of the Palestinians. So, of course, did the Egyptians, the Jordanians, the Syrians, and the Lebanese; and the greatest culprits were the Palestinians themselves. But while Israel has no need to apologize to the Palestinians for the return of the Jews to their historical homeland, she can afford to look the truth in its face. It is not nearly as ugly as some people want you to think.

Part of the present impasse is that Israel has already done much of what is required, only to reap the worst wave of suicide murders in the history of mankind. All the talk about returning to the negotiating table so as to put an end to violence overlooks the fact that there is almost nothing left to offer that was not already offered and rejected. An inch here, a centimeter there: these are not what the Palestinians spilled so much blood for. The bleak fact is that for negotiations to be more than a futile and frustrating charade, the Palestinians will have to change some of their basic positions.

Specifically, if peace is their goal, the Palestinians must offer the Israelis security, respect, and recognition.

Security is the easiest of these conditions, for it can be defined and empirically determined: peace means that Palestinians don't kill Israelis. No distinctions will be accepted between Hamas-Jihad-Islamist militants and "mainstream" PLO. We've been there already. If Palestinians keep on killing Israelis, it's not peace. If it's not peace, we won't pay for it with land.

The demand that the Palestinians respect us and recognize our right to be here, as we acknowledge theirs, will be harder to measure but no less crucial. This fundamental demand was totally overlooked in the Oslo process, which failed to stipulate that the country with whom the Palestinians were negotiating peace is the Jewish state, leaving wide open the possibility that Israel was destined eventually to become a binational state with a Palestinian majority. The essence of this demand is that both sides truly accept the legitimacy of the other, transforming the conflict from an existential to a practical one that can then be resolved by horse trading. Its most obvious requirement is that the Palestinians relinquish their demand for a right of return, which not only contradicts the essence of a Jewish state, but means essentially a "return" to pre-1948 conditions. The unjust wars they fought and lost for the destruction of Israel must have a price, and the price is that the refugees must settle where they are or in the sovereign state of Palestine in exchange for some fair and agreed-upon form of compensation. Like the Jews, in effect, the Palestinians also must look forward to a robust national life, not backward to what cannot be changed.

All the Arabic readers I have asked tell me unanimously that while some Palestinians grudgingly accept that Israel may be here to stay, none of them acknowledge the right of the Jews to be here. Hence, should Israel ever lose her overwhelming military and economic superiority, her very existence will come into question. The late Faisal Husseini, dubbed by *The Economist* "a Palestinian for coexistence with Israel," repeatedly said—in Arabic—that making peace with Israel would be merely a stage in the conflict, which would continue by other means.

There are numerous illustrations of this attitude. In July 2001, nine months into the Jerusalem *intifada* and four months into the government of Ariel Sharon, a group of some two dozen intellectuals from both sides convened to build a bridge over the ruins of peace. These were all old friends who have been meeting for many years in hope of finding enough common ground to enable the politicians to pick up the torch. Back when they started, they were unpopular pariahs in their respective communities for daring to reach out to the enemy; but over years of perseverance, they had managed to pull ever larger segments of their people behind them, and from eccentrics they had become mainstream. Between them there must have been many thousands of hours of dialogue. Intelligent, educated individuals, rational realists, there was not a hard-line militant among them.

Their idea was simple: to agree on a joint declaration calling on the warring factions to desist from their insanity and return to negotiations. The peaceniks would join hands and with their moral authority embarrass the politicians back to sanity. The Palestinians were willing to join in, stating that there should be two independent states alongside each other, but the Israelis, alerted by the fiascoes of Camp David and Taba to a nuance they had previously overlooked, demanded that the statement clearly say that Israel would be a Jewish state and Palestine an Arab one. The Palestinians refused. Jews, they said, are a religion, not a nationality, and neither need nor deserve their own state. They were welcome to live in Israel, but the Palestinian refugees would come back, and she would cease in time to be a Jewish state.

If even the peace-seeking extremes cannot agree, there is nothing left to strive for. Yet some Israelis resolved to bend even further backward in their desperate search for common ground. On September 28, 2001, eight Israeli human rights organizations published a full-page ad in the weekend edition of *Haaretz*. It took the form of an obituary, and crowded into it were the names of all those who had died in a year of violence—about eight hundred people. For those who took the time to wade through it, it was quite edifying. For example, the dead Arabs were overwhelmingly men, while a majority of dead Israelis were women. The bloodcurdling part, however, was that the names of the Palestinian suicide murderers were printed alongside their Jewish victims.

This, it soon transpired, was only half the story. The Israeli activists had initially hoped that their Palestinian colleagues would join them in mourning all the dead, no matter how they died, and the ad was to appear simultaneously in *Haaretz* and a Palestinian paper. The Palestinians refused, saying that they could not mourn dead Jewish settlers, even in the context of a call to end the violence. So the Jews ignominiously went ahead with their lonely demonstration.

Human rights may mean all sorts of things: the right to food, to dignity, to freedom, and to equality irrespective of gender, religion, or ethnicity. Their fundamental bedrock, however, is the right to life itself. Jews have a tradition that recognized this and formulated it clearly as far back as we go; the Talmud elaborated on this understanding and fleshed it out two thousand years ago. Arguably, the roots of respect for the sanctity of life that is central to Western civilization was inherited from the Jews—it certainly didn't come from the Romans. The Israeli human rights activists who published this perverse ad have lost their moral moorings, but at least their initial impulse, though foolish, springs from good intentions. Their Palestinian partners are probably the best you will find: no religious fanatics among them. Yet there is no common ground between our moral tradition and their position that Jews who live on "Arab land" deserve to die.

The Israeli demand that the Palestinians recognize our right to be here and agree with us on rules of conflict resolution is not the arrogant diktat of a colonial power trying to control its weaker neighbor. It is a commonsense requirement for living alongside each other in peace. Without it, whatever the politicians agree on will collapse, and at horrific cost, as the story of the Oslo process demonstrates. If both sides cannot do this, there will be no peace. At the moment, Israel has gone considerably further in this direction than the Palestinians. Would that it were otherwise.

Once the conceptual framework is in place, there will only remain the horse trading: Where precisely will land be swapped? Can there be a mechanism for a limited right of return for some Palestinians to their immediate families in Israel? What must be done to help the descendants of the refugees become normal citizens of their countries, to the extent they are not already integrated? What will the economic relations be between the two sovereign states? How will they regulate the use of the limited and physically intertwined water resources at their disposal? The bureaucrats will have a very full workload, and it can be expected to take months of negotiations and probably a few years of implementation. But assuming

Jerusalem in 2003
Jewish and Arab Residential Areas

Jewish residential areas

Arab residential areas

High importance to both Jews and Palestinians

Israel-Jordan Armistice Demarcation line of 1949

Israeli eastern enlargement following 1967 war

Municipal perimeter of Jerusalem today

* Mount Scopus was an Israeli enclave in Jordanian territory between 1948–1967

WEST BANK

ISRAEL

BET ZAYIT

Jerusalem

Old City

Mount Scopus*

ABU DIS

WEST BANK

0 Miles 2

0 Kilometers 2 4

the conceptual agreement, this can even be done in a mutually constructive and beneficial way.

The real test of peace will be Jerusalem. Dividing the city will ensure war; sharing it will be the proof of peace.

Jerusalem is at the heart of how we define ourselves, and the Palestinians must learn to accept this. So far they are being very clear: Not only is the Haram el-Sharif theirs alone, even the Western Wall is not Jewish. On February 20, 2001, the mufti of Jerusalem issued a religious decree (fatwa) stating that the Western Wall is Islamic property. "No stone of the Western Wall has any connection to Hebrew history," he declared, adding that the wall is simply the western side of the Al-Aqsa Mosque. It should not be called the Western Wall or the Wailing Wall, but the Al-Burak Wall, after the name of Muhammad's horse.

But as usual, the most damning positions come not from the extremists, or from the Muslim religious establishment, but from the tiny group of Palestinians who have dedicated years of their lives to the peace process, who have many personal connections with Israelis, speak fluent English, regularly publish op-eds in the most important American and European newspapers, and are welcome in the corridors of power throughout the West. In July 2001, Abu Ala gave an interview to the *Jerusalem Report,* a high-profile Jewish magazine. Seasoned politician and negotiator that he is, Ala carefully calibrated his message to his audience. Looking back on the failure of Camp David, he described the clash of positions on the Temple Mount: "The Haram is not only Palestinian. It's for all Muslims. This is a physical place on the ground. What's the intention of their asking for our recognition? To divide it? To share it? To give it up? There are two mosques there. Should we share it with the Jews? No one can accept this. It's impossible." In other words, the Jews must hand it over, and that's it. This would be unconstructive even if victorious Palestinians were dictating humiliating peace terms to a vanquished foe; as a fundamental position relating to an unvanquished enemy alongside whom you wish to live in peace, it is breathtaking in its audacity and hardly demonstrates the minimal goodwill that is an essential precondition for reconciliation.

Jerusalem meaning what it does for Jews, we will inevitably make additional symbolic gestures there, at least as serious as placing benches next to the Western Wall (1929), guiding tourists along the outside perimeter of the Temple Mount (1996), or having our politicians visit (2000). After all, it is for us the single most important place on the face of the globe. The Palestinians must accept that we have a reason for being here and a claim to the Temple Mount that is as real for us as theirs is for them. Without this kind of mutual acceptance, future clashes are inevitable. Moreover, if they back their rejection of our right to exist with violence, then violence will continue on both sides. Peace will be possible only when there are Palestinians who can address our identity as Barak addressed theirs. When that happens, we will join efforts to solve this most intractable of issues.

Division of the city will not be the solution, however, because division cannot work.

Assume that a Barak-like Israeli government overrides the deepest sentiments of many Jews and manages to collect enough democratic support for the decision to divide Jerusalem. Peace reigns as a result. Both sides forget their differences and past animosities. Relieved of the burdens of war, Israel shoots to the top of the list of the world's wealthiest countries, while independent Palestine goes the way of all non-oil-producing Arab countries and becomes a miserable third world state, replete with a corrupt leadership that mismanages everything except their own bank accounts. In Jerusalem, there are hundreds of places where the distance between Palestinian and Jewish sections is no wider than the street between them; in some places the distance is the breadth of the stone wall between two rooms. Can you conceive of a rich society and a poor one, living twenty-five feet from each other, each with its own police force, where the police that protect the rich have no jurisdiction over the poor? Such a scenario sounds like the perfect way to create animosity and violence even without any previous history.

So assume the gamble fails: peace does not reign. The past animosities smolder on, separated by twenty-five feet of street and two mutually antagonistic police forces. Bitterness, frustration, anger, hatred, violence. What comes next is not only obvious, it already exists and appears from time to time on your television screen at a place called Hebron. Since late 1996, Hebron has been a divided city in the way that the advocates of peace insist Jerusalem be divided. Someday the division of Hebron will be ended, when all the Jews leave, but this will never happen in Jerusalem.

Another way to underline the lunacy of dividing Jerusalem is to note the unhappy fact that there is not a single inch of peaceful border anywhere between the Arab world and a rich Western democratic country, unless you count Muslim Turkey, itself not fully a rich Western democracy. Israel's borders with Egypt and Jordan are patrolled twenty-four hours a day, are open solely at the designated border points, and can be crossed only after cumbersome bureaucratic procedures. Moreover, worldwide and in all of history there is no precedent for dividing a living city between warring nations as the basis of making peace. The visionaries who assure us that what exists nowhere else on the globe will somehow spring into existence in the alleys of this tortured city and soothe the rest of Islam's grudges against the West are simply hallucinating.

It grieves me to admit, but I cannot say how we will resolve the question of Jerusalem. It lies beyond my ability. At the same time, leaving it as a festering issue for our descendants to solve is not acceptable, so let me postulate that if Israelis and Palestinians manage to reach agreement on everything else, they will agree also on this. Since both have real claims to the same small place, they will have to devise an innovative solution based on sharing rather than a violent and repugnant solution based on division. Since a prerequisite for peace is mutual respect, they will no doubt devise a way of sharing that reflects this. More I cannot say, accept to add that I personally intend to vote against any peace plan put before the Israeli electorate that divides Jerusalem, not for its symbolic meaning to the Jews, but out of the practical conviction that the plan won't work.

Logically, however, there is no present reason to assume that the conflict can be resolved to the satisfaction of both sides. Historically, we know that hatred of the Jews has never disappeared and has adapted itself to every major change in history. Not always: the United States seems remarkably free of its more virulent strains, and here and there other societies have forced it out of the mainstream. The Western churches have in recent decades taken steps that may lead to a radically new position in their relations to the Jews. But nothing has changed in the Eastern churches, and much of Islam seems to be moving rapidly in the opposite direction. The centrality of antisemitism to the troubled self-perception of much of the Muslim world is growing and spreading, not diminishing, and the expectation that this deep-seated animosity will somehow vanish on the day that a Palestinian state is established is not morally or intellectually serious. Even the modest hope that the Palestinians themselves will buck this trend strains our credulity. Unless you seriously believe that the all-pervading antisemitism in Pakistan and the Muslim sections of Manchester is merely the result of Israel's alleged atrocities—in which case you are simply beyond rational appeals.

What if Israel faces an irrational hatred that cannot be resolved by rational behavior? Past experience would indicate that you do not try to appease it. Appeasing hatred merely causes it to thrive. As Churchill remarked, appeasers feed other people to the crocodiles in the hope they will be eaten last. This could explain the simple but generally overlooked fact that during the seven years of the Oslo process, terrorism was high when Rabin and Peres were at the helm, but low on Netanyahu's watch.

The second thing you don't do is despair. You must continuously be alert for ways to mitigate the practical influence of the hatred. Peace will not be possible until the Palestinians decide for it, but Israel must remain open-minded to the possibility that this might happen, and must not miss the moment, when it comes—as it well may, someday. Perhaps the single point on which I agree with Israel's critics is that the creation of additional settlements and the continued growth of those existing ones which even most Israelis agree will one day be dismantled, is destructive, since it preempts partitioning the land at that future date. Jewish construction in Jerusalem must continue, obviously.

The elections of January 2003 returned Sharon to power with an overwhelming majority. In order to understand these results, it helps to note an important but often overlooked characteristic of Israeli politics: Prime ministers almost never win two consecutive elections. In nearly thirty years, since 1974, only one has ever managed to do so—Menachem Begin in 1981—and even he needed the peace treaty with Egypt merely to scrape by with a slender majority. Israelis don't like their politicians to take them for granted, nor do they like them to get used to the comforts of power, so they rotate them with regularity; even when they elect them the first time, it is often by a very slim margin.

In January 2003, the electorate was offered four models of political behavior. The ultrahawks of the far Right hoped to gain from the emotions generated by more than two years of a murderous campaign against Israeli citizens, and they offered an iron fist against Palestinian terrorism, unbridled continuation of settlement building, and a watered-down version of partition. There was even a splinter party—Herut—which suggested that rather than partition the land, the Palestinians should be sternly encouraged to move elsewhere in the Arab world. Three religious parties and the right wing of the Likud differed from the ultrahawks on partition, which they accepted, although its terms are to be less generous than those offered by Barak at Camp David and will include no division of Jerusalem. The die-hard doves of the Left said that Israel must negotiate with the Palestinians immediately, accepting the Palestinian position that the violence would continue until a resolution to the conflict was in the offing and that the negotiations would pick up where they had stopped at Taba in January 2001. The centrists said that peace with the Palestinians is not possible at this stage and thus should not be the issue on which voters cast their ballot. When someday the Palestinians decide to sue for peace on terms Israel can live with, the centrists will be there to talk to them, but in the meantime they prefer to deal with internal Israeli matters, such as rolling back the political influence of the Orthodox.

Rather surprisingly, Labor under its new leader, Amram Mitzna, positioned itself resolutely on the left, with no attempt to lure voters from the center. Equally surprisingly, Sharon positioned himself only a tad to the right of the centrists. He announced loudly and clearly that he accepted the idea of a sovereign Palestinian state sharing the land with Israel and informed the voters that painful compromises would be called for, though he did not specify what they might be.

The elections of 2001 had been for the prime minister alone, with the Knesset remaining as elected in 1999. The elections of 2003 were thus the first full elections since the demise of the peace process, and they could be seen both as a referendum on the future of negotiations and as a judgment on Sharon's determination not to allow the Palestinians any gain whatsoever from their violence. Ultimately, the question the voters had to answer was whether Palestinian violence should be taken as a sign of their desperation, in which case a renewal of negotiations might bring peace, or of their determination to bring Israel to her knees, in which case negotiations would lead somewhere only after they had been convinced that violence would never achieve anything.

The verdict was resoundingly clear. Indeed, no elections since Begin's first victory in 1977 have given such an unequivocal result. The ultrahawks lost about a quarter of the votes they had garnered in 1999, and the extreme Herut failed to send even one representative to the Knesset. Shas, to the right of Sharon, lost a third of its power. Natan Sharansky's Russian Party lost two-thirds of its voters and folded into the Likud the week after the election, signifying the end of a block of Russians a mere twelve years after the peak of their immigration. The Arab parties lost a quarter of their votes. The most resounding loss, however, was of the Zionist Left. Labor lost a quarter of its voters, and Meretz, further to the left, lost 40 percent. The entire Left, Zionist and Arab together, hardly got more than a quarter of the votes.

There were two dramatic winners. The secular-centrist Shinui Party, a new arrival on the political scene that first ran in 1999, became the third largest party, only 4 percent smaller than Labor. And Sharon's Likud doubled its power, from nineteen MKs to thirty-eight (soon to be joined by the two Russians); for every Labor voter there were two for Likud.

Representational democracy being what it is, it is impossible to say what the politicians will do with this verdict, but Israeli public sentiment is clear. Ten years after the Oslo agreement, and two and a half years after its violent repudiation by the Palestinians, the electorate has made up its mind: *Eretz Yisrael* will be partitioned between Jews and Palestinians, each with their own sovereign state. This will happen when the Palestinians are ready to accept it. In the meantime, Palestinian violence will be met with greater Israeli force, so that in the struggle of arms, the Palestinians will lose. Since Palestinian acceptance of Israel may be a long time in coming, it is important that Israeli society remain a place in which its mainstream can continue to feel comfortable, with the extremists—right, left, *haredi,* settlers—relegated to their rightful place and not at center stage.

This is the almost consensual position of democratic Israel after two and a half years of brutal violence aimed at her citizens. Anyone who wishes to achieve peace in the Middle East must take it into account. Wishing it were otherwise will not make it so, and since the pressure exerted by the Palestinians to break Israeli society has been of the most vicious sort and has failed, it is hard to imagine what might. The Israelis are ready for peace but will not be bludgeoned into surrender.

Three weeks after my wedding, in 1982, I was mobilized and sent to war. We spent most of the night being moved from one mobilization center to the next, collecting additional reservists as we went. At two or three A.M. we finally left Jerusalem and drove north. In the blue light of predawn one of us stood in the back of the bus and prayed the morning service; he was killed later that week. When we arrived at the division, everything was hustle and bustle. The usual cynical mirth of reservists on their way into the army was subdued, though not extinguished. We went about our tasks with an unaccustomed seriousness, loading shells onto tanks, checking our equipment, spreading rumors, queuing in the canteen, listening to the CO as he drew arrows on a map, slapping backs of friends we hadn't seen for months or a year and some others we would never see again.

It wasn't the right place to be three weeks after getting married, and I was feeling rather glum. At one point I was sitting on the turret of a tank, chatting with my lieutenant, who was a few years older than I and already had a few children. Usually he was quite a clown, his main preoccupation being when he could next organize ten minutes of calm so as to brew some coffee. Dejected, I asked him how much longer this was going to go on. He peered at the machine gun he was mounting on the turret, fiddled with his wrench, and gave the only possible answer: "For as long as it takes."

So how much longer will this go on? My own opinion is that we have at least 150 years to go. The Muslim world resisted the Crusaders for 200 years until they finally gave up and left. From their perspective, we are a second wave of Crusaders, uncalled-for invaders from the West. We don't belong here, in the middle of their world, and they want us gone. Sometimes they fight us, sometimes they don't. We have resisted their pressure for 50-plus years, which is more than they expected, but they remember that the first time around it took longer, and they can wait. Perhaps we will need to outlast the Crusaders before they begin to understand that we are another story—that for us, 200 years is as nothing when compared with 2,000. If that's what it takes, so be it.

CHAPTER

11

Immoral Decisions: The Bad Faith of Israel's Detractors

The Economist (London) is one of the world's best newspapers. It is intelligent and respects the intelligence of its readers. It does its best to ascertain the facts and to present them in a cogent way; it has no qualms about publishing letters from readers who have spotted inaccuracies. Except in matters of free market economics, it keeps a cool head about the issues, carefully weighing the options open to the protagonists. It is a fine paper. Until it comes to Israel. The paper launched its coverage of the second *intifada* with a paragraph from never-never land:

> [Israel] has to abate its greed for other people's land. Occupying territory, except in the course of war, is not an acceptable state of affairs. Most Palestinians, who once lived in the land that is now Israel, have through their leaders accepted the two-state solution. It is now up to the Israelis, if they want a decent, civilized life for themselves, to allow the Palestinians a reasonably sized little state with its proper capital in East Jerusalem.[1]

At the other side of *intifada,* and the other end of the British political spectrum, Phil Reeves of *The Independent* told his readers on April 16,

[1] *The Economist,* "The Road to War," October 5, 2000.

2002, about the horrors of Jenin. It was a dramatic description, from his own "flitting through an olive orchard overlooked by two Israeli tanks" to reach the site, to his surreptitious guides: "Hidden, whispering people directed us through narrow alleys they thought were clear. When there were soldiers about, a finger would raise in warning, or a hand waved us back." There were fine dramatic effects: "The mosques, once so noisy at prayer time, were silent," as well as prophetic flairs: " 'This is mass murder committed by Ariel Sharon,' Jamel Saleh, 43, said. 'We feel more hate for Israel now than ever. Look at this boy.' He placed his hand on the tousled head of a little boy, Mohammed, the eight-year-old son of a friend. 'He saw all this evil. He will remember it all.' " Most powerful of all, the report contained a holy moral injunction: "Rajib Ahmed, from the Palestinian Energy Authority, came to try to repair the power lines. He was trembling with fury and shock. 'This is mass murder. I have come here to help but I have found nothing but devastation. Just look for yourself.' All had the same message: tell the world." So Reeves told the world:

> A monstrous war crime that Israel has tried to cover up for a fortnight has finally been exposed. . . . The sweet and ghastly reek of rotting human bodies is everywhere, evidence that it is a human tomb. The people, who spent days hiding in basements crowded into single rooms as the rockets pounded in, say there are hundreds of corpses, entombed beneath the dust, under a field of debris, crisscrossed with tank and bulldozer treadmarks. . . . A quiet sad-looking young man called Kamal Anis led us across the wasteland, littered now with detritus of what were once households, foam rubber, torn clothes, shoes, tin cans, children's toys. He suddenly stopped. This was a mass grave, he said, pointing.
>
> We stared at a mound of debris. Here, he said, he saw the Israeli soldiers pile 30 bodies beneath a half-wrecked house. When the pile was complete, they bulldozed the building, bringing its ruins down on the corpses. Then they flattened the area with a tank. We could not see the bodies. But we could smell them.
>
> A few days ago, we might not have believed Kamal Anis. But the descriptions given by the many other refugees who escaped from Jenin

camp were understated, not, as many feared and Israel encouraged us to believe, exaggerations. Their stories had not prepared me for what I saw yesterday. I believe them now.

You can't flatten a mound of rocky rubble with a tank: that snippet alone is proof that the entire story was cooked up in the mind of Kamal Anis. But Reeves knows nothing about tanks, nor do his readers, and in response to the supposed massacre at Jenin, there was an uproar of popular fury, mass demonstrations across Western Europe, and calls for a war crimes tribunal. The European Council voted for sanctions against Israel and measures of support for the Palestinians; academics in Europe and the United States initiated boycotts against Israeli colleagues and scientific research projects. The Norwegian members of the Nobel Peace Prize Commission publicly recanted for having awarded it to Shimon Peres.

Only one small fact intruded on this orgy of hatred: There had been no massacre. There hadn't even been any particularly severe war crimes, although the Palestinians' decision to base their terrorist activities in the middle of a civilian population was clearly in contravention of the Geneva Conventions.

The poor journalism of Phil Reeves is not really the issue, however. Nor is the inclination of millions to believe the worst about the Jews. The issue is that the attitude of the onlookers has itself become a part of the events. The support the Palestinians consistently garner from abroad encourages them to continue their murderous struggle, since if so many outsiders tell them they are justified in killing innocent Jews—or that there are no innocent Jews—it must be so. Moreover, the greater the external pressure on Israel, the greater the hopes of Palestinians that she will be forced to change her course.

How is this complicity to be explained? First, many of Israel's critics simply have no idea what they are talking about, and their culpability lies in allowing themselves to be manipulated. Second, they are antisemites, whether acknowledged or not, and their culpability lies in their decision to hate Jews. Third, they cannot stand first world societies that use military force; their culpability is in their hypocrisy.

Above all, the methodology of contemporary journalism does not lend itself to explaining Israel's wars. Instead it tends to obfuscate reality and dissipate clear judgments in a haze of moral relativism. Allow me to postulate eight rules by which journalists operate, six of which often give false results.

First rule: The picture is reality. What you see is what really happened, else how could there be a photograph of it? Of course, this isn't true, since often a mere picture has no context. The filmed sequence of Muhammad al-Durrah indeed showed his horrible death, but it didn't say who shot him. The same is true for the demolished homes at Jenin: only a specialist could tell if they had been blown up by charges laid by the defenders, or rocketed from the air, or bulldozed at close quarters. Moreover, such a specialist would have to be on the spot and could not determine anything from a ten-second sequence on CNN. Pictures show only what the camera sees, so if the photographer wants to spin and pan while standing in one spot, he can easily convince his viewers that one small section of Jenin is actually the entire town. Finally, pictures can prove the opposite of what you think you see. For example, the endless pictures of Palestinian civilians confronting Israeli troops prove only that in most cases the Palestinians are in very little danger. As long as they don't threaten the lives of Israelis, by dumping rocks on the heads of Jewish worshipers or harboring armed men in their ranks, there is little chance that the soldiers will shoot at them, and the demonstrators are well aware of this. This is the reason there are so many pictures of Palestinians confronting Israeli soldiers and so few comparable pictures from other military occupations of the twentieth century—Germans, Soviets, or French in Algeria. Truly brutal occupying forces would shoot such civilians on sight.

Second rule: Life is like basketball—quick, action packed, and with immediate results. The outcome can be influenced by the decisions you make, and wrong decisions will lead to the loss of the game.

It took more than five years of war to defeat Nazism. The policy of containment took four decades to topple communism. Equality for women the world over was a project that took most of the twentith century and is nowhere near completion. Likewise, it took thirty years and four wars to convince Egypt that defeating Israel militarily was not an option. It took about two years of a slowly escalating war of attrition to make Egypt abandon the goal trumpeted by Nasser when he started it. It took the Islamists the entire decade of the 1990s to topple the World Trade Center, including two years of specific preparations for the attack that ultimately succeeded. It is going to take years to beat them.

Compare these facts to daily statements in the press. To wit: Israeli measures against Palestinian terrorism are a pointless failure, since the terrorism goes on. September 11 was revenge for American support for Israel in the second *intifada*. (At one point, I saw a report that it was retaliation for the American boycott of Durban, a week before the attack, and for President Bush's decision on Kyoto, a few months earlier.) Or try this edifying sequence: America has no way to retaliate for the September 11 attack (September); if it attacks in Afghanistan, it will lose (October); bombing Afghanistan is pointless, it is merely creating further hatred (November). Less than a week into the campaign in Iraq, the media was agog with the approaching quagmire. Baghdad fell two weeks later. These and other comments reflect an astonishing lack of historical wisdom and intellectual maturity in the Western press. For journalists trained to see the world this way, the very concept of winning a war of attrition through a slow, patient, and bloody accumulation of small victories, even while sustaining heavy losses, is quite foreign.

Third rule: Foreign languages are unimportant, and a dedicated journalist can find out what is going on without them. This aspect of the journalistic mind reflects a combination of arrogance and laziness. Only rarely does a foreign journalist posted to the Middle East know either Arabic or Hebrew, and certainly not both.

If you don't know the language of the countries you are covering, you are cut off from the local reality and the experience of most of its people. In Israel, this means you are left with the official information outlets, of which most journalists are understandably leery, and the segments of society that are eager to communicate with journalists and are capable of doing so in English. This automatically puts a slant on things, since most Israelis who fit this description come from the liberal and left-leaning end of the political spectrum.

Palestinians for their part know full well that Western journalists don't follow what is said in Arabic, and often the discrepancies between what they say in English and their native tongue are terribly significant. The Israeli media employ specialists who daily read the Arab press and trawl the Arab media; they also employ Arab-speaking journalists (often Israeli

Arabs) who roam freely throughout the territories with their microphones and cameras and talk to the great and the ordinary in Arabic. Their reports are screened every single day on our prime-time newscasts. This partially explains why Israeli public opinion diverges so vastly from that of places where Arabic is never broadcast: we simply have more facts at our disposal.

Some foreign observers are as imprisoned by their own language as by their ignorance of ours. For example, the only French word that exists to describe Israeli settlements was previously used to describe French colonialism in Algeria; thus the French cannot discuss Israeli actions without thinking about their own past, whether it is relevant or not. Nor can they envision life under occupation without thinking of how it was for them to live under the Nazis. Their very vocabulary forces them to draw illegitimate analogies between Israel and the Nazis and between Israel and their own murderous regime in Algeria. This engenders slogans, not clear thinking; but it is a problem that the French must resolve, not the Israelis.

Fourth rule: A reasonably intelligent reporter can learn enough in a short time to present a reasonably accurate picture of events. This is nonsense, but not obviously so. Imagine the following being broadcast on the *BBC World News:* "In a replay of a time-honored pattern, Muslim preachers this morning incited the devout on the Haram el-Sharif to attack Jewish civilians at the nearby Western Wall. This follows the visit yesterday of Israel's opposition leader, Ariel Sharon, to the disputed Temple Mount/Haram el-Sharif. For both Muslims and Jews, the Mount is the holiest site in the land, and ever since the early 1920s Jewish attempts to assert their connection to it have sparked bloody Muslim riots." The fact that this sort of thing never occurs makes clear how very unlikely it is that your standard beat reporter will be able to explain what is happening.

Take another chimerical story: "In an updated version of an ancient lie, Yasser Arafat yesterday blamed Israelis for using radioactive shells against Palestinian towns so as to cause cancer among the populace. Such allegations have been a staple of anti-Jewish rhetoric for centuries, most famously the accusation that wells poisoned by Jews were the cause of the black plague that engulfed Europe in 1348. As a result of those accusations, many thousands of Jews were murdered. . . ." The correspondent would have to know some history to be able to write such a report, but if she doesn't know this history, her report will inevitably be wrong. Arafat's accusations were not a coincidence, there was a reason for their peculiar formulation, and unless this is part of the story, the readers aren't getting their money's worth.

Fifth rule: Discerning journalists can see through deceit. This may be a reasonable rule of thumb when applied to our own democratically elected politicians. It is demonstrably false when dealing with people for whom lying is a legitimate weapon in a war for Western hearts and minds. Listen to the late Faisal Husseini, widely hailed in the West for his commitment to peace, who said publicly in Arabic before his death in 2001: "Tactically, we may win or lose, but our eyes will continue to aspire to the strategic goal, namely, to Palestine from the [Jordan] river to the [Mediterranean] sea"—that is, to a state of Palestine in place of Israel. "Whatever we get now, cannot make us forget this supreme truth." Of course, the past master of this kind of deceit is Arafat himself, who talks peace in English and calls in Arabic for a million *shahids* (martyrs) to march on Jerusalem while authorizing payments for terrorist cells to continue their actions against Israeli citizens.

Sixth rule: Good journalists know better than natives, whose antics they observe with cool detachment. The natives, being totally submerged in their subjective perspectives, cannot pull themselves out of their dramas by their own shoelaces, but we the reporters, and you our readers, know better. This superior knowledge allows us to preach to the natives, even though they will not listen. A good example of this kind of moral preening is the editorial of *The Guardian* on August 10, 2001, after the Sbarro pizzeria attack that claimed fifteen lives:

> For Israelis, the shock of the bomb is no less appalling for its sickening familiarity. But they, too, must surely pause at this moment of greatest fear and loathing, if only for the sake of those who died. The dead do not cry out for vengeance; they cry out for peace. To do them honour, and do right by his country, Mr Sharon must gather his cohorts in turn and say: no more assassinations, no more live fire, no more air raids and bulldozing. It is time for Israel, too, to pull back from the abyss, and there is still time, just, to do it. Pull back from the frontlines of Gaza and the West Bank, curb the settlers, end the blockade. And start talking again, as Shimon Peres urges, without any more preconditions.

Seventh rule: No one remembers what journalists said last week, no one notices their mistakes, and no one cares. Unlike the first six rules, this one is true. By definition, the press deals with ephemeral events and is ephemeral itself. Today's newspapers will wrap tomorrow's fish. Newspaper reporters have up to twelve hours between an event and filing a report; CNN doesn't even have five minutes. Yet the essence of their job is to dramatize events, to get us excited enough to make us want to listen. To achieve this, they must pretend, with convincing seriousness, that they know something we don't about the significance of these events. So they stand in front of the camera or sit at their laptop and invent significance to whatever has just happened (for instance, that Sharon's electoral victory "means war" or Arafat's speech "means an end to the violence"). If they happen by some coincidence to be right, they will only be convinced of their clairvoyance; if they were very wrong, they'll still redouble their efforts, secure in the knowledge that we're not keeping track anyway.

Eighth rule: Journalists are not thinkers, they are merely purveyors of news. This rule is also true. Faced with a given set of events, journalists will understand and report on them with commonly accepted explanations. Most reporters cannot conceive of a frame of mind radically different from their own and assure us that everyone is basically motivated by the same interests, ideas, and passions. If someone is angry, someone must have angered him or her; if an entire community is furious, someone must have done something to them. If the Palestinians goad their children to kill themselves along with the Jews, then the Jews must have done something horrible to cause such fury. Eventually such reasoning collapses, else one would have to say that the Jews must have done the Germans some awesomely unique evil in order to have reaped the Holocaust. But journalists are merely technicians, not thinkers: they do not try to evolve new explanations for reality, and they are not equipped to deal with anything truly mysterious, such as a hatred that is stronger than the will to live.

Yet for all of these natural shortcomings, it is still not clear why journalists so often work against Israel and for the Arabs. The consistency of anti-Israel bias in the media requires deeper explanations. Given the longevity, potency, and centrality of antisemitism in Western culture, it would be an act of supreme gullibility to pretend that nothing about the blatant anti-Zionist strands in the international sphere has anything to do with the preceding centuries of hatred. Yet that is what many of Israel's detractors would have us believe.

Tom Paulin, he of the Zionist SS poem, was interviewed in April 2002 by the Egyptian newspaper *Al-Ahram.* He told his interviewer that "I never believed that Israel had the right to exist at all." He then went on to tell about his feelings toward "Brooklyn-born Jewish settlers": "They should be shot dead. I think they are Nazis, racists, I feel nothing but hatred for them." During the ensuing uproar, he denied being an antisemite and condemned one of his critics: "What is so galling is that people like [Neville] Nagler think that they can insinuate antisemitism and leave it at that. . . . I am a philo-Semite, and I repudiate his letter with contempt." Yet contrary to Paulin's position, whereby he (or Israel's other detractors) is the only one who can say whether or not he is antisemitic, this is not a purely subjective issue.

The term *antisemitism* was coined in 1878 by a German politician named Wilhelm Marr as a way to hate Jews and the church simultaneously. His problem was simple: How do you continue to hate Jews if you yourself no longer believe in Christ? His solution was to hate them as a race. That this would logically require him also to hate Arabs never occurred to him, nor did it matter, since he did not know any Arabs. Europeans today who are against Muslims in one form or another neither call themselves antisemites nor are labeled as such. The word is clearly reserved for the hatred of Jews.

Once the term became synonymous with Auschwitz, it also became an alibi for millions. Whoever was sincerely horrified by the mass murder of Jews could reassure himself that he was therefore not an antisemite. Antisemites kill Jews in gas chambers, which we abhor, so we can't be antisemites. Also, since antisemites hate Semites, and Arabs are also Semites, Arabs can't be antisemites.

One solution would be to desist from using the term *antisemitism* and revert to the more precise "hatred of Jews." The problem is that hatred of the Jews at its worst is tied to the word *antisemitism,* and by using a different term, we are letting the haters off the hook by disconnecting their animosities from the historical heritage they must forever own. After Auschwitz, all future haters of Jews must bear the onus of the connection between their sentiments and industrial murder. This is not to say that all dislike of Jews must, will, or even could lead to murder. There are benign and malignant forms of the illness, but they are all forms of illness, and none of them should be confused with health.

Yet the metaphor of illness should be used warily. It contains the important truth that antisemitism is an affliction of the haters, even though the suffering is borne by the victims. (Alzheimer's disease does the same: the family suffers more than the person afflicted.) Yet illnesses are caused by bugs, or genes, or other external agents. Hatred exists in the mind and thus returns us to the essence of humanity—namely, the ability to make moral choices. Hatred is an affliction that besets only those who allow it to do so, who choose to hate. There is nothing deterministic about it. Hatred is always immoral.

Israel, like any other country, makes mistakes; living at war has given her the opportunity to make some extremely stupid ones, well beyond the scope of normal societies at peace. Surely outsiders can criticize her for her wrongdoing without being immoral themselves. Surely they can do so even beyond what she thinks is fair and still retain their own morality.

Yet just as surely, the critics' good opinion of themselves can also be questioned. Adolf Eichmann professed in Jerusalem not to be an antisemite, and may even have believed it, but there is a wealth of documentation (in German) to prove that he was. Surely Israel's critics cannot be considered the sole judges of their own animosity and thus their immorality.

For this purpose, I propose the "Joschka Fischer standard." Joschka Fischer is the German foreign minister, and a rather unlikely one at that. He represents the Green Party, which since its founding in the early 1970s was an antiestablishment party of eternal opposition, and Fischer came from its loonier side. In the early 1970s, he was involved in various violent demonstrations and was close to some of the most unsavory characters that particular subculture produced. Since these people were all anti-Zionists, so was he, and in 1969 he even went to Algiers to participate in a PLO conference that reconfirmed that the only solution to the Zionist problem was Israel's destruction—standard fare for the PLO in those days.

Then, somewhere along the way, Fischer began growing up. During his early tenure as a member of the Bundestag (the German Parliament), he was conspicuous in his antiestablishment attire, demeanor, and positions, but he was already light-years away from punching policemen. At the end of the 1990s, he led the party into the federal government; and now, as foreign minister, the second highest position in the cabinet, he is about as establishment as they come.

Still, Israelis could be excused for being wary of him. When the Jerusalem *intifada* broke out, and Europe clamored for us to be nicer to the Palestinians, to appease their holy wrath and generally behave as the Europeans would have us behave, you might have expected us to brush aside the pronouncements of a Joschka Fischer with some self-righteous wrath of our own.

This never happened. True, most Israelis can't name too many European politicians, but we had our list of those we loved to hate: Jacques Chirac, obviously; Terje Roed-Larsen of Norway; Luis Michel of Belgium; Javier Solana, emissary to the Middle East of the European Union; and, of course, Kofi Annan, though he's not European. Fischer was not only not on the list, he stood at the top of another very short list of Europeans whom we actually respect. Not because he was invariably on our side, because he wasn't, but because he was consistently fair—a mensch, in the Yiddish meaning of that German word.

It just so happened that Fischer was down the block when a suicide bomber killed twenty-one teenagers at the Dolphinarium discotheque in Tel Aviv, and we could see that he was deeply shaken. He postponed his return home by four or five days, holding the fort until some top American arrived, and spent every waking moment trying to avert a war. But he did so in tones we could accept: by screaming at Arafat that this *had to stop* while pleading with Sharon to stay his hand, not for ideological reasons but pragmatically, to see if Arafat had perhaps now, finally, gotten the message. Had we been the wrathful seekers of revenge that we're routinely described as being, we'd have been scathing in our rejection of Fischer's efforts; instead we recognized him as an honest broker whose agenda was what it purported to be. He also happened to be wrong, and things probably would have been better had we turned our might on the Palestinians then and not waited until the following year. But this didn't affect our opinion of him.

Most interesting of all, the Palestinians also accept him as an honest broker. Fischer has not become a Zionist, and some of his positions have been quite critical of Israel. But that is the point of the Joschka Fischer standard: it demonstrates that it is possible to come from all the wrong European traditions and still learn to criticize Israel in an acceptable way. It also proves that when people do so, we not only refrain from calling them antisemites, but listen to their critical advice and sometimes even act upon it. Even when we don't, we still remain friends, because they also accept that while we cannot be convinced by them at certain times, at other times we can be.

The Joschka Fischer standard underlines a salient characteristic of contemporary antisemitism: that much of it, at least in the West, is no longer directed at individual Jews. In 2002, *The Economist* asked whether antisemitism *was* on the rise in Europe and concluded that it wasn't, since there was no discernible rise in anti-Jewish discrimination. Such feigned innocence was not convincing in a serious publication. In pre-Zionist times, Jews had no actual power, so their haters either had to pretend that they did (as in *The Protocols of the Elders of Zion*) or vented their animosity at individual Jews nearby. After the Holocaust, there weren't many Jews left in Europe, except in France and Britain, and democratic respect for the individual became the only accepted way of thought. The Jews, however, now had a state, and that state was using its power to promote its interests, thus opening a wide vista of previously unavailable accusations.

For a while, antisemites could claim to be merely anti-Zionist, pointing to their generally cordial relations with their Jewish neighbors as an alibi. Yet this was a flimsy line of reasoning. An overwhelming majority of Jews in the world identified with Israel; while not always agreeing with her actions, they cared for her, hoped for her success and well-being, and often supported her, and when they criticized her it was all the more intense precisely because they felt a bond they didn't feel with any other foreign country. Having an affinity with Israel is part of being a Jew, and Zionism has truly become the central Jewish project. This means that while you may certainly be critical of specific Israeli actions, as a practical matter you cannot call yourself an anti-Zionist without also being antisemitic. The Jews have made a decision to have a sovereign state, and being against it means being against them.

Eventually, even the sham of limited anti-Zionism showed itself for the travesty it is. Beyond the outright lying about Israel's actions, there was the stark irrationality and hypocrisy of the criticism and the perverse double standards, particularly at the UN and its forums. Israel is singled out for denunciation and attack again and again, while far worse culprits go unmentioned or are welcomed as colleagues in censure. Even the breathtaking Israeli offers at Taba never made a dent. Anti-Zionism obsessively puts Israel at the epicenter of world events, so that September 11 was attributed to American support for Israel (or even to an Israeli plot hatched by Sharon himself), while the murder of two hundred mostly Australian tourists at Bali—with not a single Israeli among them—was likewise Israel's fault.

Ironically, the Muslims and far-right chauvinists who attack Jewish cemeteries, synagogues, or community centers in Europe or South America understand the connection between anti-Zionism and antisemitism quite clearly. They also see through the self-righteousness of their own societies. If the entire establishment shrilly castigates Israel, it is a rejection of the *Jewish* state. Their violent actions emphasize the true significance of antisemitism and its danger to the antisemites themselves: You cannot single out a group or nation for castigation by unique standards and remain democratic. The concept of universal humanity and hatred of a specific group contradict each other.

Using the Joschka Fischer standard, Mr. Reeves, his editors, and their many accomplices will simply have to live with the fact that we regard them as antisemites. The only advantage to being at the receiving end of this phenomenon is that we get to have the final say as to who is and who is not an antisemite.

Yet compelling as it is, antisemitism cannot explain all the antagonism toward Israel. There is another, related but separate, phenomenon foreseen by one of the most important prophets of the twentieth century, Franz Kafka, when he wrote in *The Trial* that *"Die Lüge wird zur Weltordnung gemacht"* ("the Lie becomes the way of the world").

In the world of intellectual discourse, truth has become an embarrassing word. Only the unsophisticated still believe in it; the sophisticated have unveiled it for what it is: a subjective way of looking at the world, predetermined by one's material and social conditions and reflecting current relations of power, whereby the strong force their version of truth (their "narrative construction") on the weak. The mark of a true intellectual is the ability to rise above these narrow circumstances so as to understand the narratives of those who have different circumstances, different truths. They are, of course, equally subjective, but the narratives of the powerless are privileged, for power always corrupts.

This intellectual conceit has devastating implications for the making of policy. In the words of the University of Southampton's David Cesarani, "Sadly, the Enlightenment notion of perfectability has been overtaken by post-Enlightenment relativism. A left-liberal person between 1750 and 1950 would have looked at the Taliban and said: poor, benighted souls—but they have reason and the capacity for improvement so we must teach them civilization. Now the view is: well, if that's what they think and that's the way they do things, who are we to judge? The left has lost the moral vigour that once powered its social reform schemes."

Since truth is held to be subjective, the language of journalism must be sanitized of any tendency to take sides. The best example is the expunging of the word *terrorism* from the vocabulary of enlightened news reporters. Where there is no truth, there is no objective way of deciding who is and is not a terrorist; therefore you can only conclude that one man's terrorist is another man's freedom fighter. Since it is the task of the reporter to report, not take sides, the T-word must never be used, and it has been replaced by the euphemistic term *militants.* This has many disadvantages, one being that all self-styled "militants" are now implicitly allowed to kill civilians to promote their interests. Another is that the language now lacks a precise word for the intentional political killing of uninvolved civilians. Finally, deleting the T-word can aggravate readers, which is fine if the readers are Jews but deplorable if the readers are one's own taxpayers, which is why the BBC has a directive whereby in Northern Ireland there are terrorists, while in the rest of the world there are only militants. But the entire exercise is not to be taken seriously, since it applies only to one word. It would never occur to anyone, for example, to replace the term *occupied territories* with *disputed territories* on the grounds that one man's occupation might be another's liberation.

Another stratagem for avoiding the truth is through a very liberal use of parenthesis. Anything the journalist wishes not to endorse as a fact gets referred to as hearsay or an untested statement made by some spokesman. Thus, when the BBC reports the news that Israeli radio has said (or "claimed") that three dead Palestinians were wearing "explosive belts," the public can decide for itself whether or not to believe the story.

A by-product of the journalistic unwillingness to make moral judgment is the retreat to moral equivalence. One makes a list of all the things that can be done wrong and criticizes all delinquents equally. Bombing an empty police station after warning people to get out is as repugnant as bombing a mall crowded with weekend shoppers. Manning roadblocks and checkpoints that infuriate Palestinians and hamper civilian traffic is just as criminal as trying to get through them to murder civilians and is somehow seen to justify such acts. Attempting to make peace by offering almost 100 percent of the West Bank, but not parts of Jerusalem, is just as destructive as rejecting the offer and launching a wave of unprovoked violence.

The fountainhead of the loss of truth is—as Kafka expected—in Europe, where it is intertwined in the major political undertaking of our era: the annulment of history in the name of peace. Following centuries of warfare and their horrendous crescendo in the slaughter of World War I, the barbarities of fascism and communism, and the ultimate depravity of World War II, Western Europe decided to banish the use of force in international relations. Under the umbrella of American power, they created an island, severed from the rest of humanity, in which war was inconceivable and all differences are resolved by peaceful negotiation. This can be achieved only by creating a state of mind in which nothing is as important as the preservation of peace itself—neither one's tradition, nor one's national goals, nor even, as it eventually became clear, one's sovereignty itself. Nor, one might cynically add, the lives of Muslim Europeans in Bosnia, if defending them means taking up arms.

This is a radical break with standard human behavior, and is not clearly a positive development. It would have been better had the Europeans taught themselves the art of living simultaneously in peace and in true diversity—but since Europe is ultimately not such a diverse place when compared with the full gamut that mankind has to offer, they have chosen an easier way. They are investing tremendous efforts in their project, writing reams of regulations about the packaging of sausages or the structure and content of schoolbooks. Since European history demonstrated to them that they could not live peacefully with diversity, they resolved to become all alike.

Outsiders who don't agree with them, or who still insist on having values that are so important they are willing to fight for them, are regarded as primitive and anachronistic. Since the Jews were so central to European history, they of all people are expected to understand what the Europeans are doing and should want to participate; by doing the opposite, they cast doubt on the whole project in a way that Africans or Arabs could never do.

Listen to an archetypal European figure, Greta Duisenberg, wife of Wim Duisenberg, the head of the European Central Bank, and an indefatigable defender of the Palestinians. During a visit to the West Bank in January 2003, she explained that the Israeli occupation was definitely worse than the Nazi occupation of Holland, assuming one was willing to overlook the murder of more than one hundred thousand Dutch Jews, in that the Israelis demolish Palestinian homes, and even the Nazis never did that.

Actually, the Nazis did: they launched their perfidious attack on neutral Holland in 1940 with a devastating air raid on Rotterdam, destroying most of the center of the town. After that, they didn't have to demolish Dutch homes to deter any acts of resistance, because whenever such acts happened, they shot hundreds of Dutch hostages. And anyway, their murder of the Jews wasn't a footnote to the conquest of Europe, it was the centerpiece of Nazism. This was not mentioned in most of the responses I saw to Ms. Duisenberg's idiotic statements, because they came from the core of the new consensus, whereby truth is merely a subjective construct and can never be allowed to interfere with the process of reconciling everybody to everybody else.

This is the frame of mind that informs the endless preaching of so-called peace activists when calling upon disputants to desist from their foolish behavior: whatever you are fighting about isn't really important, and if you'd only listen to our wise counsel, everything would be all right. It makes for a moral equivalence accompanied by a plaintive otherworldliness that you wouldn't expect from adults. Listen to the wistful recommendations of Human Rights Watch, in its October 2002 report, "Erased in a Moment: Suicide Bombing Attacks Against Israeli Civilians":

> Human Rights Watch calls on the leaders of Hamas, Islamic Jihad, the al-Aqsa Martyrs' Brigades, and the Popular Front for the Liberation of Palestine to:
>
> ~ Cease such attacks immediately and declare publicly that they will not resort to such attacks in the future under any circumstances.
>
> ~ Commit publicly to respecting the basic principles of international humanitarian law, and instruct all members of their organizations to do so, in particular those principles applying to the protection of civil-

> ians during armed conflict and the duty to arrest and deliver to the authorities for prosecution anyone who fails to do so. . . .
>
> To President Arafat and the Palestinian Authority:
>
> Make clear that suicide bombings and other attacks on civilians constitute grave crimes; that those who incite, plan, assist, attempt or carry out such attacks will face criminal charges; and that the PA will take all possible measures to ensure that they are brought to justice.

It is as if the human rights activists really believe the Palestinians are engaging in their crimes by accident, perhaps absentmindedly; now that they've been told about it, the problem can be swiftly corrected.

The so-called peace activists of this world, whether Europeans or left-wing Americans, are trying to guide the world away not only from Europe's lethal past, but also from another part of its legacy: colonialism. On September 12, 2002, *The Guardian* published a concise history of the twentieth century from the point of view of its regular columnist Seamus Milne. Aptly titled "The Battle for History," it set forth a simple thesis: Nazism was the century's arch-evil, and communisim cannot be compared to it, both because the number of victims commonly attributed to communism are bloated and because the cruelty of communism in the 1920s propelled the USSR into modernity and enabled it to defeat the Nazis in the 1940s. But according to Milne, all this pales beside the immense viciousness of European colonialism. He even seems to be toying with the idea that colonialism was worse than Nazism, at least in terms of the sheer numbers of people who died because of it. He finishes with a call to activism:

> Those who write colonial barbarity out of 20th-century history want to legitimise the new liberal imperialism, just as those who demonise past attempts to build an alternative to capitalist society are determined to prove that there is none. The problem for the left now is not so much that it has failed to face up to its own history, but that it has become paralysed by the burden of it.

In the eyes of such people Zionism is a colonial movement, and Milne is quite clear what should be done about it, were the world not paralyzed by the burden of history: international sanctions. Asked for a response to Sharon's election, he wrote the following:

> By any reasonable reckoning, he is a war criminal. This is a man of blood, whose history of terror and violation of the rules of war stretches back to the early 50s, when his unit slaughtered Palestinian villagers, through his brutal onslaught on the refugees of Gaza in the 70s, to his central role in Israel's 1982 invasion of Lebanon in which up to 20,000 people died. . . . Israel's own Kahan commission found Sharon "personally" but "indirectly" responsible for the massacre, though whether an independent court would be so generous is open to question . . . It will be objected that Sharon has been chosen in a democratic election and that pursuing him for 18-year-old crimes will do nothing to advance the chances of a peace settlement. Such a settlement will become more likely once the majority of Israelis realize that Sharon's hard-line policies of repression will not deliver the security they crave, while sanctions seem more suitable for a state whose citizens have a say in policy, rather than for dictatorships where they have none. (*The Guardian*, February 9, 2001)

Try as you may, however, the scope for casting Israel as a colonial power is limited, even if like Milne you are willing to inflate greatly the number of dead in Israel's Lebanese campaign or to disparage the independence of Israel's courts. If you are predisposed to identify conflicts between Western powers and anyone else in terms of "liberal colonialism," rather than in empirical analysis or a universal evaluation of the morality of the protagonists, the real culprit, of course, is the United States: very big, very rich, very powerful, the mainstay of the first world.

September 11 upset the complacency of the deniers of truth. It was too big and too awful to write off as just an alternative narrative. Its evil was too great for most decent people to justify by any alleged wrong that the citizens of New York and Washington had somehow perpetrated upon the privileged sons of Egypt and Saudi Arabia. It therefore functioned for some lazy but basically decent people as a brutal call to return to their senses.

For those of us who were never allowed that kind of laziness and have been staring evil in the face for many years, the interesting thing about

September 12 was the way the responses to the attacks corresponded largely to the way people related to Israel. Our friends shook their heads in horror, affirmed or reaffirmed their moral bearings, and resolved to take action; our enemies undertook tactical damage control but changed nothing in their view of the world.

This was not only because the murderers were the cousins of our own local terrorists, but because September 11 had echoes of Nazism in being so stark an event that terms like *good* and *evil* demand to be applied. Would you choose to recognize what you had preferred to forget—that the respect for human life has enemies so potent that at times they must be killed—or would you continue to pretend that nothing is worth killing for and that if they wish to kill us, we must have done them a great injustice?

Columnist Robert Fisk of *The Independent* is the most obvious representative of those who refuse to think in universal moral terms. He is the paper's senior correspondent in the Middle East, which he has been covering for twenty-five years. Beirut is his base. He knows his stuff, meaning that he's well read and intelligent, and he knows how to write. He is also rabidly critical of Israel, while proclaiming indignantly that he is no antisemite. Yet he will happily enumerate the abusive terms Israeli politicians have thrown at Palestinians without a murmur about the Goebbels-like propaganda and antisemitic lies commonly broadcast by the Palestinians and many other Arab media. He is also incapable of making the distinction between murder and killing, but in this, as in so many other things, he doesn't stand out from the crowd.

Two of his pieces, however, do stand out: his response to September 11 and his eerie response to being attacked himself. His response to September 11, titled "The Wickedness and Awesome Cruelty of a Crushed and Humiliated People" (*The Independent,* September 12, 2001), articulately states the proposition that ties morality to political or economic well-being.

> So it has come to this. The entire modern history of the Middle East: the collapse of the Ottoman Empire, the Balfour declaration, Lawrence of Arabia's lies, the Arab revolt, the foundation of the state of Israel, four Arab-Israeli wars and the 34 years of Israel's brutal occupation of Arab land: all erased within hours as those who claim to represent a crushed, humiliated population struck back with the wickedness and awesome cruelty of a doomed people. . . . Our broken

> promises, perhaps even our destruction of the Ottoman Empire, led inevitably to this tragedy. America has bankrolled Israel's wars for so many years that it believed this would be cost-free. No longer so.

September 11 as justified retribution for World War I! Yet Fisk is a consistent man. While traveling through Pakistan two months later, he was attacked by a mob simply for being a Westerner. His description of his ordeal, published the next day, is a fascinating study of the depths one can plumb once one relativizes morality:

> And—I realised—there were all the Afghan men and boys who had attacked me who should never have done so but whose brutality was entirely the product of others, of us—of we who had armed their struggle against the Russians and ignored their pain and laughed at their civil war and then armed and paid them again for the "War for Civilisation" just a few miles away and then bombed their homes and ripped up their families and called them "collateral damage". . . . The people who were assaulted were the Afghans, the scars inflicted by us—by B-52s, not by them. And I'll say it again. If I was an Afghan refugee in Kila Abdullah, I would have done just what they did. I would have attacked Robert Fisk. Or any other Westerner I could find.[2]

Fisk seems unable to make the distinction between understanding the causes of mob violence and accepting it as a justified response to oppressive conditions. With reasoning like this, you begin to appreciate how antiwar demonstrations with hundreds of thousands of participants, especially in Europe, take on the appearance of mass rallies against Israel and America, just like in Iran under Khomeini.

There is another group that is certainly not antisemitic and knows enough not to identify Israel as a colonial power: the Israeli Zionist peace camp. They are not to be mistaken for the post-Zionists and their political representatives, some of whom would feel comfortable with the looniest Fisk-like figures. The Zionist peace camp, however, though sorely shrunken since the Palestinians broke all the rules, are still around; politically they are the voters of the left wing of Labor or much of the Meretz Party.

[2] *The Independent*, December 10, 2001.

One of their leading spokesmen is Israeli novelist David Grossman, who published *The Yellow Wind* in the mid-1980s, at a time when the PLO still officially rejected Israel's right to exist and saw in violence the only legitimate way to achieve its goal. Grossman, a sensitive person who writes with passion and intelligence, wandered around the occupied territories talking with Arabs and came back to report what he had found. His conclusion was that from a Palestinian perspective, Israelis were brutal and arrogant bastards, but if they would only start taking the Palestinians seriously, they would find them willing partners for peace. The book was immensely successful and as influential as a single book can be. In one of its most memorable passages, echoed several times elsewhere, Grossman's Palestinian interlocutors assure him with disarming frankness that should there ever be peace between the two states, they would gladly forgo maintaining an army. In the words of the Palestinians themselves, the only reason we need an army is to protect us from you, and if we were at peace, why would we want to spend money on an army?

Grossman's message was basically optimistic and purportedly came from the Palestinians themselves. Every one of the book's statements about the Palestinian position was to prove false, even long before Camp David; the Palestinian insistence on building an army far larger than the police force agreed upon was merely one of the more obvious points. Palestinian behavior since Camp David effectively demolished the entire message of the book, but Grossman never publicly had second thoughts.

In early January 2002, Israelis captured a Palestinian ship loaded with weaponry. Much of it, such as hundreds of Katyusha rockets shipped from Iran, could only have been aimed at civilian targets. Even as unlikely an observer as Osama el-Baz, senior adviser to Egyptian president Hosni Mubarak, noted in front of the cameras that should the Israeli allegation be proved, it would seriously hurt Palestinian credibility.

And Grossman? He published an article in *Yediot,* Israel's largest paper, full of surprisingly harsh language castigating Israel's politicians, generals, and press for their hypocrisy: given Israel's cruel occupation, what did we expect?

The Zionist peace camp are not antisemites. Not that Jews can't be antisemites: there is a long and strange tradition of such people. But it's hard to see how one might be a committed Zionist and an antisemite at the same time. Some of them are infected with the moral equivalence disease, and many feel an affinity for the intellectuals of Europe. Mostly, however, they are people who refuse to accept the pessimism that comes with the expectation of additional generations of Arab rejection. Like the rest of us, they see the murderous Palestinian policies close up, and they know that much of the Muslim world reeks with an antisemitism that is far beyond any rational explanation. But they still cling to an optimistic fantasy that Israel by her actions can somehow make things better. They prefer to focus on what Israel does wrong, hoping to influence the actions of their own country since they cannot influence anyone else, and tell themselves that if Israel were to do all the right things, the Arabs would reciprocate.

But while the ugliness of our occupation is *not* the defining element of the conflict, *not* its motivating source, and though removing it will unfortunately *not* bring an end to the conflict, still it is important we be reminded constantly of the human cost it demands of both sides. It is a sign of the robustness of our democracy that we have never lacked for journalists to remind us, editors to publish them, or a morally sensitive public to read them.

The ultimate difference between Israelis of the die-hard peace camp and Israel's foreign critics is that they're here and the critics are not. Should the Palestinians ever manage to destroy Israel, the throats of the peace camp Israelis will be slit along with the others; until then, the suicide bombers are murdering Israelis of all political hues. The foreign pundits, on the other hand, will tut-tut over the tale of our destruction for a week or so and go on to the next event. Being an Israeli—or, for that matter, a Palestinian—means you pay for your decisions and those of your society. Being a foreign observer means you can pontificate at will and then do something else. There is no price for being wrong at our expense.

The crescendo came in April 2002. Ever since Sharon's ascension to power, the number of dead had been rising, and by March the frequency of attacks was so high that the semblance of normal daily life was disappearing. No elected leader anywhere in the world would have restrained himself in such a situation, and the fact that Sharon, the "man of blood," was letting it happen was incredible. Even his faithful supporters wondered if he had lost his nerve, and polls showed him slipping steadily while his critics crowed that the Palestinian violence was unstoppable and Israel must concede her positions to appease it. Until the night of the seder, that symbolic night commemorating freedom. Two days later, the IDF finally got down to business.

The uproar was earsplitting. While reserve units registered more than 100 percent recruitment, a small group of Israelis stood up against their society's consensus and demonstrated in front of the Ministry of Defense. Knesset member Zahava Gal-On of Meretz had an inspired sound bite when she shouted that the commencing military operation was *"Stam! Stam! Stam!"* (*"Futile! Futile! Futile!"*). Hundreds of antisemitic or just plain clueless pro-Palestinian "peace activists" flew in from Europe, the United States, and even Australia to insert themselves into the battlefields and prove that Sharon's Israel would stop at nothing. European diplomats piled up at the airports, waiting to visit Arafat in his besieged Ramallah headquarters. Mass demonstrations against Israel—and against the Jews in general—hit the streets of Europe, even as synagogues were being attacked all over the continent. The American administration wavered, torn between its reluctance to tell Israel simply to live with terror and its fear that a larger conflagration was in the offing or that some humanitarian disaster would discredit its own efforts against the cousins of the Palestinian murderers. The United Nations, led by Nobel laureate Kofi Annan, resolved to send a commission of inquiry into the crimes committed against its wards, the descendants of refugees in Jenin. And Phil Reeves spewed out his bile.

They were all wrong. Every single one of them. As the IDF turned the tide of the murderous Palestinians, the number of casualties on both sides dropped. The "Butcher of Beirut" turned out to be striving for a decline in the violence that would leave more people *on both sides* alive; moreover, to an extent he was successful, and any reasonable observer would have to admit that the ongoing violence was the result of a conscious Palestinian decision to continue killing Jews. Meanwhile, Sharon repeatedly announced that the final stage of negotiations would be a sovereign Palestinian state alongside Israel, although he demanded that the violence end as a precondition. None of this has garnered him any credit on the international scene.

But Israel's enemies—the Palestinian ones next door, the Arab ones nearby, or the Western ones in their peaceful countries far away—are not interested in facts. They feel no need to reexamine their assumptions. A Jewish state using its power to defend itself and prepared to meet murderous intent with resolute force is not acceptable to them. End of discussion.

CHAPTER

12

Tenacity: The Decision to Endure

The Oslo process failed, and it's time to return the name to the Norwegians. Both the Americans and the Israelis took it for granted, each in their own way, and relationships taken for granted have a way of unraveling. The Americans allowed both sides to be sloppy in implementing their commitments, while the Israelis assumed the irreversibility of the process and acted irresponsibly along the way. By enlarging the settlements, Israel did not make clear her understanding that peace would only be achieved without them, while by disregarding the many Palestinian infractions, especially the systematic poisoning of minds and the ongoing terror, she did not make it sufficiently clear that they would only have a state without *them*.

Americans and Israelis both erred in assuming that at the end of the day, everybody would behave rationally and strive for the best that could be achieved rather than the best that could be imagined. They knew that ultimately, no Israeli government would permit the process to disintegrate, because the Israeli electorate wouldn't allow it. Sooner or later, an Israeli government would table a proposal that would contain all the compromises Israel could make, the Palestinians would reciprocate, and the mistakes of both sides would be annulled by the success of its resolution. But it was not to be, and those of us who supported the Oslo process for as long as it went on were wrong.

If there is nothing Israel can afford to do that will resolve the conflict, two questions remain to be addressed. Was the Oslo process worth trying? Is living with permanent war worth it?

Strictly speaking, Oslo was not worth trying. It vastly improved the Palestinian ability to kill Jews while putting the onus for the killing on the Israelis themselves. By raising the military stakes, it also vastly inflated the number of Palestinians getting killed, but that too is a reason to regret launching Oslo, since killing Palestinians is not what Zionism is about. Yet for all its deadly drawbacks, Oslo greatly strengthened Israel's resolve, and in a war of centuries, that is not something to be shrugged off.

The late 1970s saw the emergence of two fallacies among Israelis. The first, that of the hawks, was the belief that if they presented the world with a united front, eventually the Palestinian problem would go away. This was part of the rationale behind the creation of the settlements, which supplied the Palestinians with a perfect alibi for their murderous hatred. The second, that of the doves, was the equally childish belief that the Palestinians had become enlightened yeomen, yearning only for a bit of peace on their land from which to engage in free trade, environmental conservation, and liberal discourse, from which only our intransigence and chauvinism impeded them.

Both camps were tilting at windmills, and both foolishly convinced themselves that it was in the power of the Jews to determine what the Palestinians would want and do. As if that powerful will to murder, embedded so deeply in the Palestinian national project, were not the result of a mature decision but, rather, was a mistake they had slipped into because we had not been either stern or nice enough.

Oslo demonstrated what we should never have forgotten: that the will to murder Jews was never the result of oppression and cannot be solved by removing it. The fact that a sincere offer of peace sent the Palestinians into a paroxysm of violence can be explained only by their fear of its finality, the obligation to relinquish their fantasies in favor of reality, and the inevitability of becoming responsible for their own destiny within the limits of the possible rather than in their irresponsible dreams.

Oslo also destroyed the naiveté of the Israelis. The settlers know they do not have the backing of the people, and most of the electorate knows that the land must be partitioned. The peace camp, or at least its broad hinterland, without which it cannot achieve anything, knows that the true enemies are those who celebrate the deaths of our children, not other Israelis who disagree with them about the goals of Zionism.

Close to a thousand Israelis were killed by Palestinians from Oslo until the end of 2002—a steep price to pay for such clarity. Running over their names, ages, occupations, and smiling pictures, I ask whether those, like myself, who demanded we embark on the road from Oslo were too careless with human lives; if so, there can hardly be a more serious allegation.

Assuming, of course, that there had been a real alternative. Israelis were also being murdered before Oslo, though not at such a rate. But after the breakdown of consensus in the wake of the Lebanon invasion and the futility of repressing the first *intifada* while offering no alternative, Israeli society was showing serious rifts. A healthy society can afford a little discord when at war, but to many of us, Lebanon and the first *intifada* had seemed unnecessary conflicts. The collapse of Oslo focused our minds on fundamental facts: this is not a war for settlements or an attempt to deprive the Palestinians of their own state; it is a war for the right of the Jews to self-determination, in a world that is quite willing to live without them.

Israeli children of the 1950s or 1960s were expected to grow up and not have to fight in the army. By now, their children are serving in the army, as will their children's children and their children after them. A poignant but very popular Hebrew song called "We Are the Children of 1973" tells of the shock and bereavement with which the tired young men returned from the battlefields in that cold and dark winter and clung to the young women with the passion of loss. How they promised their children to make a more peaceful world. It hasn't happened, but—say the children-turned-soldiers—we still have the strength to go on and can share it with you if you're tiring.

You guide your kids through childhood, counting the years to the day they'll go off to the army—and a fighting army it is. People get killed there, and they become killers. For these eighteen-year-old inductees, the whole thing seems a gigantic lark, where one's mettle will be tested. For their parents, who have been there and have lost the feeling of immortality common to adolescents, the second time around is far more disturbing. Why do this to yourself, to your children, to your children's children?

The question is misleading, since with the exception of full-scale wars, most of the Jewish victims are civilians: children on their way to school, teenagers out on the town, young couples wandering in the fields, men shopping, women taking buses. So it has been for at least eighty years, and so it will most likely continue, with peaks and troughs of intensity. Why submit yourself to this punishment, generation after generation?

Ultimately, because that's what Jews do. Here and there over the millennia, Jews have enjoyed extended periods of peace and prosperity. It is not true that the story of the Jews is one of unmitigated and eternal disaster. Yet neither is theirs a history of peace punctuated by occasional calamities. Jews are about creativity under any conditions. They are about commitment to an ongoing and ever growing tradition. They are about dreaming of and working toward a utopian future while doing one's best in a very imperfect world. They are about ambivalence, questioning, and doubt while proclaiming the possibility of clarity and truth.

The eighteenth-century Hasidic rabbi of Kotsk famously said, "There is nothing as whole as a broken heart," and I can't think of any statement that better summarizes "Jewishness." You can't have a broken heart unless you are deeply involved in life. Being deeply involved in life will give you a broken heart. A broken heart is the last thing you want, but only once it is broken can it truly be whole. Thus, seeking any other destiny will leave you less whole. A broken heart is part of a full life—its prerequisite, its price.

At this stage in their long history, close to half of living Jews have chosen to participate in the experiment of returning to the ranks of sovereign nations—just like the Zambians, the Uzbeks, the Bolivians, and the Norwegians. Zionism was not the invention of desperate refugees from Nazi persecution—it was well on its way to achieving its goals before the Holocaust, in which most of its potential citizens were murdered. It was not the decision of fundamentalist religious fanatics to enact an age-old dream, but the invention of atheistic, realistic children of the Enlightenment. It was not an offshoot of European imperialism, nor was it a bulwark of the West or of communism. Nor was it a solution to antisemitism. Rather, it was antisemitism's best lease on life. Zionism is not a plot against the Arabs, but the most recent chapter in an ancient story, an attempt by the Jews to define their place in the modern world, and a refusal of the Jews to cease being, to die out, to fade away.

Zionism has succeeded far beyond the dreams of its inventors. Israel has yet to fulfill a single one of its utopian goals, and its creation has been accompanied by at least as much confusion, ineptitude, bad faith, waste, poor taste, callousness, and stupidity as any other large-scale human project—though there has been rather less murder than in most other nation-building projects. Imperfect as it is, is Zionism worth fighting and dying for, unto our children's children's children? Of course it is.

TIMELINE

1880–1900: Proto-Zionist immigration and settlement (first aliyah).

1887: First Zionist Congress, convened in Basle by Theodor Herzl, founds the Zionist movement and its first institutions.

1903–1914: Second aliyah. Characterized by the intense ideological drive of its participants, the second aliyah created the ethos of the pioneering Zionist settlement and formed the core of its leadership for decades.

1917: Balfour Declaration in favor of a Jewish National Home in Palestine.

1920: Attacks on Jewish settlements, including three days of rioting, looting, rape, and murder against the Jews of Jerusalem.

1921: Arab riots and attacks against Jews in Jaffa and several new settlements.

1929: 133 dead Jews in a week of pogroms, including the destruction of the ancient Jewish community of Hebron.

1936–1938: The Arab Revolt: initially a popular revolt against British rule and Jewish immigration, the violence deteriorated into Palestinian internecine bloodletting, and was eventually defeated by the British.

1947: United Nations partition plan proposes partitioning of mandatory Palestine into two sovereign states, Israel and Palestine. The Arab world rejects the plan and launches a war to destroy the nascent Jewish state.

1947–1948: Israeli War of Independence, Palestinian Naqba ("Catastrophe").

May 14th, 1948: Declaration of Israel's Independence, David Ben-Gurion provisional prime minister.

1949: Armistice agreements between Israel and Egypt, Jordan, Lebanon, and Syria reflecting the positions of the Israeli and Arab armies at the end of the fighting.

1948–1953: Ben-Gurion leads the newly founded state, absorbing hundreds of immigrants and creating most of the country's institutions and political traditions. After a brief interlude under Moshe Sharett, Ben-Gurion was again prime minister from 1955–1963.

1956: Sinai campaign. Following almost a decade of murderous infiltrations along Israel's borders, the Sinai campaign produced almost a decade of calm along the Israeli-Egyptian border—the most peaceful years Israel has ever known.

1963–1969: Prime Minister Levi Eshkol. Standing in Ben-Gurion's gigantic shadow, only in recent years has Eshkol been recognized as one of Israel's more effective prime ministers.

June 1967: Six-Day War. Instigated by President Nasser of Egypt, the Arab world's second attempt to destroy Israel resulted in Israeli control over the Sinai, the Gaza Strip, the Golan Heights, the West Bank, and the unification of Jerusalem under Israeli control.

1968–1970: The War of Attrition launched by Nasser was an attempt to dislodge Israel from its positions on the east bank of the Suez Canal, which ended when Israeli bombing attacks deep inside Egypt convinced Nasser to accept an American mediation attempt (the Rogers Plan).

1969–1974: Prime Minister Golda Meir. Remembered affectionately by American Jews, she is remembered in Israel for her destructive arrogance:

she rebuffed Egyptian negotiating feelers, preached at angry young Oriental Jews for being disrespectful, and failed to read the signs of an approaching joint Egyptian-Syrian attack.

1973: The Yom Kippur War. An attack Israel did not foresee and was not prepared for, it was repulsed at great cost in less than three weeks. Partial Arab successes enabled the Egyptians to claim that Israeli invincibility had been destroyed.

1974–1977: Prime Minister Yitzhak Rabin. A mediocre leader whose failures led to the decline of Labor as a majority party and the emergence of the more nationalistic Likud.

1977–1983: Prime Minister Menachem Begin. Contrary to his image as a hawk, Begin's historic achievement was to make peace with Egypt, evacuating the Sinai and disbanding settlements.

1977: Anwar Sadat launches peace initiative with a visit to Israel.

1978: Camp David Accords between Egypt and Israel.

1982: Completion of Israeli withdrawal from Egyptian territories in Sinai.

1982: Israeli invasion of Lebanon: Israel's sole attempt to act as a regional hegemon entangled her in a moral and military quagmire.

1983–1984: Prime Minister Yitzhak Shamir: remembered primarily for his adamant refusal to take any daring step in any direction.

1984–1986: Prime Minister Shimon Peres: in an astonishing two-year term, he withdrew the Israeli army from most of Lebanon and pulled the Israeli economy out of hyperinflation.

1985: Completion of Israeli withdrawal from Lebanon, except for a narrow strip north of the border.

1986–1992: Prime Minister Yitzhak Shamir: his single notable achievement was not to get embroiled in the first American-Iraqi war, in spite of thirty-nine Iraqi missiles shot at Israel's cities.

1987–1993: First *intifada*: a popular, mostly nonviolent uprising of Palestinians against Israeli occupation, it convinced both Israel and the PLO that an agreement must be reached.

1992–1995: Prime Minster Yitzhak Rabin. In his second term, Rabin launched a variety of significant reforms. The internal dissensions unleashed by his attempt to make peace with the Palestinians led to his assassination by an Israeli extremist.

1993: Oslo Accords between Israel and the PLO.

1994: Peace treaty between Israel and Jordan.

1995–1996: Prime Minister Shimon Peres. During his brief second term, Peres was unable to repeat any of the dramatic successes of his first term.

1996–1999: Prime Minister Benjamin Netanyahu. During his disastrous term, Netanyahu alienated everyone: the Palestinians, Israeli supporters and critics of the peace process, much of the international community, and many of his own closest aides.

1999–2001: Prime Minister Ehud Barak. Elected by an unprecedented margin to correct Netanyahu's many mistakes, Barak's actions revealed the fundamental rejection of Israel by many of her neighbors, and the willingness of much of the international community to accept this rejection.

2000: Prime Minister Ehud Barak orders unilateral Israeli withdrawal from last parts of southern Lebanon.

September 27, 2000: Outbreak of the Jerusalem *intifada* follows failed Israeli-Palestinian negotiations at Camp David and visit of Ariel Sharon to Temple Mount.

2001: Elected by a huge margin and reelected by a similar margin in 2003, Ariel Sharon was felt by most Israelis to be the only leader capable of dealing with the shambles left by his predecessor.

April 2002: Operation Defensive Shield turns the tide of the Jerusalem *intifada*.

ACKNOWLEDGMENTS

While writing this book, I was blessed by the generous assistance of many people; I am grateful to them all.

Dave Abelman, Sallyann Amdur-Sack, Leah Kabaker, Menachem Lorberbaum, and Karen Shawn all encouraged me to try my hand at this project and assisted me with their advice; Gabriel Schoenfeld also published an early version of my deliberations in the May 2001 edition of *Commentary*.

Nomi Halpern, Ronit Kamil, Malka Lozowick, Pinchas Lozowick, Ralf Oberndoerfer, Dana Porat, Irena Steinfeld, and Efraim Zuroff all read parts of the evolving manuscript and made valuable comments.

Beverly Martin at agentsresearch.com introduced me to Danny Baror of Baror International and Jimmy Vines of The Vines Agency. Danny and Jimmy demonstrated the power of literary agents at their best, propelling the manuscript into the top league of publishers and guiding me through a world I had not previously encountered.

The manuscript Adam Bellow read was the personal odyssey of my search for political and moral significance in the turmoil that was Israel in 2001. He suggested the transformation of the personal search into a report on its findings. He also showed me how to write the extensively revised book he had in mind. This revision became one of the most exciting intellectual exercises it has been my good fortune to engage in. Also at Doubleday, I was assisted by Miriam Abramowitz, Jenny Choi, and Sona Vogel.

Life in Jerusalem since September 2000 has been full of stress, and Achikam, Nechama, and Meir have had to deal with frightening challenges frankly inconceivable to their teenage peers elsewhere: the mortal danger of taking a bus or the life-threatening challenge of going downtown. It has been an honor and an education to watch them grow, morally intact no matter what was happening around them. Achikam has chosen Arabic as his major subject. Nechama has trained as a medic and carries a first-aid kit wherever she goes. And Meir has gone from being an impressionable sixteen-year-old who repeatedly missed murderous attacks by seconds or feet to a gentle nineteen-year-old serving in the IDF, facing people who would kill him and us. Their ability to keep their humanity and their determination are living proof that living by a moral code is what should be required of everyone.

My wife and partner, Sylvia Tessler-Lozowick, is a shining example of daily commitment to human rights at their essential core. Her keen and original perspectives have enriched my own thinking, and hopefully my readers have benefited from this. Her loving support has been the mainstay of my ability to be creative.

Yaacov Lozowick
Jerusalem
January 2003

INDEX